GREAT CLASSICAL MYTHS

GREAT
CLASSICAL
MYTHS

Edited, and with an Introduction, by

F. R. B. Godolphin

The Modern Library
NEW YORK

THE MODERN LIBRARY

is published by

RANDOM HOUSE, INC.

New York, New York

Manufactured in the United States of America

ACKNOWLEDGMENTS

My thanks are due the following publishers and agents for permission to reprint translations copyrighted by them:

MRS. WILMON BREWER—for selections from Ovid's *Metamorphoses*, translated by Brookes More (Marshall Jones Co.); Book I, copyright 1922, by Brookes More; Books II, III, copyright 1923, by The Cornhill Publishing Co., copyright purchased 1926, by Brookes More; Books IV, V, copyright 1933, by Brookes More; Books VI-X, copyright 1941, by Katharine More Brewer; Books XI-XV, copyright © 1957, by Katharine More Brewer.

DOUBLEDAY & COMPANY, INC.—for selections from *The Odyssey* by Homer, translated by Robert Fitzgerald, copyright © 1961, by Robert Fitzgerald.

G. G. HARRAP & COMPANY—for selections from *The Odyssey* by Homer, translated by H. B. Cotterill.

HARVARD UNIVERSITY PRESS AND THE LOEB CLASSICAL LIBRARY—for selections from *Apollodorus*, translated by J. G. Frazer; and for selections from *Hesiod*, translated by H. G. Evelyn White.

INDIANA UNIVERSITY PRESS—for selections from Ovid's *Metamorphoses*, translated by Rolfe Humphries, copyright 1955, by Indiana University Press.

LITTLE, BROWN & COMPANY—for selections from *The Iliad* by Homer, translated by Chase and Perry, copyright 1950, by Alston Hurd Chase and William G. Perry, Jr.

NEW DIRECTIONS—for the *Third* and *Fourth Pythian Odes* by

Pindar, translated by Richmond Lattimore, copyright 1942, by New Directions.

RANDOM HOUSE, INC.—for selections from *The Odyssey of Homer*, translated by Ennis Rees, copyright © 1960, by Ennis Rees.

CHARLES SCRIBNER'S SONS—for selections from *The Aeneid of Virgil*, translated by Rolfe Humphries, copyright 1951, by Charles Scribner's Sons.

UNIVERSITY OF CHICAGO PRESS—for selections from *The Iliad of Homer*, translated by Richmond Lattimore, copyright 1951, by the University of Chicago;—for selections from *The Georgics* by Virgil, translated by S. P. Bovie, copyright 1956, by the University of Chicago;—for selections from *Odes* by Pindar, translated by Richmond Lattimore, copyright 1947, by the University of Chicago;—for the selection from Aeschylus' *Agamemnon*, translated by Richmond Lattimore, copyright 1942, by the University of Chicago;—for the selection from Euripides' *Bacchae*, translated by William Arrowsmith, copyright © 1959, by the University of Chicago;—for the selection from Aeschylus' *Seven Against Thebes*, translated by David Grene, copyright © 1956, by the University of Chicago;—and for the selection from Sophocles' *Philoctetes*, translated by David Grene, copyright © 1957, by the University of Chicago.

UNIVERSITY OF KANSAS PRESS—for selections from *Myths* by Hyginus, translated by Mary Grant, copyright © 1960, by the University of Kansas Press.

UNIVERSITY OF MICHIGAN PRESS—for selections from *The Theogony* and *The Works and Days* by Hesiod, translated by Richmond Lattimore, copyright © 1959, by the University of Michigan.

VIKING PRESS, INC.—for selections from Ovid's *Metamorphoses*, translated by Horace Gregory, copyright © 1958, by the Viking Press, Inc.

YALE UNIVERSITY PRESS—for Ode 19 from *Bacchylides*, translated by Robert Fagles, copyright © 1961, by Robert Fagles.

CONTENTS

II EARLY HEROES AND HEROINES

III THE HOMERIC HEROES

1. The story of Achilles; Greeks and Trojans

2. The Wanderings of Odysseus

3. Aeneas and Rome

IV   INDIVIDUAL MYTHS

V LOVERS, IMMORTAL AND MORTAL

APPENDIX

1. The Cyclic Epics

INTRODUCTION

This volume presents the Greek myths in English translations of the Greek and Roman poets. The ancient poets drew on a great body of story material which provided the beginnings of the education of the Greeks—an education which was the basis of the humanistic tradition for Western culture. These poets' versions have caught the imagination of writers and painters of the Western world from ancient times to the present. Despite the development of other branches of knowledge and the growth of rational and scientific inquiry, Greek mythology continued to be an essential element in art, literature, and philosophy because the creative imagination which went in to the making of these myths is a primary function of man. From translation and adaptation of the myth, or a poetic shorthand of allusion and ornamentation on the one hand, to imaginative recreation on the other hand, the Greek myths beyond all others have dominated poetic feeling and use for almost three thousand years.

Since this influence went on for over a thousand years in the ancient world, and since much of Greek and Roman literature has disappeared, the ancient authors who preserved these stories came from many places and widely varying periods of the ancient world. Their attitudes and beliefs are no more homogeneous than are those of writers from Chaucer to the present. The story, likewise, is not necessarily primitive or sophisticated simply because it happens to be told by an early or a late writer. The origins and uses of the myths represent a far more complicated series of states in human thought and belief than one might suppose.

In this volume an effort has been made in the translations to reproduce something of the variety of expression in the originals by the use of prose and verse translations from the hands of translators over the last four centuries. Some sense of the changes in understanding and interpretation of Homer, for example, may be found by comparing the tone and treatment of the translations of Chapman with those of Fitzgerald and Lattimore. For the works of other ancient authors I have also selected a variety of English translators in an effort to indicate something of the complexity of Classical mythology as it appears in our literature.

To understand something of this complexity some distinctions must be drawn in the use of the term "myth," and it is also necessary to distinguish some of the theories of the origin of myth and the uses to which myths have been put. The word "myth" starts with the Greek word μῦθος, which means "that which is spoken," a story, a tale, and in the early days it was probably accepted as something actual and real. This broad definition has been limited and narrowed in various ways at different times, but perhaps contains an important warning for those of us who try to restrict its meaning too severely. To the Greeks several types of story were included under this heading, and save for the professional mythographer, this is likely still to be true for poets, artists, and most of the members of their audience.

It is, I think, well to distinguish the main types of myths or legends that were originally told within various primitive societies, although such distinctions tend to be obscured in the actual myths as we have them. The myth proper may be thought of as early man's effort to explain certain facts of experience, especially natural phenomena, by the use of his imagination rather than by the use of reason or scientific observation, neither of which was sufficiently developed to be of much help to him. For example, it rains because a God—that is some power other than himself and greater—is pouring water out of the sky. This provides an explanation if one is not too deeply concerned with questions of how and why.

Another type of myth is what is now called saga, the story of human action which is, in some measure, related to an historical event. The qualification is necessary, because the relationship to the historical may be quite changed and transformed as the story is retold by bards and poets. The best example of this is the Trojan War. Archaeology has enabled us to know that a war or wars took place in an identifiable area, at a time which can be roughly determined, and between peoples of whose culture and civilization a good deal can be learned. However, the *Iliad,* the epic poem which makes use of this historical material, is not history nor was meant to be. The Greeks in later times may have thought of it as giving an account of their early history, but Homer was providing his hearers with a mythos, a great story told by a great genius. His primary interest was the interacting of character and personality, not an historical sequence of events.

There is a third variety of story, or mythos, which has wide currency among all sorts of primitive peoples. This may be called the folktale, often designated by the German term *Märchen*. In this instance the teller's purpose is simply amusement and entertainment; there is no effort to explain anything; no historical event is reflected; no demand is made that the hearer believe or accept the probability of the story.

It is, I think, obvious that in the telling and retelling of stories these basic types were combined and blended. They are a convenience in understanding some of the elements which have gone into a story, but nothing is gained for understanding of the literary and artistic value of the myth by trying to purge it of those elements by which it is enriched and enlivened at whatever cost to the strict mythographer's conception of "pure myth."

Although other races have created myths and legends, and one of the great services of anthropology has been the extension and enrichment of our knowledge of these stories, the Greeks beyond all others were the creators and transmitters of a wide range of myths which have fascinated men, captured their imaginations, and again and again tempted them to the most varied forms of interpretation. Before turning to these Greeks in an effort to find out what manner of men they were, it would perhaps be worthwhile to sketch some of the methods of interpretation of myth which have been important at various times and many of which, indeed, are still influential in one guise or another.

One of the ancient and persistent explanations of myth is the method of allegory, by means of which deep and important meanings are found to lie beneath the ostensibly simple story. Later readers assume that the creator of the story must have had as his purpose the communication of some secret knowledge, and that it is only necessary to find the key to discover something of profound significance which is concealed from the understanding of the vulgar by a deceptively simple surface. It is hard for a later age to realize that early man did not have the intellectual grasp of a complex philosophical, religious, and scientific system on which to base the supposed allegory. This sort of allegorical interpretation of myth is far different from the use of myth by a sophisticated author for the purpose of allegory. Ovid, had he wished to, undoubtedly could have employed the myths in the fashion of the *Moralized Ovid* of the fourteenth century A.D., probably using an Orphic or Pythagorean basis, obviously not a Christian one, but it is clear that he had no such desire. Closely akin to allegorical interpretation is the method of symbolism. This avoids the implications of a systematic correspondence between the myth and a conception of a reality beyond, and indeed must be taken seriously since the imagination does seek to present a picture of reality in its own way and with its own validity. However, the symbolic method used as the basis for the interpretation of a series of myths rapidly turns into a system and is subject to the same objections as the allegorical method.

Rationalism, by means of which everything is rejected or reinterpreted in accordance with the preconceptions of fact and truth and probability, enjoyed by the interpreter has, as Socrates said in Plato's *Phaedrus*, no end, and requires a great deal of leisure if every feature of every myth is to be rationalized. This had clearly become a popular occupation among the Athenians by the end of the fifth century B.C.

A theory called Euhemerism, from its chief proponent, Euhemeros, was popular in the period after the death of Alexander the Great (323 B.C.) and does correspond to certain facts in the Greek world. According to this theory the popular gods were men who had been deified by those they had aided. The Greeks did deify some men, but this theory does not explain the concept "God" and is really only a variation on the method of rationalism insofar as the myths are concerned. Actually, in the case of some myths there are sound archaeological reasons for believing that the human beings of the myth, as in the story of Hyacinthus—even Helen of Troy herself—had been worshipped as gods in an earlier society and had been ousted from their divine status by the popularity of the Olympian deities of the later period. Helen and Ariadne are two early vegetation goddesses who become human beings in the myths. Nature myths, especially solar ones, have been thought to account for the Greek gods, if not for the body of myths. Some relationship may exist, but it is curious to note that the Greeks did not make as many connections between their gods and the manifestations of nature as we have tended to do for them. For example, we may think of Apollo as the sun god, but there is not much evidence that the Greeks did so. Helios (the Greek word for sun) is sometimes mentioned, but he seems to have had no considerable cult, and even Ovid in the story of Phaethon does not identify his father Helios with Apollo. Much has been made of vegetation spirits, and the theme of death and rebirth in nature has absorbed the attention of many writers on Greek religion and myth, but there is little evidence that this was important to the tellers of the Greek myths and the writers who transmitted them to the Greece of historical time and to the Western world.

Psychology and psychoanalysis have found many matters of interest and concern in the Greek myths. The Jungian notion of *archetypes* deep in the human unconscious is attractive. Many Greek myths may strike us as having roots in the human experience and the human predicament, but it is very difficult to get from this instinctive feeling of relationship to anything which helps to explain or interpret any particular myth. Burial customs, incest taboos, matriarchal societies, patriarchal societies, tree worship, animal cults and totems—all seem to have psychological bases. What the relationship between these psychological bases and the Greek myths may be is still unclear to most students of the myths. In the meantime it is possible to examine the source of the myth, often to determine from what branch of the Greek people it came, to see whether it is pre-Greek, to determine whether it is primarily myth proper, saga, or folk tale, and finally to compare it with other tales which have been collected from the legends of primitive peoples in various parts of the world.

So far the mythographer. It is clear that the myths must inevitably attract a variety of specialists who will find in them elements important in such fields as Religion, Philosophy, Anthropology, Archaeology, and History. As the myth itself is likely to be a composite of pure myth, saga, and folk tale it has an appeal for students of these many disciplines. What distinguishes the Greek myth from others, however, is the appeal it has had for writers and painters for nearly three thousand years. Perhaps, then, it will be profitable to try to understand some of the qualities and something of the background of racial and cultural experiences which combined to give the Greeks of the historical period their particular character.

For the Greeks almost everything began with Homer, and he was the great teacher for them of almost everything that was worth knowing. So also for us he has provided insights essential to the understanding of the beliefs and achievements of the Greeks, and pointed toward the questions which have led to our present understanding of much of the pre-Greek society of the Aegean basin.

To much that he tells us we were long blind, and until Schliemann took his Homer in one hand and a spade in the other no one thought to seek an answer to the many questions about Greeks and their predecessors that were presented in the pages of Homer. Once Schliemann had excavated at Troy, the recovery of Mycenaean civilization followed; then the Minoan civilization of Crete; and, a few years ago, the deciphering of the Cretan linear-B script and the discovery that the language was Greek but written in a script entirely different from the Phoenician alphabet adopted centuries later.

These archaeological discoveries, along with the demonstration that the Homeric epics are the product of an oral tradition, make it possible for us to have a greater understanding of the Greeks, their religion, history, literature and mythology, than was possible previously.

In the *Iliad* we can be reasonably sure that a great artist has given his own particular form to a tradition which had been developed and passed on orally for several centuries. Knowledge of some things which we can learn from archaeological excavation had vanished completely; other elements survived. The linguistic, military, religious, and mythological elements which do not make a consistent pattern no longer trouble us. If one can realize that matters of custom and practice from a period of four hundred years, 1200 to 800 B.C. along with folkways which may go back even earlier, have been combined with saga (prehistory) traditions by a bard who enjoyed the use of the artistic and literary devices of generations of predecessors, he can begin to see how the *Iliad* fuses these elements into a great artistic creation.

In terms of the myths that Homer has incorporated into the structure of the *Iliad*, we can see that he is telling of the great deeds, not literally or historically, but mythologically, of men who lived in the great days before his own time; also, that he has a sense of the great heroes who lived in earlier days still. In a sense Crete and Mycenae were as remote for Homer as they are for us. Scholars have shown that he was unfamiliar with many facts of Mycenaean civilization; what he knew of Crete does not begin to report the great days of Minoan civilization.

Excavations at Mycenae and elsewhere have shown something of the beliefs and artistic achievements of a race of conquerors who came into Greece and dominated a native population.

Excavations in Crete have demonstrated the high achievements of a non-Indo-European society which dominated the island and deeply influenced the Mycenaean civilization before it was overrun by the invaders about 1400 B.C. Clearly, at least two series of invaders from Central Europe, we may call the Achaeans and the Dorians, upset the status quo in Greece and Crete. Apparently this process included the imposition of a religious system based on the predominance of gods, presumably a patriarchal system, on a previously existing religious system where the goddess was supreme and her consort temporary and unimportant.

Many other elements in this religious complex (some of them will emerge in the telling of the myths) can be identified. Tree cults, bird epiphanies, animal (but apparently not totemic) manifestations, strange composite animal and demonic manifestations, many perhaps indicating Assyrian and Egyptian influences—all of these are a part of the pre-Homeric picture in the Greek world.

For the Greek world Homer fixed the picture of the Gods living on Olympus and ruled by their king, Zeus. For the Greeks this society of the Gods was recognizably similar to human society, and since they did not have a body of sacred writings, any dogmas or tests of orthodoxy, it was not necessary to go beyond the Homeric pictures to determine which of his Olympians had been taken over from other races and which were survivals from an earlier civilization in Greece itself. For example, the bickering and disagreements between Zeus and his wife, Hera, are humanly comprehensible and can on occasion be turned to comic purposes. To understand them it was not necessary to discover that Hera was a goddess in parts of the Peloponnese from a very early period, and that when the invaders brought in their chief god, Zeus, it had been necessary to make a compromise with existing religion by making Hera the consort of Zeus.

Athene was probably a pre-Hellenic goddess, patroness of a Mycenaean city, as later of Athens. She was brought into a special relation with Zeus by the story of her birth from his head, in order to incorporate her into the society of the Olympians.

Artemis, whose name is not Greek, seems to have been associated with a Minoan deity, the Mistress of Wild Things, by no means the virgin goddess of the historical period, but to have been brought into the society of the Olympians by being made the sister of Apollo. She was still a huntress goddess and closely concerned with birth among animals and humans, but was dissociated from procreation.

Aphrodite, although her name was associated with the Greek word for foam, and although she was widely worshipped by the Greeks, was Oriental in origin. Her cult on the island of Cyprus was very old and non-Greek. Time and time again in the myths one may note signs of her social inferiority in the Olympian pantheon.

In Homer, Hephaistos is an Olympian, son of Hera and, presumably, Zeus, but in origin he was an Oriental fire-god first in Lycia and the volcanic regions of Asia Minor and finally in the volcanic regions of the West. This may suggest the way in which Homer gave form to a variety of religious beliefs and myths which had been transmitted for centuries by the bards and singers who had at the same time developed the meter, the language, the formulae and the conventions of epic from various periods and places of the civilization of the Aegean.

We can find some traces of cults which the earliest occupants of Greece had established. There are evidences of elements which come from the Minoan civilization of Crete of the third and second millennia before Christ; many remnants point to the Mycenaean civlization of the first Greek tribes to establish themselves in Greece, the Achaeans. The early Ionians and the later Dorians are not prominent in Homer's synthesis, which focuses primarily on the heroic age of the Achaeans. An interesting indication of the preservation of connections between the Mycenaean civilization and Asia Minor appears in the part played by the Lycians. Though it was surprising and illogical, Homer had to make them allies of the Trojans in order to exploit the mythical accounts of Greek relationships, as in the story of Glaucus and Diomede, and the accounts of Bellerophon and Sarpedon.

Most of the proper names, Greek and Trojan, are Greek in origin and many of them probably go back to Mycenaean times. Naturally, Homer or his predecessors had little opportunity to obtain Trojan names. Many of the characters of the *Iliad*, however, may be the inventions of the poet, for example, Hector among the Trojans and Patroklos among the Greeks.

One further observation. Homer clearly knew other extensive myths beyond those which were relevant to his story. He has various characters in the *Iliad* tell some of them; the fact that neither Homer nor one of his characters alludes to a particular myth is still no evidence that it was later than Mycenaean or even Homeric times. Homer was no more concerned to make a compendium of myths than he was to provide a chronological or historical account of the war which was the setting of the action of the *Iliad*.

He was deeply concerned with the character and psychology of his heroes, and because of this human concern he seems frequently to have softened the rude barbaric character of his divine actors and to have altered the primitive harshness of many of the myths. It is almost as if Homer was aware of the fact that these myths were very old. They were a necessary part of the background but not to be told for their own sake, and, because they were in no sense sacred, could be refashioned in accordance with the poet's interests and beliefs. This freedom to interpret the myth in accordance with the poet's desires is an early manifestation of the vital and creative use of myth so notable later in the work of the tragic poets.

Much of what is most important in Greek mythology is closely related to the *Iliad*. What of the other great epic, the *Odyssey*? Certainly the folk tale and the romance are more characteristic of it than the heroic myth. Much of the *Odyssey* seems to be of later date than the *Iliad*. Was it, as Longinus thought, a product of Homer's old age? Were there two comparably great epic poets in the period between 800 B.C. and 700 B.C.? A natural and conservative human tendency has been to say no, but there were three great tragic poets (Aeschylus, Sophocles, Euripides) in the fifth century B.C. There were many great lyric poets in a comparable period in the seventh and sixth centuries B.C. Since we no longer have the half-dozen other epics of the Cycle once attributed to Homer, our basis for judgment is limited. Whether it was the work of Homer or of another poet, and apart from its high literary quality, the *Odyssey* established for the Greeks much mythology and a body of folk tales second only to the importance of the pictures of the Olympian Gods and the myths of the *Iliad*.

Certainly no folk tales have been more widely known by young and old than Odysseus' stories of the Sirens, the Lotoseaters, the Cyclops, Circe, Calypso, Scylla and Charybdis, and of course the touching story of Nausicaa. Traveler's tales and tales of far-off unknown places are here in abundance. All the elements, nonetheless, are combined into a skillful and well-organized plot, the work of an informing intelligence, not an accretion of details gathered only for their own sake.

Hesiod, the other early and important figure in the presentation of Greek myth, is a very different figure. Not for him the recollections of an earlier heroic age or the pictures of the Gods in action. Hesiod is rooted in the hardships of life in the dark ages of Greece, and he is concerned to present the genealogical relationship of the Gods and to set forth the theological and cosmological background against which man must lead his life of toil and make his peace with the Gods. For the most part his appeal is not to the imagination, nor does he present the Gods with poetic imagery. Yet for the "facts" of mythology his importance is great.

The *Homeric Hymns*, from various hands in the seventh and sixth centuries, often provide much more that is interesting and colorful in the way of stories about the Gods. The character and events connected with Demeter and Hermes, for example, consist largely of the details told in their hymns. Many individual items of information to do with mythology undoubtedly come from the Cyclic Epics (see the prose summaries in the Appendix) and the Hymns of the seventh and sixth centuries, although the works are lost and we find traces only in the late scholiasts and commentators who drew their information from the great collections of the library at Alexandria.

The writers of the fifth century B.C. continued the process of reshaping myths which we have seen in Homer, and in the case of the earliest, Pindar, it is quite clear that he was often dissatisfied or morally outraged by the older versions of myths and tales of the Gods. Consequently he altered them freely to bring them into accord with his religious beliefs. Aeschylus, Sophocles, and Euripides also made whatever modifications they found necessary for dramatic purposes or to convey their own insights into the relations of man and god, or man and man. We know that all three used the same myth more than once and we can see differences in their treatment. For example, in the story of Orestes' and Electra's vengeance on Clytemnestra for the murder of Agamemnon there is wide divergence in the emphasis of the different dramatists. In the case of the dramatist it is very difficult to find passages to present his treatment of a given myth, because frequently the whole play or plays is necessary to convey the interpretation fully. In the *Odyssey*, Homer has told what may be called the "basic" myth of the return of Agamemnon. It is a fascinating study, but beyond the scope of such a book as this, to trace the variations on the theme in the works of the dramatists; the interested reader should seek out the appropriate plays. When we come to the poets of the Alexandrian period, a different spirit is at work. Apollonius can exploit the old myth of the Argonauts in a series of brilliant episodes and expand the relation between Jason and Medea into the psychological drama of the third book. Theocritus takes the savage uncouth figure of the Cyclops and turns him into the love-lorn Polyphemus singing of his beloved Galatea. Both of these examples show how increased interest in the love theme result in reworking of the myth. Various Alexandrians seem to have reworked obscure myths or invented myths in order to explore eccentricities in human behavior or causes of ritual and practice in various places. These are of less importance in the stream of Western art and literature however, except insofar as they may reappear in the works of Ovid who gave some of them wide currency.

Although there are a few genuine Roman myths, for the most part the Roman poets borrowed their mythology from the Greeks and their great importance is as reshapers and transmitters of a tradition which was a thousand years old by the time Roman literature began. Vergil gave a distinctive stamp to the traditions of Rome's origin by using the story of the Trojan Aeneas to link Rome to the great cycle of Troy. Whatever hints and suggestions he may have found already in existence, it is the Vergilian formulation which has influenced many of our ideas about the fall of Troy, the journey of Aeneas, and, above all, the story of Dido and Aeneas.

Horace seldom tells a myth. His contribution to the place of myth is largely in the form of allusion and ornament, so that he is more important as a teacher of technique and method than as a mythologist.

Ovid, on the other hand, has been the source and fountainhead of Greek myth for almost 2000 years. Although he wears his learning lightly, he was steeped in the traditions of mythology and draws on an endless fund of myths as raw material for his portrayal of the vagaries of human kind. He is primarily a poet of love, and he succeeds in presenting most of the normal and abnormal variations on this theme in the dress of mythological tales of Gods and mortals, but he is also concerned with everything which concerns mankind, from theories of the Creation to the history of his own day. His intense curiosity combined with his poetic skill enabled him to be influential even under the most unlikely circumstances. The medieval passion for allegorical interpretation, combined with the belief that the ancients were valuable guides and serious of purpose, led to the *Moralised Ovid* which turns the *Metamorphoses* into vehicles of Christian doctrine and even led to the amusing and sophisticated *Art of Love* being interpreted to teach the nuns of Canterbury their Christian duty.

The richness of Greek myth and the variations of detail in individual myths from centuries of retelling by the poets led to handbooks of mythology comparable to our modern collections; of these, Apollodorus sometimes preserves the flavor and interest of his sources, and Hyginus often has interesting accounts. Apart from the poets on the one hand and the commentators on the other, many Greek prose writers used myths. Herodotus and Plato not only used pre-existing myths, but created them for the modern world (for examples see the Appendix). Plutarch often preserves them in connection with the lives of the early Greeks and Romans. Pausanias frequently tells them in his guidebook to Greece which describes the works of art which survived until the second century A.D.

I have not been concerned to present the variants of myths, nor have I been concerned to present all the Greek myths which have survived. Such a work as H. J. Rose, *Handbook of Greek Mythology*, does this admirably. This collection is designed to supply as many as possible of the myths which have influenced European art and literature in as close an approximation of the poetic form of the originals as can be obtained in English. Ever since Shakespeare used both Ovid's Latin and Golding's translation, one source of mythological knowledge in English has been the translation. Although dictionaries of mythology and handbooks are valuable aids, for most students and general readers I believe that it is more important to get the "feel" and the emotional overtone of an ancient poet's telling of a myth than it is to get the "facts" of the myth, and more important to get an account from one of the Greeks or Romans than to risk the confusion and obscurity inherent in a paraphrase which tries to take into account all the variants in the incidents and in the names of the characters.

Line references in the table of contents and headings are to standard texts of the Greek and Latin authors.

Consistency in the spelling of the names of the figures of Greek mythology is impossible; even prose translators differ and verse translations usually cannot be changed. Translators also use the Greek or the Roman names of the gods according to their personal preferences. The Glossary contains cross-references to one spelling, generally one sanctioned by usage whatever its relation to the original. For convenience of reference the Glossary also contains very brief accounts of a number of mythological figures who are not treated in the text.

Here are a number of books that are suggested as further reading in various areas having to do with classical mythology and its influence:

WILMON BREWER, *Ovid's Metamorphoses in European Cultures*. Cornhill, 1933.

E. R. CURTIUS, *European Literature and the Latin Middle Ages*. N.Y.: Pantheon, 1953.

SIR JAMES GEORGE FRAZER, *The New Golden Bough*. Ed., T. H. Gaster. N.Y.: Anchor, 1961.

GILBERT HIGHET, *The Classical Tradition*. N.Y.: Oxford, 1949.

GILBERT MURRAY, *Five Stages of Greek Religion*. N.Y.: Anchor.

DOUGLAS BUSH, *Mythology and the Renaissance Tradition in English Poetry*. Minneapolis: Univ. of Minnesota Press, 1932.

DOUGLAS BUSH, *Mythology and the Romantic Tradition in English Poetry*. Cambridge, Mass.: Harvard Univ. Press, 1937.

M. P. NILSSON, *A History of Greek Religion*. N.Y.: Oxford, 1925.

M. P. NILSSON, *The Minoan—Mycenaean Religion*. Lund: Gleerup, 2nd ed., 1950.

H. J. ROSE, *A Handbook of Greek Mythology*. London: Methuen, 5th ed., 1953.

JEAN SEZNEC, *The Survival of the Pagan Gods*. N.Y.: Pantheon, 1953.

RHYS CARPENTER, *Folk Tale Fiction and Saga in the Homeric Epics*. Berkeley: Univ. of California Press, 1956.

ARROWSMITH AND SHATTUCK, *The Craft and Context of Translation*. Austin: Univ. of Texas Press, 1961.

NORTON AND RUSHTON, *Classical Myths in English Literature*. N.Y.: Holt, Rinehart & Winston, 1952.

I

CREATION, THE GODS, AND THE UNDERWORLD

CREATION AND THE EARLY GODS

HESIOD, *Theogony*, 116-222 (Lattimore)

Hesiod's account of the Creation and the early gods was much modified by later writers, but it remains the starting point for myths and speculation on the cosmos.

First of all there came Chaos,
     and after him came
Gaia of the broad breast,
     to be the unshakable foundation
of all the immortals who keep the crests
     of snowy Olympos,
and Tartaros the foggy in the pit
     of the wide-wayed earth,
and Eros, who is love, handsomest among all
     the immortals,
who breaks the limbs' strength,
     who in all gods, in all human beings
overpowers the intelligence in the breast,
     and all their shrewd planning.
From Chaos was born Erebos, the dark,
     and black Night,
and from Night again Aither and Hemera,
     the day, were begotten,
for she lay in love with Erebos
     and conceived and bore these two.
But Gaia's first born was one
     who matched her every dimension,
Ouranos, the starry sky,

to cover her all over,
to be an unshakable standing-place
for the blessed immortals.
Then she brought forth the tall Hills,
those wild haunts that are beloved
by the goddess Nymphs who live on the hills
and in their forests.
Without any sweet act of love
she produced the barren
sea, Pontos, seething in his fury of waves,
and after this
she lay with Ouranos, and bore him
deep-swirling Okeanos
the ocean-stream; and Koios, Krios,
Hyperion, Iapetos,
and Theia too and Rheia, and Themis,
and Mnemosyne,
Phoibe of the wreath of gold,
and Tethys the lovely.
After these her youngest-born
was devious-devising Kronos,
most terrible of her children;
and he hated his strong father.
She brought forth also the Kyklopes,
whose hearts are proud and powerful,
Brontes and Steropes, and Arges
of the violent spirit,
who made the thunder and gave it to Zeus,
and fashioned the lightning.
These in all the rest of their shape
were made like gods,
but they had only one eye set in the middle
of their foreheads.
Kyklopes, wheel-eyed, was the name given them,
by reason
of the single wheel-shaped eye
that was set in their foreheads.
Strength and force, and contriving skills,
were in all their labors.
And still other children were born
to Gaia and Ouranos,
three sons, big and powerful, so great

they could never be told of,
Kottos, Briareos, and Gyes,
   overmastering children.
Each had a hundred intolerably strong arms
   bursting
out of his shoulders,
   and on the shoulders of each grew fifty
heads, above their massive bodies;
   irresistible
and staunch strength matched the appearance
   of their big bodies,
and of all children ever born
   to Gaia and Ouranos
these were the most terrible,
   and they hated their father
from the beginning, and every time each one
   was beginning
to come out, he would push them back again,
   deep inside Gaia,
and would not let them into the light,
   and Ouranos exulted
in his wicked work; but great Gaia
   groaned within for pressure
of pain; and then she thought of an evil,
   treacherous attack.
Presently creating the element of gray flint
she made of it a great sickle,
   and explained it to her own children,
and spoke, in the disturbance of her heart,
   to encourage them:
"My sons, born to me of a criminal father,
   if you are willing
to obey me, we can punish your father
   for the brutal treatment
he put upon you, for he was first to think
   of shameful dealing."
     So she spoke, but fear took hold of all,
   nor did one of them
speak, but then great devious-devising Kronos
   took courage
and spoke in return,
   and gave his gracious mother an answer:

"My mother, I will promise to undertake
    to accomplish
this act, and for our father,
    him of the evil name, I care
nothing, for he was the first
    to think of shameful dealing."
        So he spoke, and giant Gaia
        rejoiced greatly in her heart
and took and hid him in a secret ambush,
        and put into his hands
the sickle, edged like teeth, and told him
    all her treachery.
And huge Ouranos came on
    bringing night with him, and desiring
love he embraced Gaia and lay over her
    stretched out
complete, and from his hiding place his son
    reached with his left hand
and seized him, and holding in his right
    the enormous sickle
with its long blade edged like teeth,
    he swung it sharply,
and lopped the members of his own father,
    and threw them behind him
to fall where they would,
    but they were not lost away when they were flung
from his hand, but all the bloody drops
    that went splashing from them
were taken in by Gaia, the earth,
    and with the turning of the seasons
she brought forth the powerful Furies
    and the tall Giants
shining in their armor
    and holding long spears in their hands;
and the nymphs they call, on boundless earth,
    the Nymphs of the Ash Trees.
But the members themselves, when Kronos
    had lopped them with the flint,
he threw from the mainland
    into the great wash of the sea water
and they drifted a great while

on the open sea, and there spread
a circle of white foam
   from the immortal flesh, and in it
grew a girl, whose course first took her
   to holy Kythera,
and from there she afterward made her way
   to sea-washed Cyprus
and stepped ashore, a modest lovely Goddess,
   and about her
light and slender feet the grass grew,
   and the gods call her
Aphrodite, and men do too,
   and the aphro-foam-born
goddess, and garlanded Kythereia,
   because from the seafoam
she grew, and Kytheria because she had gone
   to Kythera,
and Kyprogeneia, because she came forth
   from wave-washed Cyprus,
and Philommedea, because she appeared
   from *medea*, members.
And Eros went with her, and handsome Himeros
   attended her
when first she was born, and when she joined
   the immortal community,
and here is the privilege she was given
   and holds from the beginning,
and which is the part she plays among men
   and the gods immortal:
the whispering together of girls,
   the smiles and deceptions,
the delight, and the sweetnesses of love,
   and the flattery.
     But their great father Ouranos,
   who himself begot them,
bitterly gave to those others, his sons,
   the name of Titans,
the Stretchers, for they stretched
   their power outrageously and accomplished
a monstrous thing, and they would some day
   be punished for it.

But Night bore horrible Moros, and black Ker,
 End and Fate,
and Death, and Sleep, and she bore also
 the brood of Dreams,
she, dark Night, by herself,
 and had not been loved by any god,
and then again she bore mocking Momos
 and painful Oizys,
and the Hesperides, who across
 the fabulous stream of the Ocean
keep the golden apples
 and the fruit-bearing orchards,
and she bore the destinies, the Moirai,
 and the cruelly never-forgetful
Fates, Klotho, Lachesis, and Atropos,
 who at their birth
bestow upon mortals their portion
 of good and evil,
and these control the transgressions
 of both men and divinities,
and these goddesses never remit
 their dreaded anger
until whoever has done wrong
 gives them satisfaction.

THE AGES OF MAN

HESIOD, *Works and Days*, 109-201 (Lattimore)

The theme of the Golden Age and the subsequent decline from it is widespread and, among the ancients, far more common than the notion of man's "progress" from primitivism.

In the beginning, the immortals
 who have their homes on Olympos
created the golden generation of mortal people.
These lived in Kronos' time, when he
 was the king in heaven.
They lived as if they were gods.

their hearts free from all sorrow,
by themselves, and without hard work or pain;
    no miserable
old age came their way; their hands, their feet,
    did not alter.
They took their pleasure in festivals,
    and lived without troubles.
When they died, it was as if they fell asleep.
    All goods
were theirs. The fruitful grainland
    yielded its harvest to them
of its own accord; this was great and abundant,
    while they at their pleasure
quietly looked after their works,
    in the midst of good things
prosperous in flocks, on friendly terms
    with the blessed immortals.

    Now that the earth has gathered over this generation,
these are called pure and blessed spirits;
    they live upon earth,
and are good, they watch over mortal men
    and defend them from evil;
they keep watch over lawsuits and hard dealings;
    they mantle
themselves in dark mist
    and wander all over the country;
they bestow wealth; for this right
    as of kings was given them.
    Next after these the dwellers upon Olympos created
a second generation, of silver, far worse
    than the other.
They were not like the golden ones either in shape
    or spirit.
A child was a child for a hundred years,
    looked after and playing
by his gracious mother, kept at home,
    a complete booby.
But when it came time for them to grow up
    and gain full measure,
they lived for only a poor short time;
    by their own foolishness

they had troubles, for they were not able
　　to keep away from
reckless crime against each other,
　　nor would they worship
the gods, nor do sacrifice on the sacred altars
　　of the blessed ones,
which is the right thing among the customs of men,
　　and therefore
Zeus, son of Kronos, in anger engulfed them,
　　for they paid no due
honors to the blessed gods who live on Olympos.

　　But when the earth had gathered over this generation
also—and they too are called blessed spirits
　　by men, though under
the ground, and secondary, but still
　　they have their due worship—
then Zeus the father created the third generation
　　of mortals,
the age of bronze. They were not like
　　the generation of silver.
They came from ash spears. They were terrible
　　and strong, and the ghastly
action of Ares was theirs, and violence.
　　They ate no bread,
but maintained an indomitable and adamantine spirit.
None could come near them; their strength was big,
　　and from their shoulders
the arms grew irresistible on their ponderous bodies.
The weapons of these men were bronze,
　　of bronze their houses,
and they worked as bronzesmiths. There was not yet
　　any black iron.
Yet even these, destroyed beneath the hands
　　of each other,
went down into the moldering domain of cold Hades;
nameless; for all they were formidable black death
seized them, and they had to forsake
　　the shining sunlight.

Now when the earth had gathered over this generation
also, Zeus, son of Kronos, created yet another

fourth generation on the fertile earth,
    and these were better and nobler,
the wonderful generation of hero-men, who are also
called half-gods, the generation before our own
    on this vast earth.
But of these too, evil war and the terrible carnage
took some; some by seven-gated Thebes
    in the land of Kadmos
as they fought together over the flocks of Oidipous;
    others
war had taken in ships over the great gulf
    of the sea,
where they also fought for the sake
    of lovely-haired Helen.
There, for these, the end of death was misted
    about them.
But on others Zeus, son of Kronos, settled a living
    and a country
of their own, apart from human kind,
    at the end of the world.
And there they have their dwelling place,
    and hearts free of sorrow
in the islands of the blessed
    by the deep-swirling stream of the ocean,
prospering heroes, on whom in every year
    three times over
the fruitful grainland bestows its sweet yield.
    These live
far from the immortals, and Kronos
    is king among them.
For Zeus, father of gods and mortals,
    set him free from his bondage,
although the position and the glory still belong
    to the young gods.

After this, Zeus of the wide brows
    established yet one more
generation of men, the fifth, to be
    on the fertile earth.

And I wish that I were not any part
    of the fifth generation

of men, but had died before it came,
  or been born afterward.
For here now is the age of iron. Never by daytime
will there be an end to hard work and pain,
  nor in the night
to weariness, when the gods will send anxieties
  to trouble us.
Yet here also there shall be some good things
  mixed with the evils.
But Zeus will destroy this generation of mortals
  also,
in the time when children, as they are born,
  grow gray on the temples,
when the father no longer agrees with the children,
  nor children with their father,
when guest is no longer at one with host,
  nor companion to companion,
when your brother is no longer your friend,
  as he was in the old days.
Men will deprive their parents of all rights,
  as they grow old,
and people will mock them too,
  babbling bitter words against them,
harshly, and without shame in the sight of the gods;
  not even
to their aging parents will they give back
  what once was given.
Strong of hand, one man shall seek
  the city of another.
There will be no favor for the man
  who keeps his oath, for the righteous
and the good man, rather men shall give their praise
  to violence
and the doer of evil. Right will be in the arm.
  Shame will
not be. The vile man will crowd his better out,
  and attack him
with twisted accusations and swear an oath
  to his story.
The spirit of Envy, with grim face
  and screaming voice, who delights
in evil, will be the constant companion

of wretched humanity,
and at last Nemesis and Aidos, Decency and Respect,
    shrouding
their bright forms in pale mantles, shall go
    from the wide-wayed
earth back on their way to Olympos,
    forsaking the whole race
of mortal men, and all that will be left by them
    to mankind
will be wretched pain. And there shall be no defense
    against evil.

THE FLOOD

OVID, *Metamorphoses*, Book 1. 285-418, with omissions (Dryden)

*Ovid introduces his account of the Flood and repopulation
of the earth with his own version of the Ages of Man.*

The Golden Age was first; when man yet new,
No rule but uncorrupted reason knew;
And, with a native bent, did good pursue.
Unforc'd by punishment, unaw'd by fear,
His words were simple, and his soul sincere:
Needless was written law, where none opprest;
The law of man was written in his breast:
No suppliant crowds before the judge appear'd:
No court erected yet, nor cause was hear'd;
But all was safe, for conscience was their guard.
The mountain trees in distant prospect please,
E're yet the pine descended to the seas;
E're sails were spread, new oceans to explore;
And happy mortals, unconcern'd for more,
Confin'd their wishes to their native shore.
No walls were yet; nor fence, nor moat nor mound;
Nor drum was heard, nor trumpets' angry sound:
Nor swords were forg'd; but, void of care and crime,
The soft creation slept away their time.
The teeming earth, yet guiltless of the plough,

And unprovok'd, did fruitful stores allow:
Content with food, which Nature freely bred,
On wildings, and on strawberries they fed;
Cornels and bramble-berries gave the rest,
And falling acorns furnisht out a feast.
The flow'rs unsown, in fields and meadows reign'd,
And western winds immortal spring maintain'd.
In following years, the bearded corn ensu'd
From earth unask'd, nor was that earth renew'd.
From veins of valleys, milk and nectar broke;
And honey sweating through the pores of oak.
  But when good Saturn, banish'd from above,
Was driv'n to Hell, the world was under Jove.
Succeeding times a Silver Age behold,
Excelling brass, but more excell'd by gold.
Then summer, autumn, winter did appear;
And spring was but a season of the year.
The sun his annual course obliquely made,
Good days contracted, and enlarg'd the bad.
Then air with sultry heats began to glow,
The wings of winds were clogg'd with ice and snow;
And shivering mortals, into houses driven,
Sought shelter from th' inclemency of Heav'n.
Those houses, then, were caves, or homely sheds,
With twining oziers fenc'd; and moss their beds.
Then ploughs, for seed, the fruitful furrows broke,
And oxen labor'd first beneath the yoke.
  To this next came in course the Brazen Age:
A warlike offspring prompt to bloody rage,
Not impious yet—
  —Hard Steel succeeded then;
And stubborn as the metal, were the men.
Truth, Modesty, and Shame, the world forsook:
Fraud, Avarice, and Force, their places took.
Then sails were spread, to every wind that blew;
Raw were the sailors, and the depths were new:
Trees rudely hollow'd, did the waves sustain;
E're ships in triumph plough'd the watry plain.
  Then landmarks limited to each his right:
For all before was common, as the light.
Nor was the ground alone requir'd to bear
Her annual income to the crooked share:

But greedy mortals, rummaging her store,
Digg'd from her entrails first the precious ore;
Which next to Hell the prudent Gods had laid;
And that alluring ill to sight displaid.
Thus cursed steel, and more accursed gold,
Gave mischief birth, and made that mischief bold:
And double death did wretched man invade,
By steel assaulted, and by gold betray'd.
Now (brandish'd weapons glitt'ring in their hands)
Mankind is broken loose from moral bands;
No rights of hospitality remain:
The guest by him who harbor'd him, is slain:
The son-in-law pursues the father's life;
The wife her husband murders, he the wife.
The step-dame poison for the son prepares;
The son inquires into his father's years.
Faith flies, and Piety in exile mourns;
And Justice, here opprest, to Heav'n returns.

   Nor were the Gods themselves more safe above;
Against beleagur'd heav'n, the giants move.
Hills piled on hills, on mountains, mountains lie,
To make their mad approaches to the sky.
Till Jove, no longer patient, took his time
T' avenge with thunder their audacious crime:
Red light'ning play'd along the firmament,
And their demolish't works to pieces rent.

    . . . .

"Mankind's a monster, and th' ungodly times,
Confed'rate into guilt, are sworn to crimes.
All are alike involv'd in ill, and all
Must by the same relentless fury fall."
   Thus ended he; the greater Gods assent,
By clamors urging his severe intent;
The less fill up the cry for punishment.
Yet still with pity they remember man;
And mourn as much as heav'nly spirits can.
They ask, when those were lost of human birth,
What he wou'd do with all this waste of earth:
If his dispeopl'd world he would resign
To beasts, a mute, and more ignoble line;
Neglected altars must no longer smoke,
If none were left to worship and invoke.

To whom the Father of the Gods reply'd:
"Lay that unnecessary fear aside:
Mine be the care, new people to provide.
I will from wondrous principles ordain
A race unlike the first, and try my skill again."
    Already had he toss'd the flaming brand,
And roll'd the thunder in his spacious hand;
Preparing to discharge on seas and land:
But stopp'd, for fear thus violently driv'n,
The sparks should catch his axle-tree of Heav'n.
Rememb'ring, in the Fates, a time when fire
Shou'd to the battlements of Heav'n aspire,
And all his blazing worlds above shou'd burn,
And all th' inferior globe to cinders turn.
His dire Artill'ry thus dismist, he bent
His thoughts to some securer punishment:
Concludes to pour a watry deluge down;
And what he durst not burn, resolves to drown.
    The Northern breath, that freezes floods, he binds;
With all the race of cloud-dispelling winds
The South he loos'd, who night and horror brings;
And fogs are shaken from his flaggy wings.
From his divided beard, two streams he pours;
His head and rheumy eyes distil in showers.
With rain his robe and heavy mantle flow:
And lazy mists are lowring on his brow.
Still as he swept along, with his clench't fist,
He squeez'd the clouds; th' imprison'd clouds resist:
The skies, from pole to pole, with peals resound:
And show'rs inlarg'd come pouring on the ground.
Then, clad in colors of a various dye,
Junonian Iris breeds a new supply
To feed the clouds: impetuous rain descends;
The bearded corn beneath the burden bends:
Defrauded clowns deplore their perish'd grain;
And the long labors of the year are vain.
    Nor from his patrimonial heav'n alone
Is Jove content to pour his vengeance down:
Aid from his brother of the seas he craves,
To help him with auxiliary waves.
The watry tyrant calls his brooks and floods,
Who roll from mossy caves (their moist abodes;)

And with perpetual urns his palace fill:
To whom in brief, he thus imparts his will.
   Small exhortation needs; your pow'rs employ:
And this bad world, so Jove requires, destroy.
Let loose the reins to all your watry store:
Bear down the dams, and open every door.
   The floods, by nature enemies to land,
And proudly swelling with their new command,
Remove the living stones, that stopt their way,
And gushing from their source, augment the sea.
Then, with his mace, their monarch struck the ground:
With inward trembling, Earth receiv'd the wound;
And rising streams a ready passage found.
Th' expanded waters gather on the plain,
They float the fields, and over-top the grain;
Then rushing onwards, with a sweepy sway,
Bear flocks, and folds, and lab'ring hinds away.
Nor safe their dwellings were; for, sapp'd by floods,
Their houses fell upon their household gods.
The solid piles, too strongly built to fall,
High o'er their heads, behold a watry wall:
Now seas and earth were in confusion lost;
A world of waters, and without a coast.
   One climbs a cliff; one in his boat is born,
And ploughs above, where late he sow'd his corn.
Others o'er chimney tops and turrets row,
And drop their anchors on the meads below:
Or downward driv'n, they bruise the tender vine,
Or tost aloft, are knock't against a pine.
And where of late the kids had cropt the grass,
The monsters of the deep now take their place.
Insulting Nereids on the cities ride,
And wondring dolphins o'er the palace glide.
On leaves and masts of mighty oaks they browse,
And their broad fins entangle in the boughs.
The frighted wolf now swims amongst the sheep;
The yellow lion wanders in the deep;
His rapid force no longer helps the boar.
The stag swims faster than he ran before.
The fowls, long beating on their wings in vain,
Despair of land, and drop into the main.
Now hills and vales no more distinction know,

And levell'd nature lies oppress'd below.
The most of mortals perish in the flood:
The small remainder dies for want of food.
A mountain of stupendous height there stands
Betwixt th' Athenian and Boeotian lands,
The bound of fruitful fields, while fields they were,
But then a field of waters did appear:
Parnassus is its name; whose forky rise
Mounts through the clouds, and mates the lofty skies.
High on the summit of this dubious cliff,
Deucalion wafting, moor'd his little skiff.
He with his wife were only left behind
Of perish'd man; they two were human kind.
The mountain nymphs and Themis they adore,
And from her oracles relief implore.
The most upright of mortal men was he;
The most sincere and holy woman, she.

When Jupiter, surveying Earth from high,
Beheld it in a lake of water lie,
That, where so many millions lately liv'd,
But two, the best of either sex, surviv'd,
He loos'd the northern wind; fierce Boreas flies
To puff away the clouds, and purge the skies:
Serenely, while he blows, the vapors, driven,
Discover Heav'n to Earth, and Earth to Heaven.
The billows fall, while Neptune lays his mace
On the rough sea, and smooths its furrow'd face,
Already Triton, at his call appears
Above the waves; a Tyrian robe he wears;
And in his hand a crooked trumpet bears.
The sovereign bids him peaceful sounds inspire,
And give the waves the signal to retire.
His writhen shell he takes; whose narrow vent
Grows by degrees into a large extent;
Then gives it breath; the blast, with doubling sound,
Runs the wide circuit of the world around.
The sun first heard it, in his early East,
And met the rattling echo's in the West.
The waters, listening to the trumpets' roar,
Obey the summons, and forsake the shore.

A thin circumference of land appears;
And earth, but not at once, her visage rears,

And peeps upon the seas from upper grounds:
The streams, but just contain'd within their bounds,
By slow degrees into their channels crawl
And earth increases as the waters fall.
In longer time the tops of trees appear,
Which mud on their dishonor'd branches bear.
  At length the world was all restor'd to view,
But desolate, and of a sickly hue:
Nature beheld herself, and stood aghast,
A dismal desert, and a silent waste.
  Which when Deucalion, with a piteous look,
Beheld, he wept, and thus to Pyrrha spoke:
"Oh wife, oh sister, oh oh all thy kind
The best and only creature left behind,
By kindred, love, and now by dangers join'd;
Of multitudes, who breath'd the common air,
We two remain; a species in a pair;
The rest the seas have swallow'd; nor have we
Ev'n of this wretched life a certainty.
The clouds are still above; and, while I speak,
A second deluge o'er our heads may break.
Shou'd I be snatch'd from hence, and thou remain,
Without relief, or partner of thy pain,
How cou'd'st thou such a wretched life sustain?
Shou'd I be left, and thou be lost, the sea,
That bury'd her I lov'd, shou'd bury me.
Oh cou'd our father his old arts inspire,
And make me heir of his informing fire,
That so I might abolisht man retrieve,
And perisht people in new souls might live.
But Heav'n is pleas'd, nor ought we to complain,
That we, th' examples of mankind remain."
He said: the careful couple join their tears,
And then invoke the Gods, with pious prayers.
Thus, in devotion having eas'd their grief,
From sacred oracles they seek relief:
And to Cephysus' brook their way pursue:
The stream was troubl'd, but the ford they knew.
With living waters in the fountain bred,
They sprinkle first their garments, and their head,
Then took the way which to the temple led.
The roofs were all defil'd with moss and mire,

The desert altars void of solemn fire.
Before the gradual, prostrate they ador'd,
The pavement kiss'd, and thus the saint implor'd.
  "O righteous Themis, if the pow'rs above
By pray'rs are bent to pity, and to love;
If human miseries can move their mind;
If yet they can forgive, and yet be kind;
Tell how we may restore, by second birth,
Mankind, and people-desolated earth."
Then thus the gracious Goddess, nodding, said;
"Depart, and with your vestments veil your head;
And stooping lowly down, with loosn'd zones,
Throw each behind your backs, your mighty mother's bones."
Amaz'd the pair; and mute with wonder, stand,
Till Pyrrha first refus'd the dire command.
"Forbid it heav'n," said she, "that I shou'd tear
Those holy reliques from the sepulcher."
They ponder'd the mysterious words again,
For some new sense; and long they sought in vain.
At length Deucalion clear'd his cloudy brow,
And said; "The dark enigma will allow
A meaning, which, if well I understand,
From sacrilege will free the God's command:
This earth our mighty mother is, the stones
In her capacious body, are her bones.
These we must cast behind." With hope and fear,
The woman did the new solution hear:
The man diffides in his own augury,
And doubts the Gods; yet both resolve to try.
Descending from the mount, they first unbind
Their vests, and veil'd, they cast the stones behind:
The stones (a miracle to mortal view,
But long tradition makes it pass for true)
Did first the rigor of their kind expell,
And suppl'd into softness as they fell;
Then swell'd, and swelling, by degrees grew warm;
And took the rudiments of human form;
Imperfect shapes: in marble such are seen,
When the rude chisel does the man begin;
While yet the roughness of the stone remains,
Without the rising muscles, and the veins.
The sappy parts, and next resembling juice,

Were turn'd to moisture, for the bodies' use:
Supplying humors, blood, and nourishment:
The rest (too solid to receive a bent)
Converts to bones; and what was once a vein,
Its former name and nature did retain.
By help of pow'r divine, in little space,
What the man threw, assum'd a manly face;
And what the wife, renew'd the female race.
Hence we derive our nature, born to bear
Laborious life; and harden'd into care.
    The rest of animals, from teeming earth
Produc'd, in various forms receiv'd their birth.
The native moisture, in its close retreat,
Digested by the sun's ethereal heat,
As in a kindly womb, began to breed:
Then swell'd and quicken'd by the vital seed.
And some in less, and some in longer space,
Were ripen'd into form, and took a several face.
Thus when the Nile from Pharian fields is fled,
And seeks, with ebbing tides, his ancient bed,
The fat manure with heav'nly fire is warm'd;
And crusted creatures, as in wombs are form'd:
These, when they turn the glebe, the peasants find:
Some rude, and yet unfinish'd in their kind:
Short of their limbs, a lame imperfect birth;
One half alive; and one of lifeless earth.
    For heat and moisture, when in bodies join'd,
The temper that results from either kind,
Conception makes; and fighting, till they mix,
Their mingl'd atoms in each other fix.
Thus Nature's hand the genial bed prepares
With friendly discord, and with fruitful wars.
    From hence the surface of the ground with mud
And slime besmear'd (the feces of the flood),
Receiv'd the rays of Heav'n; and sucking in
The seeds of heat, new creatures did begin:
Some were of sev'ral sorts produc'd before;
But of new monsters, earth created more.

THE GODS OF DELPHI

AESCHYLUS, *Eumenides*, 1-19 (Campbell)

The priestess of Apollo gives an account of the early days of the shrine.

"First in my prayer I sanctify the power
Of Earth, first prophetess; and then of her,
Themis, who next upon her mother's throne
Of divination sat, as legends tell.
Third came and by consent was 'stablished here
Another Titan daughter of the ground,
Phoebe, who gave, in honor of his birth,
This place to Phoebus, near to her in name.
He left the Delian reef and the broad sea,
Landed on Pallas' ship-receiving shore,
And sought these pastures, 'neath Parnassus' height,
Led by Hephaestus' sons, his worshippers,
Good pioneers who make rough countries smooth.
This people, at his coming, and their king,
Delphos, sage pilot of the land, enriched him
With reverent offerings, while Zeus inspired
His heart with wisdom, and established him
Fourth holder of this high prophetic seat.
Here Phoebus dwells, his Sire's interpreter.
These names I make the prelude of my prayer.
Then, praising Pallas of the vestibule,
And the fair nymphs, where the Corycian cave,
Beloved of birds, owns presence more divine,
Nor yet forgetting him, who haunts this land
Since, leading forth his Bacchanals to war,
He hunted Pentheus like a hare;—once more,
Naming the springs of Pleistos and the strong
Poseidon, and the absolute perfectness
Of Zeus, I mount to my prophetic throne."

ZEUS

HOMER, *Iliad*, Book 16. 384-393 (Lattimore)

Zeus, the god of the sky, is concerned with a wide variety of phenomena. Although his amorous proclivities are mentioned even by the earliest writers, he is always a god of stature, concerned with man's political and moral life. In this simile Homer shows Zeus' concern for righteousness.

As underneath the hurricane all the black earth is burdened
on an autumn day, when Zeus sends down the most violent waters
in deep rage against mortals after they stir him to anger
because in violent assembly they pass decrees that are crooked,
and drive righteousness from among them and care nothing for
    what the gods think,
and all the rivers of these men swell current to full spate
and in the ravines of their water-courses rip all the hillsides
and dash whirling in huge noise down to the blue sea, out of
the mountains headlong, so that the works of men are diminished;
so huge rose the noise from the horses of Troy in their running.

ZEUS

AESCHYLUS, *Agamemnon*, 160-183 (Morshead)

The chorus gives an account of the nature of Zeus, the successor of Uranus and Cronus.

Zeus—if to The Unknown
    That name of many names seem good—
Zeus, upon Thee I call.
    Thro' the mind's every road
I passed, but vain are all,
Save that which names thee Zeus, the Highest One,

Were it but mine to cast away the load,
The weary load, that weighs my spirit down.

He that was Lord of old,
In full-blown pride of place and valor bold,
    Hath fallen and is gone, even as an old tale told!
    And he that next held sway,
    By stronger grasp o'erthrown
    Hath pass'd away!
And whoso now shall bid the triumph-chant arise
    To Zeus, and Zeus alone,
He shall be found the truly wise.

'Tis Zeus alone who shows the perfect way
    Of knowledge: He hath ruled,
Men shall learn wisdom, by affliction schooled.

ZEUS, HERA, AND HEPHAESTUS

HOMER, *Iliad*, Book 1. 533-611 (Lattimore)

A picture of life on Olympus.

Zeus went back to his own house, and all the gods rose up
from their chairs to greet the coming of their father, not one had
        courage
to keep his place as the father advanced, but stood up to greet him.
Thus he took his place on the throne; yet Hera was not
ignorant, having seen how he had been plotting counsels
with Thetis the silver-footed, the daughter of the sea's ancient,
and at once she spoke revilingly to Zeus son of Kronos:
"Treacherous one, what god has been plotting counsels with you?
Always it is dear to your heart in my absence to think of
secret things and decide upon them. Never have you patience
frankly to speak forth to me the thing that you purpose."
    Then to her the father of gods and men made answer:
"Hera, do not go on hoping that you will hear all my
thoughts, since these will be too hard for you, though you are my
        wife.

Any thought that it is right for you to listen to, no one
neither man nor any immortal shall hear it before you.
But anything that apart from the rest of the gods I wish to
plan, do not always question each detail nor probe me."
    Then the goddess the ox-eyed lady Hera answered:
"Majesty, son of Kronos, what sort of thing have you spoken?
Truly too much in time past I have not questioned nor probed
    you,
but you are entirely free to think out whatever pleases you.
Now, though, I am terribly afraid you were won over
by Thetis the silver-footed, the daughter of the sea's ancient.
For early in the morning she sat beside you and took your
knees, and I think you bowed your head in assent to do honor
to Achilleus, and to destroy many beside the ships of the
    Achaians."
    Then in return Zeus who gathers the clouds made answer:
"Dear lady, I never escape you, you are always full of suspicion.
Yet thus you can accomplish nothing surely, but be more
distant from my heart than ever, and it will be the worse for you.
If what you say is true, then that is the way I wish it.
But go then, sit down in silence, and do as I tell you,
for fear all the gods, as many as are on Olympos, can do nothing
if I come close and lay my unconquerable hands upon you."
    He spoke, and the goddess the ox-eyed lady Hera was frightened
and went and sat down in silence wrenching her heart to obedi-
    ence,
and all the Uranian gods in the house of Zeus were troubled.
Hephaistos the renowned smith rose up to speak among them,
to bring comfort to his beloved mother, Hera of the white arms:
"This will be a disastrous matter and not endurable
if you two are to quarrel thus for the sake of mortals
and bring brawling among the gods. There will be no pleasure
in the stately feast at all, since vile things will be uppermost.
And I entreat my mother, though she herself understands it,
to be ingratiating toward our father Zeus, that no longer
our father may scold her and break up the quiet of our feasting.
For if the Olympian who handles the lightning should be minded
to hurl us out of our places, he is far too strong for any.
Do you therefore approach him again with words made gentle,
and at once the Olympian will be gracious again to us."
    He spoke, and springing to his feet put a two-handled goblet
into his mother's hands and spoke again to her once more:

"Have patience, my mother, and endure it, though you be sad-
    dened,
for fear that, dear as you are, I see you before my own eyes
struck down, and then sorry though I be I shall not be able
to do anything. It is too hard to fight against the Olympian.
There was a time once before now I was minded to help you,
and he caught me by the foot and threw me from the magic thresh-
    old,
and all day long I dropped helpless, and about sunset
I landed in Lemnos, and there was not much life left in me.
After that fall it was the Sintian men who took care of me."
    He spoke, and the goddess of the white arms Hera smiled at
    him,
and smiling she accepted the goblet out of her son's hand.
Thereafter beginning from the left he poured drinks for the other
gods, dipping up from the mixing bowl the sweet nectar.
But among the blessed immortals uncontrollable laughter
went up as they saw Hephaistos bustling about the palace.
    Thus thereafter the whole day long until the sun went under
they feasted, nor was anyone's hunger denied a fair portion,
nor denied the beautifully wrought lyre in the hands of Apollo
nor the antiphonal sweet sound of the Muses singing.
    Afterwards when the light of the flaming sun went under
they went away each one to sleep in his home where
for each one the far-renowned strong-handed Hephaistos
had built a house by means of his craftsmanship and cunning.
Zeus the Olympian and lord of the lightning went to
his own bed, where always he lay when sweet sleep came on him.
Going up to the bed he slept and Hera of the gold throne beside
    him.

~~~~~

POSEIDON, ZEUS, AND HADES

HOMER, *Iliad*, Book 15. 187-195 (Chase and Perry)

*Poseidon describes to Iris the division of rule among the sons
of Cronus.*

Greatly angered, the famous Earth-shaker addressed her: "Indeed, mighty as he may be, he has spoken with arrogance, if by

force and against my will he plans to restrain me who am his equal in honor. We are three brothers, sprung from Cronus, born of Rhea, Zeus and I and the third one, Hades, who rules over those beneath the earth. All things were divided in three ways and each one had his share of honor. When the lots were cast, mine was the gray sea, to dwell therein forever, and Hades drew the misty realms of shadows. Zeus drew broad heaven, amid the air and clouds. But earth and high Olympus are still held by all in common. Therefore I will not live after the mind of Zeus. Let him, though mightier, abide in peace in his appointed third. Let him not try to scare me by might of hand as though I were a weakling, for it were better to upbraid with dreadful words his sons and daughters whom he himself begot, who will perforce give ear when he commands."

POSEIDON

HOMER, *Iliad*, Book 13. 17-38 (Chase and Perry)

Poseidon goes to rouse the Greeks, hard pressed by the Trojans.

Yet the mighty Earth-shaker kept no careless watch, for gazing in wonder at the war and battle he sat high on the loftiest peak of wooded Samothrace. Thence all Ida lay plain before him, and plain before him lay Priam's city and the ships of the Achaeans. He had risen from the sea and gone and sat there; he pitied the Achaeans as they were worsted by the Trojans, and he was greatly angered at Zeus.

At once he went down from the rugged mountain with quick strides, and the long ridges and the woods trembled beneath the immortal feet of Poseidon as he passed. Three strides he made and with the fourth he reached his goal, Aegae, where in the depths of the sea his glorious house is built, golden and glittering, indestructible forever. There he came, and put to his chariot his bronze-hoofed horses, swift-flying, with manes of gold. He clad himself in gold and grasped a well-wrought golden whip, and mounted his chariot and set out across the waves. The creatures of the sea arose on all sides from the depths and gamboled near him, nor did they fail to know their lord. With joy the sea parted before him, and the horses flew right swiftly; the bronze axle was not even wet beneath, and with easy stride they bore him toward the ships of the Achaeans.

There is a broad cavern in the depths of the deep sea, midway between Tenedos and rugged Imbros. There earth-shaking Poseidon stopped the horses and loosed them from the chariot and cast before them ambrosial food to eat. He cast golden hobbles about their feet, unbreakable, unloosable, that they might continually there await their master's return, and he himself departed for the camp of the Achaeans.

~~~~~

APOLLO

Homeric Hymns, 1-178, with omissions (Lang)

Apollo is the most characteristically Greek of all the gods. He is beautiful, the patron of medicine and music, the interpreter of the will of Zeus. His name is probably not Greek, but he was enthusiastically adopted and naturalized throughout Greece.

Mindful, ever mindful, will I be of Apollo the Far-darter. Before him, as he fares through the hall of Zeus, the Gods tremble, yea, rise up all from their thrones as he draws near with his shining bended bow. But Leto alone abides by Zeus, the Lord of Lightning, till Apollo has slackened his bow and closed his quiver. Then, taking with her hands from his mighty shoulders the bow and quiver, she hangs them against the pillar beside his father's seat from a pin of gold, and leads him to his place and seats him there, while the father welcomes his dear son, giving him nectar in a golden cup; then do the other Gods welcome him; then they make him sit, and Lady Leto rejoices, in that she bore the Lord of the Bow, her mighty son.

. . . .

How shall I hymn thee aright, although thou art, in sooth, not hard to hymn? for to thee, Phoebus, everywhere have fallen all the ranges of song, both on the mainland, nurse of young kine, and among the isles; to thee all the cliffs are dear, and the steep mountain crests and rivers running onward to the salt sea, and beaches sloping to the foam, and havens of the deep? Shall I tell how Leto bore thee first, a delight of men, couched by the Cynthian Hill in the rocky island, in sea-girt Delos—on either hand the black wave drives landward at the word of the shrill winds—whence arising thou art Lord over all mortals?

. . . .

The lands trembled sore, and were adread, and none, nay not the richest, dared to welcome Phoebus, not till Lady Leto set foot on Delos, and speaking winged words besought her:

"Delos, would that thou were minded to be the seat of my Son, Phoebus Apollo, and to let him build therein a rich temple! No other God will touch thee, nor none will honor thee, for I think thou art not to be well seen in cattle or in sheep, in fruit or grain, nor wilt thou grow plants unnumbered. But were thou to possess a temple of Apollo the Far-darter; then would all men bring thee hecatombs, gathering to thee, and ever wilt thou have savor of sacrifice . . . from others' hands, although thy soil is poor."

Thus spoke she, and Delos was glad and answered her saying:

"Leto, daughter most renowned of mighty Coeus, right gladly would I welcome the birth of the Archer Prince, for verily of me there goes an evil report among men, and thus would I wax mightiest of renown. But at this Word, Leto, I tremble, nor will I hide it from thee, for the saying is that Apollo will be mighty of mood, and mightily will lord it over mortals and immortals far and wide over the earth, the grain-giver. Therefore, I deeply dread in heart and soul lest, when first he looks upon the sunlight, he disdain my island, for rocky of soil am I, and spurn me with his feet and drive me down in the gulfs of the salt sea. Then should a great sea-wave wash mightily above my head forever, but he will fare to another land, which so pleases him, to fashion him a temple and groves of trees. But in me would many-footed sea-beasts and black seals make their chambers securely, no men dwelling by me. Nay, still, if thou hast the heart, Goddess, to swear a great oath that here first he will build a beautiful temple, to be the shrine oracular of men—thereafter among all men let him raise him shrines, since his renown shall be the widest."

So spake she, but Leto swore the great oath of the Gods:

"Bear witness, Earth, and the wide heaven above, and dropping water of Styx—the greatest oath and the most dread among the blessed Gods—that verily here shall ever be the fragrant altar and the portion of Apollo, and thee will he honor above all."

When she had sworn and done that oath, then Delos was glad in the birth of the Archer Prince. But Leto, for nine days and nine nights continually was pierced with pangs of childbirth beyond all hope. With her were all the Goddesses, the goodliest, Dione and Rhea, and Ichnaean Themis, and Amphitrite of the moaning sea, and the other deathless ones—save white-armed Hera. Alone she knew not of it, Eilithyia, the helper in difficult travail. For she sat on the crest of Olympus beneath the golden clouds, by the wile of white-armed Hera, who held her afar in jealous grudge, because even then fair-tressed Leto was about bearing her strong and noble son.

But the Goddesses sent forth Iris from the fair-established isle, to bring Eilithyia, promising her a great necklet, golden with amber studs, nine cubits long. Iris they bade to call Eilithyia apart from white-armed Hera, lest even then the words of Hera might turn her from her going. But wind-footed swift Iris heard, and fleeted forth, and swiftly she devoured the space between. As soon as she came to steep Olympus, the dwelling of the Gods, she called forth Eilithyia from hall to door, and spake winged words, even all that the Goddesses of Olympian mansions had bidden her. Thereby she won the heart in Eilithyia's breast, and forth they fared, like timid wild doves in their going.

When Eilithyia, the helper in sore travailing, set foot in Delos, then labor took hold on Leto, and a passion to bring to the birth. Around a palm tree she cast her arms, and set her knees on the soft meadow, while earth beneath smiled, and forth leaped the babe to light, and all the Goddesses raised a cry. Then, great Phoebus, the Goddesses washed thee in fair water, holy and purely, and wound thee in white swaddling bands, delicate, new woven, with a golden girdle round thee. Nor did his mother suckle Apollo the golden-sworded, but Themis with immortal hands first touched his lips with nectar and sweet ambrosia, while Leto rejoiced, in that she had borne her strong son, the bearer of the bow.

Then, Phoebus, as soon as thou had tasted the food of Paradise, the golden bands were not proof against thy pantings, nor bonds could bind thee, but all their ends were loosened. Straightway among the Goddesses spoke Phoebus Apollo: "Mine be the dear lyre and bended bow, and I will utter to men the unerring counsel of Zeus."

So speaking, he began to fare over the wide ways of earth, Phoebus of the locks unshorn, Phoebus the Far-darter. Thereon all the Goddesses were in amaze, and all Delos blossomed with gold, as when a hilltop is heavy with woodland flowers, beholding the child of Zeus and Leto, and glad because the God had chosen her wherein to set his home, beyond mainland and isles, and loved her most at heart.

But thyself, O Prince of the Silver Bow, far-darting Apollo, did now pass over rocky Cynthus, now wander among temples and men. Many are thy temples and groves, and dear are all the headlands, and high peaks of lofty hills, and rivers flowing onward to the sea; but with Delos, Phoebus, art thou most delighted at heart, where the long-robed Ionians gather in thine honor, with children and shame-free wives. Mindful of thee they delight thee with boxing, and dances, and minstrelsy in their games. Whoever then encountered them at the gathering of the Ionians, would say that they are exempt from age and death, beholding them so gracious, and would be glad at heart, looking on the men and fair-girdled women, and their much wealth, and their swift galleys. Moreover, there is this great marvel of renown imperishable, the Delian damsels, hand-maidens of the Far-darter. They, when first they have hymned Apollo, and next Leto and Artemis the Archer, then sing in memory of the men and women of old time, enchanting the tribes of mortals. And they are skilled to mimic the notes and dance music of all men, so that each would say himself were singing, so well woven is their fair chant.

But now come, be gracious, Apollo, be gracious, Artemis; and ye maidens all, farewell, but remember me even in time to come, when any of earthly men, yea, any stranger that much has seen and much endured, comes hither and asks:

"Maidens, who is the sweetest to you of singers here conversant, and in whose song are you most glad?"

Then do you all with one voice make answer:

"A blind man is he, and he dwells in rocky Chios; his songs will ever have the mastery, ay, in all time to come."

But I shall bear my renown of you as far as I wander over earth to the fairest cities of men, and they will believe my report, for my word is true. But, for me, never shall I cease singing of Apollo of the Silver Bow, the Far-darter, whom fair-tressed Leto bore.

O Prince, Lycia is thine, and pleasant Maeonia, and Miletus, a winsome city by the sea, and thou, too, are the mighty lord of sea-washed Delos.

~~~~

ARTEMIS

Homeric Hymns, 1-20 (Lang)

The goddess Artemis, the virgin huntress, sister of Apollo, is non-Greek in origin. She was a mother-goddess, closely connected with the birth of all living things, and was worshipped in many places outside Greece.

I sing of Artemis of the Golden Distaff, Goddess of the loud chase, a maiden revered, the slayer of stags, the archer, very sister of Apollo of the golden blade. She through the shadowy hills and the windy headlands rejoicing in the chase draws her golden bow, sending forth shafts of sorrow. Then tremble the crests of the lofty mountains, and terribly the dark woodland rings with din of beasts, and the earth shudders, and the teeming sea. Meanwhile she of the stout heart turns about on every side slaying the race of wild beasts. When the Archer Huntress has taken her delight, and has gladdened her heart, she slackens her bended bow, and goes to the great hall of her dear Phoebus Apollo, to the rich Delphian land; and arrays the lovely dance of Muses and Graces. There hangs she up her bended bow and her arrows, and all graciously clad about she leads the dances, first in place, while the others utter their immortal voice in hymns to fair-ankled Leto, how she bore such children pre-eminent among the Immortals in counsel and in deed. Hail, ye children of Zeus and fair-tressed Leto.

~~~~

ATHENE

Homeric Hymns, 1-17 (Lang)

Athene, the warlike patron of Athens, becomes a goddess of handicrafts and, ultimately, of wisdom in general.

Of fairest Athene, renowned Goddess, I begin to sing, of the Gray-eyed, the wise; her of the relentless heart, the maiden revered, the succor of cities, the strong Tritogeneia. Her did Zeus the counsellor himself beget from his holy head, all armed for war in shining golden mail, while in awe did the other Gods behold it. Quickly did the Goddess leap from the immortal head, and stood before Zeus, shaking her sharp spear, and high Olympus trembled in dread beneath the strength of the gray-eyed Maiden, while earth rang terribly around, and the sea was boiling with dark waves, and suddenly broke forth the foam. Yea, and the glorious son of Hyperion checked for long his swift steeds, till the maiden took from her immortal shoulders her divine armor, even Pallas Athene: and Zeus the counsellor rejoiced. Hail to thee, thou child of aegis-bearing Zeus, ever shall I be mindful of thee.

HERMES

Homeric Hymns, 1-578 (Lang)

Hermes is a versatile god, concerned with a wide variety of activities. Of no great importance among the Olympians, he is a messenger and errand boy, but among men he is a friendly and sociable god.

Of Hermes sing, O Muse, the son of Zeus and Maia, Lord of Cyllene, and Arcadia rich in sheep, the fortune-bearing Herald of the Gods, him whom Maia bore, the fair-tressed nymph, that lay in the arms of Zeus; a shamefaced nymph was she, shunning the assembly of the blessed Gods, dwelling within a shadowy cave. Therein did Cronion embrace the fair-tressed nymph in the deep of night, when sweet sleep held white-armed Hera, the immortal Gods knowing it not, nor mortal men.

But when the mind of great Zeus was fulfilled, and over her the tenth moon stood in the sky, the babe was born to light, and all was made manifest; yea, then she bore a child of many a wile and cunning counsel, a robber, a driver of the cattle, a captain of raiders, a watcher of the night, a thief of the gates, who soon should show forth deeds renowned among the deathless Gods. Born in the dawn, by midday well he harped, and in the evening stole the cattle of Apollo the Far-darter, on that fourth day of the month wherein lady Maia bore him. Who, when he leaped from the immortal knees of his mother, lay not long in the sacred cradle, but sped forth to seek the cattle of Apollo, crossing the threshold of the high-roofed cave. There found he a tortoise, and won endless delight, for lo, it was Hermes that first made of the tortoise a minstrel. The creature met him at the outer door as she fed on the rich grass in front of the dwelling, waddling along, at sight whereof the luck-bringing son of Zeus laughed, and straightway spoke, saying:

"Lo, a lucky omen for me, not by me to be mocked! Hail, darling and dancer, friend of the feast, welcome! whence got thou the gay garment, a speckled shell, thou, a mountain-dwelling tortoise? Nay, I will carry thee within, and a boon shalt thou be to me, not by me to be scorned, nay, thou shall first serve my turn. Best it is to bide at home, since danger is abroad. Living shall thou be a spell against ill witchery, and dead, then a right sweet music-maker."

So spoke he, and raising in both hands the tortoise, went back within the dwelling, bearing the glad treasure. Then he choked the creature, and with a gouge of gray iron he scooped out the marrow of the hill tortoise. And as a swift thought wings through the breast of one that crowding cares are haunting, or as bright glances fleet from the eyes, so swiftly devised renowned Hermes both deed and word. He cut to measure stalks of reed, and fixed them in through holes bored in the stony shell of the tortoise, and cunningly stretched round it the hide of an ox, and put in the horns of the lyre, and to both he fitted the bridge, and stretched seven harmonious chords of sheep gut.

Then took he his treasure, when he had fashioned it, and touched the strings in turn with the plectrum, and wondrously it sounded under his hand, and fair sang the God to the notes, improvising his chant as he played, like lads exchanging taunts at festivals. Of Zeus Cronides and fair-sandalled Maia he sang how they had lived in loving dalliance, and he told out the tale of his begetting, and sang the handmaids and the goodly halls of the Nymph, and the tripods in the house, and the store of cauldrons. So then he sang, but dreamed of other deeds; then bore he the hollow lyre and laid it in the sacred cradle; then, in longing for flesh of cattle he sped from the fragrant hall to a place of outlook, with such a design in his heart as robbers pursue in the dark of night.

The sun had sunk down beneath earth into ocean, with horses and chariot, when Hermes came running to the shadowy hills of Pieria, where the deathless cattle of the blessed Gods had ever their haunt; there fed they on the fair unshorn meadows. From their number did the keen-sighted Argeiphontes, son of Maia, cut off fifty loud-lowing cattle, and drove them hither and thither over the sandy land, reversing their tracks, and, mindful of his cunning, confused the hoof-marks, the front behind, the hind in front, and himself fared down again. Straightway he wove sandals on the sea-sand (things undreamed he wrought, works wonderful, unspeakable) mingling myrtle twigs and tamarisk, then binding together a bundle of the fresh young wood, he shrewdly fastened it for light sandals beneath his feet, leaves and all,—brushwood that the renowned slayer of Argos had plucked on his way from Pieria.

Then an old man that was laboring a fruitful vineyard marked the God faring down to the plain through grassy Onchestus, and to him spoke first the son of renowned Maia:

"Old man that bowest thy shoulders over thy hoeing, thou shall have wine enough when all these vines are bearing. . . . See thou, and see not; hear thou, and hear not; be silent, so long as nothing of thine is harmed."

Therewith he drove on together the sturdy heads of cattle. And over many a shadowy hill, and through echoing hollows and flowering plains drove renowned Hermes. Then stayed for the more part his darkling ally, the sacred Night, and swiftly came morning when men can work, and sacred Selene, daughter of Pallas, mighty prince, climbed to a new place of outlook, and then the strong son of Zeus drove the broadbrowed cattle of Phoebus Apollo to the river Alpheius. Unwearied they came to the high-roofed stall and the watering-places in front of the fair meadow. There, when he had foddered the deep-voiced cattle, he herded them huddled together into the barn, munching lotus and dewy marsh marigold; next brought he much wood, and set himself to the craft of fire-kindling. Taking a goodly shoot of the daphne, he peeled it with the knife, fitting it to his hand, and the hot vapor of smoke arose. Then took he many dry faggots, great plenty, and piled them in the trench, and flame began to break, sending far the breath of burning fire. And when the force of renowned Hephaestus kept the fire aflame, then downward dragged he, so mighty his strength, two bellowing cattle of twisted horn; close up to the fire he dragged them, and cast them both panting upon their backs to the ground. Then bending over them he turned them upwards and cut their throats . . . task upon task, and sliced off the fat meat, pierced it with spits of wood, and broiled it—flesh, and chine, the joint of honor, and blood in the bowels, all together—then laid all there in its place. The hides he stretched out on a broken rock, as even now they are used, such as are to be enduring, long after that ancient day. Then glad Hermes dragged the fat portions onto a smooth ledge, and cut twelve messes sorted out by lot, to each its due he gave. Then a longing for the rite of the sacrifice of flesh came on renowned Hermes: for the sweet savor irked him, immortal as he was, but not even so did his strong heart yield. . . . The fat and flesh he placed in the high-roofed stall, the rest he swiftly raised aloft, a trophy of his robbery, and, gathering dry faggots, he burned heads and feet entire with the vapor of flame. When the God had duly finished all, he cast his sandals into the deep swirling pool of Alpheius, quenched the embers, and all night long spread smooth the black dust: Selene lighting him with her lovely light. Back to the crests of Cyllene came the God at dawn, nor blessed God, on that long way, nor mortal man encountered him; nay, and no dog barked. Then Hermes, son of Zeus, bearer of boon, bowed his head, and entered the hall through the hole of the bolt, like mist on the breath of autumn. Then, standing erect, he sped to the rich inmost chamber of the cave, lightly treading noiseless on the floor. Quickly to his cradle came glorious Hermes and wrapped the swaddling bands about his shoulders, like a witless babe, playing with the wrapper about his knees. So lay he, guarding his dear lyre at his left hand. But his Goddess mother the God did not deceive; she spoke, saying:

"Wherefore, thou cunning one, and whence comest thou in the night, thou clad in shamelessness? Methinks thou will go forth at Apollo's hands, with bonds about thy sides that may not be broken, sooner than be a robber in the glens. Go to, wretch, thy Father begot thee for a trouble to deathless Gods and mortal men."

But Hermes answered her with words of guile: "Mother mine, why would thou scare me so, as though I were an untutored child, with little craft in his heart, a trembling babe that dreads his mother's chidings? Nay, but I will essay the wiliest craft to feed thee and me forever. We two are not to endure to abide here, of all the deathless Gods alone unapproached with sacrifice and prayer, as thou commandest. Better it is eternally to be conversant with Immortals, richly, nobly, well seen in wealth of grain, than to be homekeepers in a darkling cave. And for honor, I too will have my dues of sacrifice, even as Apollo. Even if my Father give it me not I will endeavor, for I am of avail, to be a captain of robbers. And if the son of renowned Leto make inquest for me, methinks some worse thing will befall him. For to Pytho I will go, to break into his great house, whence I shall sack goodly tripods and cauldrons enough, and gold, and gleaming iron, and much raiment. Thyself, if thou hast a mind, shall see it."

So held they converse one with another, the son of Zeus of the Aegis, and Lady Maia. Then Morning the Daughter of Dawn was arising from the deep stream of Oceanus, bearing light to mortals, what time Apollo came to Onchestus in his journeying, the gracious grove, a holy place of the loud Girdler of the Earth: there he found an old man grazing his ox, the stay of his vineyard, on the roadside. To him the son of renowned Leto.

"Old man, hedger of grassy Onchestus; hither am I come seeking cattle from Pieria, all the crook-horned cattle out of my herd: my black bull was wont to graze apart from the rest, and my four bright-eyed hounds followed, four of them, wise as men and all of one mind. These were left, the hounds and the bull, a marvel; but the cattle wandered away from their soft meadow and sweet pasture, at the going down of the sun. Tell me, thou old man of ancient days, if thou hast seen any man faring after these cattle?"

Then to him the old man spoke and answered:

"My friend, hard it were to tell all that a man may see: for many wayfarers go by, some full of ill intent, and some of good: and it is difficult to be certain regarding each. Nevertheless, the whole day long till sunset I was digging about my vineyard plot, and methought I marked—but I know not surely—a child that went after the horned cattle; right young he was, and held a staff, and kept going from side to side, and backwards he drove the cattle, their faces fronting him."

So spoke the old man, but Apollo heard, and went fleeter on his path. Then marked he a bird long of wing, and he knew that the thief had been the son of Zeus Cronion. Swiftly sped the Prince, Apollo, son of Zeus, to goodly Pylos, seeking the shambling cattle, while his broad shoulders were swathed in purple cloud. Then the Far-darter marked the tracks, and spoke:

"Verily, a great marvel mine eyes behold! These are the tracks of high-horned cattle, but all are turned back to the meadow of asphodel. But these are not the footsteps of a man, nay, nor of a woman, nor of gray wolves, nor bears, nor lions, nor, methinks, of a shaggy-maned Centaur, whosoever with fleet feet makes such mighty strides! Dread to see they are that backwards go, more dread they that go forwards."

So speaking, the Prince sped on, Apollo, son of Zeus. To the Cyllenian hill he came, that is clad in forests, to the deep shadow of the hollow rock, where the deathless nymph brought forth the child of Zeus Cronion. A fragrance sweet was spread about the goodly hill, and many tall sheep were grazing the grass. Thence he went fleetly over the stone threshold into the dusky cave, Apollo, the Far-darter.

Now when the son of Zeus and Maia beheld Apollo thus in wrath for his cattle, he sank down within his fragrant swaddling bands, being covered as piled embers of burnt tree-roots are covered by thick ashes, so Hermes coiled himself up, when he saw the Far-darter; and curled himself, feet, head, and hands, into small space summoning sweet sleep, though in truth wide awake, and his tortoise-shell he kept beneath his armpit. But the son of Zeus and Leto marked them well, the lovely mountain nymph and her dear son, a little babe, all wrapped in cunning wiles. Gazing round all the chamber of the vasty dwelling, Apollo opened three cupboards with the shining key; full were they of nectar and glad ambrosia, and much gold and silver lay within, and much raiment of the Nymph, purple and glistening, such as are within the dwellings of the mighty Gods. When he had searched out the chambers of the great hall, the son of Leto spoke to renowned Hermes:

"Child, in the cradle lying, tell me straightway of my cattle: or speedily between us two will be unseemly strife. For I will seize and cast thee into murky Tartarus, into the darkness of doom where none is of avail. Nor shall thy father or mother redeem thee to the light: nay, under earth shall thou roam, a robber among folk fordone."

Then Hermes answered with words of craft: "Apollo, what ungentle word hast thou spoken? And is it thy cattle of the homestead thou come here to seek? I saw them not, heard not of them, gave ear to no word of them: of them I can tell no tidings, nor win the fee of him who tells. Not like a lifter of cattle, a stalwart man, am I: no task is this of mine: hitherto I have other cares; sleep, and mother's milk, and about my shoulders swaddling bands, and warmed baths. Let none know whence this feud arose! And verily great marvel among the Immortals it would be, that a new-born child should cross the threshold after cattle of the homestead.

Yesterday was I born, my feet are tender, and rough is the earth below. But if thou wish I shall swear the great oath by my father's head, that neither I myself am to blame, nor have I seen any other thief of thy cattle: whatever cattle be, for I know but by hearsay."

So spoke he with twinkling eyes, and twisted brows, glancing hither and thither, with long-drawn whistling breath, hearing Apollo's word as a vain thing. Then lightly laughing spoke Apollo the Far-darter:

"Oh, thou rogue, thou crafty one; I think that many a time thou will break into established homes, and by night leave many a man bare, silently pillaging through his house, such is thy speech today! And many herdsmen will thou vex in the mountain glens, when in lust for flesh thou come upon the herds and sheep thick of fleece. Nay come, lest thou sleep the last and longest slumber, come forth from thy cradle, thou companion of black night! For surely this honor hereafter thou shall have among the Immortals, to be called for ever the captain of robbers."

So spoke Phoebus Apollo, and lifted the child, but even then strong Argus-bane had his device, and, in the hands of the God, let forth an Omen, an evil belly-tenant, with tidings of worse, and a speedy sneeze thereafter. Apollo heard, and dropped renowned Hermes on the ground, then sat down before him, eager as he was to be gone, chiding Hermes, and thus he spoke:

"Take heart, swaddling one, child of Zeus and Maia. By these thine Omens shall I find the sturdy cattle, and thou shall lead the way."

So spoke he, but swiftly arose Cyllenian Hermes, and swiftly fared, pulling about his ears his swaddling bands that were his shoulder wrapping. Then spoke he:

"Whither bearest thou me, Far-darter, of Gods most vehement? Is it for wrath about thy cattle that thou thus provoke me? Would that the race of cattle might perish, for thy cattle have I not stolen, nor seen another steal, whatsoever cattle may be; I know but by hearsay, I! But let our suit be judged before Zeus Cronion."

Now were lone Hermes and the splendid son of Leto point by point disputing their pleas, Apollo with sure knowledge was righteously seeking to convict renowned Hermes for the sake of his cattle, but he with craft and cunning words sought to beguile —the Cyllenian to beguile the God of the Silver Bow. But when the wily one found one as wily, then speedily he strode forward through the sand in front, while behind came the son of Zeus and Leto. Swiftly they came to the crests of fragrant Olympus, to father Cronion they came, these goodly sons of Zeus, for there were set for them the balances of doom. Quiet was snowy Olympus, but they who know not decay or death were gathering after gold-throned Dawn. Then stood Hermes and Apollo of the Silver Bow before the knees of Zeus, the Thunderer, who inquired of his glorious Son, saying:

"Phoebus, whence drive thou such mighty spoil, a new-born babe like a Herald? A mighty matter this, to come before the gathering of the Gods!"

Then answered him the Prince, Apollo the Far-darter:

"Father, thou shall hear no empty tale; tauntest thou me, as though I were the only lover of booty? This boy have I found, a finished robber, in the hills of Cyllene, a long way to wander; so fine a knave as I know not among Gods or men, of all robbers on earth. My cattle he stole from the meadows, and went driving them at eventide along the loud sea shores, straight to Pylos. Wondrous were the tracks, a thing to marvel on, work of a glorious god. For the black dust showed the tracks of the cattle making backward to the mead of asphodel; but this child intractable fared neither on hands nor feet, through the sandy land, but this other strange craft had he, to tread the paths as if shod on with oaken shoots. While he drove the cattle through a land of sand, right plain to discern were all the tracks in the dust, but when he had crossed the great tract of sand, straightway on hard ground his traces and those of the cattle were ill to discern. But a mortal man beheld him, driving straight to Pylos the cattle broad of brow. Now when he had stalled the cattle in quiet, and confused his tracks on either side the way, he lay dark as night in his cradle, in the dusk of a shadowy cave. The keenest eagle could not have spied him, and much he rubbed his eyes, with crafty purpose, and bluntly spoke his word:

" 'I saw not, I heard not aught, nor learned another's tale; nor tidings could I give, nor win reward of tidings.' "

Therewith Phoebus Apollo sat him down, but another tale did Hermes tell, among the Immortals, addressing Cronion, the master of all Gods:

"Father Zeus, verily the truth will I tell thee: for true am I, nor know the way of falsehood. Today at sunrise came Apollo to our house, seeking his shambling cattle. No witnesses of the Gods brought he, nor no Gods who had seen the fact. But he bade me declare the thing under duress, threatening often to cast me into wide Tartarus, for he wears the tender flower of glorious youth, but I was born but yesterday, as well he knows, and in naught am I like a stalwart lifter of cattle. Believe, for thou give thyself out to be my father, that may I never be well if I drove home the cattle, nay, or crossed the threshold. The Sun I greatly revere, and other gods, and Thee I love, and *him* I dread. Nay, thyself know that I am not to blame; and thereto I will add a great oath: by these fair-wrought porches of the Gods I am guiltless, and one day yet I shall avenge me on him for this pitiless accusation, mighty as he is; but do thou aid the younger!"

So spoke Cyllenian Argus-bane, and winked, with his wrapping on his arm: he did not cast it down. But Zeus laughed aloud at the sight of his evil-witted child, so well and wittily he pled denial about the cattle. Then he bade them both be of one mind, and so seek the cattle, with Hermes as guide to lead the way, and show without guile where he had hidden the sturdy cattle. The Son of Cronos nodded, and glorious Hermes obeyed, for lightly persuadeth the counsel of Zeus of the Aegis.

Then sped both of them, the fair children of Zeus, to sandy Pylos, at the ford of Alpheius, and to the fields they came, and the stall of lofty roof, where the booty was tended in the season of darkness. There Hermes went to the side of the rocky cave, and began driving the sturdy cattle into the light. But the son of Leto, glancing aside, saw the flayed skins on the high rock, and quickly asked renowned Hermes:

"How could thou, oh crafty one, flay two cattle; new-born and childish as thou are? For time to come I dread thy might: no need for thee to be growing long, thou son of Maia!"

Then the strong Argus-bane with twinkling glances looked down at the ground, wishful to hide his purpose. But that harsh son of renowned Leto, the Far-darter, did he lightly soothe to his will; taking his lyre in his left hand he tuned it with the plectrum: and wondrously it rang beneath his hand. Thereat Phoebus Apollo laughed and was glad, and the winsome note passed through to his very soul as he heard. Then Maia's son took courage, and sweetly harping with his harp he stood at Apollo's left side, playing his prelude, and thereon followed his winsome voice. He sang the renowns of the deathless Gods, and the dark Earth, how all things were at the first, and how each God got his portion.

To Mnemosyne, first of Gods, he gave the gift of minstrelsy, to the Mother of the Muses, for the Muse came upon the Son of Maia.

Then all the rest of the Immortals, in order of rank and birth, did he honor, the splendid son of Zeus, telling duly all the tale, as he struck the lyre on his arm. But on Apollo's heart in his breast came the stress of desire, who spoke to him winged words:

"Thou crafty slayer of cattle, thou comrade of the feast; thy song is worth the price of fifty oxen! Henceforth, methinks, shall we be peacefully made at one. But, come now, tell me this, thou wily Son of Maia, have these marvels been with thee even since thy birth, or is it that some immortal, or some mortal man, has given thee the glorious gift and shown thee song divine? For marvellous is this new song in mine ears, such as, I think, none has known, either of men, or of Immortals who have mansions in Olympus, save thyself, thou robber, thou Son of Zeus and Maia! What art is this, what charm against the stress of cares? What a path of song! for verily here is choice of all three things, joy, and love, and sweet sleep. For truly though I be conversant with the Olympian Muses, to whom dances are a charge, and the bright minstrel hymn, and rich song, and the lovesome sound of flutes, yet never has anything been so dear to my heart, dear as the skill in the festivals of the Gods. I marvel, Son of Zeus, at this, the music of thy minstrelsy. But now since, despite thy youth, thou hast such glorious skill, to thee and to thy Mother I speak this word: verily, by this shaft of cornel wood, I shall lead thee renowned and fortunate among the Immortals, and give thee glorious gifts, nor in the end deceive thee."

Then Hermes answered him with cunning words:

"Shrewdly thou question me, Far-darter, nor do I grudge thee to enter upon my art. This day shalt thou know it: and to thee would I be kind in word and will: but within thyself thou well know all things, for first among the Immortals, Son of Zeus, is thy place. Mighty art thou and strong, and Zeus of wise counsels loves thee well with reverence due, and has given thee honor and goodly gifts. Nay, they tell that thou know soothsaying, Far-darter, by the voice of Zeus: for from Zeus are all oracles, wherein I myself now know thee to be all-wise. Thy province it is to know whatever thou wish. Since, then, thy heart bids thee play the lyre, harp thou and sing, and let joys be thy care, taking this gift from me; and to me, friend, gain glory. Sweetly sing with my shrill comrade in thy hands, that knows speech good and fair and in order due. Freely do thou bear it hereafter into the glad feast, and the winsome dance, and the glorious revel, a joy by night and day. Whatsoever skilled hand shall inquire of it artfully and wisely, surely its voice shall teach him all things joyous, being easily played by gentle practice, fleeing dull toil. But if an unskilled hand first impetuously inquires of it, vain and discordant shall the false notes sound. But thine it is of nature to know what things thou will: so to thee will I give this lyre, thou glorious son of Zeus. But we for our part will let graze thy cattle of the field on the pastures of hill and plain, thou Far-darter. So shall the cattle, consorting with the bulls, bring forth calves male and female, great store, and no need there is that thou, wise as thou are, should be vehement in anger."

So spoke he, and held forth the lyre that Phoebus Apollo took, and pledged his shining whip in the hands of Hermes, and set him over the herds. Gladly the son of Maia received it; while the glorious son of Leto, Apollo, the Prince, the Far-darter, held the lyre in his left hand, and tuned it orderly with the plectrum. Sweetly it sounded to his hand, and fair thereto was the song of the God.

Then the two turned the cattle to the rich meadow, but themselves, the glorious children of Zeus, hastened back to snow-clad Olympus, rejoicing in the lyre: ay, and Zeus, the counsellor, was glad of it. But Hermes withal invented the skill of a new art, the far-heard music of the reed pipes.

Then spoke the son of Leto to Hermes thus:

"I fear me, Son of Maia, thou leader, thou crafty one, lest thou steal from me both my lyre and my bent bow. For this gift thou hast from Zeus, to establish the ways of barter among men on the fruitful earth. Wherefore I wish that thou would swear me the great oath of the Gods, with a nod of the head or by the showering waters of Styx, that thy doings shall ever to my heart be kind and dear."

Then, with a nod of his head, did Maia's son vow that never would he steal the possessions of the Far-darter, nor draw near his strong dwelling. And Leto's son made vow and band of love and alliance, that none other among the Gods should be dearer of Gods or men the seed of Zeus.

"Thereafter shall I give thee a fair wand of wealth and fortune, a golden wand, three-pointed, which shall guard thee harmless, accomplishing all things good of word and deed that it is mine to learn from the voice of Zeus. But as touching the art prophetic, oh best of fosterlings of Zeus, concerning which thou inquire, for thee it is not fit to learn that art, nay, nor for any other Immortal. That lies in the mind of Zeus alone. Myself did make pledge, and promise, and strong oath, that, save me, none other of the eternal Gods should know the secret counsel of Zeus. And thou, my brother of the Golden Wand, bid me not tell thee what awful purposes is planning the far-seeing Zeus.

"One mortal shall I harm, and another shall I bless, with many a turn of fortune among hapless men. Of my oracle shall he have profit whosoever comes in the wake of wings and voice of birds of omen: he shall have profit of my oracle: him I will not deceive. But whoso, trusting birds not ominous, approaches my oracle, to inquire beyond my will, and know more than the eternal Gods, shall come, I say, on a bootless journey, yet his gifts shall I receive. Yet another thing will I tell thee, thou Son of renowned Maia and of Zeus of the Aegis, thou bringer of boon; there be certain Thriae, sisters born, three maidens rejoicing in swift wings. Their heads are sprinkled with white barley flour, and they dwell beneath a glade of Parnassus; apart they dwell, teachers of soothsaying. This art I learned while yet a boy I tended the cattle, and my Father heeded not. Thence they flit continually hither and thither, feeding on honeycombs and bringing all things to fulfilment. They, when they are full of the spirit of soothsaying, having eaten of the pale honey, delight to speak forth the truth. But if they be bereft of the sweet food divine, then lie they all confused. These I bestow on thee, and do thou, inquiring clearly, delight thine own heart, and if thou instruct any man, he will often hearken to thine oracle, if he have the good fortune. These be thine, O Son of Maia, and the cattle of the field with twisted horn do thou tend, and horses, and toilsome mules. . . . And be lord over the burning eyes of lions, and white-toothed swine, and dogs, and sheep that wide earth nourishes, and over all flocks be glorious Hermes lord. And let him alone be herald appointed to Hades, who, though he be giftless, will give him highest gift of honor."

With such love, in all kindness, did Apollo pledge the Son of Maia, and thereto Cronion added grace. With all mortals and immortals he consorts. Somewhat does he bless, but ever through the dark night he beguiles the tribes of mortal men.

DEMETER

Homeric Hymns, 1-495 (Lang)

*Demeter, an Aryan mother-goddess, was merged with an
earlier pre-Hellenic matriarchal goddess and became particu-
larly important in the rites at Eleusis.*

Of fair-tressed Demeter, Demeter holy Goddess, I begin to sing:
of her and her slim-ankled daughter whom Hades snatched away,
the gift of wide-beholding Zeus; but Demeter knew it not, she that
bears the Seasons, the giver of goodly crops. For her daughter was
playing with the deep-bosomed maidens of Oceanus, and was
gathering flowers—roses, and crocuses, and fair violets in the soft
meadow, and lilies, and hyacinths, and the narcissus which the
earth brought forth as a snare to the fair-faced maiden, by the
counsel of Zeus and to pleasure the Lord with many guests. Wondrously bloomed the flower, a marvel for all to see, whether deathless gods or deathly men. From its root grew forth a hundred blossoms, and with its fragrant odor the wide heaven above and the
whole earth laughed, and the salt wave of the sea. Then the
maiden marvelled, and stretched forth both her hands to seize the
fair plaything, but the wide-wayed earth gaped in the Nysian
plain, and up rushed the Prince, the host of many guests, the
many-named son of Cronos, with his immortal horses. Against her
will he seized her, and drove her off weeping in his golden chariot,
but she shrilled aloud, calling on Father Cronides, the highest of
gods and the best.
    But no immortal god or deathly man heard the voice of her,
. . . save the daughter of Persaeus, Hecate of the shining head-
gear, as she was thinking delicate thoughts, who heard the cry
from her cave and Prince Helios, the glorious son of Hyperion,
the maiden calling on Father Cronides. But he far off sat apart
from the gods in his temple haunted by prayers, receiving goodly
victims from mortal men. By the design of Zeus did the brother of
Zeus lead the maiden away, the lord of many, the host of many
guests, with his deathless horses; right sore against her will, even
he of many names the son of Cronos. Now, so long as the God-

dess beheld the earth, and the starry heaven, and the tide of the teeming sea, and the rays of the sun, and still hoped to behold her mother dear, and the tribes of the eternal gods; even so long, despite her sorrow, hope warmed her high heart; then rang the mountain peaks, and the depths of the sea to her immortal voice, and her lady mother heard her. Then sharp pain caught at her heart, and with her hands she tore the wimple about her ambrosial hair, and cast a dark veil about her shoulders, and then sped she like a bird over land and sea in her great yearning; but to her there was none that would tell the truth, none, either of Gods, or deathly men, nor even a bird came near her, a soothsaying messenger. Thereafter for nine days did Lady Deo roam the earth, with torches burning in her hands, nor ever in her sorrow tasted she of ambrosia and sweet nectar, nor laved her body in the baths. But when at last the tenth morn came to her with the light, Hecate met her, a torch in her hands, and spoke a word of tidings, and said:

"Lady Demeter, thou that bring the Seasons, thou giver of glad gifts, which of the heavenly gods or deathly men has ravished away Persephone, and brought thee sorrow: for I heard a voice but I saw not who the ravisher might be?"

So spoke Hecate, and the daughter of fair-tressed Rhea answered her not, but swiftly rushed on with her, bearing torches burning in her hands. So came they to Helios that watches both for gods and men, and stood before his car, and the lady Goddess questioned him:

"Helios, have pity on me that am a goddess, if ever by word or deed I gladdened thy heart. My daughter, whom I bore, a sweet plant and fair to see; it was her shrill voice I heard through the air unharvested, even as of one violently entreated, but I saw her not with my eyes. But do thou that look down with thy rays from the holy air upon all the land and sea, do thou tell me truly concerning my dear child, if thou did behold her; who it is that has gone off and ravished her away from me against her will, who is it of gods or mortal men?"

So spoke she, and Hyperionides answered her:

"Daughter of fair-tressed Rhea, Queen Demeter, thou shall know it; for greatly do I pity and revere thee in thy sorrow for thy slim-ankled child. There is none other guilty of the Immortals but Zeus himself that gathers the clouds, who gave thy daughter to Hades, his own brother, to be called his lovely wife; and Hades has ravished her away in his chariot, loudly shrilling, beneath the dusky gloom. But, Goddess, cease from thy long lamenting. It behooves not thee thus vainly to cherish anger unassuaged. No unseemly lord for thy daughter among the Immortals is Aidoneus, the lord of many, thine own brother and of one seed with thee, and for his honor he won, since when was made the threefold division, to be lord among those with whom he dwells."

So spoke he, and called upon his horses, and at his call they swiftly bore the fleet chariot on like long-winged birds. But grief more dread and bitter fell upon her, and angry thereafter was she with Cronion that has dark clouds for his dwelling. She held apart from the gathering of the Gods and from tall Olympus, and disfiguring her form for many days she went among the cities and rich fields of men. Now no man knew her that looked on her, nor no deep-bosomed woman, till she came to the dwelling of Celeus, who then was Prince of fragrant Eleusis. There sat she at the wayside in sorrow of heart, by the Maiden Well whence the townsfolk came to draw water. In the shade she sat; above her grew a thick olive-tree; and in fashion she was like an ancient crone who knows no more of child-bearing and the gifts of Aphrodite, the lover of garlands. Such she was as are the nurses of the children of law-pronouncing kings. Such are the housekeepers in their echoing halls.

Now the daughters of Celeus beheld her as they came to fetch the fair-flowing water, to carry in bronze vessels to their father's home. Four were they, like unto goddesses, all in the bloom of youth, Callidice, and Cleisidice, and winsome Demo, and Callithoe the eldest of them all, nor did they know her, for the Gods are hard to be known by mortals, but they stood near her and spoke winged words:

"Who art thou and whence, old woman, of ancient folk, and why were thou wandering apart from the town, nor do draw near to the houses where are women of thine own age, in the shadowy halls, even such as thou, and younger women, too, who may kindly entreat thee in word and deed?"

So spoke they, and the lady Goddess answered:

"Dear children, whoever ye be, of womankind I bid you hail, and I will tell you my story. Seemly it is to answer your questions truly. Deo is my name that my lady mother gave me; but now, look you, from Crete am I come hither over the wide ridges of the sea, by no will of my own, nay, by violence have sea-rovers brought me hither under duress, who thereafter touched with their ship at Thoricos where the women and they themselves embarked on land. Then were they busy about supper beside the hawsers of the ship, but my heart heeded not delight of supper; no, stealthily setting forth through the dark land I fled from these overweening masters, that they might not sell me whom they had never bought and gain my price. Thus hither have I come in my wandering, nor know I at all what land is this, nor who they be that dwell therein. But to you may all they that hold mansions in Olympus give husbands and lords, and such children to bear as parents desire; but me do ye maidens pity in your kindness, till I come to the house of woman or of man, that there I may work zealously for them in such tasks as fit a woman of my years. I could carry in my arms a new-born babe, and nurse it well, and keep the house, and strew my master's bed within the well-builded chambers, and teach the maids their tasks."

So spoke the Goddess, and straightway answered her the maid unwed, Callidice, the fairest of the daughters of Celeus:

"Mother, what things soever the Gods do give must men, though sorrowing, endure, for the Gods are far stronger than we; but this will I tell thee clearly and truly, namely, what men they are who here have most honor, and who lead the people, and by their counsels and just laws do safeguard the bulwarks of the city. Such are wise Triptolemus, Diocles, Polyxenus, and noble Eumolpus, and Dolichus, and our lordly father. All their wives keep their houses, and not one of them would at first sight condemn thee and thrust thee from their halls, but gladly they will receive thee: for thine aspect is divine. So, if thou will, abide here, that we may go to the house of my father, and tell out all this tale to my mother, the deep-bosomed Metaneira, if perchance she will bid thee come to our house and not seek the homes of others. A dear son born in her later years is nurtured in the well-builded hall, a child of many prayers and a welcome. If thou would nurse him till he comes to the measure of youth, then whatsoever woman saw thee should envy thee; such gifts of fosterage would my mother give thee."

So spoke she and the Goddess nodded assent. So rejoicing they filled their shining pitchers with water and bore them away. Swiftly they came to the high hall of their father, and quickly they told their mother what they had heard and seen, and speedily she bade them run and call the strange woman, offering goodly hire. Then as deer or calves in the season of Spring leap along the meadow, when they have had their fill of pasture, so lightly they tucked up the folds of their lovely gowns, and ran along the hollow chariot-way, while their hair danced on their shoulders, in color like the crocus flower. They found the glorious Goddess at the wayside, even where they had left her, and led her to their father's house. But she paced behind in heaviness of heart, her head veiled, and the dark robe floating about her slender feet divine. Speedily they came to the house of Celeus, the fosterling of Zeus, and they went through the corridor where their lady mother was sitting by the doorpost of the well-wrought hall, with her child in her lap, a young blossom, and the girls ran up to her, but the Goddess stood on the threshold, her head touching the roof-beam, and she filled the doorway with the light divine. Then wonder, and awe, and pale fear seized the mother, and she gave place from her high seat, and bade the Goddess be seated. But Demeter the bearer of the Seasons, the Giver of goodly gifts, would not sit down upon the shining high seat. Nay, in silence she waited, casting down her lovely eyes, till the wise Iambe set for her a well-made stool, and cast over it a glistening fleece. Then sat she down and held the veil before her face: long in sorrow and silence sat she so, and spoke to no man nor made any sign, but smileless she sat, nor tasted meat nor drink, wasting with long desire for her deep-bosomed daughter.

So abode she till wise Iambe with jests and many mockeries beguiled the lady, the holy one, to smile and laugh and hold a happier heart, and pleased her moods even thereafter. Then Metaneira filled a cup of sweet wine and offered it to her, but she refused it, saying, that it was not permitted for her to drink red wine; but she bade them mix meal and water with the tender herb of mint, and give it to her to drink. Then Metaneira made a potion and gave it to the Goddess as she bade, and Lady Deo took it and made libation, and to them fair-girdled Metaneira said:

"Hail, lady, for methinks thou art not of mean parentage, but goodly born, for grace and honor shine in thine eyes as in the eyes of law-dealing kings. But the gifts of the Gods, even in sorrow, we men of necessity endure, for the yoke is laid upon our necks; yet now that thou art come hither, such things as I have shall be thine. Rear me this child that the Gods have given in my later years and beyond my hope; and he is to me a child of many prayers. If thou rear him, and he come to the measure of youth, verily each woman that sees thee will envy thee, such shall be my gifts of fosterage."

Then answered her again Demeter of the fair garland:

"And may thou too, lady, fare well, and the Gods give thee

all things good. Gladly will I receive thy child that thou bid me nurse. Never, methinks, by the folly of his nurse shall charm or sorcery harm him; for I know an antidote stronger than the wild wood herb, and a goodly salve I know for the venomed spells."

So spoke she, and with her immortal hands she placed the child on her fragrant breast, and the mother was glad at heart. So in the halls she nursed the goodly son of wise Celeus, even Demophoon, whom deep-breasted Metaneira bare, and he grew like a god, upon no mortal food, nor on no mother's milk. For Demeter anointed him with ambrosia as though he had been a son of a God, breathing sweetness over him, and keeping him in her bosom. So worked she by day, but at night she hid him in the force of fire like a brand, his dear parents knowing it not. Nay, to them it was great marvel how flourished he and grew like the Gods to look upon. And, verily, she would have made him exempt from age and death forever, had not fair-girdled Metaneira, in her witlessness, spied on her in the night from her fragrant chamber. Then wailed she, and smote both her thighs, in terror for her child, and in anguish of heart, and lamenting she spoke winged words: "My child Demophoon, the stranger is concealing thee in the heart of the fire; bitter sorrow for me and lamentation."

So spoke she, wailing, and the lady Goddess heard her. Then in wrath did the fair-garlanded Demeter snatch out of the fire with her immortal hands and cast upon the ground that woman's dear son, whom beyond all hope she had borne in the halls. Dread was the wrath of Demeter, and she spoke to fair-girdled Metaneira. "Oh ill-advised and uncounselled race of men, that know not beforehand the fate of coming good or coming evil. For, lo, thou hast wrought upon thyself a bane incurable, by thine own witlessness; for by the oath of the Gods, the relentless water of Styx, I would have made thy dear child deathless and exempt from age forever, and would have given him glory imperishable. But now in nowise may he escape the Fates and death, yet glory imperishable will ever be his, since he has lain on my knees and slept within my arms; but as the years go round, and in his day, the sons of the Eleusinians will ever wage war and dreadful strife one upon the other. Now I am honored Demeter, the greatest good and gain of the Immortals to deathly men. But, come now, let all the people build me a great temple and an altar thereby, below the town, and the steep wall, above Callichorus on the jutting rock. But the rites I myself will prescribe, that in time to come ye may pay them duly and appease my power."

Therewith the Goddess changed her shape and height, and cast off old age, and beauty breathed about her, and the sweet scent was breathed from her fragrant robes, and afar shone the light from the deathless body of the Goddess, the yellow hair flowing about her shoulders, so that the goodly house was filled with the splendor as of lightning fire, and forth from the halls went she.

But anon the knees of the woman were loosened, and for long time she was speechless, nay, nor did she even mind of the child, her best beloved, to lift him from the floor. But the sisters of the child heard his pitiful cry, and leapt from their fair-strewn beds; one of them, lifting the child in her hands, laid it in her bosom; and another lit fire, and the third ran with smooth feet to take her mother forth from the fragrant chamber. Then gathered they about the child, and bathed and clad him lovingly, yet his mood was not softened, for meaner nurses now and handmaids held him.

They the long night through were adoring the renowned Goddess, trembling with fear, but at the dawning they told truly to mighty Celeus all that the Goddess had commanded; even Demeter of the goodly garland. Thereon he called into the market-place the many people, and bade them make a rich temple, and an altar to fair-tressed Demeter, upon the jutting rock. Then they heard and obeyed his voice, and as he bade they builded. And the child increased in strength by the Goddess's will.

Now when they had done their work, and rested from their labors, each man started for his home, but yellow-haired Demeter, sitting there apart from all the blessed Gods, abided, wasting away with desire for her deep-bosomed daughter. Then the most dread and terrible of years did the Goddess bring for mortals upon the fruitful earth, nor did the earth send up the seed, for Demeter of the goodly garland concealed it. Many crooked ploughs did the oxen drag through the furrows in vain, and much white barley fell fruitless upon the land. Now would the whole race of mortal men have perished utterly from the stress of famine, and the Gods that hold mansions in Olympus would have lost the share and renown of gift and sacrifice, if Zeus had not conceived a counsel within his heart.

First he roused Iris of the golden wings to speed forth and call the fair-tressed Demeter, the lovesome in beauty. So spoke Zeus, and Iris obeyed Zeus, the son of Cronos, who has dark clouds for his tabernacle, and swiftly she sped down the space between heaven and earth. Then came she to the citadel of fragrant Eleusis, and in the temple she found Demeter clothed in dark raiment, and speaking winged words addressed her: "Demeter, Father Zeus, whose counsels are imperishable, bids thee back unto the tribes of the eternal Gods. Come thou, then, lest the word of Zeus be of no avail." So spoke she in her prayer, but the Goddess yielded not. Thereafter the Father sent forth all the blessed Gods, all of the Immortals, and coming one by one they bade Demeter return, and gave her many splendid gifts, and all honors that she might choose among the immortal Gods. But none availed to persuade by turning her mind and her angry heart, so stubbornly she refused their sayings. For she deemed no more forever to enter fragrant Olympus, and no more to allow the earth to bear her fruit, until her eyes should behold her fair-faced daughter.

But when far-seeing Zeus, the lord of the thunder-peal, had heard the thing, he sent to Erebus the slayer of Argus, the God of the golden wand, to win over Hades with soft words, and persuade him to bring up holy Persephone into the light, and among the Gods, forth from the murky gloom, so that her mother might behold her, and that her anger might relent. And Hermes disobeyed not, but straightway and speedily went forth beneath the hollow places of the earth, leaving the home of Olympus. That King he found within his dwelling, sitting on a couch with his chaste bedfellow, who sorely grieved for desire of her mother, that still was cherishing a fell design against the ill deeds of the Gods. Then the strong slayer of Argos drew near and spoke: "Hades of the dark locks, thou Prince of men outworn, Father Zeus bade me bring the dread Persephone forth from Erebus among the Gods, that her mother may behold her, and relent from her anger and terrible wrath against the Immortals, for now she contrives a mighty deed, to destroy the feeble tribes of earth-born men by withholding the seed under the earth. Thereby the honors of the Gods are lessened and fierce is her wrath, nor mingles she with the Gods, but sits apart within the fragrant temple in the steep citadel of Eleusis."

So spoke he, and smiling were the brows of Aidoneus, Prince of the dead, nor did he disobey the commands of King Zeus, as speedily he bade the wise Persephone: "Go, Persephone, to thy dark-mantled mother, go with a gentle spirit in thy breast, nor be thou beyond all other folk disconsolate. Verily I shall be no unseemly lord of thine among the Immortals, I that am the brother of Father Zeus, and while thou art here shall thou be mistress over all that lives and moves, but among the Immortals shall thou have

the greatest renown. Upon them that wrong thee shall vengeance
be unceasing, upon them that solicit not thy power with sacrifice,
and pious deeds, and every acceptable gift."

So spoke he, and wise Persephone was glad; and joyously and
swiftly she arose, but the God himself, stealthily looking around
her, gave her sweet pomegranate seed to eat, and this he did that
she might not abide forever beside revered Demeter of the dark
mantle. Then openly did Aidoneus, the Prince of all, get ready the
steeds beneath the golden chariot, and she climbed up into the
golden chariot, and beside her the strong Slayer of Argus took
reins and whip in hand, and drove forth from the halls, and gladly
sped the two horses. Speedily they devoured the long way; nor
sea, nor rivers, nor grassy glades, nor cliffs, could stay the rush of
the deathless horses; nay, far above them they cleft the deep air
in their course. Before the fragrant temple he drove them, and
checked them where dwelt Demeter of the goodly garland, who,
when she beheld them, rushed forth like a Maenad down a dark
mountain woodland.

Persephone on the other side rejoiced to see her mother dear,
and leaped to meet her; but the mother said, "Child, in Hades
hast thou eaten any food? for if thou hast not then with me and
thy father the son of Cronos, who has dark clouds for his tabernacle, shall thou ever dwell honored among all the Immortals. But
if thou hast tasted food, thou must return again, and beneath the
hollows of the earth must dwell in Hades a third portion of the
year; yet two parts of the year thou shall abide with me and the
other Immortals. When the earth blossoms with all manner of fragrant flowers, then from beneath the murky gloom shall thou
come again, a mighty marvel to Gods and to mortal men. Now
tell me by what wile the strong host of many guests deceived
thee? . . ."

Then fair Persephone answered her august mother: "Behold,
I shall tell thee all the truth without fail. I leaped up for joy when
good Hermes, the swift messenger, came from my father Cronides
and the other heavenly Gods, with the message that I was to return out of Erebus, so that thou mightest behold me, and cease
thine anger and dread wrath against the Immortals. Thereon
Hades himself compelled me to taste of a sweet pomegranate seed
against my will. And now I will tell thee how, through the crafty
device of Cronides my father, he ravished me, and bore me away
beneath the hollows of the earth. All that thou askest I will tell
thee. We were all playing in the lovely meadows. We were playing

there, and plucking beautiful blossoms with our hands; crocuses mingled, and iris, and hyacinth, and roses, and lilies, a marvel to behold, and narcissus, that the wide earth bore, a wile for my un-doing. Gladly was I gathering them when the earth gaped be-neath, and therefrom leaped the mighty Prince, the host of many guests, and he bore me against my will despite my grief beneath the earth, in his golden chariot; and shrilly did I cry. This all is true that I tell thee."

So the livelong day in oneness of heart did they cheer each other with love, and their minds ceased from sorrow, and great gladness did either win from other. Then came to them Hekate of the fair wimple, and often did she kiss the holy daughter of De-meter, and from that day was her queenly comrade and hand-maiden; but to them for a messenger did far-seeing Zeus of the loud thunder-peal send fair-tressed Rhea to bring dark-mantled Demeter among the Gods, with pledge of what honor she might choose among the Immortals. He vowed that her daughter, for the third part of the revolving year, should dwell beneath the murky gloom, but for the other two parts she should abide with her mother and the other gods.

Thus he spoke, and the Goddess disobeyed not the com-mands of Zeus. Swiftly she sped down from the peaks of Olym-pus, and came to fertile Rarion; fertile of old, but now no longer fruitful; for fallow and leafless it lay, and hidden was the white barley grain by the device of fair-ankled Demeter. Nonetheless with the growing of the Spring the land was to teem with tall ears of corn, and the rich furrows were to be heavy with corn, and the corn to be bound in sheaves. There first did she land from the un-harvested ether, and gladly the Goddesses looked on each other, and rejoiced in heart, and thus first did Rhea of the fair wimple speak to Demeter:

"Hither, child; for he calleth thee, far-seeing Zeus, the lord of the deep thunder, to come among the Gods, and has promised thee such honors as thou wish, and has decreed that thy child, for the third of the rolling year, shall dwell beneath the murky gloom, but the other two parts with her mother and the rest of the Im-mortals. So does he promise that it shall be and thereto nods his head; but come, my child, obey, and be not too unrelenting against the Son of Cronos, the lord of the dark cloud. And do thou increase the grain that brings life to men."

So spoke she, and Demeter of the fair garland obeyed. Speedily she sent up the grain from the rich field, and the wide earth was heavy with leaves and flowers: and she hastened, and showed the thing to the kings, the dealers of law; to Triptolemus and Diocles the charioteer, and mighty Eumolpus, and Celeus the leader of the people; she showed them the manner of her rites, and taught them her goodly mysteries, holy mysteries which none may violate, or search into, or noise abroad, for the great curse from the Gods restrains the voice. Happy is he among deathly men who hath beheld these things! and he that is uninitiate, and has no lot in them, has never equal lot in death beneath the murky gloom.

Now when the Goddess had given instruction in all her rites, they went to Olympus, to the gathering of the other Gods. There the Goddesses dwell beside Zeus the lord of the thunder, holy and revered are they. Right happy is he among mortal men whom they dearly love; speedily do they send as a guest to his lofty hall Plutus, who giveth wealth to mortal men. But come thou that holdest the land of fragrant Eleusis, and sea-girt Paros, and rocky Antron, come, Lady Deo! Queen and giver of goodly gifts, and bringer of the Seasons; come thou and thy daughter, beautiful Persephone, and of your grace grant me goodly substance in requital of my song; but I will mind me of thee, and of other minstrelsy.

HEPHAESTUS

HOMER, *Iliad*, Book 18. 368-405 (Lang, Leaf, and Myers)

Thetis comes to Hephaestus, the craftsman, to obtain new arms for her son Achilles.

Thetis of the silver feet came unto the house of Hephaistos, imperishable, starlike, far seen among the dwellings of Immortals, a house of bronze, wrought by the crook-footed god himself. Him found she sweating in toil and busy about his bellows, for he was forging tripods twenty in all to stand around the wall of his established hall, and beneath the base of each he had set golden wheels, that of their own motion they might enter the assembly of the gods and again return unto his house, a marvel to look upon. Thus much were they finished that not yet were the ears of cunning work set thereon; these was he making ready, and welding chains. While thereat he was laboring with wise intent, then drew nigh unto him Thetis, goddess of the silver feet. And Charis went forward and beheld her, fair Charis of the shining chaplet whom the renowned lame god had wed. And she clasped her hand in hers and spoke and called her by her name: "Wherefore, long-robed Thetis, come thou to our house, honored that thou art and dear? No frequent comer art thou hitherto. But come onward with me that I may set guest-cheer before thee."

Thus spike the bright goddess and led her on. Then set she her on a silver-studded throne, goodly, of cunning work, and a footstool was beneath her feet; and she called to Hephaistos, the famed artificer, and said unto him: "Hephaistos, come forth hither, Thetis has need of thee."

And the renowned lame god made answer to her: "Verily a dread and honored goddess in my sight is she that is within, seeing that she delivered me when pain came upon me from my great fall though the ill-will of my shameless mother who would have fain hid me away, for that I was lame. Then had I suffered anguish of heart had not Eurynome and Thetis taken me into their bosom —Eurynome daughter of Ocean that floweth back ever upon himself. Nine years with them I wrought much cunning work of bronze, brooches and spiral arm-bands and cups and necklaces, in the hollow cave, while around me the stream of Ocean with murmuring foam flowed infinite. Neither knew thereof any other of gods or of mortal men, save only Thetis and Eurynome who delivered me. And now comes Thetis to our house; wherefore it behooves me in all ways to repay fair-tressed Thetis for the saving of my life. But do thou now set beside her fair entertainment, while I put away my bellows and all my gear."

He said, and from the anvil rose limping, a huge bulk, but under him his slender legs moved nimbly. The bellows he set away from the fire, and gathered all his gear wherewith he worked into a silver chest; and with a sponge he wiped his face and hands and sturdy neck and shaggy breast, and put on his doublet, and took a stout staff and went forth limping; but there were hand-maidens of gold that moved to help their lord, the semblances of living maids. In them is understanding at their hearts, in them are voice and strength, and they have skill of the immortal gods. These moved beneath their lord, and he got him haltingly near to where Thetis was, and set him on a bright seat, and clasped her hand in his and spoke and called her by her name: "Wherefore,

long-robed Thetis, come thou to our house, honored that thou art
and dear? No frequent comer art thou hitherto. Speak what thou
hast at heart; my soul desires to accomplish it, if accomplish it I
can, and if it be appointed for accomplishment."

APHRODITE

Homeric Hymns, 1-292 (Lang)

*Oriental influences are strong in the character of Aphrodite,
and her title "Kypris" connects her with a very old shrine
on the island of Cyprus. As a goddess of love and beauty
she was popular and was worshipped all over the Greek
world.*

Tell me, Muse, of the deeds of golden Aphrodite, the Cyprian,
who rouses sweet desire among the Immortals, and vanquishes the
tribes of deathly men, and birds that wanton in the air, and all
beasts, even all the clans that earth nurtures, and all in the sea. To
all are dear the deeds of the garlanded Cyprian.

Yet three hearts there be that she cannot persuade or beguile:
the daughter of Zeus of the Aegis, gray-eyed Athene: not to her
are dear the deeds of golden Aphrodite, but war and the work of
Ares, battle and broil, and the mastery of noble arts. First was she
to teach earthly men the fashioning of war chariots and cars fair
wrought with bronze. And she teaches to tender maidens in the
halls all goodly arts, breathing skill into their minds. Nor ever
does laughter-loving Aphrodite conquer in desire Artemis of the
Golden Distaff, rejoicing in the sound of the chase, for the bow
and arrow are her delight, and slaughter of the wild beasts on the
hills: the lyre, the dance, the clear hunting halloo, and shadowy
glens, and cities of righteous men.

Nor to the revered maiden Hestia are the feats of Aphrodite a
joy, eldest daughter of crooked-counselled Cronos, youngest, too,
by the design of Zeus of the Aegis, that lady whom both Poseidon
and Apollo sought to win. But she would not, nay stubbornly she
refused; and she swore a great oath fulfilled, with her hand on the
head of Father Zeus of the Aegis, to be a maiden forever, that
lady Goddess. And to her Father Zeus gave a goodly gift of honor,

in lieu of wedlock; and in mid-hall she sat her down choosing the best portion: and in all temples of the Gods is she honored, and among all mortals is chief of Gods.

Of these she cannot win or beguile the hearts. But of all others there is none, of blessed Gods or mortal men, that has escaped Aphrodite. Yea, even the heart of Zeus the Thunderer she led astray; of him that is greatest of all, and has the highest lot of honor. Even his wise wit she has beguiled at her will, and lightly laid him in the arms of mortal women; Hera not knowing of it, his sister and his wife, the fairest in goodliness of beauty among the deathless Goddesses. To highest honor did they beget her, crooked-counselled Cronos and Mother Rhea; and Zeus of imperishable counsel made her his chaste and duteous wife.

But into Aphrodite herself Zeus sent sweet desire, to lie in the arms of a mortal man. This wrought he so that not even she might be unconversant with a mortal bed, and might not some day with sweet laughter make her boast among all the Gods, the smiling Aphrodite, that she had given the Gods to mortal paramours, and they for deathless Gods bore deathly sons, and that she mingled Goddesses in love with mortal men. Therefore Zeus sent into her heart sweet desire of Anchises, who as then was pasturing his cattle on the steep hills of many-fountained Ida, a man in semblance like the Immortals. Him thereafter did smiling Aphrodite see and love, and measureless desire took hold on her heart. To Cyprus went she, within her fragrant shrine: even to Paphos, where is her sacred enclosure and odorous altar. Thither went she in, and shut the shining doors, and there the Graces bathed and anointed her with oil ambrosial, such as is on the bodies of the eternal Gods, sweet fragrant oil that she had by her. Then clad she her body in goodly raiment, and bedecked herself with gold, the smiling Aphrodite; then sped to Troy, leaving fragrant Cyprus, and high among the clouds she swiftly accomplished her way.

To many-fountained Ida she came, mother of wild beasts, and made straight for the farm through the mountain, while behind her came fawning the beasts, gray wolves, and lions fiery-eyed, and bears, and swift leopards, insatiate pursuers of the roe deer. Glad was she at the sight of them, and sent desire into their breasts, and they went coupling two by two in the shadowy dells. But she came to the well-builded huts, and him she found left alone in the huts with no company, the hero Anchises, graced with beauty from the Gods. All the rest were faring after the cattle through the grassy pastures, but he, left lonely at the huts, walked up and down, harping sweet and shrill. In front of him stood the daughter of Zeus, Aphrodite, in semblance and stature like an un-wed maid, lest he should be adread when he beheld the Goddess. And Anchises marvelled when he beheld her, her height, and beauty, and glistening raiment. For she was clad in vesture more shining than the flame of fire, and with twisted armlets and glis-tening earrings of flower-fashion. About her delicate neck were lovely jewels, fair and golden: and like the moon's was the light on her fair breasts, and love came upon Anchises, and he spoke unto her:

"Hail, Queen, whosoever of the Immortals thou art that comest to this house; whether Artemis, or Leto, or golden Aphro-dite, or high-born Themis, or gray-eyed Athene. Or perchance thou art one of the Graces come hither, who dwell friendly with the Gods, and have a name to be immortal; or of the nymphs that dwell in this fair glade, or in this fair mountain, and in the well-heads of rivers, and in grassy dells. But to thee on some point of outlook, in a place far seen, will I make an altar, and offer to thee goodly victims in every season. But for thy part be kindly, and grant me to be a man pre-eminent among the Trojans, and give goodly seed of children to follow me; but for me, let me live long, and see the sunlight, and come to the limit of old age, being ever in all things fortunate among men."

Then Aphrodite the daughter of Zeus answered him:

"Anchises, most renowned of men on earth, behold no God-dess am I—why liken me to the Immortals? Nay, mortal am I, and a mortal mother bore me, and my father is famous Otreus, if thou perchance have heard of him, who reigns over strong-warded Phrygia. Now I well know both your tongue and our own, for a Trojan nurse reared me in the hall, and nurtured me ever, from the day when she took me at my mother's hands, and while I was but a little child. Thus it is, you see, that I well know thy tongue as well as my own. But even now the Argus-slayer of the Golden Wand has ravished me away from the choir of Artemis, the God-dess of the Golden Distaff, who loves the noise of the chase. Many nymphs, and maids beloved of many wooers, were we there at play, and a great circle of people was about us. But thence did he bear me away, the Argus-slayer, he of the Golden Wand, and bore me over much tilled land of mortal men, and many wastes untilled and uninhabited, where wild beasts roam through the shadowy dells. So fleet we passed that I seemed not to touch the fertile earth with my feet. Now Hermes said that I was bidden to be the bride of Anchises, and mother of thy goodly children. But when he had spoken and shown the thing, lo, instantly he went back among the immortal Gods—the renowned Slayer of Argus. But I come to thee, strong necessity being laid upon me, and by Zeus I beseech thee and thy good parents—for none ill folk may get such a son as thee—by them I implore thee to take me, a maiden as I am and untried in love, and show me to thy father and thy discreet mother, and to thy brothers of one lineage with thee. No unseemly daughter to these, and sister to those will I be, but well worthy; and do thou send a messenger swiftly to the Phrygians of the dappled steeds, to tell my father of my fortunes, and my sorrowing mother: gold enough and woven raiment will they send, and many and goodly gifts shall be thine. Do thou all this, and then prepare the winsome wedding-feast, that is honorable among both men and immortal Gods."

So speaking, the Goddess brought sweet desire into his heart, and love came upon Anchises, and he spoke, and said:

"If indeed thou art mortal and a mortal mother bore thee, and if renowned Otreus is thy father, and if thou art come hither by the will of Hermes, the immortal Guide, and are to be called my wife forever, then neither mortal man nor immortal God shall hold me from my desire before I lie with thee in love, now and anon; nay, not even if Apollo the Far-darter himself were to send the shafts of sorrow from the silver bow! Nay, thou lady like the Goddesses, willing were I to go down within the house of Hades, if but first I had climbed into thy bed."

So spoke he and took her hand; while laughter-loving Aphrodite turned, and crept with fair downcast eyes toward the bed. It was strewn for the Prince with soft garments: and above it lay skins of bears and deep-voiced lions that he had slain in the lofty hills. When then they two had gone up into the well-wrought bed, first Anchises took from her body her shining jewels, brooches, and twisted armlets, earrings and chains: and he loosed her girdle, and unclad her of her glistening raiment, that he laid on a silver-studded chair. Then through the Gods' will and design, by the immortal Goddess lay the mortal man, not knowing what he did.

Now in the hour when herdsmen drive back the cattle and sturdy sheep to the farm from the flowery pastures, even then the Goddess poured sweet sleep into Anchises, and clad herself in her goodly raiment. Now when she was wholly clad, the lady Goddess, her head touched the beam of the lofty roof: and from her cheeks shone forth immortal beauty, even the beauty of fair-garlanded Cytherea. Then she aroused him from sleep, and spoke, and said:

"Rise, son of Dardanus, why now slumber thou so deeply? Consider, am I even in aspect such as I was when first thine eyes beheld me?"

So spoke she, and straightway he started up out of slumber and was adread, and turned his eyes away when he beheld the neck and the fair eyes of Aphrodite. His goodly face he veiled again in a cloak, and imploring her, he spoke winged words:

"Even so soon as mine eyes first beheld thee, Goddess, I knew thee for divine: but not truly did thou speak to me. But by Zeus of the Aegis I implore thee, suffer me not to live a strengthless shadow among men, but pity me: for no man lives in strength that has couched with immortal Goddesses."

Then answered him Aphrodite, daughter of Zeus:

"Anchises, most renowned of mortal men, take courage, nor fear overmuch. For no fear is there that thou shall suffer harm from me, nor from others of the blessed Gods, for dear to the Gods art thou. And to thee shall a dear son be born, and bear sway among the Trojans, and children's children shall arise after him continually. Lo, Aeneas shall his name be called, since dread sorrow held me when I came into the bed of a mortal man. And of all mortal men these who spring from thy race are always nearest to the immortal Gods in beauty and stature; witness how wise-counselling Zeus carried away golden-haired Ganymede, for his beauty's sake, that he might abide with the Immortals and be the cup-bearer of the Gods in the house of Zeus, a marvellous thing to behold, a mortal honored among all the Immortals, as he draws the red nectar from the golden mixing bowl. But grief incurable possessed the heart of Tros, nor knew he where the wild wind had blown his dear son away, therefore day by day he lamented continually till Zeus took pity upon him, and gave him as a ransom of his son high-stepping horses that bear the immortal Gods. These he gave him for a gift, and the Guide, the Slayer of Argus, told all these things by the command of Zeus, even how Ganymede should be forever exempt from old age and death, even as are the Gods. Now when his father heard this message of Zeus he rejoiced in his heart and lamented no longer, but was gladly charioted by the wind-fleet horses.

"So too did Dawn of the Golden Throne carry off Tithonus, a man of your lineage, one like unto the Immortals. Then went she to pray to Cronion, who has dark clouds for his tabernacle, that her lover might be immortal and exempt from death forever. Thereto Zeus consented and granted her desire, but foolish of heart was the Lady Dawn, nor did she deem it good to ask for eternal youth for her lover, and to keep him unwrinkled by grievous old age. Now so long as winsome youth was his, in joy did he dwell with the Golden-throned Dawn, the daughter of Morning, at the world's end beside the streams of Oceanus, but as soon as gray hairs began to flow from his fair head and goodly chin, the Lady Dawn held aloof from his bed, but kept and cherished him in her halls, giving him food and ambrosia and beautiful raiment. But when hateful old age had utterly overcome him, and he could not move or lift his limbs, to her this seemed the wisest counsel; she laid him in a chamber, and shut the shining doors, and his voice flows on endlessly, and no strength now is his such as once there was in his limbs. Therefore I would not have thee to be immortal and live forever in such fashion among the deathless Gods, but if, being such as thou art in beauty and form, thou could live on, and be called my lord, then this grief would not overshadow my heart.

"But it may not be, for swiftly will pitiless old age come upon thee, old age that stands close by mortal men; wretched and weary, and detested by the Gods: but among the immortal Gods shall great blame be mine forever, and all for love of thee. For the Gods were accustomed to dread my words and wiles wherewith I had subdued all the Immortals to mortal women in love, my purpose overcoming them all; now, my mouth will no longer suffice to speak forth this boast among the Immortals, for deep and sore has been my folly, wretched and not to be named; and distraught have I been who carry a child beneath my girdle, the child of a mortal. Now as soon as he sees the light of the sun the deep-bosomed mountain nymphs will rear him for me; the nymphs who haunt this great and holy mountain, being of the clan neither of mortals nor of immortal Gods. Long is their life, and immortal food do they eat, and they join in the goodly dance with the immortal Gods. With them the Sileni and the keen-sighted Slayer of Argus live in dalliance in the recesses of the dark caves. At their birth there sprang up pine trees or tall-crested oaks on the fruitful earth, flourishing and fair, and on the lofty mountain they stand, and are called the groves of the immortal Gods, which in no wise does man cut down with the steel. But when the fate of death approaches, first do the fair trees wither on the ground, and the bark about them moulders, and the twigs fall down, and even as the tree perishes so the soul of the nymph leaves the light of the sun.

"These nymphs will keep my child with them and rear him; and him when first he enters on lovely youth shall these Goddesses bring here to thee, and show thee. But to thee, that I may tell thee all my mind, will I come in the fifth year bringing my son. At the sight of him thou will be glad when thou behold him with thine eyes, for he will be divinely fair, and thou will lead him straightway to windy Ilios. But if any mortal man asks of thee what mother bore this thy dear son, be mindful to answer him as I command: say that he is thy son by one of the flower-faced nymphs who dwell in this forest-clad mountain, but if in thy folly thou speak out, and boast to have been the lover of fair-garlanded Cytherea, then Zeus in his wrath will smite thee with the smoldering thunderbolt. Now all is told to thee: do thou be wise, and keep thy counsel, and speak not my name, but revere the wrath of the Gods."

So spoke she, and soared up into the windy heaven.

~~~~~

ARES

HOMER, *Iliad*, Book 5. 825-898 (Chase and Perry)

The low esteem in which Ares was held appears in a scene where Diomede is encouraged to deeds of valor by Athene.

Then the bright-eyed goddess Athena answered him: "Son of Tydeus, Diomedes, dear to my heart, fear neither Ares, in this case, nor any other of the immortals, such a helper am I to you. Come, drive your single-hoofed horses against Ares first and strike him in close combat and do not dread impetuous Ares, that madman, a born plague, that renegade, who lately spoke to Hera and to me and promised to fight against the Trojans and aid the Achaeans, and who now joins with the Trojans and forgets the others."

So speaking, she drew back Sthenelus with her hand and thrust him from the chariot to the ground, and he instantly sprang away. The goddess eagerly mounted the chariot beside godlike Diomedes and loudly did the oaken axle groan beneath its burden, for it carried a dread goddess and the bravest of men. Then Pallas Athena grasped the whip and reins and quickly drove the single-hoofed horses against Ares first. Now he was despoiling of his armor huge Periphas, by far the best of the Aetolians, Ochesius' glorious son; him was bloodstained Ares stripping. Then Athena put on the helmet of Hades, lest mighty Ares see her.

When Ares, bane of mortals, saw godlike Diomedes, he left huge Periphas to lie where first he had slain him and taken away his life, and he went straight toward Diomedes, tamer of horses. When they came close to one another in their onset, Ares thrust forward his brazen spear over the yoke and reins of the horses. eager to take away his life. But the bright-eyed goddess Athena caught the spear in her hand and thrust it up over the chariot to fly uselessly away. Then Diomedes of the mighty war cry attacked with his brazen spear. And Pallas Athena guided it to the nethermost part of Ares' belly, where he was girt by a belt. There Diomedes hit and wounded him and pierced the fair skin and drew forth the spear again. Brazen Ares bellowed as loud as nine thousand warriors, or ten thousand, shout in battle as they join in Ares' strife. A trembling fell alike upon Achaeans and Trojans, in their fear, so loudly bellowed Ares, insatiate of war.

As a black gloom appears in the clouds, when after burning heat a storm wind rises, so to Diomedes, Tydeus' son, did brazen Ares seem as he passed through the clouds to the broad heaven. Swiftly he came to the dwelling of the gods, to steep Olympus, and he sat down, grieved at heart, near Zeus, the son of Cronus. He pointed to the ambrosial blood pouring from his wounds and spoke winged words in lamentation: "Father Zeus, are you not angry to behold these violent deeds? Ever indeed do we gods suffer most cruelly through one another's will, when we show favor to men. We are all aroused against you, for you gave birth to a heedless maiden, accursed, whose mind is ever set on violent deeds. All we other gods, as many as are in Olympus, obey you and are each subject to you. But her you reprove neither by word nor deed; rather, you set her on, since you yourself bore this insolent child. She has now stirred up Tydeus' son, the mighty Diomedes, madly to attack the immortal gods. First he wounded Cypris upon the hand's edge in close combat, and next he rushed upon me like a god. But my swift feet bore me away, else I would have endured long anguish there among the grim heaps of the dead or lived on strengthless from the woundings of the bronze."

Looking at him scornfully, cloud-gathering Zeus replied: "Do not sit beside me, fickle one, and whimper. You are to me the most hateful of the gods who dwell upon Olympus. For dear to you always are strife and wars and battles. You have your mother Hera's intolerable, unyielding spirit. Hardly can I restrain her with words. Therefore I think that it is at her promptings that you suffer thus. But still I will not long endure that you suffer pain, for you are my offspring and your mother bore you to me. If you had been born so insolent of any other of the gods, long ago would you have been lower than the sons of heaven."

DIONYSUS

Homeric Hymns, 1-21 (Lang)

Dionysus was a latecomer and a foreigner of Phrygian and Thracian origin. This emerges in the conflicting tales of his birth and the un-Greek story of his birth from the thigh of Zeus, with the curious epithet, "In-Sewn." By the sixth century B.C. *he replaces Hestia among the Olympians, is joined with Apollo at Delphi, and becomes the patron god of the dramatic festivals in Athens.*

Some say that Semele bore thee to Zeus the lord of thunder in Dracanon, and some in windy Icarus, and some in Naxos, thou seed of Zeus, In-Sewn; and others by the deep-swelling river Alpheius, and others, O Prince, say that thou were born in Thebes. Falsely speak they all: for the Father of Gods and men begot thee far away from men, while white-armed Hera knew it not. There is a hill called Nyse, a lofty hill, flowering into woodland, far away from Phoenicia, near the streams of Aegyptus. . . .

"And to thee will they raise many statues in the temples: as these thy deeds are three, so men will sacrifice to thee hecatombs every three years."

So spake Zeus the counsellor, and nodded with his head. Be gracious, thou wild lover, In-Sewn, from thee, beginning and ending with thee, we minstrels sing: in nowise is it possible for him who forgets thee to be mindful of sacred song. Hail to thee, Dionysus In-Sewn, with thy mother Semele, whom men call Thyone.

DIONYSUS AND THE SAILORS

Homeric Hymns, 1-59 (Lang)

Concerning Dionysus the son of renowned Semele shall I sing; how once he appeared upon the shore of the sea unharvested, on a jutting headland, in form like a man in the bloom of youth, with his beautiful dark hair waving around him, and on his strong shoulders a purple robe. Anon came in sight certain men that were pirates; in a well-wrought ship sailing swiftly on the dark seas: Tyrsenians were they, and Ill Fate was their leader, for they beholding him nodded each to other, and swiftly leaped forth, and hastily seized him, and set him aboard their ship rejoicing in heart, for they deemed that he was the son of kings, the foster-lings of Zeus, and they were of a mind to bind him with grievous bonds. But him the fetters held not, and the bonds fell far from his hands and feet. There sat he smiling with his dark eyes, but the steersman saw it, and spoke aloud to his companions: "Fools, what God have ye taken and bound? a strong God is he, our trim ship may not contain him. Surely this is Zeus, or Apollo of the Silver Bow, or Poseidon; for he is nowise like mortal man, but like the Gods who have mansions in Olympus. Nay, come let us instantly release him upon the dark mainland, nor lay your hands upon him, lest, being wroth, he rouse against us masterful winds and rushing storm."

So spoke he, but their captain rebuked him with a hateful word: "Fool, look thou to the wind, and haul up the sail, and grip to all the gear, but this fellow will be for men to meddle with. Methinks he will come to Egypt, or to Cyprus, or to the Hyperboreans, or further far; and at the last he will tell us who his friends are, and concerning his wealth, and his brethren, for the God has delivered him into our hands."

So spoke he, and let raise the mast and hoist the mainsail, and the wind filled the sail, and they made taut the ropes all round. But soon strange matters appeared to them: first there flowed through all the swift black ship a sweet and fragrant wine, and the ambrosial fragrance arose, and fear fell upon all the mariners that beheld it. And straightway a vine stretched hither and thither along the sail, hanging with many a cluster, and dark ivy twined round the mast blossoming with flowers, and gracious fruit and garlands grew on all the tholepins; and they that saw it bade the steersman drive straight to land. Meanwhile within the ship the God changed into the shape of a lion at the bow; and loudly he roared, and in midship he made a shaggy bear: such marvels he showed forth: there stood it raging, and on the deck glared the lion terribly. Then the men fled in terror to the stern, and there stood in fear round the honest pilot. But suddenly sprang forth the lion and seized the captain, and the men all at once leaped overboard into the strong sea, shunning dread doom, and there were changed into dolphins. But the God took pity upon the steersman, and kept him, and gave him all good fortune, and spoke, saying, "Be of good courage, Sir, dear art thou to me, and I am Dionysus of the noisy rites whom Cadmeian Semele bore to the love of Zeus." Hail, thou child of beautiful Semele, none that is mindless of thee can fashion sweet minstrelsy.

DIONYSUS

EURIPIDES, *Bacchae*, 1-54 (Arrowsmith)

Euripides puts into the mouth of Dionysus an account of his birth, travels, influence, and of his intention to punish Pentheus for failure to recognize his divinity.

"I am Dionysus, the son of Zeus,
come back to Thebes, this land where I was born.
My mother was Cadmus' daughter, Semele by name,
midwived by fire, delivered by the lightning's
blast.
      And here I stand, a god incognito,
disguised as man, beside the stream of Dirce
and the waters of Ismenus. There before the palace
I see my lightning-married mother's grave,
and there upon the ruins of her shattered house
the living fire of Zeus still smolders on
in deathless witness of Hera's violence and rage
against my mother. But Cadmus wins my praise:

he has made this tomb a shrine, sacred to my mother.
It was I who screened her grave with the green
of the clustering vine.

> Far behind me lie
those golden-rivered lands, Lydia and Phrygia,
where my journeying began. Overland I went,
across the steppes of Persia where the sun strikes hotly
down, through Bactrian fastness and the grim waste
of Media. Thence to rich Arabia I came;
and so, along all Asia's swarming littoral
of towered cities where Greeks and foreign nations,
mingling, live, my progress made. There
I taught my dances to the feet of living men,
establishing my mysteries and rites
that I might be revealed on earth for what I am:
a god.

> And thence to Thebes.

> This city, first
in Hellas, now shrills and echoes to my women's cries,
their ecstasy of joy. Here in Thebes
I bound the fawn-skin to the women's flesh and armed
their hands with shafts of ivy. For I have come
to refute that slander spoken by my mother's sisters—
those who least had right to slander her.
They said that Dionysus was no son of Zeus,
but Semele had slept beside a man in love
and fathered off her shame on Zeus—a fraud, they sneered,
contrived by Cadmus to protect his daughter's name.
They said she lied, and Zeus in anger at that lie
blasted her with lightning.
Because of that offense
I have stung them with frenzy, hounded them from home
up to the mountains where they wander, crazed of mind,
and compelled to wear my orgies' livery.
Every woman in Thebes—but the women only—
I drove from home, mad. There they sit,
rich and poor alike, even the daughters of Cadmus,
beneath the silver firs on the roofless rocks.
Like it or not, this city must learn its lesson:
it lacks initiation in my mysteries;
that I shall vindicate my mother Semele
and stand revealed to mortal eyes as the god

she bore to Zeus.
             Cadmus the king has abdicated,
leaving his throne and power to his grandson Pentheus;
who now revolts against divinity, in *me*;
thrusts *me* from his offerings; forgets *my* name
in his prayers. Therefore I shall *prove* to him
and every man in Thebes that I am god
indeed. And when my worship is established here,
and all is well, then I shall go my way
and be revealed to other men in other lands.
But if the men of Thebes attempt to force
my Bacchae from the mountainside by threat of arms,
I shall marshal my Maenads and take the field.
To these ends I have laid my deity aside
and go disguised as man."

PROMETHEUS

HESIOD, *Works and Days*, 49-82 (Lattimore)

*Prometheus, the champion of mankind, is a demigod or cul-
ture hero who is credited with all sorts of service to men.*

Zeus thought up dismal sorrows
    for mankind.
He hid fire; but Prometheus, the powerful son
    of Iapetos,
stole it again from Zeus of the counsels,
    to give to mortals.
He hid it out of the sight of Zeus
    who delights in thunder
in the hollow fennel stalk. In anger
    the cloud-gatherer spoke to him:
"Son of Iapetos, deviser of crafts beyond all others,
    you are happy that you stole the fire,
    and outwitted my thinking;
but it will be a great sorrow to you,
    and to men who come after.
As the price of fire I will give them an evil.

and all men shall fondle
this, their evil, close to their hearts,
   and take delight in it."
     So spoke the father of gods and mortals;
   and laughed out loud.
He told glorious Hephaistos to make haste, and plaster
earth with water, and to infuse it with a human voice
and vigor, and make the face
   like the immortal goddesses,
the bewitching features of a young girl;
   meanwhile Athene
was to teach her her skills, and how
   to do the intricate weaving,
while Aphrodite was to mist her head
   in golden endearment
and the cruelty of desire and longings
   that wear out the body,
but to Hermes, the guide, the slayer of Argos,
   he gave instructions
to put in her the mind of a hussy,
   and a treacherous nature.
     So Zeus spoke. And all obeyed Lord Zeus,
   the son of Kronos.
The renowned strong smith modeled her figure of earth,
   in the likeness
of a decorous young girl, as the son of Kronos
   had wished it.
The goddess gray-eyed Athene dressed and arrayed her;
   the Graces,
who are goddesses, and hallowed Persuasion
   put necklaces
of gold upon her body, while the Seasons,
   with glorious tresses,
put upon her head a coronal of spring flowers,
and Pallas Athene put all decor upon her body.
But into her heart Hermes, the guide,
   the slayer of Argos,
put lies, and wheedling words
   of falsehood, and a treacherous nature,
put a voice inside her, and gave her
   the name of woman,
Pandora, because all the gods

who have their homes on Olympos
had given her each a gift, to be a sorrow to men
who eat bread.

PROMETHEUS

AESCHYLUS, *Prometheus*, 199-243; 436-506 (More)

*Prometheus gives an account of how Zeus became ruler of
the gods and then explains how mankind has been benefitted
by Prometheus' concern.*

"Painful are these things to relate, painful is silence, and all is
wretchedness. When first the gods knew wrath, and faction raised
its head amongst them, and some would tear old Cronos from his
throne that Zeus might take his place, and others were determined that Zeus should never reign over the gods, then I with
wise counsel sought to guide the Titans, children of Earth and
Sky, — but all in vain. My crafty schemes they disdained, and in
their pride of strength thought it were easy to make themselves
lords by force. Often to me my mother Themis (or call her Earth,
for many names she hath, being one) had foretold in oracles what
was to be, with warning that not by might or brutal force should
victory come, but by guile alone. So I counselled them, but they
turned their eyes from me in impatience. Of the courses which
then lay open, far the best, it seemed, was to take my mother as
my helper and to join my will with the will of Zeus. By my advice the cavernous gloom of Tartarus now hides in night old
Cronos and his peers. Thus the new tyrant of heaven took profit
of me, and thus rewards me with these torments. 'Tis the disease
of tyranny, no more, to take no heed of friendship. You ask why
he tortures me; hear now the reason. No sooner was he established on his father's throne than he began to award various
offices to the different gods, ordering his government throughout.
Yet no care was in his heart for miserable men, and he was fain
to blot out the whole race and in their stead create another. None
save me opposed his purpose; I only dared; I rescued mankind
from the heavy blow that was to cast them into Hades. Therefore
I am bowed down by this anguish, painful to endure, pitiable to

behold. Mercy I had for mortals, but found no mercy for myself: so piteously I am disciplined, an ignoble spectacle for Zeus."

. . . .

"Think not I am silent through pride or insolence; dumb rage gnaws at my very heart for this outrage upon me. Yet who but I established these new gods in their honors? But I speak not of this, for already you are aware of the truth. Rather listen to the sad story of mankind, who like children lived until I gave them understanding and a portion of reason; yet not in disparagement of men I speak, but meaning to set forth the greatness of my charity. For seeing they saw not, and hearing they understood not, but like as shapes in a dream they wrought all the days of their life in confusion. No houses of brick raised in the warmth of the sun they had, nor fabrics of wood, but like the little ants they dwelt underground in the sunless depth of caverns. No certain sign of approaching winter they knew, no harbinger of flowering spring or fruitful summer; ever they labored at random, till I taught them to discern the seasons by the rising and the obscure setting of the stars. Numbers I invented for them, the chiefest of all discoveries; I taught them the grouping of letters, to be a memorial and record of the past, the mistress of the arts and mother of the Muses. I first brought under the yoke beasts of burden, who by draft and carrying relieved men of their hardest labors; I yoked the proud horse to the chariot, teaching him obedience to the reins, to be the adornment of wealth and luxury. I too contrived for sailors sea-faring vessels with their flaxen wings. Alas for me! such inventions I devised for mankind, but for myself I have no cunning to escape disaster.

"Hear but the rest, and you will wonder more at my inventions and many arts. If sickness visited them, they had no healing drug, no salve or soothing potion, but wasted away for want of remedies, and this was my greatest boon; for I revealed to them the mingling of bland medicaments for the banishing of all diseases. And many modes of divination I appointed: from dreams I first taught them to judge what should befall in waking state; I found the subtle interpretation of words half heard or heard by chance, and of meetings by the way; and the flight of taloned birds with their promise of fortune or failure I clearly denoted, their various modes of life, their mutual feuds, their friendships and consortings; I taught men to observe the smooth plumpness of entrails, and the color of the gall pleasing to the gods, and the mottled symmetry of liver-lobe. Burning the thigh-bones wrapt in fat and the long chine, I guided mankind to a hidden art, and read to them the intimations of the altar-flames that before were meaningless. So much then for these inventions. And the secret treasures of the earth, all benefits to men, copper, iron, silver, gold,—who but I could boast their discovery? No one, I ween, unless in idle vaunting. Nay, hear the whole matter in a word,—all human arts are from Prometheus."

THE GOLDEN BOUGH

VERGIL, *Aeneid*, Book 6. 125-148 (Mackail)

The Cumaean Sibyl tells Aeneas how he may obtain admission to the Underworld.

"O sprung of gods' blood, child of Anchises of Troy, easy is the descent into hell; all night and day the gate of dark Dis stands open; but to recall thy steps and issue to upper air, this is the task, this the burden. Some few of gods' lineage have availed, such as Jupiter's gracious favor or virtue's ardor has upborne to heaven. Midway all is muffled in forest, and the black sliding coils of Cocytus circle it round. Yet if thy soul is so passionate and so desirous twice to float across the Stygian lake, twice to see dark Tartarus, and thy pleasure is to plunge into the mad task, learn what must first be accomplished. Hidden in a shady tree is a bough with leafage and pliant shoot all of gold, consecrate to nether Juno, wrapped in the depth of woodland and shut in by dim dusky vales. But to him only who first has plucked the golden-tressed fruitage from the tree is it given to enter the hidden places of the earth. This has beautiful Proserpine ordained to be borne to her for her proper gift. The first torn away, a second fills the place with gold, and the spray burgeons with even such ore again. So let thine eyes trace it home, and thine hand pluck it duly when found; for lightly and unreluctant will it follow if thine is fate's summons; else will no strength of thine avail to conquer it nor hard steel to cut it away."

~~~

THE ISLAND OF THE BLESSED

PINDAR, *Olympian*, 2. 61-83 (Lattimore)

But they who endure thrice over
in the world beyond to keep their souls from all sin
have gone God's way to the tower of Kronos; there
winds sweep from the Ocean
across the Island of the Blessed. Gold flowers to flame
on land in the glory of trees; it is fed in the water,
whence they bind bracelets to their arms and go chapleted

under the straight decrees of Rhadamanthys,
whom the husband of Rhea, high throned above all,
our great father, keeps in the chair of state beside him.
They say Peleus is there, and Kadmos,
and his mother with prayer softening Zeus' heart
carried Achilles thither,

who felled Hektor, Troy's unassailable
tall column of strength, who gave death to Kyknos
and the Aithiop, Dawn's child.

~~~

THE UNDERWORLD

HOMER, *Odyssey*, Book 11. 568-600 (Butler)

*Odysseus tells of famous figures of the Underworld, especially
of those undergoing punishment.*

"Then I saw Minos son of Zeus with his golden scepter in his
hand, sitting in judgment on the dead, and the ghosts were gathered sitting and standing round him in the spacious house of
Hades, to learn his sentences upon them.

"After him I saw huge Orion in a meadow full of asphodel,
driving the ghosts of the wild beasts that he had killed upon the

mountains, and he had a great bronze club in his hand, unbreakable for ever and ever.

"And I saw Tityus son of Gaia stretched upon the plain and covering some nine acres of ground. Two vultures on either side of him were digging their beaks into his liver, and he kept on trying to beat them off with his hands, but could not; for he had violated Zeus' mistress Leto as she was going through Panopeus on her way to Pytho.

"I saw also the dreadful fate of Tantalus, who stood in a lake that reached his chin. He was dying to quench his thirst, but could never reach the water, for whenever the poor creature stooped to drink, it dried up and vanished, so that there was nothing but dry ground—parched by the spite of heaven. There were tall trees, moreover, that shed their fruit over his head—pears, pomegranates, apples, sweet figs and juicy olives, but whenever the poor creature stretched out his hand to take some, the wind tossed the branches back again to the clouds.

"And I saw Sisyphus at his endless task raising his prodigious stone with both his hands. With hands and feet he tried to roll it up to the top of the hill, but always, just before he could roll it over on to the other side, its weight would be too much for him, and the pitiless stone would come thundering down again on to the plain. Then he would begin trying to push it up hill again, and the sweat ran off him and the steam rose after him."

IXION

PINDAR, *Pythian*, 2.21-48 (Lattimore)

It is by gods' work that they say Ixion,
fixed on his winged wheel, spun in a circle,
cries aloud this message to mortals:
To your benefactor return ever with kind dealing rendered.

He learned that lesson well. By favor of the sons of Kronos,
he was given a life of delight but could not abide blessedness
    long; in his delirious heart
he loved Hera, dedicated to the high couch
of Zeus. That outrage hurled him into conspicuous
ruin. He was a man and endured beyond all others

distress full merited. Two sins flowered
to pain in his life: a hero, he first
infected the mortal breed with kindred bloodshed, not without treachery;

also, in the great secret chambers of Zeus he strove to ravish
the Queen. A man should look at himself and learn well his
   own stature.
The coupling unnatural brought accumulation of evil
on him, even in success; it was a cloud he lay with,
and he in his delusion was given the false loveliness.
A phantom went in the guise of that highest daughter
of Uranian Kronos; a deceit visited upon him
by the hands of Zeus, a fair evil thing. Zeus likewise wrought
   the crucifixion on the wheel,

Ixion's bane; and, spinning there, limbs fast
to the ineluctable circle, he makes the message a thing that
   all may know.
But she, graceless, spawned
a child of violence.
There was none like her, nor her son; no honor was his
   portion in the usage of god or man.
Nursing him, she named him Kentauros, and he coupled
with the Magnesian mares on the spurs of Pelion;
and a weird breed was engendered
in the favor of either parent:
the mare's likeness in the parts below, and the manlike father
   above.

<hr>

THE DANAÏDS

HORACE, *Odes*, 3.11.13-52 (Marris)

*Horace invokes Mercury and the lyre to tell the story of the
Danaïds, and especially Hypermnestra, as a warning to the
young Lyde of sins against love.*

And thou canst draw the beasts and woods
   To follow thee, and stay the floods:

The porter of the gate of Hell,
Grim Cerberus, confessed thy spell,

Though round his Gorgon head he shakes
His fillet of a hundred snakes,
And though from out his triple mouth
Pour fetid breath and bloody froth,

Ixion, too, was forced to smile,
And Tityus: the urn awhile
Stood empty as the Danaïd throng
Drew comfort from thy soothing song.

Tell Lyde of their tragedy;
The famous weird these maidens dree—
Filling their jar, whence night and day
The wasting water leaks away.

So doom awaiteth at the last
The sinner dead, and who surpassed
Their infamy, that with the sword
Could slay each one her wedded lord.

Yet one deserved the name of bride;
One only, who superbly lied
To her deceitful father—Fame
Shall ever consecrate her name.

"Awake!" she cried, "my lord, my love!
Ere from a snare thou think'st not of
Come longer slumber! Up, and go
Before my sire and sisters know.

"Lo! they are lions, lighting on
A herd, and rending one by one:
But I am softer—I'll not wound
Nor hold thee fast in prison bound.

"My sire may load me down with chains;
Or far to Africa's domains
May ship me, for that I, your wife,
Was pitiful and spared thy life.

"Go, get thee gone, o'er land and flood
While Night and Love are kind, and good
The omens; grave upon my tomb
One word of sorrow for my doom."

I I

EARLY HEROES
AND
HEROINES

HERACLES

Homeric Hymns, 1-8 (Lang)

Heracles was by far the most popular of heroes and attracted to himself so many legends that it is impossible to recount them all. Two great centers provide the background for many of the tales: the Peloponnese where he was located in Tiryns but compelled to perform the twelve labors at the bidding of Eurystheus of Mycenae; and Thebes, in Boeotia, usually identified as his birthplace.

Accounts of the twelve labors are not consistent, but they usually include the following: (1) The Nemean lion, (2) The Hydra of Lerna, (3) The Cerynitian hind, (4) The Erymanthian boar, (5) The Stymphalian birds, (6) The Augean stables, (7) The Cretan bull, (8) The horses of Diomede, (9) Hippolyte's girdle, (10) The cattle of Geryon, (11) The apples of the Hesperides, (12) Cerberus.

In addition to his numerous amorous adventures, Heracles had two human wives, the Theban Megara whom he killed with her children in a fit of madness sent on him by Hera, his constant enemy, and Deianeira who caused his death by smearing the blood of the centaur Nessus on his robe in an effort to regain his affection when she learned of his love for Iole.

So widespread was the fame of Heracles that when the Dorians came into Greece they represented themselves as the Heracleidae, the children of Heracles, seeking to regain their inheritance.

Of Heracles the son of Zeus will I sing, mightiest of mortals, whom Alcmena bore in Thebes of the fair dancing places, for she had lain in the arms of Cronion, the lord of the dark clouds. Of old the hero wandered endlessly over land and sea, at the bidding of Eurystheus the prince, and himself wrought many deeds of fateful might, and many he endured; but now in the fair haunts of snowy Olympus he dwells in joy, and has white-ankled Hebe for his wife. Hail prince, son of Zeus, and give to us valor and good fortune.

LABORS OF HERACLES

EURIPIDES, *Heracles*, 348-429 (Coleridge)

The chorus recounts many of the labors of Heracles, while despairing of his return from Hades where he had gone to bring back Cerberus.

Phoebus is singing a plaintive dirge to drown his happier strains, striking with key of gold his sweet-tongued lyre; so too would I sing a song of praise, a crown to all his toil, concerning him who is gone to the gloom beneath the nether world, whether I am to call him son of Zeus or of Amphitryon. For the praise of noble toils accomplished is a glory to the dead. First he cleared the grove of Zeus of a lion, and put its skin upon his back, hiding his auburn hair in its fearful gaping jaws;

Then on a day, with murderous bow he wounded the race of wild Centaurs, that range the hills, slaying them with winged shafts; Peneus, the river of fair eddies, knows him well, and those far fields unharvested, and the farms on Pelion and they who haunt the glens of Homole bordering thereupon, whence they rode forth to conquer Thessaly, arming themselves with pines for clubs; likewise he slew that dappled hind with horns of gold, that preyed upon the country-folk, glorifying Artemis, huntress queen of Oenoe;

Next he mounted on a car and tamed with the bit the steeds of Diomede, that greedily champed their bloody food at gory mangers with jaws unbridled, devouring with hideous joy the flesh of men; then crossing Hebrus' silver stream he still toiled on to perform the commands of the tyrant of Mycenae, till he came to the strand of the Malian gulf by the streams of Anaurus, where he slew with his arrows Cycnus, murderer of his guests, the savage wretch who dwelt in Amphanae;

Also he came to those minstrel maids, to their orchard in the west, to pluck from the leafy apple tree its golden fruit, when he had slain the tawny dragon, whose awful coils were twined all round to guard it; and he made his way into ocean's lairs, bringing calm to men that use the oar; moreover he sought the home of Atlas, and stretched out his hands to uphold the firmament, and on his manly shoulders took the starry mansions of the gods;

Then he went through the waves of heaving Euxine against the mounted host of Amazons dwelling round Maeotis, the lake that is fed by many a stream, having gathered to his standard all his friends from Hellas, to fetch the gold-embroidered raiment of the warrior queen, a deadly quest for a girdle. And Hellas won those glorious spoils of the barbarian maid, and safe in Mycenae are they now. On Lerna's murderous hound, the many-headed hydra, he set his branding-iron, and smeared its venom on his darts, wherewith he slew the shepherd of Erytheia, a monster with three bodies;

And many another glorious achievement he brought to a happy issue; to Hades' house of tears hath he now sailed, the goal of his labors, where he is ending his career of toil, nor cometh he thence again.

LABORS OF HERACLES

APOLLODORUS, *The Library*, II. 5.5-6 (Frazer)

Apollodorus recounts in great detail the labors assigned to Heracles by Eurystheus, other of Heracles' labors, and the children sired by him. Here are a few of the labors.

The fifth labor he laid on him was to carry out the dung of the cattle of Augeas in a single day. Now Augeas was king of Elis; some say that he was a son of the Sun, others that he was a son of Poseidon, and others that he was a son of Phorbas; and he had many herds of cattle. Hercules accosted him, and without revealing the command of Eurystheus, said that he would carry out the dung in one day, if Augeas would give him the tithe of the cattle. Augeas was incredulous, but promised. Having taken Augeas's son Phyleus to witness, Hercules made a breach in the foundations of the cattle-yard, and then, diverting the courses of the Alpheus and Peneus, which flowed near each other, he turned them into the yard, having first made an outlet for the water through another opening. When Augeas learned that this had been accomplished at the command of Eurystheus, he would not pay the reward; nay more, he denied that he had promised to pay it and on that point he professed himself ready to submit to arbitration. The arbitrators having taken their seats, Phyleus was called by Hercules and bore witness against his father, affirming that he had agreed to give him a reward. In a rage Augeas, before the voting took place, ordered both Phyleus and Hercules to get out of Elis. So Phyleus went to Dulichium and dwelt there, and Hercules repaired to Dexamenus at Olenus. He found Dexamenus on the point of betrothing perforce his daughter Mnesimache to the centaur Eurytion, and, being called upon by him for help, he slew Eurytion when that centaur came to fetch his bride. But Eurystheus would not admit this labor either among the ten, alleging that it had been performed for hire.

The sixth labor he enjoined on him was to chase away the Stymphalian birds. Now at the city of Stymphalus in Arcadia was the lake called Stymphalian, embosomed in a deep wood. To it countless birds had flocked for refuge, fearing to be preyed upon by the wolves. So when Hercules was at a loss how to drive the birds from the wood, Athena gave him brazen castanets, which she had received from Hephaestus. By clashing these on a certain mountain that overhung the lake, he scared the birds. They could not abide the sound, but fluttered up in a fright, and in that way Hercules shot them.

The seventh labor he enjoined on him was to bring the Cretan bull. Acusilaus says that this was the bull that ferried across Europa for Zeus; but some say it was the bull that Poseidon sent up from the sea when Minos promised to sacrifice to Poseidon what should appear out of the sea. And they say that when he saw the beauty of the bull he sent it away to the herds and sacrificed another to Poseidon; at which the god was angry and made the bull savage. To attack this bull Hercules came to Crete, and when, in reply to his request for aid, Minos told him to fight and catch the bull for himself, he caught it and brought it to Eurystheus, and having shown it to him he let it afterwards go free.

~~~~

HERACLES AND CERBERUS

HOMER, *Odyssey*, Book 11. 601-626 (Butler)

Odysseus sees the phantom of Heracles in the underworld.

"I saw mighty Heracles; but it was his phantom only, for he is feasting ever with the immortal gods, and has lovely Hebe to wife, who is daughter of Zeus and Hera. The ghosts were screaming round him like scared birds flying all whithers. He looked black as night with his bare bow in his hands and his arrow on the string, glaring around as though ever on the point of taking aim. About his breast there was a wondrous golden belt adorned in the most marvelous fashion with bears, wild boars, and lions with gleaming eyes; there was also war, battle, and death. The man who made that belt, do what he might, would never be able to make another like it. Heracles knew me at once when he saw me and spoke piteously, saying, 'My poor Odysseus, noble son of Laertes, are you too leading the same sorry kind of life that I did when I was above ground? I was son of Zeus, but I went through an infinity of suffering, for I became bondsman to one who was far beneath me—a low fellow who set me all manner of labors. He once sent me here to fetch the hell-hound—for he did not think he could find anything harder for me than this, but I got the hound out of Hades and brought him to him, for Hermes and Athene helped me.' "

~~~~

INCIDENTAL LABORS OF HERACLES

HYGINUS, *Myths*, 31 (Grant)

Among the collections of the deeds of Heracles is that of Hyginus.

He slew Antaeus, son of Earth, in Libya. This man would compel visitors to wrestle with him, and when they were exhausted would kill them. He slew them in wrestling. [He slew] in Egypt Busiris, whose custom it was to sacrifice visitors. When Hercules heard of his customary practice, he allowed himself to be led to the altar with the fillet of sacrifice, but when Busiris was about to invoke the gods, Hercules with his club killed him and the attendants at the sacrifice as well. He killed Cygnus, son of Mars, conquering him by force of arms. When Mars came there, and wanted to contend with him in arms because of his son, Jove hurled a thunderbolt between them. He killed at Troy the sea-monster to whom Hesione was offered. Laomedon, Hesione's father, he killed with arrows because he did not give her back. The shining eagle which was eating out the heart of Prometheus he killed with arrows. He killed Lycus, son of Neptune, because he was planning to kill his wife Megara, daughter of Creon, and their sons Therimachus and Ophites. The River Achelous used to change himself into all sorts of shapes. When he fought with Hercules to win Dejanira in marriage, he changed himself into a bull. Hercules tore off his horn, presenting it to the Hesperides or the Nymphs, and the goddesses filled it with fruits and called it Cornucopia. He killed Neleus and his ten sons for refusing to cleanse him or purify him at the time when he had killed his wife Megara, daughter of Creon, and his sons Therimachus and Ophites. He killed Eurytus because he refused him when he sought his daughter Iole in marriage. He killed Eurytion the Centaur because he wooed Dejanira, daughter of Dexamenus, his hoped-for bride.

HERACLES AND HYLAS

THEOCRITUS, *Idylls*, 13. 36-67, with omissions (Lang)

In the fifth century B.C. Heracles was turned into a glutton and buffoon by the poets; later, the Stoics made him a savior and benefactor of mankind, while the pastoral poets made him a romantic figure.

Hylas of the yellow hair, with a vessel of bronze in his hand, went to draw water against suppertime, for Heracles himself, and the steadfast Telamon, for these two comrades supped ever at one table. Soon was he aware of a spring, in a hollow land, and the rushes grew thickly round it, and dark swallow-wort, and green maiden-hair, and blooming parsley, and deer-grass spreading through the marshy land. In the midst of the water the nymphs were arraying their dances, the sleepless nymphs, dread goddesses of the country people, Eunice, and Malis, and Nycheia, with her April eyes. And now the boy was holding out the wide-mouthed pitcher to the water, intent on dipping it, but the nymphs all clung to his hand, for love of the Argive lad had fluttered the soft hearts of all of them. Then down he sank into the black water, headlong all, as when a star shoots flaming from the sky. Then the nymphs held the weeping boy on their laps, and with gentle words were striving to comfort him. But the son of Amphitryon was troubled about the lad, and went forth, carrying his bended bow in Scythian fashion, and the club that is ever grasped in his right hand. Thrice he shouted "Hylas!" as loud as his deep throat could call, and thrice again the boy heard him, and thin came his voice from the water, and, hard by though he was, he seemed very far away. And as when a bearded lion, a ravening lion on the hills, hears the bleating of a fawn afar off, and rushes forth from his lair to seize it, his readiest meal, even so the mighty Heracles, in longing for the lad, sped through the trackless briars, and ranged over much country.

Reckless are lovers: great toils did Heracles bear, in hills and thickets wandering, and Jason's quest was all postponed to this. He, wheresoever his feet might lead him, went wandering in his fury, for the cruel Goddess of love was rending his heart within him.

Thus loveliest Hylas is numbered with the Blessed, but for a runaway they girded at Heracles, the heroes, because he roamed from Argo of the sixty oarsmen.

HERCULES AND CACUS

VERGIL, *Aeneid*, Book 8. 193-267 (Humphries)

Vergil connects Hercules with Rome by means of King Evander's account to Aeneas.

"Look up at the cliff
Hung on the high rocks yonder, see the scattered

Rubble of rock, the ruin of a dwelling,
The jumble of toppled crags. There was a cave there
Once on a time; no man had ever measured
Its awful depth, no sunlight ever cheered it.
The half-man, Cacus, terrible to look at,
Lived in that cave, and the ground was always reeking
With the smell of blood, and nailed to the doors, the faces
Of men hung pale and wasted. Vulcan fathered
This monster; you would know it if you saw him
With the black fire pouring from mouth and nostrils,
A bulk of moving evil. But time at last
Brought us the help we prayed for; a great avenger,
A god, came to our rescue, Hercules,
Proud in the death and spoil of triple Geryon,
Drove his huge bulls this way, the great herd filling
Valley and river. And the crazy Cacus,
Who never would lose a chance for crime or cunning,
Made off with four of the bulls and four sleek heifers,
Dragging them by their tails; the tracks would never
Prove he had driven them to his rocky cavern.
He hid them in the darkness; whoever looked
Would think they had gone not to, but from, the cave.
Meanwhile, as Hercules drove the well-fed herd
Out of the stables to the road again,
Some of them lowed in protest; hill and grove
Gave back the sound, and from the cave one heifer
Lowed in return. That was the doom of Cacus.
Black bile burned hot in Hercules; he grabbed
His weapons, his great knotted club, went rushing
Up to the mountain-top. Never before
Had men seen terror in the eyes of Cacus.
Swifter than wind, he dove into his cavern,
Shut himself in, shattered the links of iron
That held aloft the giant boulder, dropped it
To block the doorway, and Hercules came flinging
His angry strength against it, to no purpose.
This way he faced, and that, and gnashed his teeth
In sheer frustration; he went around the mountain
Three times, in burning rage; three times he battered
The bulkhead of the door; three times he rested,
Breathless and weary, on the floor of the valley.
Above the cavern ridge, a pointed rock.

All flint, cut sharp, with a sheer drop all around it,
Rose steep, a nesting place for kites and buzzards.
It leaned a little leftward toward the river.
This Hercules grabbed and shook, straining against it;
His right hand pushed and wrenched it loose; he shoved it,
With a sudden heave, down hill, and the heaven
 thundered,
The river ran backward and the banks jumped sideways,
And Cacus' den stood open, that great palace
Under the rock, the chambered vault of shadows.
An earthquake, so, might bring to light the kingdoms
Of the world below the world, the pallid regions
Loathed by the gods, the gulf of gloom, where phantoms
Shiver and quake as light descends upon them.
So there was Cacus, desperate in the light,
Caught in the hollow rock, howling and roaring
As Hercules rained weapons down upon him,
Everything he could use, from boughs to millstones,
But Cacus still had one way out of the danger:
A cloud of smoke rolled out of his jaws; the cave
Darkened to utter blackness, thick night rolling
With fitful glints of fire. This was too much
For Hercules in his fury; he jumped down through it,
Through fire, where the smoke came rolling forth the
 thickest,
Where the black billows seethed around the cavern.
And Cacus, in the darkness, to no purpose
Poured forth his fire and smoke. Hercules grabbed him,
Twisted him into a knot, hung on and choked him
Till the eyes bulged out and the throat was dry of blood.
He tore the doors loose, and the house was open;
People could see the lost and stolen plunder,
And Hercules dragged the shapeless ugly carcass
Out by the feet, a fascinating object
For the gaze of men, the terrible eyes, the muzzle,
The hairy chest, and the fire dead in the gullet."

JASON

PINDAR, *Pythian*, 4.66-255 (Lattimore)

The expedition of the Argonauts was led by Jason to recover the golden fleece of the ram who carried Helle and Phrixus over the sea toward Colchis. In this early myth are many variations in the names of the Argonauts, their adventures on the journey, and the geography, depending on the interests and knowledge of the tellers of the tale. The Oriental sorceress Medea, with her violent emotions and magical powers, tends to obscure the original details of the saga.

What, then, was the beginning of their adventure?
What danger nailed them fast in the strength of steel? The
    word of God ran that Pelias
must die at the hands, or the unyielding contrivance, of some
    proud scion of Aiolos.
The stark prophecy came to his wary mind
spoken beside the naveled center of leafy Earth, our mother:
"Beware and hold in all guard him of the single sandal
when he comes down from the steep steadings
to the rising round of famed Iolkos,

stranger be he or citizen." And he came in his time,
a man terrible with twin javelins; and a twofold guise was
    on him.
A tunic of Magnesian fashion fitted close his magnificent
    limbs,
and across it a panther's hide held off the shivering rains.
Nor did the glory of his streaming locks go shorn,
but blazed the length of his back. Striding apace
he stood, and tested his unfaltering will
in the market place that filled with people.

They knew him not; yet awe-struck one man would say to
    another:
"This cannot be Apollo, surely, nor Aphrodite's lord,
he of the brazen chariot. And in shining Naxos they say

Iphimedeia's children died, Otos, and you, lord Ephialtes the
    reckless.
And Artemis' arrows, cast from the might of her quiver,
struck down Tityos in the speed of his desire,
that any man hereafter may long rather to catch at loves he
    has power to take."

So they questioned one another and made
answer. But with his polished car and mules Pelias urgently
drove up. He stared as he saw the sandal conspicuous
on the right foot, and there only. But, veiling the fear
in his heart, he spoke: "What manner of land, my friend,
might you claim as your own? What groundling woman let
    you forth
from a sere womb? See that you stain not your race
with lies, that to all men are most hateful."

He boldly but in speech of gentleness made answer:
"I think I can carry Chiron's discipline. For I come from his
    cave
and the side of Chariklo and Philyra, where the Centaur's
    stainless daughters brought me to manhood.
With twenty years gone to fulfilment and no deed
done, no word spoken to offend them, I have come
home, bringing back my father's lordship (administered
now by no right) that Zeus of old granted, privilege
of Aiolos, leader of men, and his sons thereafter.

"For I hear that Pelias, unrighteously and in persuasion of his
    pale heart,
has stripped the power by force from my fathers, the kings
    of old.
They, when I first saw light, fearing the proud
chief's violence, made dark mourning as if I had died
in the house; under the cloak of women's mingled
lamentation they sent me away in my splendid raiment;
they made their way by night and brought me to Chiron,
    Kronos' son, to be reared.

"But the heads of all these chapters you know well.
Point me now clearly, honored citizens, the house of my
    fathers, lords of white horses.

I am one of you, Aison's child, and this soil I tread is not
    alien.
And the divine beast when he spoke to me called me Jason."
He said; and his father's eyes, as he came in the house, knew
    him,
and tears gathered and fell from the withered eyelids
for joy in his heart, as he saw his chosen son
a man, and splendid beyond all others.
And from either side his two brothers
came at the rumor of him: from near at hand, Pheres, leaving
    the spring Hypereian,
and from far Messana, Amythaon; and with speed came
    Admetos also and Melampos
to their cousin's side. And in the feast's spell
with words of love Jason gave them entertainment,
appointing the feast of fellowship with all delight for these
    men
assembled, reaping five nights together and five days
the hallowed blossoming of life's luxury.

But on the sixth he laid all the urgent tale open from the
    beginning
to his kinsmen. And they followed his guidance. Suddenly
    from their benches
they sprang up, he and they together. They came to the hall
    of Pelias
and thronging strode within. At the noise of their coming
    he, lovely-haired
Tyro's child, stood forth to meet them. But Jason,
letting his voice flow gently into quiet discourse,
cast down the foundation-stone of wise argument: "Son of
    Poseidon

"of the Rock: the hearts of mortals are all too rapid
to take the crooked way of gain over righteousness, though
    they edge withal to the rough reckoning day.
But it beseems you and me, tempering our passion, to weave
    wealth in our time.
You know well what I mean. One dam mothered Kretheus
and reckless Salmoneus, whence, in the third generation
born, you and I gaze on the golden strength of the sun.

The very Fates, their faces veiled for shame, stand apart
before hatred growing among blood kinsmen.

"It is not for us by brazen edge of the sword
or with spears to divide our great patrimony. Behold: I
    release to you
the sheep, and all the tawny herds of cattle you wrested once
from my people, and administer to make fat your wealth.
It grieves me nothing that thereby you advanced your estate
    so far.
But the scepter of single rule and the throne, where Aison,
    Kretheus' son, in his sessions
made straight the dooms for a knightly multitude—
these, with no strife joined between us,

"surrender to me; lest you make some fresh disaster to rise."
He spoke, and mildly in his turn Pelias made answer: "Such
    a man
will I be. But the elder spell of life
is on me, while your youth gathers even now to its blossom-
    ing. You have strength to lift
the wrath of the undergods. Phrixos calls us to journey
to Aietes' house, and bring home his ghost
and the deep fleece of the ram whereby he fled death at sea

"and the godless weapons of his stepmother.
The weird dream-shape haunts me and speaks. And I have
    taken counsel at the shrine by Kastalia
what shift to make; the god's behest is in speed to appoint a
    sea-venture.
Take this endeavor upon yourself and achieve it; I swear
I will yield you the whole kingship. Let Zeus
of our fathers be witness, to bind us under a strong oath."
These two assenting to the compact were parted.
But Jason now in his own right

Sped heralds abroad with news of the voyage that was be-
    ginning.
In speed came three sons of Kronian Zeus, heroes wearied
    never in battle,
Alkmena's son and two by Leda of the glancing eyes; and
    two deep-haired men

sprung of Poseidon, heroes whose thoughts were of valor
from Pylos and the rock of Tainaron; thereby splendor
of glory was brought to fulfilment for Euphamos, and for
    you, Periklymenos the mighty.
And of Apollo's blood the harper came and father of lyric
voices, Orpheus the admired.

Hermes also of the golden staff sent twin sons on this labor
    relentless,
Erytos and Echion in the laughing pride of their youth. And
    two
that were swift came, dwellers beside the Pangaios pastures.
For of his own will and with heart favorable, Boreas, king
    of the winds,
their father, sent Zetes and Kalais, men with backs
ruffled to two red wings.
And Hera inflamed overpowering sweet desire in the demi-
    gods

for the ship Argo; lest any, left at home,
sit mulling beside his mother a life with no danger; rather
    against death even
they found the fairest defense that essence of valor in their
    own fellowship.
Such company, flower of seafarers, came down to the sea
    at Iolkos,
and Jason assembled them and admired all. The seer
Mopsos, making prophecy by birds and the sacred lots,
sent with good augury the host on board; and when
they had slung the anchors at the cutwater,

the leader, taking a golden bowl in his hands
at the stern, intreated Uranian Zeus our father, of the thun-
    derspear, invoked
fleet-running currents of the waves, winds, nights, and the
    sea's ways
and days to be favorable, and the dear doom of homecoming
    at the end.
And out of the clouds Zeus, answering, called back a mantic
peal of thunder; and the bright branches of sheer lightning
    broke in flame.

The heroes, trusting the signs apparent of God,
drew breath; and the prophet cried aloud,

bespeaking glad expectations, to bend to their sweeps;
and slakeless the oars went dipping from the speed in their
hands.
On a following southwest wind they came to the Euxine
mouth,
and founded there a holy precinct to the sea-god Poseidon,
and a red herd of Thracian bulls was dedicated
with the slab of an altar new-founded upon piled stones.
Straining now into deep danger, they supplicated the lord of
ships

to escape the stark collision of the Clashing
Rocks. These were two, and alive; they rolled together with
shock more fleet
than the battalions of thunderous winds; but even now that
sailing
of demigods brought their death. To Phasis thereafter
they came, to meet in their strength the dark men of Kolchis
at the house of King Aietes. But Aphrodite, lady of Kypros,
mistress of rending arrows, sent down from Olympos the
bright wryneck,
binding crosswise over a breakless wheel

the passionate bird, that was brought that time first
to mortal man; and she made Aisonides, Jason, wise in
charm and incantation
that he might loosen Medeia's shame for her parents, and
Hellas be all her desire,
that her heart ablaze under the lash of longing be set in
tumult.
And she revealed forthwith the secret of the trials her father
would set,
and with oil medicating simples against stark pain
gave them for his use. And they compacted marriage to be
joined thereafter in all delight between them.

Now when Aietes before them all had driven home the steel
plowshare,

those oxen, that blew from their tawny jaws the flame of
    ravening fire
and tore the soil with brazen hoofs as they passed,
these he led and forced their necks to the yoke, single-handed;
    then, running the furrow straight,
drove, and ripped six feet deep the back of earth.
He spoke then: "Let the king, whoever he be,
lord of the ship, do this for me; then take away the robe
    unperishing,

"the bright fleece tasseled in gold."
He ended, and Jason, reliant on God, threw down his saffron
    mantle
and stepped to the work. Flame, by craft of the strange witch-
    maiden, harmed him not.
Gripping the plow, he bent the necks of the oxen under,
binding the yoke upon them, and by main strength of his
    shoulders,
with the fell goad laid on, plowed the whole length perforce.
Aietes, even in pained and speechless amazement,
gasped, admiring that act of strength;

and his friends held out their arms to the man in his might
and with leaf-woven garlands crowned him, and spoke him
    fair with admiring words.
Straightway Helios' wonderful son spoke of the shining
    fleece
where Phrixos' knife had flayed and hung it.
His hope was that not even so could the man accomplish that
    labor,
for it was set in a thicket, and guarded by the rending fangs
    of a great snake
that for measure and thickness outpassed a galley of fifty oars
the ax's stroke has labored to build.

The high road is long for me to travel, and time closes. I
    know
a short path, I that guide many another in the craft of singers.
By guile he slew the green-eyed serpent of the burnished
    scales,
O Arkesilas, and stole away Medeia, with her good will, she
    that was bane to Pelias.

They touched the gulfs of Ocean and the Red Sea,
and at Lemnos the breed of women that had slain their
    lords;
and there in games, for prize of raiment, displayed the
    strength in their limbs.

They lay with these women.

JASON AND MEDEA

EURIPIDES, *Medea*, 1-43; 1323-1343; 1377-1388
(Coleridge, revised)

> *When the Argonauts finally returned after strange wander-*
> *ings in Europe and Africa, Medea persuaded the daughters*
> *of Pelias that they could renew his youth by boiling him in*
> *a cauldron, but she neglected to supply them with her magic*
> *herbs. As a result of Pelias' death Jason and Medea were*
> *forced to flee to Corinth with their children. There Jason*
> *abandoned Medea to marry the daughter of King Creon.*
> *Medea's nurse describes the situation in Corinth after Jason*
> *has left Medea for his new bride.*
>
>   *The nurse's premonitions are borne out by Medea's*
> *murder of her sons. Medea and Jason have a final exchange*
> *of words before Medea leaves in her dragon car with the*
> *bodies of her children, hoping to find refuge with Aegeus,*
> *the king of Athens.*

Ah! would to Heaven the good ship Argo ne'er had sped its
course to the Colchian land through the misty blue Symplegades,
nor ever in the glens of Pelion the pine been felled to furnish
with oars the chieftain's hands, who went to fetch the golden
fleece for Pelias; for then would my own mistress Medea never
have sailed to the turrets of Iolcos, her soul with love for Jason
smitten, nor would she have beguiled the daughters of Pelias to
slay their father and come to live here in the land of Corinth with
her husband and children, where her exile found favor with the
citizens to whose land she had come, and in all things of her own
accord was she at one with Jason, the greatest safeguard this when
wife and husband do agree; but now their love is all turned to

hate, and tenderest ties are weak. For Jason betrayed his own children and my mistress dear for the love of a royal bride, for he wedded the daughter of Creon, lord of this land. While Medea, his hapless wife, thus scorned, appeals to the oaths he swore, recalls the strong pledge his right hand gave, and bids heaven be witness what requital she is finding from Jason. And here she lies fasting, yielding her body to her grief, wasting away in tears ever since she learned that she was wronged by her husband, never lifting her eye nor raising her face from off the ground; and she lends as deaf an ear to her friend's warning as if she were a rock or ocean billow, save when she turns her snow-white neck aside and softly to herself bemoans her father dear, her country, and her home, which she gave up to come hither with the man who now holds her in dishonor. She, poor lady, has by sad experience learned how good a thing it is never to quit one's native land. And she hates her children now and feels no joy at seeing them; I fear she may contrive some untoward scheme; for her mood is dangerous nor will she brook her cruel treatment; full well I know her, and I much do dread that she will plunge the keen sword through their hearts, stealing without a word into the chamber where their marriage couch is spread, or else that she will slay the prince and bridegroom too, and so find some calamity still more grievous than the present; for dreadful is her wrath; verily the man that incurs her hate will have no easy task to raise over her a song of triumph. Lo! where her sons come here from their childish sports; little they think of their mother's woes, for the soul of the young is no friend to sorrow.

· · · ·

JASON

Accursed woman! by gods, by me and all mankind abhorred as never woman was, who had the heart to stab your children, you their mother, leaving me undone and childless; this you did and still you gaze upon the sun and earth after this deed most impious. Curses on you! I now perceive what then I missed in the day I brought you, fraught with doom, from your home in a barbarian land to dwell in Hellas, traitress to your father and to the land that nurtured you. On me the gods have hurled the curse that dogged your steps, for you slew your brother at his hearth before you came aboard our fair ship, Argo. Such was the outset of your life of crime; then you married me, and having borne me sons to glut your passion's lust, you now have slain them. Not one amongst the wives of Hellas ever had dared this deed; yet before them all I chose you for my wife, wedding a foe to be my doom, no woman, but a lioness fiercer than Tyrrhene Scylla in nature. But with reproaches heaped a thousandfold I cannot wound you, so brazen is your nature. Perish, vile sorceress, murderess of your children! While I must mourn my luckless fate, for I shall never enjoy my new-found bride, nor shall I have the children, whom I bred and reared, alive to say the last farewell to me; nay, I have lost them.

MEDEA

To this speech I could have made a long reply, but Father Zeus knows well all I have done for you, and the treatment you have given me. Yet you were not ordained to scorn my love and lead a life of joy in mockery of me, nor was your royal bride nor Creon, who gave you a second wife, to thrust me from this land and rue it not. Wherefore, if you will, call me a lioness, and Scylla, whose home is in the Tyrrhene land; for I in turn have wrung your heart, as well I might.

. . . .

JASON

Give up to me those dead, to bury and lament.

MEDEA

No, never! I will bury them myself, bearing them to Hera's sacred field who watches over the Cape, that none of their foes may insult them by pulling down their tombs; and in this land of Sisyphus I will ordain hereafter a solemn feast and mystic rites to atone for this impious murder. I will now go to the land of Erechtheus, to dwell with Aegeus, Pandion's son. But you as well you may, shalt die a scoundrel's death, your head crushed beneath a shattered relic of Argo, when you have seen the bitter ending of my marriage.

~~~~

THESEUS

PLUTARCH, *Lives*, "Theseus," with omissions (Dryden)

Theseus is a curious figure. Praised by the Athenians as a hero comparable to Heracles, he was slandered by many in the other Greek cities as faithless and unreliable. In his biography Plutarch has preserved the main outlines of the myth, although he has been hard pushed on occasion to create an impression of historicity.

The lineage of Theseus, by his father's side, ascends as high as to Erechtheus and the first inhabitants of Attica. By his mother's side he was descended of Pelops. For Pelops was the most powerful of all the kings of Peloponnesus, not so much by the greatness of his riches as the multitude of his children, having married many daughters to chief men, and put many sons in places of command in the towns round about him. One of whom named Pittheus, grandfather to Theseus, was governor of the small city of the Troezenians and had the repute of a man of the greatest knowledge and wisdom of his time. Aegeus, being desirous of children, and consulting the oracle of Delphi, received the celebrated answer which forbade him the company of any woman before his return to Athens. But the oracle being so obscure as not to satisfy him that he was clearly forbid this, he went to Troezen, and communicated to Pittheus the voice of the god, which was in this manner,—

> "Loose not the wine-skin foot, thou chief of men,
> Until to Athens thou art come again."

Pittheus, therefore, taking advantage from the obscurity of the oracle, prevailed upon him, it is uncertain whether by persuasion or deceit, to lie with his daughter Aethra. Aegeus afterwards, knowing her whom he had lain with to be Pittheus's daughter, and suspecting her to be with child by him, left a sword and a pair of shoes, hiding them under a great stone that had a hollow in it exactly fitting them; and went away making her only privy to it, and commanding her, if she brought forth a son who, when he came to man's estate, should be able to lift up the stone and take away what he had left there, she should send him to him with those things with all secrecy, and with injunctions to him as much as possible to conceal his journey from everyone; for he greatly feared the Pallantidae, who were continually mutinying against him, and despised him for his want of children, they themselves being fifty brothers, all sons of Pallas.

When Aethra was delivered of a son, some say that he was immediately named Theseus, from the tokens which his father had *put* under the stone; others that he had received his name afterwards at Athens, when Aegeus *acknowledged* him for his son. He was brought up under his grandfather Pittheus.

. . . .

Aethra for some time concealed the true parentage of Theseus, and a report was given out by Pittheus that he was begotten by Neptune; for the Troezenians pay Neptune the highest veneration. He is their tutelar god; to him they offer all their first fruits, and in his honor stamp their money with a trident.

Theseus displaying not only great strength of body, but equal bravery, and a quickness alike and force of understanding, his mother Aethra, conducting him to the stone, and informing him who was his true father, commanded him to take from thence the tokens that Aegeus had left, and sail to Athens. He without any difficulty set himself to the stone and lifted it up; but refused to take his journey by sea, though it was much the safer way, and though his mother and grandfather begged him to do so. For it was at that time very dangerous to go by land on the road to Athens, no part of it being free from robbers and murderers.

. . . .

It was therefore a very hazardous journey to travel by land from Athens to Peloponnesus; and Pittheus, giving him an exact account of each of the robbers and villains, their strength, and the cruelty they used to all strangers, tried to persuade Theseus to go by sea. But he, it seems, had long since been secretly fired by the glory of Hercules, held him in the highest estimation, and was never more satisfied than in listening to any that gave an account of him; especially those that had seen him, or had been present at any action or saying of his. . . . Besides, they were related, being born of cousins-german. For Aethra was daughter of Pittheus, and Alcmena of Lysidice; and Lysidice and Pittheus were brother and sister, children of Hippodamia and Pelops. He thought it therefore a dishonorable thing, and not to be endured, that Hercules should go out everywhere, and purge both land and sea from wicked men, and he himself should fly from the like adventures that actually came in his way; disgracing his reputed father by a mean flight by sea, and not showing his true one as good evidence of the greatness of his birth by noble and worthy actions, as by the token that he brought with him the shoes and the sword.

With this mind and these thoughts, he set forward with a design to do injury to nobody, but to repel and revenge himself of all those that should offer any. And first of all, in a set combat, he slew Periphetes, in the neighborhood of Epidaurus, who used a club for his arms and thence had the name of Corynetes, or the club-bearer; who seized upon him, and forbade him to go forward in his journey. Being pleased with the club, he took it, and made it his weapon, continuing to use it as Hercules did the lion's skin, on whose shoulders that served to prove how huge a beast he had killed; and to the same end Theseus carried about him this club; overcome indeed by him, but now in his hands, invincible.

Passing on further towards the Isthmus of Peloponnesus, he slew Sinnis, often surnamed the Bender of Pines, after the same manner in which he himself had destroyed many others before. And this he did without having either practiced or ever learned the art of bending these trees, to show that natural strength is above all art. This Sinnis had a daughter of remarkable beauty and stature, called Perigune, who, when her father was killed, fled, and was sought after everywhere by Theseus; and coming into a place overgrown with brushwood, shrubs, and asparagus-thorn, there, in a childlike innocent manner, prayed and begged them, as if they understood her, to give her shelter, with vows that if she escaped she would never cut them down nor burn them. But Theseus calling upon her, and giving her his promise that he would use her with respect, and offer her no injury, she came forth, and in due time bore him a son, named Melanippus.

. . . . .

The Crommyonian sow, which they called Phaea, was a savage and formidable wild beast, by no means an enemy to be despised. Theseus killed her, going out of his way on purpose to meet and engage her, so that he might not seem to perform all his great exploits out of mere necessity; being also of opinion that it was the part of a brave man to chastise villainous and wicked men when attacked by them, but to seek out and overcome the more noble wild beasts. Others relate that Phaea was a woman, a robber full of cruelty and lust, that lived in Crommyon, and had the name of Sow given her from the foulness of her life and manners, and afterwards was killed by Theseus. He slew also Sciron, upon the borders of Megara, casting him down from the rocks, being, as most report, a notorious robber of all passengers, and, as others add, accustomed, out of insolence and wantonness, to stretch forth his feet to strangers, commanding them to wash them, and then while they did it, with a kick to send them down the rock into the sea.

. . . .

In Eleusis he killed Cercyon, the Arcadian, in a wrestling match. And going on a little farther, in Erineus, he slew Damastes, otherwise called Procrustes, forcing his body to the size of his own bed, as he himself was used to do with all strangers; this he did in imitation of Hercules, who always returned upon his assailants the same sort of violence that they offered to him; sacrificed Busiris, killed Antaeus in wrestling, and Cycnus in single combat, and Termerus by breaking his skull in pieces (whence, they say, comes the proverb of "a Termerian mischief"), for it seems Termerus killed passengers that he met by running with his head against them. And so also Theseus proceeded in the punishment of evil men, who underwent the same violence from him which they had inflicted upon others, justly suffering after the manner of their own injustice.

As he went forward on his journey, and was come as far as the river Cephisus, some of the race of the Phytalidae met him and saluted him, and upon his desire to use the purifications, then in custom, they performed them with all the usual ceremonies, and, having offered propitiatory sacrifices to the gods, invited him and entertained him at their house, a kindness which, in all his journey hitherto, he had not met.

On the eighth day of Cronius, now called Hecatombaeon, he arrived at Athens, where he found the public affairs full of all confusion, and divided into parties and factions, Aegeus also, and his whole private family, laboring under the same distemper; for Medea, having fled from Corinth, and promised Aegeus to make him, by her art, capable of having children, was living with him. She first was aware of Theseus, whom as yet Aegeus did not know, and he being in years, full of jealousies and suspicions, and fearing everything by reason of the faction that was then in the city, she easily persuaded him to kill him by poison at a banquet, to which he was to be invited as a stranger. He, coming to the entertainment, thought it not fit to discover himself at once, but willing to give his father the occasion of first finding him out, the

meat being on the table, he drew his sword as if he designed to
cut with it; Aegeus, at once recognizing the token, threw down
the cup of poison, and, questioning his son, embraced him, and
having gathered together all his citizens, owned him publicly before them, who, on their part, received him gladly for the fame of
his greatness and bravery; and it is said, that when the cup fell,
the poison was spilt there where now is the enclosed space in the
Delphinium; for in that place stood Aegeus's house, and the figure of Mercury on the east side of the temple is called the Mercury of Aegeus's gate.

The sons of Pallas, who before were quiet upon expectation
of recovering the kingdom after Aegeus's death, who was without
issue, as soon as Theseus appeared and was acknowledged the successor, highly resenting that Aegeus first, an adopted son only of
Pandion, and not at all related to the family of Erechtheus,
should be holding the kingdom, and that after him, Theseus, a
visitor and stranger, should be destined to succeed to it, broke
out into open war. And dividing themselves into two companies,
one part of them marched openly from Sphettus, with their father,
against the city, the other, hiding themselves in the village of
Gargettus, lay in ambush, with a design to set upon the enemy on
both sides. They had with them a crier of the township of Agnus,
named Leos, who discovered to Theseus all the designs of the Pallantidae. He immediately fell upon those that lay in ambuscade,
and cut them all off; upon tidings of which Pallas and his company fled and were dispersed.

. . . .

Theseus, longing to be in action, and desirous also to make
himself popular, left Athens to fight with the bull of Marathon,
which did no small mischief to the inhabitants of Tetrapolis. And
having overcome it, he brought it alive in triumph through the
city, and afterwards sacrificed it to the Delphinian Apollo. The
story of Hecale, also, of her receiving and entertaining Theseus in
this expedition, seems to be not altogether void of truth; for the
townships round about, meeting upon a certain day, used to offer
a sacrifice which they called Hecalesia, to Jupiter Hecaleius, and
to pay honor to Hecale, whom, by a diminutive name, they called
Hecalene, because she, while entertaining Theseus, who was quite
a youth, addressed him, as old people do, with similar endearing
diminutives; and having made a vow to Jupiter for him as he was
going to the fight, that, if he returned in safety, she would offer
sacrifices in thanks of it, and dying before he came back, she had

these honors given her by way of return for her hospitality, by the command of Theseus.

Not long after arrived the third time from Crete the collectors of the tribute which the Athenians paid them upon the following occasion. Androgeus having been treacherously murdered in the confines of Attica, not only Minos, his father, put the Athenians to extreme distress by a perpetual war, but the gods also laid waste their country; both famine and pestilence lay heavy upon them, and even their rivers were dried up. Being told by the oracle that, if they appeased and reconciled Minos, the anger of the gods would cease and they should enjoy rest from the miseries they labored under, they sent heralds, and with much supplication were at last reconciled, entering into an agreement to send to Crete every nine years a tribute of seven young men and as many virgins; and the most poetical story adds, that the Minotaur destroyed them, or that, wandering in the labyrinth, and finding no possible means of getting out, they miserably ended their lives there; and that this Minotaur was (as Euripides hath it)—

"A mingled form where two strange shapes combined,
    And different nature, bull and man, were joined."

. . . .

Now, when the time of the third tribute was come, and the fathers who had any young men for their sons were to proceed by lot to the choice of those that were to be sent, there arose fresh discontents and accusations against Aegeus among the people, who were full of grief and indignation that he who was the cause of all their miseries was the only person exempt from the punishment; adopting and settling his kingdom upon a bastard and foreign son, he took no thought, they said, of their destitution and loss, not of bastards, but lawful children. These things sensibly affected Theseus, who, thinking it but just not to disregard, but rather partake of, the sufferings of his fellow-citizens, offered himself for one without any lot. All else were struck with admiration for the nobleness and with love for the goodness of the act; and Aegeus, after prayers and entreaties, finding him inflexible and not to be persuaded, proceeded to the choosing of the rest by lot. Hellanicus, however, tells us that the Athenians did not send the young men and virgins by lot, but that Minos himself used to come and make his own choice, and pitched upon Theseus before all others; according to the conditions agreed upon between them, namely, that the Athenians should furnish them with a ship and that the young men that were to sail with him should carry no weapons of war; but that if the Minotaur was destroyed, the tribute should cease.

On the two former occasions of the payment of the tribute, entertaining no hopes of safety or return, they sent out the ship with a black sail, as to unavoidable destruction; but now, Theseus encouraging his father, and speaking greatly of himself, as confident that he should kill the Minotaur, he gave the pilot another sail, which was white, commanding him, as he returned, if Theseus were safe, to make use of that; but if not, to sail with the black one, and to hang out that sign of his misfortune.

. . . .

When he arrived at Crete, having a clue of thread given him by Ariadne, who had fallen in love with him, and being instructed by her how to use it so as to conduct him through the windings of the labyrinth, he escaped out of it and slew the Minotaur, and sailed back, taking along with him Ariadne and the young Athenian captives.

. . . .

There are yet many other traditions concerning Ariadne, all inconsistent with each other. Some relate that she hung herself, being deserted by Theseus. Others that she was carried away by his sailors to the isle of Naxos, and married to Oenarus, priest of Bacchus; and that Theseus left her because he fell in love with another.

. . . .

But the more famous of the legendary stories everybody (as I may say) has in his mouth. In Paeon, however, the Amathusian, there is a story given, differing from the rest. For he writes that Theseus, being driven by a storm upon the isle of Cyprus, and having aboard with him Ariadne, big with child, and extremely discomposed with the rolling of the sea, set her on shore, and left her there alone, to return himself and help the ship, when, on a sudden, a violent wind carried him again out to sea. That the women of the island received Ariadne very kindly, and did all they could to console and alleviate her distress at being left behind. That they counterfeited kind letters, and delivered them to her, as sent from Theseus, and, when she fell in labor, were diligent in performing to her every needful service; but that she died before she could be delivered, and was honorably interred. That soon after Theseus returned, and was greatly afflicted for her loss, and at his departure left a sum of money among the people of the island, ordering them to do sacrifice to Ariadne; and caused two little images to be made and dedicated to her, one of silver and the other of brass. Moreover, that on the second day of Gorpiaeus, which is sacred to Ariadne, they have this ceremony among their sacrifices, to have a youth lie down and with his voice and gesture represent the pains of a woman in travail; and that the Amathusians call the grove in which they show her tomb, the grove of Venus Ariadne.

Differing yet from this account, some of the Naxians write that there were two Minoses and two Ariadnes, one of whom, they say, was married to Bacchus, in the isle of Naxos, and bore the children Staphylus and his brother; but that the other, of a later age, was carried off by Theseus, and, being afterwards deserted by him, retired to Naxos, with her nurse Corcyna, whose grave they yet show. That this Ariadne also died there, and was worshipped by the island, but in a different manner from the former; for her day is celebrated with general joy and revelling, but all the sacrifices performed to the latter are attended with mourning and gloom.

Now Theseus, in his return from Crete, put in at Delos, and having sacrificed to the god of the island, dedicated to the temple the image of Venus which Ariadne had given him, and danced with the young Athenians a dance that, in memory of him, they say is still preserved among the inhabitants of Delos, consisting in certain measured turnings and returnings, imitative of the windings and twistings of the labyrinth. And this dance, as Dicaearchus writes, is called among the Delians the Crane. This he danced around the Ceratonian Altar, so called from its consisting of horns taken from the left side of the head. They say also that he instituted games in Delos, where he was the first that began the custom of giving a palm to the victors.

When they were come near the coast of Attica, so great was the joy for the happy success of their voyage, that neither Theseus himself nor the pilot remembered to hang out the sail which should have been the token of their safety to Aegeus, who, in despair at the sight, threw himself headlong from a rock, and perished in the sea.

. . . . .

Now, after the death of his father Aegeus, forming in his mind a great and wonderful design, he gathered together all the inhabitants of Attica into one town, and made them one people of one city, whereas before they lived dispersed, and were not easy to assemble upon any affair for the common interest. Nay, differences and even wars often occurred between them, which he by his persuasions appeased, going from township to township, and from tribe to tribe. And those of a more private and mean condition readily embracing such good advice, to those of greater power he promised a commonwealth without monarchy, a democracy, or people's government, in which he should only be continued as their commander in war and the protector of their laws, all things else being equally distributed among them;—and by this means brought a part of them over to his proposal. The rest, fearing his power, which was already grown very formidable, and knowing his courage and resolution, chose rather to be persuaded than forced into a compliance.

. . . .

It is true, indeed, that Theseus married Phaedra, but that was after the death of Antiope, by whom he had a son called Hippolytus, or, as Pindar writes, Demophon. The calamities which befell Phaedra and this son, since none of the historians have contradicted the tragic poets that have written of them, we must suppose happened as represented uniformly by them.

. . . .

The celebrated friendship between Theseus and Pirithous is said to have been thus begun; the fame of the strength and valor of Theseus being spread through Greece, Pirithous was desirous to make a trial and proof of it himself, and to this end seized a herd of oxen which belonged to Theseus, and was driving them away from Marathon, and, when the news was brought that Theseus pursued him in arms, he did not fly, but turned back and went to meet him. But as soon as they had viewed one another, each so admired the gracefulness and beauty, and was seized with such respect for the courage of the other, that they forgot all thoughts of fighting; and Pirithous, first stretching out his hand to Theseus, bade him be judge in this case himself, and promised to submit willingly to any penalty he should impose. But Theseus not only forgave him all, but entreated him to be his friend and brother in arms; and they ratified their friendship by oaths. After this Pirithous married Deidamia, and invited Theseus to the wedding, entreating him to come and see his country, and make acquaintance with the Lapithae; he had at the same time invited the Centaurs to the feast, who growing hot with wine and beginning to be insolent and wild, and offering violence to the women, the Lapithae took immediate revenge upon them, slaying many of them upon the place, and afterwards, having overcome them in battle, drove the whole race of them out of their country, Theseus all along taking their part and fighting on their side.

. . . .

About this time, Menestheus, the son of Peteus, grandson of Orneus, and great-grandson of Erechtheus, the first man that is recorded to have affected popularity and ingratiated himself with the multitude, stirred up and exasperated the most eminent men of the city, who had long borne a secret grudge to Theseus, conceiving that he had robbed them of their several little kingdoms and lordships, and having pent them all up in one city, was using them as his subjects and slaves.

. . . .

And at last, despairing of any good success of his affairs in Athens, Theseus sent away his children privately to Euboea, commending them to the care of Elephenor, the son of Chalcodon; and he himself having solemnly cursed the people of Athens in the village of Gargettus, in which there yet remains the place called Araterion, or the place of cursing, sailed to Scyros, where he had lands left him by his father, and friendship, as he thought, with those of the island. Lycomedes was then king of Scyros. Theseus, therefore, addressed himself to him and desired to have his lands put into his possession, as designing to settle and to dwell there, though others say that he came to beg his assistance against the Athenians. But Lycomedes, either jealous of the glory of so great a man, or to gratify Menestheus, having led him up to the highest cliff of the island, on pretence of showing him from thence the lands that he desired, threw him headlong down from the rock, and killed him. At that time there was no notice taken, nor were any concerned for his death, but Menestheus quietly possessed the kingdom of Athens. His sons were brought up in a private condition, and accompanied Elephenor to the Trojan war, but, after the decease of Menestheus in that expedition, returned to Athens, and recovered the government. But in succeeding ages, besides several other circumstances that moved the Athenians to honor Theseus as a demigod, in the battle which was fought at Marathon against the Medes, many of the soldiers believed they saw an apparition of Theseus in arms, rushing on at the head of them against the barbarians. And after the Median war, Phaedo being archon of Athens, the Athenians, consulting the oracle at Delphi, were commanded to gather together the bones of Theseus, and, laying them in some honorable place, keep them as sacred in the city. But it was very difficult to recover those relics, or so much as to find out the place where they lay, on account of the inhospitable and savage temper of the barbarous people that inhabited the island. Nevertheless, afterwards, when Cimon took the island and had a great ambition to find out the place where Theseus was buried, he, by chance, spied an eagle upon a rising ground pecking with her beak and tearing up the earth with her talons, when on the sudden it came into his mind, as it were by some divine inspiration, to dig there, and search for the bones of Theseus. There were found in that place a coffin of a man of more than ordinary size, and a brazen spear-head, and a sword lying by it, all which he took aboard his galley and brought with him to Athens. Upon which the Athenians, greatly delighted, went out to meet and receive the relics with splendid processions and sacrifices, as if it were Theseus himself returning alive to the city. He lies interred in the middle of the city, near the present gymnasium. His tomb is a sanctuary and refuge for slaves, and all those of mean condition that fly from the persecution of men in power, in memory that Theseus while he lived was an assister and protector of the distressed, and never refused the petitions of the afflicted that fled to him.

THESEUS, ARIADNE, AND DIONYSUS

CATULLUS, 64. 246-264 (Martin)

Through the device of an embroidered coverlet, Catullus tells the story of Theseus' desertion of Ariadne and of Dionysus' rescue of her.

When proud Theseus with exulting tread
The threshold crossed, where lay his father dead,
A sorrow smote him, kin to that his scorn
Had wrought to Minos' daughter, left forlorn,
Who, torn with passions manifold and dark,
Still gazed and gazed on his receding bark.

Elsewhere upon that coverlet of sheen,
Bounding along was blooming Bacchus seen,

With all his heart aflame with love for thee,
Fair Ariadne! And behind him, see,
Where Satyrs and Sileni whirl along,
With frenzy fired, a fierce tumultuous throng!
Evöe! they yell, Evöe! that jocund rout,
And clap their hands, and toss their heads about.
There some wave thyrsi wreathed with ivy, here
Some toss the limbs of a dismembered steer;
Around their waists some coiling serpents twine,
While others work the mysteries divine
With arks of osiers, mysteries of fear,
Which the profane desire in vain to hear.
Others with open palms the timbrel smite,
Or with thin brazen rods wake tinklings light;
And many a hoarse resounding horn is blown,
And fifes barbarian shriek with hideous drone.

MELEAGER

HOMER, *Iliad*, Book 9. 529-599, with omissions (Derby)

*Homer's account of Meleager is suggestive of the early heroic
saga. The story may have existed long before additional details were invented or borrowed from the realm of folk tale
to reshape it in Ovid's version.*

Time was, that with Aetolia's warlike bands
Round Calydon the Acarnanians fought
With mutual slaughter: these to save the town,
The Acarnanians burning to destroy.
This curse of war the golden-throned Queen
Diana sent, in anger that from her
Oeneus the first-fruits of his field withheld.
The other Gods their hecatombs receiv'd;
Diana's shrine alone no off'rings deck'd,
Neglected, or o'erlook'd; the sin was great;
And in her wrath the arrow-darting Queen
A savage wild-boar sent, with gleaming tusks,
Which, Oeneus' vineyard haunting, wrought him harm.

There laid he prostrate many a stately tree,
With root and branch, with blossom and with fruit.
Him Meleager, son of Oeneus, slew,
With youths and dogs from all the neighboring towns
Collected; smaller force had not avail'd,
So huge he was, so fierce; and many a youth
Had by his tusks been laid upon the bier.
A fierce contention then the Goddess rais'd,
For the boar's head and bristly hide, between
The Acarnanian and th' Aetolian bands.
While warlike Meleager kept the field,
So long the Acarnanians far'd but ill;
Nor dar'd, despite the numbers of their host,
Maintain their ground before the city walls.
When he to anger yielded, which sometimes
Swells in the bosom ev'n of wisest men,
Incens'd against his mother, he withdrew
To Cleopatra fair, his wedded wife.

         . . . .

With her, retiring from the field, he nurs'd
His wrath; resenting thus his mother's curse,
Althaea; she her brother's death bore hard,
And pray'd to Heav'n above, and with her hands
Beating the solid earth, the nether pow'rs,
Pluto and awful Proserpine, implor'd,
Down on her knees, her bosom wet with tears,
Death on her son invoking; from the depths
Of Erebus Erinnys heard her pray'r,
Gloom-haunting Goddess, dark and stern of heart.
Soon round the gates the din of battle rose,
The tow'rs by storm assaulted; then his aid
Th' Aetolian Elders and the sacred priests
With promises of great reward implor'd.
A fruitful plot they bade him set apart,
The richest land in lovely Calydon,
Of fifty acres: half for vineyard meet,
And half of fertile plain, for tillage clear'd.
Upon the threshold of his lofty rooms
Old Oeneus stood, and at the portals clos'd
He knock'd in vain, a suppliant to his son.
His sisters and his brother join'd their pray'rs,
But sterner his rejection of their suit;

The friends he valued most, and lov'd the best,
Yet they too fail'd his fix'd resolve to shake;
Till to his very doors the war had reach'd,
The foe upon the tow'rs, the town in flames:
Then Meleager's beauteous wife, at length,
In tears, beseeching him, the thousand ills
Recall'd, which on a captur'd town attend;
The slaughter'd men, the city burnt with fire,
The helpless children and deep-bosom'd dames
A prey to strangers. List'ning to the tale,
His spirit was rous'd within him; and again
He took the field, and donn'd his glitt'ring arms.
Thus did his act from doom th' Aetolians save
Spontaneous; yet he gain'd not, though he sav'd,
The rich reward they once were pledg'd to give.

~~~~~

MELEAGER

OVID, *Metamorphoses*, Book 8. 273-532, with omissions (More)

The nation had a fruitful year,
For which the good king Oeneus had decreed
That all should offer the first fruits of corn
To Ceres—and to Bacchus wine of grapes—
And oil of olives to the golden haired
Minerva. Thus, the Gods were all adored,
Beginning with the lowest to the highest,
Except alone Diana, and of all the Gods
Her altars only were neglected. No
Frankincense unto her was given! Neglect
Enrages even Deities.
        "Am I
To suffer this indignity?" she cried,
"Though I am thus dishonored, I will not
Be unrevenged!" And so the boar was sent
To ravage the fair land of Calydon.
    And this avenging boar was quite as large
As bulls now feeding on the green Epirus,
And larger than the bulls of Sicily.
A dreadful boar.—His burning, bloodshot eyes

Seemed coals of living fire, and his rough neck
Was knotted with stiff muscles, and thick-set
With bristles like sharp spikes. A seething froth
Dripped on his shoulders, and his tusks
Were like the spoils of Ind. Discordant roars
Reverberated from his hideous jaws;
And lightning—belched forth from his horrid throat—
Scorched the green fields. He trampled the green corn
And doomed the farmer to lament his crops,
In vain the threshing-floor has been prepared,
In vain the barns await the promised yield.
Long branches of the vine and heavy grapes
Are scattered in confusion, and the fruits
And branches of the olive tree, whose leaves
Should never wither, are cast on the ground.

His spleen was vented on the simple flocks,
Which neither dogs nor shepherd could protect;
And the brave bulls could not defend their herds.
The people fled in all directions from the fields,
For safety to the cities. Terror reigned.
There seemed no remedy to save the land,
Till Meleager chose a band of youths,
United for the glory of great deeds.

And Atalanta, virgin of the groves,
Of Mount Lycaeus, glory of her sex;
A polished buckle fastened her attire;
Her lustrous hair was fashioned in a knot;
Her weapons rattled in an ivory case,
Swung from her white left shoulder, and she held
A bow in her left hand. Her face appeared
As maidenly for boy, or boyish for girl.

When Meleager saw her, he at once
Longed for her beauty, though some God forbade.
The fires of love flamed in him; and he said,
"Happy the husband who shall win this girl!"
Neither the time nor his own modesty
Permitted him to say another word.
But now the dreadful contest with the boar
Engaged this hero's energy and thought.

A wood, umbrageous, not impaired with age,
Slopes from a plain and shadows the wide fields,
And there this band of valiant heroes went—

Eager to slay the dreaded enemy,
Some spread the nets and some let loose the dogs,
Some traced the wide spoor of the monster's hoofs.
    There is a deep gorge where the rivulets
That gather from the rain, discharge themselves;
And there the bending willow, the smooth sedge,
The marsh-rush, ozier and tall tangled reed
In wild profusion cover up the marsh.
Aroused from this retreat the startled boar,
As quick as lightning from the clashing clouds
Crashed all the trees that cumbered his mad way.—
    The young men raised a shout, leveled their spears,
And brandished their keen weapons; but the boar
Rushed onward through the yelping dogs,
And scattered them with deadly sidelong stroke.
    Echion was the first to hurl his spear,
But slanting in its course it only glanced
A nearby maple tree, and next the spear
Of long-remembered Jason cut the air;
So swiftly hurled it seemed it might transfix
The boar's back, but with over-force it sped
Beyond the monster. Poising first his dart,
The son of Ampyx, as he cast it, he
Implored Apollo, "Grant my prayer if I
Have truly worshiped you, harken to me
As always I adore you! Let my spear
Unerring strike its aim." Apollo heard,
And guided the swift spear, but as it sped
Diana struck the iron head from the shaft,
And the blunt wood fell harmless from his hide.
    Then was the monster's savage anger roused;
As the bright lightning's flash his red eyes flamed;
His breath was hot as fire. As when a stone
Is aimed at walls or strong towers, which protect
Encompassed armies,—launched by the taut rope
It strikes with dreaded impact; so the boar
With fatal onset rushed among this band
Of noble lads, and stretched upon the ground
Eupalamon and Pelagon whose guard
Was on the right; and their companions bore
Their bodies from the field.
                    Another youth,

The brave son of Hippocoon received
A deadly wound—while turning to escape,
The sinew of his thigh was cut and failed
To bear his tottering steps.—And Nestor might
Have perished then, so long before he fought
The heroes of old Troy, but ever wise,
He vaulted on his long lance from the ground
Into the branches of a sheltering tree;
Where in a safe position, he could look
Down on his baffled foe. The raging boar
Whetted his gleaming tushes on an oak.

      Then with his sharpened tusks he gored the thigh
Of mighty Hippasus. Observed of all,
And mounted on their horses—whiter than
The northern snow—the twins (long afterward
Transformed to constellations) sallied forth,
And brandishing their lances, poised in air,
Determined to destroy the bristling boar.
It thwarted their design by hiding in
A thicket intricate; where neither steed
Nor lance could penetrate. But Telamon
Pursued undaunted, and in haste tripped up
By tangled roots, fell headlong.—Peleus stooped
To rescue him.

             While he regained his feet,
The virgin, Atalanta, took her bow
And fitting a sharp arrow to the notch,
Twanged the tight cord. The feathered shaft
Quivered beneath the monster's ear, the red blood
Stained his hard bristles.

             Flushed with her success
Rejoiced the maid, but not more gladly than
The hero Meleager. He it was
Who first observed the blood, and pointed out
The stain to his companions as he cried,
"Give honor to the courage of a maid!"
Unwilling to be worsted by a maid,
The rushing heroes raised a mighty cry
And as they shouted in excitement, hurled
Their weapons in confusion; and so great
The multitude their actions interfered.

      Behold! Ancaeus wielding his war-axe,

And rushing madly to his fate, exclaimed,
"Witness it! See the weapons of a man
Excel a woman's! Ho, make way for my
Achievement! Let Diana shield the brute!
Despite her utmost effort my right hand
Shall slaughter him!" So mighty in his boast
He puffed himself; and, lifting with both hands
His double-edged axe, he stood erect,
On tiptoe fiercely bold. The savage boar
Caught him, and ripped his tushes through his groin,
A spot where death is sure.—Ancaeus fell;
And his torn entrails and his crimson blood
Stained the fair verdure of the spot with death.

    Ixion's doughty son was running straight
Against the monster, shaking his long lance
With nervous vigor in his strong right hand;
But Theseus, standing at a distance called:
"Beware! beware, O, dearest of my friends;
Be valiant at a distance, or the fate
Of rashly-bold Ancaeus may be yours!"

    Even as he spoke he balanced in his hand
His brazen-pointed lance of cornel wood;
With aim so true it seemed the great boar's death
Was certain, but an evergreen oak branch
Shielded the beast.—Then Jason hurled his dart,
Which turned by chance, transfixed a luckless dog
And pinned him yelping, to the sanguine earth.—

    So fared those heroes. Better fortune gave
Success to Meleager; first he threw
A spear that missed and quivered in the ground;
But next he hurled a spear with certain aim.
It pierced the middle of the monster's back;
And rushing in upon the dreaded beast,
While raging it was whirling round and round,
The fearless prince provoked to greater rage
The wounded adversary. Bloody froth
Dripped down his champing jaws—his purple blood
Poured from a rankling wound. Without delay
The mighty Meleager plunged a spear
Deep in the monster's shoulder. All his friends
Raised a glad shout, and gathering round him, tried
To grasp his hand.—With wonder they beheld

The monster's bulk stretched out upon the plain;
And fearful still to touch him, they began
To stain their weapons in his spouting blood.
        At length the hero Meleager pressed
His conquering foot upon the monster's head
And said, "O Atalanta, glorious maid,
Of Nonacris, to you is yielded spoil,
My lawful right, and I rejoice to share
The merit of this glorious victory."
        And while he spoke, he gave to her the pelt,
Covered with horrid bristles, and the head
Frightful with gory tusks: and she rejoiced
In Meleager and his royal gift.
        But all the others, envious, began
To murmur; and the sons of Thestius
Levelled their pointed spears, and shouted out;
"Give up the prize! Let not the confidence
Of your great beauty be a snare to you!
A woman should not interfering filch
The manly honors of a mighty hunt!
Aside! and let your witless lover yield!"
So threatened they and took from her the prize;
And forcibly despoiled him of his rights.
        The warlike prince, indignant and enraged,—
Roused with resentment, shouted out. "What! Ho!
You spoilers of this honor that is ours,
Brave deeds are different far from craven threats!"
And with his cruel sword he pierced the breast
Of rash Plexippus, taken unawares,
And while his brother, Toxeus, struck with fear,
Stood hesitating whether to avenge
Or run to safety, Meleager plunged
The hot sword, smoking with a brother's blood,
In his breast also. And so perished they.

        Ere this, Althaea, mother of the prince,
And sister of the slaughtered twain,—because
Her son had killed the boar, made haste to bear
Rich offerings to the temples of the Gods;
But when she saw her slaughtered brothers borne
In sad procession, she began to shriek,

And filled the city with her wild lament.
Unwilling to abide her festal robes
She dressed in sable.—When she was informed
Her own son Meleager was the cause,
She banished grief and lamentations,—
Thirsting for vengeance.
                  She remembered well,
How, when she lay in childbirth round her stood
The three attendant sisters of his fate.
There was a billet in the room, and this
They took and cast upon the wasting flames,
And as they spun and drew the fatal threads
They softly chanted, "Unto you we give,
O child new-born! only the life of this;
The period of this billet is your life."
And having spoken so, they vanished in the smoke.
    Althaea snatched the billet from the fire,
And having quenched it with drawn water, hid
It long and secretly in her own room,
Where, thus preserved, it acted as a charm
To save the life of Meleager. This
The mother now brought forth, and fetched a pile
Of seasoned tinder ready for the torch.
She lit the torches and the ready pile,
And as the flames leaped up, four times prepared
To cast the fatal billet in the midst;
And four times hesitated to commit
The dreadful deed,—so long the contest veered
Between the feelings of a mother's breast
And the fierce vengeance of a sister's rage.
    Now is the mother's visage pale with fear,
And now the sister's sanguinary rage
Glows in her eyes. Her countenance contorts
With cruel threats and in bewildered ways
Dissolves compassionate: And even when
The heat of anger had dried up her eyes
The conflict of her passion brought new tears.
    As when the wind has seized upon a ship
And blows against a tide of equal force,
The vexed vessel feels repellent powers,
And with unsteady motion sways to both;
So did Althaea hesitate between

The conflict of her passions: when her rage
Had cooled, her fury was as fast renewed:
But always the unsatisfied desire
Of blood, to ease the disembodied shades
Of her slain brothers, seemed to overcome
The mother-instinct; and intensity
Of conduct proved the utmost test of love.

    She took the billet in her arms and stood
Before the leaping flames, and said, "Alas,
Be this the funeral pyre of my own flesh!"
And as she held in her relentless hand
The destiny of him she loved, and stood
Before the flames, in all her wretchedness
She moaned, "You sad Eumenides attend!
Relentless Gods of punishment,—turn, turn
Your dreadful vision on these baneful rites!
I am avenging and committing crime!
With death must death be justified and crime
Be added unto crime! Let funerals
Upon succeeding funerals attend!

    "Let these accumulating woes destroy
A wicked race. Shall happy Oeneus bask
In the great fame of his victorious son,
And Thestius mourn without slaughtered ones?
'Tis better they should both lament the deed!
Witness the act of my affection, shades
Of my departed brothers! and accept
My funeral offering, given at a cost
Beyond my strength to bear. Ah wretched me!
Distracted is my reason! Pity me,
The yearnings of a stricken mother's heart
Withholding me from duty! Aye, although
His punishment be just, my hands refuse
The office of such vengeance. What, shall he
Alive, victorious, flushed with his success,
Inherit the broad realms of Calydon,
And you, my slaughtered brothers, unavenged,
Dissolved in ashes, float upon the air,
Unpalpitating phantoms? How can I
Endure the thought of it? Oh let the wretch
Forever perish, and with him be lost
The hopes of his sad father, in the wreck

Of his distracted kingdom. Where are now
The love and feelings of a mother; how
Can I forget the bitter pangs endured
While twice times five the slow moon waxed and waned?
      "O had you perished in your infancy
By those first fires, and I had suffered it!
Your life was in my power! and now your death
Is the result of wrongs which you have done—
Take now a just reward for what you did:
Return to me the life I gave and saved.
When from the flames I snatched the fatal brand.
Return that gift or take my wretched life,
That I may hasten to my brothers' tomb.
      "What dreadful deed can satisfy the law,
When I for love against my love am forced?
For even as my brothers' wounds appear
In visions dreadful to denounce my son,
The love so nurtured in a mother's breast
Breaks down the resolution! Wretched me!
Such vengeance for my brothers overcomes
First at your birth I gave it, and again
The yearning of a mother for her son!
Let not my love denounce my vengeance!
My soul may follow with its love the shade
Of him I sacrifice, and following him
My shade and his and yours unite below."
      She spoke and as she turned her face away,
She threw the fatal billet on the fire,
And as the flames devoured it, a strange groan
Was heard to issue from the burning wood.
      But Meleager at a distance knows
Of naught to wreck his hour of victory,
Until he feels the flame of burning wood
Scorching with secret fire his forfeit life.
Yet with a mighty will, disdaining pain
He grieves his bloodless and ignoble death.
He calls Ancaeus happy for the wounds
That caused his death. With sighs and groans he called
His aged father's name, and then the names
Of brothers, sisters, and his wife—and last,
They say he called upon his mother's name.
      His torment always with the fire increased,

Until, as little of the wood remained,—
His pain diminished with the heat's decrease;
And as the flames extinguished, so his life
Slowly ascended in the rising air.

    And all the mighty realm of Calydon
Was filled with lamentations—young and old,
The common people and the nobles mourned;
And all the wailing women tore their hair.
His father threw his body on the ground,
And as he covered his white hair and face
With ashy dust, bewailed his aged days.

    Althaea, maddened in her mother's grief,
Has punished herself with a ruthless hand;
She pierced her heart with iron.

PERSEUS

OVID, *Metamorphoses*, Book 4. 610-803 (More)

    Acrisius,
The son of Abas, of the Cadmean race,
Remained to banish Bacchus from the walls
Of Argos, and to lift up hostile arms
Against that deity, who he denied
Was born to Jove. He would not even grant
That Perseus from the loins of Jupiter
Was got of Danaë in the showering gold.

    So mighty is the hidden power of truth
Acrisius soon lamented that affront
To Bacchus, and that ever he refused
To own his grandson; for the one achieved
High heaven, and the other, (as he bore
The viperous monster-head) on sounding wings
Hovered a conqueror in the fluent air,
Over sands, Libyan, where the Gorgon-head
Dropped clots of gore, that, quickening on the ground,
Became unnumbered serpents; fitting cause
To curse with vipers that infested land.

    Thence wafted by the never-constant winds

Through boundless latitudes, now here now there,
As flits a vapor-cloud in dizzy flight,
Down-looking from the lofty skies on earth,
Removed far, so compassed he the world.
    Three times did he behold the frozen Bears,
Times thrice his gaze was on the Crab's bent arms.
Now shifting to the west, now to the east,
How often changed his course? Time came, when day
Declining, he began to fear the night,
By which he stopped his flight far in the west—
The realm of Atlas—where he sought repose
Till Lucifer might call Aurora's fires;
Aurora chariot of the Day.
                 There dwelt
Huge Atlas, vaster than the race of man:
Son of Iapetus, his lordly sway
Extended over those extreme domains,
And over oceans that command their waves
To take the panting coursers of the Sun,
And bathe the wearied Chariot of the Day.
    For him a thousand flocks, a thousand herds
O'erwandered pasture fields; and neighbor tribes
Might none disturb that land. Aglint with gold
Bright leaves adorn the trees,—boughs golden-wrought
Bear apples of pure gold. And Perseus spoke
To Atlas, "O my friend, if thou art moved
To hear the story of a noble race,
The author of my life is Jupiter;
If valiant deeds perhaps are thy delight
Mine may deserve thy praise.—Behold, of thee
Kind treatment I implore—a place of rest."
    But Atlas, mindful of an oracle
Long since by Themis, the Parnassian, told,
Recalled these words, "O Atlas! mark the day
A son of Jupiter shall come to spoil;
For when thy trees are stripped of golden fruit,
The glory shall be his."
                 Fearful of this,
Atlas had builded solid walls around
His orchard, and secured a dragon, huge,
That kept perpetual guard, and thence expelled
All strangers from his land. Wherefore he said,

"Begone! The glory of your deeds is all
Pretense; even Jupiter will fail your need."
    With that he added force and strove to drive
The hesitating alien from his doors;
Who pled reprieve or threatened with bold words.
Although he dared not rival Atlas' might,
Perseus made this reply; "For that my love
You hold in light esteem, let this be yours."
He said no more, but turning his own face,
He showed upon his left Medusa's head,
Abhorrent features.—Atlas, huge and vast,
Becomes a mountain—His great beard and hair
Are forests, and his shoulders and his hands
Mountainous ridges, and his head the top
Of a high peak;—his bones are changed to rocks.
    Augmented on all sides, enormous height
Attains his growth; for so ordained it, ye,
O mighty Gods! who now the heavens' expanse
Unnumbered stars, on him command to rest.

    In their eternal prison, Aeolus,
Grandson of Hippotas, had 'mured the winds;
And Lucifer, reminder of our toil,
In splendor rose upon the lofty sky:
And Perseus bound his wings upon his feet,
On each foot bound he them; his sword he girt
And sped wing-footed through the liquid air.
    Innumerous kingdoms far behind were left,
Till peoples Ethiopic and the lands
Of Cepheus were beneath his lofty view.
    There Ammon, the unjust, had made decree
Andromeda, the innocent, should grieve
Her mother's tongue. They bound her fettered arms
Fast to the rock. When Perseus her beheld
As marble he would deem her, but the breeze
Moved in her hair, and from her streaming eyes
The warm tears fell. Her beauty so amazed
His heart, unconscious captive of her charms,
That almost his swift wings forgot to wave.—
    Alighted on the ground, he thus began;
"O fairest! whom these chains become not so,
But worthy are for links that lovers bind,

Make known to me your country's name and yours
And wherefore bound in chains." A moment then,
As overcome with shame, she made no sound:
Were not she fettered she would surely hide
Her blushing head; but what she could perform
That did she do—she filled her eyes with tears.

    So pleaded he that lest refusal seem
Implied confession of a crime, she told
Her name, her country's name, and how her charms
Had been her mother's pride. But as she spoke
The mighty ocean roared. Over the waves
A monster fast approached, its head held high,
Abreast the wide expanse.—The virgin shrieked;—
No aid her wretched father gave, nor aid
Her still more wretched mother; but they wept
And mingled lamentations with their tears—
Clinging distracted to her fettered form.

    And thus the stranger spoke to them, "Time waits
For tears, but flies the moment of our need:
Were I, who am the son of regal Jove
And her whom he embraced in showers of gold,
Leaving her pregnant in her brazen cell,—
I, Perseus, who destroyed the Gorgon, wreathed
With snake-hair, I, who dared on waving wings
To cleave etherial air—were I to ask
The maid in marriage, I should be preferred
Above all others as your son-in-law.
Not satisfied with deeds achieved, I strive
To add such merit as the Gods permit;
Now, therefore, should my valor save her life,
Be it conditioned that I win her love."

    To this her parents gave a glad assent,
For who could hesitate? And they entreat,
And promise him the kingdom as a dower.

    As a great ship with steady prow speeds on;
Forced forwards by the sweating arms of youth
It plows the deep; so, breasting the great waves,
The monster moved, until to reach the rock
No further space remained than might the whirl
Of Balearic string encompass, through
The middle skies, with plummet-mold of lead.

    That instant, spurning with his feet the ground,

The youth rose upwards to a cloudy height;
And when the shadow of the hero marked
The surface of the sea, the monster sought
Vainly to vent his fury on the shade.
　　　As the swift bird of Jove, when he beholds
A basking serpent in an open field,
Exposing to the sun its mottled back,
And seizes on its tail; lest it shall turn
To strike with venomed fang, he fixes fast
His grasping talons in the scaly neck;
So did the winged youth, in rapid flight
Through yielding elements, press down
On the great monster's back, and thrust his sword,
Sheer to the hilt, in its right shoulder—loud
Its frightful torture sounded o'er the waves.—
So fought the hero-son of Inachus.
　　　Wild with the grievous wound, the monster rears
High in the air, or plunges in the waves;—
Or wheels around as turns the frightened boar,
Shunning the hounds, around him in full cry.
　　　The hero on his active wings avoids
The monster's jaws, and with his crooked sword
Tortures its back wherever he may pierce
Its mail of hollow shell, or strikes betwixt
The ribs each side, or wounds its lashing tail,
Long, tapered as a fish.
　　　　　　　　　　　　The monster spouts
Forth streams—incarnadined with blood—
That spray upon the hero's wings; who drenched,
And heavy with the spume, no longer dares
To trust existence to his dripping wings;
But he discerns a rock, which rises clear
Above the water when the sea is calm,
But now is covered by the lashing waves.
On this he rests; and as his left hand holds
Firm on the upmost ledge, he thrusts his sword,
Times more than three, unswerving in his aim,
Sheer through the monster's entrails.—Shouts of praise
Resound along the shores, and even the Gods
May hear his glory in their high abodes.
　　　Her parents, Cepheus and Cassiope,
Most joyfully salute their son-in-law;

Declaring him the savior of their house.
And now, her chains struck off, the lovely cause
And guerdon of his toil, walks on the shore.
  The hero washes his victorious hands
In water newly taken from the sea:
But lest the sand upon the shore might harm
The viper-covered head, he first prepared
A bed of springy leaves, on which he threw
Weeds of the sea, produced beneath the waves.
On them he laid Medusa's awful face,
Daughter of Phorcys;—and the living weeds,
Fresh taken from the boundless deep, imbibed
The monster's poison in their spongy pith:
They hardened at the touch, and felt in branch
And leaf unwonted stiffness. Sea-Nymphs, too,
Attempted to perform that prodigy
On numerous other weeds, with like result:
So pleased at their success, they raised new seeds,
From plants wide-scattered on the salt expanse.
  Even from that day the coral has retained
Such wondrous nature, that exposed to air
It hardens.—Thus, a plant beneath the waves
Becomes a stone when taken from the sea.
  Three altars to three Gods he made of turf.
To thee, victorious Virgin, did he build
An altar on the right, to Mercury
An altar on the left, and unto Jove
An altar in the midst. He sacrificed
A heifer to Minerva, and a calf
To Mercury, the Wingfoot, and a bull
To thee, O greatest of the Deities.
  Without a dower he takes Andromeda,
The guerdon of his glorious victory,
Nor hesitates.—Now pacing in the van,
Both Love and Hymen wave the flaring torch,
Abundant perfumes lavished in the flames.
  The houses are bedecked with wreathed flowers;
And lyres and flageolets resound, and songs—
Felicit notes that happy hearts declare.
The portals opened, sumptuous halls display
Their golden splendors, and the noble lords
Of Cepheus' court take places at the feast,

Magnificently served.
                    After the feast,
When every heart was warming to the joys
Of genial Bacchus, then, the grandson sprung
Of Abas, told how they had lived and what
Their customs. And, of such things speaking, Perseus,
Lyncides, dwelt upon the manners, laws,
And habits of that land, which quite complete,
Much more than this, the valiant Perseus told,
The story of the deed, that all may know,
And what the arts and power prevailed, when he
Struck off the serpent-covered head.
                            "There is,"
Continued that descendant of Abas,
"There is a spot beneath cold Atlas, where
In bulwarks of enormous strength, to guard
Its rocky entrance, dwelt two sisters, born
Of Phorcys. These were wont to share in turn
A single eye between them: this by craft
I got possession of, when one essayed
To hand it to the other.—I put forth
My hand and took it as it passed between:
Then, far, remote, through rocky pathless crags,
Over wild hills that bristled with great woods,
I thence arrived to where the Gorgon dwelt.

    "Along the way, in fields and by the roads,
I saw on all sides men and animals—
Like statues—turned to flinty stone at sight
Of dread Medusa's visage. Ne'er-the-less
Reflected on the brazen shield, I bore
Upon my left, I saw her horrid face.

    "When she was helpless in the power of sleep,
And even her serpent-hair was slumber-bound,
I struck, and took her head sheer from the neck.—
To winged Pegasus the blood gave birth,
His brother also, twins of rapid wing."
    So did he speak, and truly told besides
The perils of his journey, arduous
And long—He told of seas and lands that far
Beneath him he had seen, and of the stars
That he had touched while on his waving wings.
    And yet, before they were aware, the tale

Was ended; he was silent. Then rejoined
A noble with enquiry why alone
Of those three sisters, snakes were interspersed
In dread Medusa's locks. And he replied:—
    "Because, O Stranger, it is your desire
To learn what worthy is for me to tell,
Hear ye the cause: Beyond all others she
Was famed for beauty, and the envious hope
Of many suitors. Words would fail to tell
The glory of her hair, most wonderful
Of all her charms—A friend declared to me
He saw its lovely splendor. Fame declares
The Sovereign of the Sea attained her love
In chaste Minerva's temple. While enraged
She turned her head away and held her shield
Before her eyes. To punish that great crime
Minerva changed the Gorgon's splendid hair
To serpents horrible. And now to strike
Her foes with fear, she wears upon her breast
Those awful vipers—creatures of her rage."

OEDIPUS

AESCHYLUS, *Seven against Thebes*, 742-791 (Grene)

*The chorus recalls Laius and Oedipus and foresees the fate
of Eteocles and Polyneices.*

Old is the tale of sin I tell
but swift in retribution:
to the third generation it abides.
Thrice in Pythian prophecies
given at Navel-of-Earth
Apollo had directed
King Laius all issueless to die
and save his city so . . .

but he was mastered by loving folly
and begot for himself a doom,

father-murdering Oedipus,
who sowed his mother's sacred womb,
whence he had sprung himself,
with bloody root, to his heartbreak.
Madness was the coupler
of this distracted pair.

Now, as it were, a sea
drives on the wave:
one sinks, another rises,
triple-crested around the prow
of the city, and breaks in foam.
Our defense between is but a little thing
no bigger than a wall in width.
I fear that with our princes
our city be subdued.

For heavy is the settlement
of ancient curses, to fulfilment brought.
That evil when fulfilled
passes not away.
Prosperity grown over fat
of men, gain seeking,
compels jettisoning
of all goods, utterly.

What man has earned such admiration
of Gods and men that shared his city
and of the general throng of mortal men,
as Oedipus—who ever had such honor
as he that from his land had banished
the Sphinx, that ate men up?

But when in misery he knew
the meaning of his dreadful marriage,
in pain distraught, in heart distracted
he brought a double sorrow to fulfilment.
With patricidal hand
he reft himself of eyes
that dearer to him were than his own children.
And on those children savage
maledictions he launched

for their cruel tendance of him
and wished they might divide
with iron-wielding hand his own possessions.
And now I fear
that nimble-footed Fury bring those wishes to fulfilment.

JOCASTA

EURIPIDES, *Phoenissae*, 10-87 (Coleridge)

Jocasta tells her story.

"O sun-god, who cleavest thy way along the starry sky, mounted on golden-studded car, rolling on thy path of flame behind fleet coursers, how curst the beam thou did shed on Thebes, the day that Cadmus left Phoenicia's realm beside the sea and reached this land! He it was that in days long gone wed Harmonia, the daughter of Cypris, and begot Polydorus from whom they say sprung Labdacus, and Laius from him. I am known as the daughter of Menoeceus, and Creon is my brother by the same mother. Men called me Jocasta, for so my father named me, and I am married to Laius. Now when he was still childless after being wed to me a long time, he went and questioned Phoebus, craving moreover that our love might be crowned with sons born to his house. But the god said, "King of Thebes for horses famed! seek not to beget children against the will of heaven; for if thou beget a son, that child shall slay thee, and all thy house shall wade through blood." But he, yielding to his lust in a drunken fit, begat a son of me, and when his babe was born, conscious of his sin and of the god's warning, he gave the child to shepherds to expose in Hera's meadow on mount Cithaeron, after piercing his ankles with iron spikes; whence it was that Hellas named him Oedipus. But the keepers of the horses of Polybus finding him took him home and laid him in the arms of their mistress. So she suckled the child that I had borne and persuaded her husband she was its mother. Soon as my son was grown to man's estate, the tawny beard upon his cheek, either because he had guessed the fraud or learned it from another, he set out for the shrine of Phoebus, eager to know for certain who his parents were; and likewise Laius, my husband, was on his way there, anxious to find out if the child he had exposed was dead. And they met where the branching roads to Phocis unite; and the charioteer of Laius called to him, "Out of the way, stranger, room for my lord!" But he, with never a word, strode on in his pride; and the horses with their hoofs drew blood from the tendons of his feet. Then—but why need I tell aught beyond the sad issue?—son slew father, and taking his chariot gave it to Polybus his foster-father. Now when the Sphinx was grievously harrying our city after my husband's death, my brother Creon proclaimed that he would wed me to any who should guess the riddle of that crafty maiden. By some strange chance, my own son, Oedipus, guessed the Sphinx's riddle, and so he became king of this land and received its scepter as his prize, and married his mother, all unwitting, luckless wretch! nor did I his mother know that I was wedded to my son; and I bore him two sons, Eteocles and the hero Polyneices, and two daughters as well; the one her father called Ismene, the other, which was the elder, I named Antigone. Now when Oedipus, that awful sufferer, learned that I his wedded wife was his mother too, he inflicted a ghastly outrage upon his eyes, tearing the bleeding orbs with a golden brooch. But since my sons have grown to bearded men, they have confined their father closely, that his misfortune, needing as it did full many a shift to hide it, might be forgotten. He is still living in the palace, but his misfortunes have so unhinged him that he imprecates the most unholy curses on his sons, praying that they may have to draw the sword before they share this house between them. So they, fearful that heaven may accomplish his prayer if they dwell together, have made an agreement, arranging that Polyneices, the younger, should first leave the land in voluntary exile, while Eteocles should stay and hold the scepter for a year and then change places. But as soon as Eteocles was seated high in power, he refused to give up the throne, and drove Polyneices into exile from the kingdom; so Polyneices went to Argos and married into the family of Adrastus, and having collected a numerous force of Argives is leading them hither; and he is come up against our seven-gated walls, demanding the scepter of his father and his share in the kingdom. Wherefore I, to end their strife, have prevailed on one son to meet the other under truce, before appealing to arms; and the messenger I sent tells me that he will come. O Zeus, whose home is heaven's radiant vault, save us, and grant that my sons may be reconciled! For thou, if thou art really wise, must not suffer the same poor mortal to be forever wretched."

ANTIGONE

SOPHOCLES, *Antigone*, 891-928 (Jebb, revised)

Antigone, condemned to the tomb by Creon for the burial of her brother Polyneices, makes her final statement.

"Tomb, bridal-chamber, eternal prison in the caverned rock, where I go to find my own, those many who have perished, and whom Persephone has received among the dead! Last of all shall I pass thither, and far most miserably of all, before the term of my life is spent. But I cherish good hope that my coming will be welcome to my father, and pleasant to you, my mother, and welcome, brother, to you: for, when you died, with my own hands I washed and dressed you, and poured drink-offerings at your graves; and now, Polyneices, it is for tending your corpse that I win such recompense as this.

"And yet I honored you, as the wise will think, rightly. Never, had I been a mother of children, or if a husband had been mouldering in death, would I have taken this task upon me in the city's despite. What law, you ask, is my warrant for that word? The husband lost, another might have been found, and child from another, to replace the first-born; but, father and mother hidden with Hades, no brother's life could ever bloom for me again. Such was the law whereby I held you first in honor; but Creon considered me guilty of error therein, and of outrage, ah brother mine! And now he leads me thus, a captive in his hands; no bridal bed, no bridal song has been mine, no joy of marriage, no portion in the nurture of children; but thus, forlorn of friends, unhappy one, I go living to the vaults of death.

"And what law of heaven have I transgressed? Why, hapless one, should I look to the gods any more,—what ally should I invoke,—when by piety I have earned the name of impious? Nay, then, if these things are pleasing to the gods, when I have suffered my doom, I shall come to know my sin; but if the sin is with my judges, I could wish them no fuller measure of evil than they, on their part, do wrongfully to me."

~~~~~

TIRESIAS

SOPHOCLES, *Oedipus the King*, 447-462 (Jebb, revised)

Tiresias, under compulsion, tells Oedipus what will prove to be the truth about him.

"I will go when I have done my errand, fearless of your frown: for you can never destroy me. And I tell you—the man you have long been seeking, uttering threats, and proclaiming a search into the murder of Laius—that man is here,—seemingly, an alien sojourner, but soon he shall be found a native Theban, and shall not be glad of his fortune. A blind man, he who now has sight, a begger, who now is rich, he shall make his way to a strange land, feeling the ground before him with his staff. And he shall be found at once brother and father of the children with whom he consorts; son and husband of the woman who bore him; heir to his father's bed, shedder of his father's blood.

"So go you in and think on that; and if you find that I have been at fault, say then that I have no wit in prophecy."

~~~~~

THE SEVEN AGAINST THEBES

SOPHOCLES, *Oedipus at Colonus*, 1309-1329 (Jebb, revised)

Polyneices tells Oedipus his preparations for the seven to attack Thebes and asks in vain for his blessing.

"I have been driven, an exile, from my fatherland, because, as eldest born, I claimed to sit in your sovereign seat. Eteocles, though the younger, thrust me from the land, when he had neither worsted me in argument, nor come to trial of might and deed,—no, but won the city over. And of this I think it most likely that the curse on your house is the cause; then from soothsayers also I so hear. For when I came to Dorian Argos, I took the daughter of Adrastus to wife and I bound to me by oath all of the Apian land who are foremost in renown of war, that with them I might levy the sevenfold host of spearmen against Thebes, and die in my just cause, or cast the doers of this wrong from the realm.

"Well, and why have I come here now? With suppliant prayers, my father, unto you—my own, and the prayers of my allies, who now, with seven hosts behind their seven spears, have set their leaguer round the plain of Thebes; of whom is swift-speared Amphiaraus, matchless warrior, matchless augur; then the son of Oeneus, Aetolian Tydeus; Eteoclus third, of Argive birth; the fourth, Hippomedon, sent by Talaos, his sire; while Capaneus, the fifth, vaunts that he will burn Thebes with fire, unto the ground; and sixth, Arcadian Parthenopaeus rushes to the war, named from that virgin of other days whose marriage in after-time gave him birth, trusty son of Atalanta. Last, I, your son,—or if not yours, but offspring of an evil fate, yet yours at least in name, —lead the fearless host of Argos unto Thebes.

"And we, by these your children and by your life, my father, implore you all, praying you to remit your stern wrath against me, as I go forth to chastise my brother, who has thrust me out and robbed me of my fatherland. For if any truth is told by oracles, they said that victory should be with those whom you should join."

<hr />

THE HEROINES

HOMER, *Odyssey*, Book 11. 235-327 (Butler)

Odysseus tells of the great heroines of old.

"The first I saw was Tyro. She was daughter of Salmoneus and wife of Cretheus the son of Aeolus. She fell in love with the river Enipeus, who is much the most beautiful river in the whole world. Once when she was taking a walk by his side as usual, Poseidon, disguised as her lover, lay with her at the mouth of the river, and a huge blue wave arched itself like a mountain over them to hide both woman and god, whereon he loosed her virgin girdle and laid her in a deep slumber. When the god had accomplished the deed of love, he took her hand in his own and said, "Tyro, rejoice in all good will; the embraces of the gods are not fruitless, and you will have fine twins about this time twelve months. Take great care of them. I am Poseidon, so now go home, but hold your tongue and do not tell anyone.'

"Then he dived under the sea, and she in due course bore Pelias and Neleus, who both of them served Zeus with all their might. Pelias was a great breeder of sheep and lived in Iolcus, but the other lived in Pylos. The rest of her children were by Cretheus, namely, Aeson, Pheres, and Amythaon, who was a mighty warrior and charioteer.

"Next to her I saw Antiope daughter of Asopus, who could boast of having slept in the arms of even Zeus himself, and who bore him two sons, Amphion and Zethus. These founded Thebes with its seven gates, and built a wall all round it; for strong though they were they could not hold Thebes till they had walled it.

"Then I saw Alcmena, the wife of Amphitryon, who also bore to Zeus indomitable Heracles; and Megara, who was daughter to great King Creon, and married the redoubtable son of Amphitryon.

"I also saw fair Epicaste [Jocasta], mother of King Oedipus, whose awful lot it was to marry her own son without suspecting it. He married her after having killed his father, but the gods proclaimed the whole story to the world; whereon he remained king of Thebes, in great grief for the spite the gods had borne him; but Epicaste went to the house of the mighty jailor Hades, having hanged herself for grief, and the avenging spirits haunted him as for an outraged mother—to his ruing bitterly thereafter.

"Then I saw Chloris, whom Neleus married for her beauty, having given priceless presents for her. She was youngest daughter to Amphion, son of Iasus and king of Minyan Orchomenus, and was queen in Pylos. She bore Nestor, Chromius, and Periclymenus, and she also bore that marvelously lovely woman Pero, who was wooed by all the country round; but Neleus would only give her to him who should raid the cattle of Iphicles from the grazing grounds of Phylace, and this was a hard task. The only man who would undertake to raid them was a certain excellent seer [Melampus], but the will of heaven was against him, for the rangers of the cattle caught him and put him in prison. Nevertheless, when a full year had passed and the same season came round again, Iphicles set him at liberty, after he had expounded all the oracles of heaven. Thus, then, was the will of Zeus accomplished.

"And I saw Leda the wife of Tyndarus, who bore him two famous sons, Castor, breaker of horses, and Pollux, the mighty boxer. Both these heroes are lying under the earth, though they are still alive, for by a special dispensation of Zeus, they die and come to life again, each one of them every other day throughout all time, and they have the rank of gods.

"After her I saw Iphimedeia wife of Aloeus, who boasted the embrace of Poseidon. She bore two sons, Otus and Ephialtes, but both were short lived. They were the finest children that were ever born in this world, and the best looking, Orion only excepted; for at nine years old they were nine fathoms high, and measured nine cubits round the chest. They threatened to make war with the gods in Olympus, and tried to set Mount Ossa on the top of Mount Olympus, and Mount Pelion on the top of Ossa, that they might scale heaven itself, and they would have done it too if they had been grown up. But Apollo, son of Leto, killed both of them, before they had got so much as a sign of hair upon cheeks or chin.

"Then I saw Phaedra, and Procris, and fair Ariadne, daughter of the magician Minos, whom Theseus was carrying off from Crete to Athens, but he did not enjoy her, for before he could do so Artemis killed her in the island of Dia on account of what Dionysus had said against her.

"I also saw Maera and Clymene and hateful Eriphyle, who sold her own husband for gold."

III

THE
HOMERIC
HEROES

1. The Story of Achilles; Greeks and Trojans

THE DESIGN OF THE ILIAD

HOMER, *Iliad*, Book 1. 1-7 (Lang, Leaf, and Myers)

The opening lines state the theme of the Iliad and make it clear that the poet is not going to tell the whole story of the Trojan War.

Sing, goddess, the wrath of Achilles Peleus' son, the ruinous wrath that brought on the Achaians woes innumerable, and hurled down into Hades many strong souls of heroes, and gave their bodies to be a prey to dogs and all winged fowls; and so the counsel of Zeus wrought out its accomplishment from the day when first strife parted Atreides king of men and noble Achilles.

THE BIRTH OF ACHILLES

PINDAR, *Isthmian*, 8. 27-59 (Lattimore)

Zeus and bright Poseidon came to strife over Thetis,
each desirous to be wed to her beauty
and possess her; the passion was on them.
But the will of the gods did not accomplish such union,

for they had heard things foretold. Themis,
lady of good counsel, rose up among them and spoke

how it was destined for this sea-goddess to bring to birth a lord
stronger than his father, to wield in his hand a shaft heavier than the thunderbolt
or the weariless trident, if she lay with Zeus or his brothers.
"Let her go.
She must come rather into a mortal bed.
Let her look upon her son slain in battle,
but a son like Ares for strength of hand, like the thundershaft for speed of his feet.
For my part, I say grant the divine grace
of this marriage to Aiakos' son, Peleus,
rumored the most upright man that dwells in Iolkos plain.

"And let the messages go straightway
to Chiron's immortal cave.
Let not Nereus' daughter put twice in our hands the leaf-ballots of our contention.
By full moon at evening let her break
the fastening of her lovely virginity for the hero." The goddess spoke before the Kronians; they
nodded with immortal brows. The words' harvest
faded not. They say the two kings consented
to Thetis' marriage; and the lips of poets
have published to those who knew not of it the young strength of Achilles;
who stained the Mysian vineyards
with the dark blood of Telephos, drenching the plain;

and made a bridge to bring the Atreidai home,
and set Helen free, cutting
with the spear's edge the sinews of Troy, that had fought him off in deadly battle
as he did great deeds in the plain; Memnon the mighty
and impetuous Hektor, others, chiefs among men; Achilles,
the staunch Aiakid, showed them Persephone's house
and revealed the glory of Aigina and the stock he came of.
Even in death, songs did not leave him,
but, standing beside his pyre and his grave, the maidens
of Helikon let fall upon him their abundant dirge.
Even the immortals were pleased

to bestow on a brave man, though perished, the song of
  goddesses.

~~~~~

ACHILLES' VERSION OF THE QUARREL

HOMER, *Iliad*, Book 1. 366-412 (Bryant)

*Achilles asks his mother Thetis to obtain the assistance of
Zeus in avenging Agamemnon's insult to his honor.*

Achilles, swift of foot, sighed heavily,
And said: "Thou know'st already. Why relate
These things to thee, who art apprised of all?
   "To Thebe, to Eetion's sacred town,
We marched, and plundered it, and hither brought
The booty, which was fairly shared among
The sons of Greece, and Agamemnon took
The fair-cheeked maid Chryseis as his prize.
But Chryses, priest of Phoebus, to the fleet
Of the Achaian warriors, brazen-mailed,
Came, to redeem his daughter, offering
Ransom uncounted. In his hand he bore
The fillets of Apollo, archer-god,
Upon the golden scepter, and he sued
To all the Greeks, but chiefly to the sons
Of Atreus, the two leaders of the host.
Then all the other chiefs, applauding, bade
Revere the priest and take the liberal gifts
He offered; but the counsel did not please
Atrides Agamemnon: he dismissed
The priest with scorn, and added threatening
   words.
The aged man indignantly withdrew;
And Phoebus—for the priest was dear to him—
Granted his prayer and sent among the Greeks
A deadly shaft. The people of the camp
Were perishing in heaps. His arrows flew
Among the Grecian army, far and wide.

A seer expert in oracles revealed
The will of Phoebus, and I was the first
To counsel that the god should be appeased.
But Agamemnon rose in sudden wrath,
Uttering a threat, which he has since fulfilled.
And now the dark-eyed Greeks are taking back
His child to Chryses, and with her they bear
Gifts to the monarch-god; while to my tent
Heralds have come, and borne away the maid
Briseis, given me by the sons of Greece.
But succor thou thy son, if thou hast power;
Ascend to heaven and bring thy prayer to Jove,
If e'er by word or act thou gav'st him aid.
For I remember, in my father's halls
I often heard thee, glorying, tell how thou,
Alone of all the gods, did interpose
To save the cloud-compeller, Saturn's son,
From shameful overthrow, when all the rest
Who dwell upon Olympus had conspired
To bind him,—Juno, Neptune, and with them
Pallas Athene. Thou did come and loose
His bonds, and call up to the Olympian heights
The hundred-handed, whom the immortal gods
Have named Briareus, but the sons of men
Aegeon, mightier than his sire in strength;
And he, rejoicing in the honor, took
His seat by Jove, and all the immortals shrank
Aghast before him, and let fall the chains.
Remind him of all this, and, sitting down,
Embrace his knees, and pray him to befriend
The Trojans, that the Greeks, hemmed in and slain
Beside their ships and by the shore, may learn
To glory in their king, and even he,
Wide-ruling Agamemnon, may perceive
How grievous was his folly when he dared
To treat with scorn the bravest of the Greeks."
    And Thetis answered, weeping as she spoke:—
"Alas, my son, why did I rear thee, born
To sorrow as thou were? O would that thou
Unwronged, and with no cause for tears, could dwell
Beside thy ships, since thou must die so soon.
I brought thee forth in an unhappy hour.

Short-lived and wronged beyond all other men.
Yet will I climb the Olympian height among
Its snows and make my suit to Jupiter
The Thunderer, if perhaps he may yield
To my entreaties. Thou, meanwhile, abide
By thy swift ships, incensed against the Greeks,
And take no part in all their battles more.
But yesterday did Jove depart to hold
A banquet far in Ocean's realm, among
The blameless Ethiopians, and with him
Went all the train of gods. Twelve days must pass
Ere he return to heaven, and I will then
Enter his brazen palace, clasp his knees,
And hope to move his purpose by my prayers."

ACHILLES' THREAT

HOMER, *Iliad*, Book 1. 225-244 (Derby)

*Athene prevents Achilles from attacking Agamemnon, but
allows him to speak his mind.*

"Thou sot, with eye of dog, and heart of deer!
Who never dares to lead in armed fight
The assembled host, nor with a chosen few
To man the secret ambush—for you fear
To look on death—no doubt 'tis easier far,
Girt with thy troops, to plunder of his right
Whoe'er may venture to oppose your will!
A tyrant King, because you rule over slaves!
Were it not so, this insult would be your last.
But this I say, and with an oath confirm,
By this my royal staff, which never more
Shall put forth leaf nor spray, since first it left
Upon the mountain-side its parent stem,
Nor blossom more, since all around the axe
Has lopped both leaf and bark, and now 'tis borne
Emblem of justice, by the sons of Greece,
Who guard the sacred ministry of law

Before the face of Jove! a mighty oath!
The time shall come, when all the sons of Greece
Shall mourn Achilles' loss; and you the while,
Heart-rent, shalt be all-impotent to aid,
When by the warrior-slayer Hector's hand
Many shall fall; and then your soul shall mourn
The slight on Grecia's bravest warrior cast."
     Thus spoke Pelides; and upon the ground
He cast his staff, with golden studs embossed
And took his seat; on the other side, in wrath,
Atrides burned; but Nestor interposed;
Nestor, the leader of the Pylian host,
The smooth-tongued chief, from whose persuasive lips
Sweeter than honey flowed the stream of speech.
Two generations of the sons of men
For him were past and gone, who with himself
Were born and bred on Pylos' lovely shore,
And o'er the third he now held royal sway.
He thus with prudent words the chiefs addressed:
     "Alas, alas! what grief is this for Greece!
What joy for Priam, and for Priam's sons!
What exultation for the men of Troy,
To hear of feuds 'tween you, of all the Greeks
The first in council, and the first in fight!
Yet, hear my words, I pray; in years, at least,
You both must yield to me; and in times past
I lived with men, and they despised me not,
Abler in counsel, greater than yourselves."

THE EMBASSY

HOMER *Iliad*, Book 9. 622-668 (Lattimore)

*As a result of the promise of Zeus, the Greeks are driven
back and discouraged, despite the mighty deeds of Diomede.
For the first time the Trojans camp on the plain outside
the city. The Greeks hold a council and, on the advice of
Nestor, Agamemnon sends an embassy to promise rich gifts
to Achilles if he will cease from his wrath. Achilles and Patroclus receive the embassy cordially, but Achilles is cold to*

the plea of Odysseus that he should accept the gifts and the
urging of Phoenix that he should accept the gifts and help
before the situation becomes desperate. Achilles promises
in the morning to consider whether to return home or stay
in the Greek camp. Finally, Ajax speaks.

"Son of Laertes and seed of Zeus, resourceful Odysseus:
let us go. I think that nothing will be accomplished
by argument on this errand; it is best to go back quickly
and tell this story, though it is not good, to the Danaans
who sit there waiting for us to come back, seeing that Achilleus
has made savage the proud-hearted spirit within his body.
He is hard, and does not remember that friends' affection
wherein we honored him by the ships, far beyond all others.
Pitiless. And yet a man takes from his brother's slayer
the blood price, or the price for a child who was killed, and the
        guilty
one, when he has largely repaid, stays still in the country,
and the injured man's heart is curbed, and his pride, and his
        anger
when he has taken the price; but the gods put in your breast a
        spirit
not to be placated, bad, for the sake of one single
girl. Yet now we offer you seven, surpassingly lovely,
and much beside these. Now make gracious the spirit within you.
Respect your own house; see, we are under the same roof with
        you,
from the multitude of the Danaans, we who desire beyond all
others to have your honor and love, out of all the Achaians."
    Then in answer to him spoke Achilleus of the swift feet:
"Son of Telamon, seed of Zeus, Aias, lord of the people:
all that you have said seems spoken after my own mind.
Yet still the heart in me swells up in anger, when I remember
the disgrace that he wrought upon me before the Argives,
the son of Atreus, as if I were some dishonored vagabond.
Do you then go back to him, and take him this message:
that I shall not think again of the bloody fighting
until such time as the son of wise Priam, Hektor the brilliant,
comes all the way to the ships of the Myrmidons, and their shel-
        ters,
slaughtering the Argives, and shall darken with fire our vessels.
But around my own shelter, I think, and beside my black ship
Hektor will be held, though he be very hungry for battle."

He spoke, and they taking each a two-handled cup poured out
a libation, then went back to their ships, and Odysseus led them.
Now Patroklos gave the maids and his followers orders
to make up without delay a neat bed for Phoinix.
And these obeyed him and made up the bed as he had commanded,
laying fleeces on it, and a blanket, and a sheet of fine linen.
There the old man lay down and waited for the divine Dawn.
But Achilleus slept in the inward corner of the strong-built shelter,
and a woman lay beside him, one he had taken from Lesbos,
Phorbas' daughter, Diomede of the fair coloring.
In the other corner Patroklos went to bed; with him also
was a girl, Iphis the fair-girdled, whom brilliant Achilleus
gave him, when he took sheer Skyros, Enyeus' citadel.

ACHILLES SENDS PATROCLUS TO INQUIRE ABOUT A WOUNDED GREEK

HOMER, *Iliad*, Book 11. 596-615 (Chase and Perry)

*After the failure of the embassy and the night expedition
of Diomede and Odysseus against the spy Dolon and King
Rhesus, the fighting resumes.*

So they fought, like shining fire. But the Neleian horses, sweating, bore Nestor from the battle and Machaon, too, shepherd of
the people. Swift-footed, godlike Achilles saw and noted him, for
he stood on the stern of his wide-bellied ship, watching the hard
toil and tearful onset. At once he spoke to his comrade Patroclus,
calling from the ship, and Patroclus, hearing him from the tent,
came out, like to Ares; and this was the beginning of misfortune
for him. The brave son of Menoetius first said to Achilles: "Why
do you call me, Achilles? What need have you of me?"

Swift-footed Achilles answered him and said: "Godlike son of
Menoetius, dear to my heart, now I think the Achaeans will fall
at my knees in supplication, for a need no longer endurable
has come upon them. Go now, Patroclus, dear to Zeus, ask

Nestor whom he brings there wounded from the battle. From the rear it seems in all ways like Machaon, Asclepius' son, but I could not see the man's eyes, for the horses rushed by me, speeding onward."

So he spoke, and Patroclus obeyed his dear companion and went running past the tents and ships of the Achaeans.

───≈───

NESTOR ADDRESSES PATROCLUS

HOMER, *Iliad*, Book 11. 783-805 (Lattimore)

"Peleus the aged was telling his own son, Achilleus,
to be always best in battle and pre-eminent beyond all others,
but for you, Menoitios, Aktor's son, had this to say to you:
'My child, by right of blood Achilleus is higher than you are,
but you are the elder. Yet in strength he is far the greater.
You must speak solid words to him, and give him good counsel,
and point his way. If he listens to you it will be for his own good.'
This is what the old man told you, you have forgotten. Yet even
now you might speak to wise Achilleus, he might be persuaded.
Who knows if, with God helping, you might trouble his spirit
by entreaty, since the persuasion of a friend is a strong thing.
But if he is drawing back from some prophecy known in his own
　　heart
and by Zeus' will his honored mother has told him of something,
let him send you out, at least, and the rest of the Myrmidon
　　people
follow you, and you may be a light given to the Danaans.
And let him give you his splendid armor to wear to the fighting,
if perhaps the Trojans might think you are he, and give way
from their attack, and the fighting sons of the Achaians get wind
again after hard work. There is little breathing space in the fight-
　　ing.
You, unwearied, might with a mere cry pile men wearied
back upon their city, and away from the ships and the shelters."

So he spoke, and stirred the feeling in the breast of Patroklos,
and he went on the run along the ships to the son of Aiakos,
Achilleus.

ZEUS ADDRESSES HERA

HOMER, *Iliad*, Book 15. 49-77 (Derby)

After reproaching Hera for aiding the Greeks, Zeus tells her the course the action will take.

"If, ox-eyed Queen, in synod of the Gods
Thy counsels shall indeed with mine agree,
Neptune, how strong soe'er his wish, must change
His course, obedient to your will and mine;
And if in all sincerity you speak,
Go to the assembled Gods, and send
Iris, and Phoebus of the silver bow;
That she may to the Grecian camp repair,
And bid that Neptune from the battlefield
Withdraw, and to his own domain retire;
While Phoebus Hector to the fight restores,
Inspiring new-born vigor, and allaying
The mortal pains which bow his spirit down;
Then, heartless fear infusing in the Greeks,
Put them to flight, that flying they may fall
Beside Achilles' ships; his comrade then,
Patroclus, he shall send to battle forth
To be by Hector slain, in front of Troy;
Yet not to fall till many valiant youths
Have felt his prowess; and, amid the rest,
My son, Sarpedon; by his comrade's death
Enraged, Achilles Hector shall subdue;
Thenceforth my counsel is, that from the ships
The Trojan force shall still be backward driven,
Until at length, by Pallas' deep designs,
The Greeks possess the lofty walls of Troy.
Yet will not I my anger intermit,
Nor suffer other of the immortal Gods
To aid the Greeks; till Peleus' son behold
His wish accomplished, and the boon obtained
I promised once, and with a nod confirmed,

That day when sea-born Thetis clasped my knees,
And prayed me to avenge her warrior son."

PATROCLUS URGES ACHILLES

HOMER, *Iliad*, Book 16. 20-100 (Bryant)

The Trojans drive the Greeks back to the ships and approach them with fire. This is too much for Patroclus.

Meanwhile Patroclus stood beside his friend
The shepherd of the people, Peleus' son,
And shed hot tears, as when a fountain sheds
Dark waters streaming down a precipice.
The great Achilles, swift of foot, beheld
And pitied him, and spoke these winged words:—
"Why weepest thou, Patroclus, like a girl,—
A little girl that by her mother's side
Runs, importuning to be taken up,
And plucks her by the robe, and stops her way,
And looks at her, and cries, until at last
She rests within her arms? Thou art like her,
Patroclus, with thy tears. Dost thou then bring
Sad tidings to the Myrmidons or me?
Or hast thou news from Phthia? It is said
That still Menoetius, son of Actor, lives,
And Peleus also, son of Aeacus,
Among the Myrmidons. Full bitterly
Should we lament to hear that either died.
Or mournest thou because the Achaians fall
Through their own folly by the roomy ships?
Speak, and hide nothing, for I too would know."
And thou, O knight Patroclus, with a sigh
Deep-drawn, did answer thus: "Be not displeased,
Achilles, son of Peleus, bravest far
Of all the Achaian army! for the Greeks
Endure a bitter lot. The chiefs who late
Were deemed their mightiest are within the ships,
Wounded or stricken down. There Diomed,

The gallant son of Tydeus, lies, and there
Ulysses, the great spearman, wounded both;
And Agamemnon; and Eurypylus,
Driven from the field, an arrow in his thigh.
Round them the healers, skilled in remedies,
Attend and dress their painful wounds, while thou,
Achilles, sittest here implacable.
O, never be such fierce resentments mine
As thou dost cherish, who art only brave
For mischief! Whom wilt thou hereafter aid,
If now thou rescue not the perishing Greeks?
O merciless! it cannot surely be
That Peleus was thy father, or the queen
Thetis thy mother; the green sea instead
And rugged precipices brought thee forth,
For savage is thy heart. But if thou heed
The warning of some god, if thou hast heard
Aught which thy goddess-mother has received
From Jove, send me at least into the war,
And let me lead thy Myrmidons, that thus
The Greeks may have some gleam of hope. And give
The armor from thy shoulders. I will wear
Thy mail, and then the Trojans, at the sight,
May think I am Achilles, and may pause
From fighting, and the warlike sons of Greece,
Tired as they are, may breathe once more, and gain
A respite from the conflict. Our fresh troops
May easily drive back upon their town
The weary Trojans from our tents and fleet."
    So spoke he, sighing; rash and blind, he asked
Death for himself and evil destiny.
Achilles the swift-footed also drew
A heavy sigh, and thus in turn he spoke:—
    "What, O divine Patroclus, hast thou said?
I fear no omen yet revealed to me;
Nor has my goddess-mother told me aught
From Jove; but ever in my heart and soul
Rankles the painful sense of injury done
By one who, having greater power, deprives
An equal of his right, and takes away
The prize he won. This is my wrong, and this
The cause of all my bitterness of heart.

Her whom the sons of Greece bestowed on me
As my reward, a trophy of my spear,
After the sack of a fenced city,—her
Did Agamemnon, son of Atreus, take
Out of my hands, as if I were a wretch,
A worthless outcast. But let that affront
Be with the things that were. It is not well
To bear a grudge forever. I have said
My anger should not cease to burn until
The clamor of the battle and the assault
Should reach the fleet. But go thou and put on
My well-known armor; lead into the field
My Myrmidons, men that rejoice in war,
Since like a lowering cloud the men of Troy
Surround the fleet, and the Achaians stand
In narrow space close pressed beside the sea,
And all the city of Ilium flings itself
Against them, confident of victory,
Now that the glitter of my helm no more
Flashes upon their eyes. Yet very soon.
Their flying host would fill the trenches here
With corpses, had but Agamemnon dealt
Gently with me; and now their squadrons close
Around our army. Now no more the spear
Is wielded by Tydides Diomed
In rescue of the Greeks; no more the shout
Of Agamemnon's hated throat is heard;
But the man-queller Hector, lifting up
His voice, exhorts the Trojans, who, in throngs,
Raising the war-cry, fill the plain, and drive
The Greeks before them. Gallantly lead on
The charge, Patroclus; rescue our good ships;
Let not the enemy give them to the flames,
And cut us off from our desired return.
Follow my counsel; bear my words in mind;
So shall thou win for me among the Greeks
Great honor and renown, and they shall bring
The beautiful maiden back with princely gifts.
When thou hast driven the assailants from the fleet,
Return thou hither. If the Thunderer,
Husband of Juno, suffer thee to gain
That victory, seek no further to prolong

The combat with the warlike sons of Troy,
Apart from me, lest I be brought to shame,
Nor, glorying in the battle and pursuit,
Slaying the Trojans as thou goest, lead
Thy men to Troy, lest from the Olympian mount
One of the ever-living gods descend
Against thee: Phoebus loves the Trojans well.
But come as soon as thou shall see the ships
In safety; leave the foes upon the plain
Contending with each other. Would to Jove
The All-Father, and to Pallas, and the god
Who bears the bow, Apollo, that of all
The Trojans, many as they are, and all
The Greeks, not one might be reprieved from death,
While thou and I alone were left alive
To overthrow the sacred walls of Troy."

~~~~~

THETIS COMES TO ACHILLES

HOMER, *Iliad*, Book 18. 78-126 (Lattimore)

*Patroclus is killed by Hector who seizes the armor of Achilles.
Thetis comes, hoping to console Achilles.*

Then sighing heavily Achilleus of the swift feet answered her:
"My mother, all these things the Olympian brought to accomplishment.
But what pleasure is this to me, since my dear companion has
perished,
Patroklos, whom I loved beyond all other companions,
as well as my own life. I have lost him, and Hektor, who killed
him,
has stripped away that gigantic armor, a wonder to look on
and splendid, which the gods gave Peleus, a glorious present,
on that day they drove you to the marriage bed of a mortal.
I wish you had gone on living then with the other goddesses
of the sea, and that Peleus had married some mortal woman.
As it is, there must be on your heart a numberless sorrow
for your son's death, since you can never again receive him

won home again to his country; since the spirit within does not
　drive me
to go on living and be among men, except on condition
that Hektor first be beaten down under my spear, lose his life
and pay the price for stripping Patroklos, the son of Menoitios."
　Then in turn Thetis spoke to him, letting the tears fall:
"Then I must lose you soon, my child, by what you are saying,
since it is decreed your death must come soon after Hektor's."
　Then deeply disturbed Achilleus of the swift feet answered her:
"I must die soon, then; since I was not to stand by my companion
when he was killed. And now, far away from the land of his fa-
　thers,
he has perished, and lacked my fighting strength to defend him.
Now, since I am not going back to the beloved land of my fa-
　thers,
since I was no light of safety to Patroklos, nor to my other
companions, who in their numbers went down before glorious
　Hektor,
but sit here beside my ships, a useless weight on the good land,
I, who am such as no other of the bronze-armored Achaians
in battle, though there are others also better in council—
why, I wish that strife would vanish away from among gods and
　mortals,
and gall, which makes a man grow angry for all his great mind,
that gall of anger that swarms like smoke inside of a man's heart
and becomes a thing sweeter to him by far than the dripping of
　honey.
So it was here that the lord of men Agamemnon angered me.
Still, we will let all this be a thing of the past, and for all our
sorrow beat down by force the anger deeply within us.
Now I shall go, to overtake that killer of a dear life,
Hektor; then I will accept my own death, at whatever
time Zeus wishes to bring it about, and the other immortals.
For not even the strength of Herakles fled away from destruction,
although he was dearest of all to lord Zeus, son of Kronos,
but his fate beat him under, and the wearisome anger of Hera.
So I likewise, if such is the fate which has been wrought for me,
shall lie still, when I am dead. Now I must win excellent glory,
and drive some one of the women of Troy, or some deep-girdled
Dardanian woman, lifting up to her soft cheeks both hands
to wipe away the close bursts of tears in her lamentation,
and learn that I stayed too long out of the fighting. Do not

hold me back from the fight, though you love me. You will not persuade me."

~~~~~~~~

RECONCILIATION

HOMER, *Iliad*, Book 19. 55-144 (Lang, Leaf, and Myers)

Thetis obtains new armor for Achilles from Hephaestus, and Achilles calls a gathering of the Greeks.

Noble Achilles went down the beach of the sea, crying his terrible cry, and roused the Achaian warriors. And they who before had kept within the circle of the ships, and they who were helmsmen and kept the steerage of the ships, or were stewards there and dealt out food, even these came then to the place of assembly, because Achilles was come forth, after long ceasing from grievous war. Limping came two of Ares' company, Tydeus' son staunch in fight and noble Odysseus, each leaning on his spear, for their wounds were grievous still; and they went and sat down in the forefront of the assembly. And last came Agamemnon, king of men, with his wound upon him, for him too in the stress of battle Koon Antenor's son had wounded with his bronze-tipped spear. But when all the Achaians were gathered, then uprose fleet-footed Achilles and spoke in their midst: "Son of Atreus, was this in any way the better way for both you and me, what time with grief at our hearts we waxed fierce in soul-devouring strife for the sake of a girl? Would that Artemis had slain her with her arrow at the ships, on the day whereon I took her to me, when I had spoiled Lyrnessos; so should not then so many Achaians have bitten the wide earth beneath their enemies' hands, by reason of my exceeding wrath. It has been well for Hector and the Trojans, but the Achaians I think shall long remember the strife that was between you and me. But begones will we let be, for all our pain, and curb under necessity the spirit within our breasts. I now will stay my anger: it beseems me not implacably forever to be angry; but come rouse speedily to the fight the flowing-haired Achaians, that I may go forth against the men of Troy and put them yet again to the proof, if they come hard by the ships. I think that some among them shall be glad to rest their knees when they are fled out of the fierceness of the battle, and from before our spear."

He spoke, and the well-greaved Achaians rejoiced that the great-hearted son of Peleus had made renouncement of his wrath. Then among them spoke Agamemnon, king of men, speaking from the place where he sat, not arisen to stand forth in their midst: "O Danaan friends and heroes, men of Ares' company, seemly is it to listen to him who stands up to speak, nor should we break in upon his words: even toward a skilled man that were hard. For amid the uproar of many men how should one listen, or yet speak? even the clearest-voiced speech is marred. To the son of Peleus I will declare myself, but you other Argives give heed, and each mark well my word. Often have the Achaians spoken thus to me, and upbraided me; but it is not I who am the cause, but Zeus and Destiny and Erinys that walk in the darkness, who put into my soul fierce madness on the day when in the assembly I, even I, took from Achilles his due. What could I do? it is God who accomplishes all. Eldest daughter of Zeus is Ate who blinds all, a power of bane: delicate are her feet, for not upon earth she goes, but walks over the heads of men, making men to fall; and entangles this one or that. Yea even Zeus was blinded one time, he who they say is greatest among gods and men; yet even him Hera with female wile deceived, on the day when Alkmene in fair-crowned Thebes was to bring forth the strength of Herakles. For then proclaimed he solemnly among all the gods: 'Hear me ye all, both gods and goddesses, while I utter the counsel of my soul within my heart. This day shall Eileithuia, the help of travailing women, bring to the light a man who shall be lord over all that dwell round about, among the race of men who are sprung of me by blood.' And to him in subtlety queen Hera spoke: 'Thou will play the cheat and not accomplish thy word. Come now, Olympian, swear me a firm oath that verily and indeed shall that man be lord over all that dwell round about, who this day shall fall between a woman's feet, even he among all men who are of the lineage of thy blood.' So spoke she, and Zeus did not perceive her subtlety, but swore a mighty oath, and therewith was he sore blinded. For Hera darted from Olympus' peak, and came swiftly to Achaian Argos, where she knew was the stately wife of Sthenelos son of Perseus, who also was great with child, and her seventh month was come. Her son Hera brought to the light, though his tale of months was untold, but she stayed Alkmene's bearing and kept the Eileithuiai from her aid. Then she brought the tidings herself and to Kronos' son Zeus she spoke: 'Father Zeus of the bright lightning, a word will I speak to thee for thy heed. Today is born a man of valor who shall rule among the Argives, Eurystheus, son of Sthenelos the son of Perseus, of thy lineage; not unmeet is it that he be lord among Argives.' She said, but sharp pain smote him in the depths of his soul, and straightway he seized Ate by her bright-haired head in the anger of his soul, and swore a mighty oath that never again to Olympus and the starry heaven should Ate come, who blinds all alike. He said, and whirling her in his hand flung her from the starry heaven, and quickly came she down among the works of men. Yet ever he groaned against her when he beheld his beloved son in cruel travail at Eurystheus' behest. Thus also I, what time great Hector of the glancing helm was slaying Argives at the sterns of our ships, could not be unmindful of Ate, who blinded me at the first. But since thus blinded was I, and Zeus bereft me of my wit, now would I make amends, and recompense manifold for the wrong. Only arise to the battle and rouse the rest of the host. Gifts am I ready to offer, even all that noble Odysseus went yesterday to promise in thy hut. So, if thou will, stay a while, though eager, from battle, and squires shall take the gifts from my ship and carry them to thee, that thou may see that what I give suffices thee."

Then answered him Achilles swift of foot: "Most noble son of Atreus, Agamemnon king of men, for the gifts, to give them as it beseemeth, if so thou wilt, or to withhold, is in thy choice. But now let us think of battle with all speed; this is no time to dally here with subtleties, for a great work is yet undone. Once more must Achilles be seen in the forefront of the battle, laying waste with his brazen spear the battalions of the men of Troy. Thereof let each of you think as he fights with his man."

BRISEIS' RETURN

HOMER, *Iliad*, Book 19. 282-302 (Bryant)

Agamemnon's gifts are sent to Achilles and with them the girl Briseis.

When the maid
Briseis, beautiful as Venus, saw

Patroclus lying gashed with wounds, she sprang
And threw herself upon the dead, and tore
Her bosom, her fair cheeks and delicate neck;
And thus the graceful maiden, weeping, said:—
 "Patroclus, dear to my unhappy heart!
I left thee in full life, when from this tent
They led me; I return and find thee dead,
O chieftain of the people! Thus it is
That sorrow upon sorrow is my lot.
Him to whose arms my father, in my youth,
And gracious mother gave me as a bride,
I saw before our city pierced and slain,
And the three brothers whom my mother bore
Slain also,—brothers whom I dearly loved.
Yet thou, when swift Achilles struck to earth
My hapless husband, and laid waste the town
Of godlike Mynes, would not suffer me
To weep despairingly; for thou did give
Thy word to make me yet the wedded wife
Of great Achilles, bear me in the fleet
To Phthia, and prepare the wedding feast
Among the Myrmidons. O ever kind!
I mourn thy death, and cannot be consoled."
 Weeping she spoke; the women wept with her
Seemingly for the dead, but each, in truth,
For her own griefs.

HECTOR AND ACHILLES

HOMER, *Iliad*, Book 22. 131-138 (Lang, Leaf, and Myers)

Achilles hurls himself into the battle, the gods join in, and finally Hector decides that he must make a stand.

"Better is it to join battle with all speed: let us know upon which of us the Olympian shall bestow renown."

Thus pondered he as he stood, but near to him came Achilles, peer of Enyalios, warrior of the waving helm, brandishing from his right shoulder the Pelian ash, his terrible spear; and all around the bronze on him flashed like the gleam of blazing fire or of the Sun as he arises. And trembling seized Hector as he was aware of him, nor endured he to abide in his place, but left the gates behind him and fled in fear. And the son of Peleus darted after him, trusting in his swift feet.

THE PURSUIT

homer, *Iliad*, Book 22. 188-213 (Derby)

Meanwhile on Hector, with untiring hate,
The swift Achilles pressed: as when a hound,
Through glen and tangled brake, pursues a fawn,
Roused from its lair upon the mountain side;
And if awhile it should evade pursuit,
Low crouching in the copse, yet quests he back,
Searching unwearied, till he find the trace;
So Hector sought to baffle, but in vain,
The keen pursuit of Peleus' active son.
Oft as he sought the shelter of the gates
Beneath the well-built towers, if perhaps from there
His comrades' weapons might some aid afford;
So oft his foeman, with superior speed,
Would cut him off, and turn him to the plain.
He toward the city still essayed his flight;
And as in dreams, when one pursues in vain,
One seeks in vain to fly, the other seeks
As vainly to pursue; so could not now
Achilles reach, nor Hector quit, his foe.
Yet how should Hector now the doom of death
Have 'scaped, had not Apollo once again
And for the last time, to his rescue come,
And given him strength and suppleness of limb?
Then to the crowd Achilles with his head
Made sign that none at Hector should presume
To cast a spear, lest one might wound, and so
The greater glory obtain, while he himself
Must be contented with the second place.
But when the fourth time in their rapid course

The founts were reached, the Eternal Father hung
His golden scales aloft, and placed in each
The lots of doom, for great Achilles one,
For Hector one, and held them by the midst:
Down sank the scale, weighted with Hector's death,
Down to the shades, and Phoebus left his side.

HECTOR FACES ACHILLES

HOMER, *Iliad*, Book 22. 239-272 (Lattimore)

Athene, in the likeness of Hector's brother Deiphobus, encourages him to face Achilles.

"My brother, it is true our father and the lady our mother, taking
my knees in turn, and my companions about me, entreated
that I stay within, such was the terror upon all of them.
But the heart within me was worn away by hard sorrow for you.
But now let us go straight on and fight hard, let there be no sparing
of our spears, so that we can find out whether Achilleus
will kill us both and carry our bloody war spoils back
to the hollow ships, or will himself go down under your spear."
  So Athene spoke and led him on by beguilement.
Now as the two in their advance were come close together,
first of the two to speak was tall helm-glittering Hektor:
"Son of Peleus, I will no longer run from you, as before this
I fled three times around the great city of Priam, and dared not
stand to your onfall. But now my spirit in turn has driven me
to stand and face you. I must take you now, or I must be taken.
Come then, shall we swear before the gods? For these are the highest
who shall be witnesses and watch over our agreements.
Brutal as you are I will not defile you, if Zeus grants
to me that I can wear you out, and take the life from you.
But after I have stripped your glorious armor, Achilleus,
I will give your corpse back to the Achaians. Do you do likewise."
  Then looking darkly at him swift-footed Achilleus answered:

"Hektor, argue me no agreements. I cannot forgive you.
As there are no trustworthy oaths between men and lions,
nor wolves and lambs have spirit that can be brought to agree-
     ment
but forever these hold feelings of hate for each other,
so there can be no love between you and me, nor shall there be
oaths between us, but one or the other must fall before then
to glut with his blood Ares the god who fights under the shield's
     guard.
Remember every valor of yours, for now the need comes
hardest upon you to be a spearman and a bold warrior.
There shall be no more escape for you, but Pallas Athene
will kill you soon by my spear. You will pay in a lump for all those
sorrows of my companions you killed in your spear's fury."

~~~

ACHILLES AND HECTOR FIGHT

HOMER, *Iliad*, Book 22. 317-366 (Chase and Perry)

*They close in battle. When Hector calls for another spear
and discovers that his brother is not with him, he realizes the
deceit of Athene. Nevertheless, he draws his sword and
charges.*

He drew the sharp sword that hung great and mighty at his side,
and he crouched and darted like a high-soaring eagle that
swoops earthward through dark clouds to seize a tender lamb or
cowering hare. So Hector darted, brandishing his sharp sword.
Achilles rushed forward, and his heart was filled with a wild fury.
He held his fair and subtly fashioned shield before his breast and
his helmet nodded with its shining, four-ridged crest, and around
it waved the fair golden plumes which Hephaestus had set
thick upon it. As the evening star moves among the other stars in
the darkness of the night—it is the fairest star that stands in
heaven—such was the radiance from the sharp spear point
which Achilles brandished in his right hand with evil purpose
against godlike Hector as he looked at his fair flesh, to see where
it would be most yielding. All the rest of Hector's flesh was covered by the fair bronze armor he had taken when he slew mighty

Patroclus, but it showed through where the collarbones separate the neck from the shoulder, the hollow of the throat, where life's destruction is swiftest. There godlike Achilles struck him with his spear as he rushed forward, and the point pierced straight through his soft neck. But the bronze-weighted ash did not sever his windpipe, so that he might speak to him and answer him with words. He fell in the dust, and godlike Achilles boasted:"Hector, you thought to be safe in despoiling Patroclus and took no heed of me, who was far away, fool that you were. I, his far mightier comrade, was left behind, far off by the hollow ships, I who have loosed your knees. You the dogs and birds shall rend shamefully, but him the Achaeans shall give burial."

Weakly, Hector of the glancing helmet said to him: "I beg you by your life, by your knees and by your parents, do not let the dogs of the Achaeans devour me beside the ships but accept ample bronze and gold, the gifts my father and my queenly mother will give to you, and give my body back home, that the Trojans and the Trojans' wives may give to me in death the meed of fire."

Swift-footed Achilles looked at him scornfully and said: "Dog, beseech me neither by my knees nor by my parents. Would that my angry heart would let me cut off your raw flesh and eat it, for what you have done to me. There is none who could ward the dogs off from your head, not though they bring ten and twenty times your ransom and weigh it out here and promise yet more besides; not even though Dardanian Priam should bid them buy you for your weight in gold, not even so shall your queenly mother lay you in your bed and weep for you she bore herself, but the dogs and birds shall devour you entirely."

Then, as he died, Hector of the glancing helmet said to him: "Well do I know you as I look upon you; there was no hope that I could move you, for surely your heart is iron in your breast. Take care now lest I be cause of anger of the gods against you on that day when Paris and Phoebus Apollo shall slay you for all your valor at the Scaean gates."

As he said this, the end of death enwrapped him. His soul fled from his limbs and passed into the house of Death, bewailing its fate and forsaking manliness and youth. Even when he had died, godlike Achilles said to him: "Die, and my fate I will accept whenever Zeus and the other immortal gods desire to fulfill it."

~~~~~

ACHILLES MALTREATS THE BODY OF HECTOR

HOMER, *Iliad*, Book 22. 395-409 (Lang, Leaf, and Myers)

He devised foul entreatment of noble Hector. The tendons of both feet behind he slit from heel to ankle-joint, and thrust therethrough thongs of ox-hide, and bound him to his chariot, leaving his head to trail. And when he had mounted the chariot and lifted therein the famous armor, he lashed his horses to speed, and they eagerly flew on. And dust rose around him that was dragged, and his dark hair flowed loose on either side, and in the dust lay all his once fair head, for now had Zeus given him over to his foes to entreat foully in his own native land.

Thus was his head all grimed with dust. But his mother when she beheld her son, tore her hair and cast far from her her shining veil, and cried aloud with an exceeding bitter cry. And piteously moaned his father, and around them the folk fell to crying and moaning throughout the town.

~~~~~

THE WILD GRIEF OF ACHILLES

HOMER, *Iliad*, Book 23. 17-23 (Lattimore)

Achilles violates the code of civilized warfare.

Peleus' son led the thronging chant of their lamentation,
and laid his manslaughtering hands over the chest of his dear
  friend:
"Good-bye, Patroklos. I hail you even in the house of the death
  god.
All that I promised you in time past I am accomplishing,
that I would drag Hektor here and give him to the dogs to feed
  on

raw, and before your burning pyre to behead twelve glorious
children of the Trojans for my anger over your slaying."

THE SHADE OF PATROCLUS

HOMER, *Iliad*, Book 23. 60-84 (Pope)

Patroclus demands burial and foretells Achilles' death.

But great Pelides, stretch'd along the shore,
Where dash'd on rocks the broken billows roar,
Lies inly groaning; while on either hand
The martial Myrmidons confusedly stand:
Along the grass his languid members fall,
Tired with his chase around the Trojan wall;
Hush'd by the murmurs of the rolling deep,
At length he sinks in the soft arms of sleep.
When lo! the shade before his closing eyes
Of sad Patroclus rose, or seem'd to rise:
In the same robe he living wore, he came,
In stature, voice, and pleasing look, the same.
The form familiar hover'd o'er his head,
And, "Sleeps Achilles" (thus the phantom said),
"Sleeps my Achilles, his Patroclus dead?
Living, I seem'd his dearest, tenderest care,
But now forgot, I wander in the air:
Let my pale corse the rites of burial know,
And give me entrance in the realms below;
Till then, the spirit finds no resting-place,
But here and there th' unbodied spectres chase
The vagrant dead around the dark abode,
Forbid to cross th' irremeable flood.
Now give thy hand; for to the farther shore
When once we pass, the soul returns no more.
When once the last funereal flames ascend,
No more shall meet Achilles and his friend;
No more our thoughts to those we love make known,
Or quit the dearest to converse alone.
Me Fate has sever'd from the sons of earth,

The Fate foredoom'd that waited from my birth:
Thee too it waits; before the Trojan wall
Ev'n great and godlike thou art doom'd to fall.
Hear then; and as in Fate and love we join,
Ah, suffer that my bones may rest with thine!
Together have we liv'd, together bred,
One house receiv'd us, and one table fed!
That golden urn thy goddess-mother gave,
May mix our ashes in one common grave."

THE GODS INTERVENE

HOMER, *Iliad*, Book 24. 31-45 (Lattimore)

Achilles holds funeral games for Patroclus and in his rage continues to mistreat the body of Hector until the gods are moved to act.

But now, as it was the twelfth dawn after the death of Hektor,
Phoibos Apollo spoke his word out among the immortals:
"You are hard, you gods, and destructive. Now did not Hektor
burn thigh pieces of oxen and unblemished goats in your honour?
Now you cannot bring yourselves to save him, though he is only
a corpse, for his wife to look upon, his child and his mother
and Priam his father, and his people, who presently thereafter
would burn his body in the fire and give him his rites of burial.
No, you gods; your desire is to help this cursed Achilleus
within whose breast there are no feelings of justice, nor can
his mind be bent, but his purposes are fierce, like a lion
who when he has given way to his own great strength and his haughty
spirit, goes among the flocks of men, to devour them.
So Achilleus has destroyed pity, and there is not in him
any shame; which does much harm to men but profits them also."

PRIAM GOES TO RANSOM
THE BODY OF HECTOR

HOMER, *Iliad*, Book 24. 477-533 (Derby)

Thetis is instructed to tell Achilles of the gods' anger. The messenger Iris tells Priam to ransom the body of Hector and Hermes takes him to the hut of Achilles.

Great Priam enter'd, unperceived of all;
And standing by Achilles, with his arms
Embraced his knees, and kissed those fearful hands.
Blood-stained, which many of his sons had slain.
As when a man, by cruel fate pursued,
In his own land hath shed another's blood,
And flying, seeks beneath some wealthy house
A foreign refuge; wond'ring, all behold:
On godlike Priam so with wonder gazed
Achilles; wonder seized th' attendants all,
And one to other looked; then Priam thus
To Peleus' son his suppliant speech addressed:
"Think, great Achilles, rival of the Gods,
Upon thy father, even as I myself
Upon the threshold of unjoyous age:
And perhaps he, from them that dwell around
May suffer wrong, with no protector near
To give him aid; yet he, rejoicing, knows
That you still live; and day by day may hope
To see his son returning safe from Troy;
While I, all hapless, that have many sons,
The best and bravest through the breadth of Troy,
Begotten, think that none are left me now.
Fifty there were, when came the sons of Greece;
Nineteen the offspring of a single womb;
The rest, the women of my household bore.
Of these have many by relentless Mars
Been laid in dust; but he, my only one,
The city's and his brethren's sole defense,

He, bravely fighting in his country's cause,
Hector, but lately by thy hand has fallen:
On his behalf I venture to approach
The Grecian ships; for his release to you
To make my prayer, and priceless ransom pay.
Then you, Achilles, reverence the Gods;
And, for your father's sake, look pitying down
On me, more needing pity; since I bear
Such grief as never man on earth hath borne,
Who stoop to kiss the hand that slew my son."

    Thus as he spoke, within Achilles' breast
Fond memory of his father rose; he touched
The old man's hand, and gently put him by;
Then wept they both, by various mem'ries stirred:
One, prostrate at Achilles' feet, bewailed
His warrior son; Achilles for his sire,
And for Patroclus wept, his comrade dear;
And through the house their weeping loud was heard.
But when Achilles had indulged his grief,
And eased the yearning of his heart and limbs,
He rose, and with his hand the aged sire
He raised, and thus with gentle words addressed:
    "Alas, what sorrows, poor old man, are yours!
How could you venture to the Grecian ships
Alone, and to the presence of the man
Whose hand has slain so many of your sons,
Many and brave? an iron heart is yours!
But sit you on this seat; and in our hearts,
Though filled with grief, let us that grief suppress;
For woeful lamentation nought avails.
Such is the thread the Gods for mortals spin,
To live in woe, while they from cares are free.
Two coffers lie beside the door of Jove,
With gifts for man: one good, the other ill;
To whom from each the Lord of lightning gives,
Him sometimes evil, sometimes good befalls;
To whom the ill alone, him foul disgrace
And grinding misery o'er the earth pursue:
By God and man alike despised he roams."

~~~~~~

ACHILLES ACCEPTS THE RANSOM

HOMER, *Iliad*, Book 24. 572-595 (Lattimore)

Achilles accepts the ransom and places the body on the wagon, thereby redeeming himself, although he knows that his own death will soon follow.

The son of Peleus bounded to the door of the house like a lion,
nor went alone, but the two henchmen followed attending,
the hero Automedon and Alkimos, those whom Achilleus
honored beyond all companions after Patroklos dead. These two
now set free from under the yoke the mules and the horses,
and led inside the herald, the old king's crier, and gave him
a chair to sit in, then from the smooth-polished mule wagon
lifted out the innumerable spoils for the head of Hektor,
but left inside it two great cloaks and a finespun tunic
to shroud the corpse in when they carried him home. Then Achilleus
called out to his serving-maids to wash the body and anoint it
all over; but take it first aside, since otherwise Priam
might see his son and in the heart's sorrow not hold in his anger
at the sight, and the deep heart in Achilleus be shaken to anger;
that he might not kill Priam and be guilty before the god's orders.
Then when the serving-maids had washed the corpse and anointed it
with olive oil, they threw a fair great cloak and a tunic
about him, and Achilleus himself lifted him and laid him
on a litter, and his friends helped him lift it to the smooth-polished
mule wagon. He groaned then, and called by name on his beloved companion:
"Be not angry with me, Patroklos, if you discover,
though you be in the house of Hades, that I gave back great Hektor
to his loved father, for the ransom he gave me was not unworthy.
I will give you your share of the spoils, as much as is fitting."

ODYSSEUS MEETS ACHILLES
IN THE UNDERWORLD

HOMER, *Odyssey*, Book 11. 471-491 (Palmer)

*Achilles was killed at Troy by Paris and Apollo. Later Odys-
seus meets him in the Underworld.*

And now there came the spirit of Achilles, son of Peleus, and of
Patroclus too, of gallant Antilochus, and of Ajax who was first
in beauty and in stature of all the Danaans after the gallant son
of Peleus. But the spirit of swift-footed Aeacides knew me, and
sorrowfully said in winged words:

"High-born son of Laertes, ready Odysseus, rash as you are,
what will you undertake more desperate than this! How dared
you come down hither to the house of Hades, where dwell the
senseless dead, specters of toil-worn men?"

So he spoke, and answering him said I: "Achilles, son of
Peleus, foremost of the Achaeans, I came for consultation with
Teiresias, hoping that he might give advice for reaching rugged
Ithaca. I have not yet been near Achaea nor once set foot upon
my land, but have had constant trouble; while as for you, Achilles,
no man was in the past more fortunate, nor in the future shall be;
for formerly, during your life, we Argives gave you equal honor
with the gods, and now you are a mighty lord among the dead,
when here. Then do not grieve at having died, Achilles."

So I spoke, and straightway answering me said he: "Mock not
at death, glorious Odysseus. Better to be the hireling of a
stranger, and serve a man of mean estate whose living is but small,
than be the ruler over all these dead and gone."

GREEK LEADERS AT TROY

HOMER, *Iliad*, Book 3. 139-244 (Derby)

Helen, summoned by Iris to see the single combat between Paris and Menelaus, describes the Greek leaders to the Trojan elders.

Thus as she spoke, in Helen's breast arose
Fond recollection of her former Lord,
Her home, and parents; o'er her head she threw
A snowy veil; and shedding tender tears
She issued forth, not unaccompanied;
For with her went fair Aethra, Pittheus' child,
And stag-eyed Clymene, her maidens twain.
They quickly at the Scaean gate arrived.
   Attending there on aged Priam, sat
The Elders of the city; Panthous,
And Lampus, and Thymaetes; Clytius,
Bold Icetaon, and Ucalegon,
With sage Antenor, wise in council both:
All these were gathered at the Scaean gate;
By age exempt from war, but in discourse
Abundant, as the cricket, that on high
From topmost boughs of forest tree sends forth
His delicate music; so on Ilium's towers
Sat the sage chiefs and councillors of Troy.
Helen they saw, as to the tower she came;
And, " 'tis no marvel," one to other said,
"The valiant Trojans and the well-greaved Greeks
For beauty such as this should long endure
The toils of war; for goddess-like she seems;
And yet, despite her beauty, let her go,
Nor bring on us and on our sons a curse."
   Thus they; but aged Priam Helen called:
"Come here, my child, and sitting by my side,
From whence you can discern your former Lord,
His kindred, and your friends (not you I blame,

But to the Gods I owe this woeful war),
Tell me the name of yonder mighty chief
Among the Greeks a warrior brave and strong:
Others in height surpass him; but my eyes
A form so noble never yet beheld,
Nor so august; he moves, a King indeed!"
　To whom in answer, Helen, heavenly fair:
"With reverence, dearest father, and with shame
I look on thee: oh would that I had died
That day when hither with your son I came,
And left my husband, friends, and darling child,
And all the loved companions of my youth:
That I died not, with grief I pine away.
But to your question: I will tell you true;
Yon chief is Agamemnon, Atreus' son,
Wide-reigning, mighty monarch, ruler good,
And valiant warrior; in my husband's name,
Lost as I am, I called him brother once."
　She spoke: the old man admiring gazed, and cried,
"Oh blessed Atrides, child of happy fate,
Favored of Heav'n! how many noble Greeks
Obey thy rule! In vine-clad Phrygia once
I saw the hosts of Phrygian warriors wheel
Their rapid steeds; and with them, all the bands
Of Otreus, and of Mygdon, godlike King,
Who lay encamped beside Sangarius' stream:
I too with them was numbered, in the day
When met them in the field the Amazons,
The woman-warriors; but their forces all
Reached not the number of the keen-eyed Greeks."
　Ulysses next the old man saw, and asked,
"Tell me again, dear child, who this may be,
In stature less than Atreus' royal son,
But broader-shouldered, and of ampler chest.
His arms are laid upon the fertile plain,
But he himself is moving through the ranks,
Inspecting, like a full-fleeced ram, that moves
Majestic through a flock of snow-white ewes."
　To whom Jove's offspring, Helen, thus replied:
"The wise Ulysses that, Laertes' son:
Though bred in rugged Ithaca, yet versed
In ev'ry stratagem, and deep device."

"O woman," then the sage Antenor said,
"Of these your words I can the truth avouch;
For hither when on your account to treat,
Brave Menelaus and Ulysses came,
I lodged them in my house, and loved them both,
And studied well the form and mind of each.
As they with Trojans mixed in social guise,
When both were standing, o'er his comrade high
With broad-set shoulders Menelaus stood;
Seated, Ulysses was the nobler form:
Then, in the great Assembly, when to all
Their public speech and argument they framed,
In fluent language Menelaus spoke,
In words though few, yet clear; though young in years,
No wordy babbler, wasteful of his speech:
But when the skilled Ulysses rose to speak,
With down-cast visage would he stand, his eyes
Bent on the ground; the staff he bore, neither back
He waved, nor forward, but like one untaught,
He held it motionless; who only saw
Would say that he was mad, or void of sense:
But when his chest its deep-toned voice sent forth,
With words that fell like flakes of wintry snow,
No mortal with Ulysses could compare:
Then little recked we of his outward show."
    At sight of Ajax next the old man enquired;
"Who is that other warrior, brave and strong,
Towering o'er all with head and shoulders broad?"
    To whom, in answer, Helen, heavenly fair:
"Gigantic Ajax that, the prop of Greece;
And by his side Idomeneus of Crete
Stands godlike, circled round by Cretan chiefs.
The warlike Menelaus welcomed him
Oft in our palace, when from Crete he came.
Now all the other keen-eyed Greeks I see,
Whom once I knew, and now could call by name;
But two I miss, two captains of the host,
My own two brethren, and my mother's sons,
Castor and Pollux; Castor, horseman bold,
Pollux, unmatched in pugilistic skill.
In Lacedaemon have they stayed behind?
Or can it be, in ocean-going ships

That they have come indeed, but shun to join
The fight of warriors, fearful of the shame,
And deep disgrace that on my name attend?"
Thus she; unconscious that in Sparta they,
Their native land, beneath the sod were laid.

~~~~~

HELEN

HOMER, *Iliad*, Book 6. 344-358 (Chase and Perry)

Helen speaks to Hector of herself and Paris.

Helen addressed Hector with humble words: "Brother of mine, horrible, malicious vixen that I am, would that on the day when first my mother bore me, some evil blast of a storm had come to bear me away to the mountain or to the billow of the resounding sea where the waves would have swept me away before these things came to pass. But since the gods so decreed these things, would that I had been the wife of a better man, who knew the meaning of disgrace and men's numerous reproaches. But this man's heart is not firm now nor shall it ever be hereafter. Therefore I think that he shall reap its fruits. Come now, enter and sit down upon this chair, my brother, since weariness has fallen most upon your heart because of my shamelessness and Alexander's folly. Upon us both Zeus sent an evil fate, that we should make matter for song for men who shall be hereafter."

~~~~~

HELEN

EURIPIDES, *Helen*, 18-59 (Coleridge, revised)

Euripides puts into the mouth of Helen an account of her adventures which exonerates her. Perhaps the fact that there were shrines in Argos where Helen was worshipped as a goddess accounts for this variant from the usual story.

My fatherland, Sparta, is not unknown to fame, or my sire Tyndareus; for a legend tells how Zeus winged his way to my mother Leda's breast, in the semblance of a swan, and thus as he fled from an eagle's pursuit, achieved by guile his amorous purpose, if this tale be true. My name is Helen, and I will now recount the sorrows I have suffered. To a hollow vale on Ida came three goddesses to Paris, for beauty's prize contending, Hera and Cypris, and the virgin child of Zeus, eager to secure his verdict on their loveliness. Now Cypris held out my beauty,—if anything so wretched deserves that name,—as a bride before the eyes of Paris, saying he should marry me; and so she won the day, wherefore the shepherd of Ida left his farm, and came to Sparta, thinking to win me for his bride. But Hera, indignant at not defeating the goddesses, brought to nothing my marriage with Paris, and gave to Priam's princely son not Helen, but a phantom endowed with life, that she made in my image out of the breath of heaven; and Paris thought that I was his, although I never was,—an idle fancy! Moreover, the counsels of Zeus added further troubles to these; for upon the land of Hellas and the hapless Phrygians he brought a war, that he might lighten mother-earth of her myriad hosts of men, and to the bravest of the sons of Hellas bring renown. So I was set up as a prize for all the chivalry of Hellas, to test the might of Phrygia, yet not I, but my name alone; for Hermes caught me up in the embracing air, and veiled me in a cloud; for Zeus was not unmindful of me; and he set me down here in the house of Proteus, judging him to be the most virtuous of all mankind; that so I might preserve my marriage with Menelaus free from taint. Here then I abide, while my hapless lord has gathered an army, and is setting out for the towers of Ilium to track and recover me. And there by Scamander's streams has many a life breathed out its last, and all for me; and I, that have endured all this, am accursed, and seem to have embroiled all Hellas in a mighty war by proving a traitress to my husband. Why, then, do I prolong my life? Because I heard Hermes declare, that I should yet again make my home on Sparta's glorious soil, with my lord,—for Hermes knew I never went to Ilium,—that so I might never submit to any other's wooing.

HELEN AND MENELAUS

HOMER, *Odyssey*, Book 4. 219-289 (Fitzgerald)

Helen and Menelaus, happily reunited after the Trojan War, entertain Telemachus at Sparta.

But now it entered Helen's mind
to drop into the wine that they were drinking
an anodyne, mild magic of forgetfulness.
Whoever drank this mixture in the wine bowl
would be incapable of tears that day—
though he should lose mother and father both,
or see, with his own eyes, a son or brother
mauled by weapons of bronze at his own gate.
The opiate of Zeus's daughter bore
this canny power. It had been supplied her
by Polydamna, mistress of Lord Thon,
in Egypt, where the rich plantations grow
herbs of all kinds, maleficent and healthful;
and no one else knows medicine as they do,
Egyptian heirs of Paian, the healing god.
She drugged the wine, then, had it served, and said—
taking again her part in the conversation—
"O Menelaos, Atreus' royal son,
and you that are great heroes' sons, you know
how Zeus gives all of us in turn
good luck and bad luck, being all powerful.
So take refreshment, take your ease in hall,
and cheer the time with stories. I'll begin.
Not that I think of naming, far less telling,
every feat of that rugged man, Odysseus,
but here is something that he dared to do
at Troy, where you Akhaians endured the war.
He had, first, given himself an outrageous beating
and thrown some rags on—like a household slave—
then slipped into that city of wide lanes
among his enemies. So changed, he looked

as never before upon the Akhaian beachhead,
but like a beggar, merged in the townspeople;
and no one there remarked him. But I knew him—
even as he was, I knew him,
and questioned him. How shrewdly he put me off!
But in the end I bathed him and anointed him,
put a fresh cloak around him, and swore an oath
not to give him away as Odysseus to the Trojans,
till he got back to camp where the long ships lay.
He spoke up then, and told me
all about the Akhaians, and their plans—
then sworded many Trojans through the body
on his way out with what he learned of theirs.
The Trojan women raised a cry—but my heart
sang—for I had come round, long before,
to dreams of sailing home, and I repented
the mad day Aphrodite
drew me away from my dear fatherland,
forsaking all—child, bridal bed, and husband—
a man without defect in form or mind."

Replied the red-haired captain, Menelaos:

"An excellent tale, my dear, and most becoming.
In my life I have met, in many countries,
foresight and wit in many first rate men,
but never have I seen one like Odysseus
for steadiness and a stout heart. Here, for instance,
is what he did—had the cold nerve to do—
inside the hollow horse, where we were waiting,
picked men all of us, for the Trojan slaughter,
when all of a sudden, you came by—I dare say
drawn by some superhuman
power that planned an exploit for the Trojans;
and Deïphobos, that handsome man, came with you.
Three times you walked around it, petting it everywhere,
and called by name the flower of our fighters,
making your voice sound like their wives, calling.
Diomêdês and I crouched in the center
along with Odysseus; we could hear you plainly;
and listening, we two were swept
by waves of longing—to reply, or go.

Odysseus fought us down, despite our craving,
and all the Akhaians kept their lips shut tight,
all but Antiklos. Desire moved his throat
to hail you, but Odysseus' great hands clamped
over his jaws, and held. So he saved us all,
till Pallas Athena led you away at last."

HELEN AND MENELAUS

HOMER, *Odyssey*, Book 4. 561-569 (Morris)

Proteus prophesies immortality for Menelaus and Helen.

"But, Zeus-cherished Menelaus, to thee it shall not come
In the horse-kind land of Argos to meet thy death and doom.
But unto the fields Elysian and the wide world's utmost end,
Where dwells tawny Rhadamanthus, the Deathless thee shall send,
Wherein are the softest life-days that men may ever gain;
No snow and no ill weather, nor any drift of rain;
But Ocean ever wafteth the wind of the shrilly west,
On menfolk ever breathing, to give them might and rest;
Because thou hast wedded Helen, and God's son art said to be."

IPHIGENEIA

AESCHYLUS, *Agamemnon*, 183-253 (Lattimore)

*By the command of the seer Calchas, Agamemnon sacrifices
Iphigeneia; this action is one of the causes of Clytemnestra's
subsequent revenge.*

On that day the elder king
of the Achaean ships, no more
strict against the prophet's word,
turned with the crosswinds of fortune,
when no ship sailed, no pail was full,

and the Achaean people sulked
fast against the shore at Aulis
facing Chalcis, where the tides ebb and surge:

and winds blew from the Strymon, bearing
sick idleness, ships tied fast, and hunger,
distraction of the mind, carelessness
for hull and cable;
with time's length bent to double measure
by delay crumbled the flower and pride
of Argos. Then against the bitter wind
the seer's voice clashed out
another medicine
more hateful yet, and spoke of Artemis, so that the kings
dashed their staves to the ground and could not hold their tears.

The elder lord spoke aloud before them:
"My fate is angry if I disobey these,
but angry if I slaughter
this child, the beauty of my house,
with maiden blood shed staining
these father's hands beside the altar.
What of these things goes now without disaster?
How shall I fail my ships
and lose my faith of battle?
For them to urge such sacrifice of innocent blood
angrily, for their wrath is great—it is right. May all be well yet."

But when necessity's yoke was put upon him
he changed, and from the heart the breath came bitter
and sacrilegious, utterly infidel,
to warp a will now to be stopped at nothing.
The sickening in men's minds, tough,
reckless in fresh cruelty brings daring. He endured then
to sacrifice his daughter
to stay the strength of war waged for a woman,
first offering for the ships' sake.

Her supplications and her cries of father
were nothing, nor the child's lamentation
to kings passioned for battle.
The father prayed, called to his men to lift her

with strength of hand swept in her robes aloft
and prone above the altar, as you might lift
a goat for sacrifice, with guards
against the lips' sweet edge, to check
the curse cried on the house of Atreus
by force of bit and speech drowned in strength.

Pouring then to the ground her saffron mantle
she struck the sacrificers with
the eyes' arrows of pity,
lovely as in a painted scene, and striving
to speak—as many times
at the kind festive table of her father
she had sung, and in the clear voice of a stainless maiden
with love had graced the song
of worship when the third cup was poured.

What happened next I saw not, neither speak it.
The crafts of Calchas fail not of outcome.
Justice so moves that those only learn
who suffer: and the future
you shall know when it has come; before then, forget it.
It is grief too soon given.

AGAMEMNON AND CLYTEMNESTRA

HOMER, *Odyssey*, Book 1. 35-43 (Fitzgerald)

*Homer used the story of the death of Agamemnon to provide
contrasts with the return of Odysseus. The knowledge or bias
of different tellers of this story makes for interesting variety.
The following is Zeus's version.*

In the bright hall of Zeus upon Olympos
the other gods were all at home, and Zeus,
the father of gods and men, made conversation.
For he had meditated on Aigisthos, dead
by the hand of Agamemnon's son, Orestes,
and spoke his thought aloud before them all:

"My word, how mortals take the gods to task!
All their afflictions come from us, we hear.
And what of their own failings? Greed and folly
double the suffering in the lot of man.
See how Aigisthos, for his double portion,
stole Agamemnon's wife and killed the soldier
on his homecoming day. And yet Aigisthos
knew that his own doom lay in this. We gods
had warned him, sent down Hermes Argeiphontes,
our most observant courier, to say:
'Don't kill the man, don't touch his wife,
or face a reckoning with Orestes
the day he comes of age and wants his patrimony.'
Friendly advice—but would Aigisthos take it?
Now he has paid the reckoning in full."

AGAMEMNON AND CLYTEMNESTRA

HOMER, *Odyssey*, Book 3. 247-312 (Fitzgerald)

Telemachus asks Nestor how Agamemnon died.

"Nestor, Neleus' son, true sage, say how
did the Lord of the Great Plains, Agamemnon, die?
What was the trick Aigisthos used
to kill the better man? And Menelaos,
where was he? Not at Argos in Akhaia,
but blown off course, held up in some far country,
is that what gave the killer nerve to strike?"

Lord Nestor of Gerenia made answer:

"Well, now, my son, I'll tell you the whole story.
You know, yourself, what would have come to pass
if red-haired Menelaos, back from Troy,
had caught Aigisthos in that house alive.
There would have been no burial mound for him,
but dogs and carrion birds to huddle on him
in the fields beyond the wall, and not a soul

bewailing him, for the great wrong he committed.
While we were hard-pressed in the war at Troy
he stayed safe inland in the grazing country,
making light talk to win Agamemnon's queen.
But the Lady Klytaimnestra, in the first days,
rebuffed him, being faithful still;
then, too, she had at hand as her companion
a minstrel Agamemnon left attending her,
charged with her care, when he took ship for Troy.
Then came the fated hour when she gave in.
Her lover tricked the poet and marooned him
on a bare island for the seabirds' picking,
and took her home, as he and she desired.
Many thighbones he burned on the gods' altars
and many a woven and golden ornament
hung to bedeck them, in his satisfaction;
he had not thought life held such glory for him.

Now Menelaos and I sailed home together
on friendly terms, from Troy,
but when we came off Sunion Point in Attika,
the ships still running free, Onetor's son
Phrontis, the steersman of Menelaos' ship,
fell over with a death grip on the tiller:
some unseen arrow from Apollo hit him.
No man handled a ship better than he did
in a high wind and sea, so Menelaos
put down his longing to get on, and landed
to give this man full honor in funeral.
His own luck turned then. Out on the winedark sea
in the murmuring hulls again, he made Cape Malea,
but Zeus who views the wide world sent a gloom
over the ocean, and a howling gale
came on with seas increasing, mountainous,
parting the ships and driving half toward Krete
where the Kydonians live by Iardanos river.
Off Gortyn's coastline in the misty sea there
a reef, a razorback, cuts through the water,
and every westerly piles up a pounding
surf along the left side, going toward Phaistos—
big seas buffeted back by the narrow stone.
They were blown here, and fought in vain for sea room;

the ships kept going in to their destruction,
slammed on the reef. The crews were saved. But now
those five that weathered it got off to southward,
taken by wind and current on to Egypt;
and there Menelaos stayed. He made a fortune
in sea traffic among those distant races,
but while he did so, the foul crime was planned
and carried out in Argos by Aigisthos,
who ruled over golden Mykenai seven years.
Seven long years, with Agamemnon dead,
he held the people down, before the vengeance.
But in the eighth year, back from exile in Attika,
Orestes killed the snake who killed his father.
He gave his hateful mother and her soft man
a tomb together, and proclaimed the funeral day
a festal day for all the Argive people.
That day Lord Menelaos of the great war cry
made port with all the gold his ships could carry."

AGAMEMNON AND CLYTEMNESTRA

HOMER, *Odyssey*, Book 4. 512-537 (Fitzgerald)

Proteus' account to Menelaus.

"Meanwhile your brother left that doom astern
in his decked ships—the Lady Hera saved him;
but as he came round Malea
a fresh squall caught him, bearing him away
over the cold sea, groaning in disgust,
to the Land's End of Argos, where Thyestes
lived in the days of old, and then his son,
Aigisthos. Now, again, return seemed easy:
the high gods wound the wind into the east,
and back he sailed, this time to his own coast.
He went ashore and kissed the earth in joy,
hot tears blinding his eyes at sight of home.
But there were eyes that watched him from a height—
a lookout, paid two bars of gold to keep

vigil the year round for Aigisthos' sake,
that he should be forewarned, and Agamemnon's
furious valor sleep unroused.
Now this man with his news ran to the tyrant,
who made his crooked arrangements in a flash,
stationed picked men at arms, a score of men
in hiding; set a feast in the next room;
then he went out with chariots and horses
to hail the king and welcome him to evil.
He led him in to banquet, all serene,
and killed him, like an ox felled at the trough;
and not a man of either company
survived that ambush in Aigisthos' house.''

AGAMEMNON SPEAKS TO ODYSSEUS

HOMER, *Odyssey*, Book 11. 387-434 (Fitzgerald)

Agamemnon, in the Underworld, gives his account.

"The soul of Agamemnon, son of Atreus,
came before me, somber in the gloom,
and others gathered round, all who were with him
when death and doom struck in Aigisthos' hall.
Sipping the black blood, the tall shade perceived me,
and cried out sharply, breaking into tears;
then tried to stretch his hands toward me, but could not,
being bereft of all the reach and power
he once felt in the great torque of his arms.
Gazing at him, and stirred, I wept for pity,
and spoke across to him:

                                    'O son of Atreus,
illustrious Lord Marshal, Agamemnon,
what was the doom that brought you low in death?
Were you at sea, aboard ship, and Poseidon
blew up a wicked squall to send you under,
or were you cattle-raiding on the mainland

or in a fight for some strongpoint, or women,
when the foe hit you to your mortal hurt?'

But he replied at once:

'Son of Laertes,
Odysseus, master of land ways and sea ways,
neither did I go down with some good ship
in any gale Poseidon blew, nor die
upon the mainland, hurt by foes in battle.
It was Aigisthos who designed my death,
he and my heartless wife, and killed me, after
feeding me, like an ox felled at the trough.
That was my miserable end—and with me
my fellows butchered, like so many swine
killed for some troop, or feast, or wedding banquet
in a great landholder's household. In your day
you have seen men, and hundreds, die in war,
in the bloody press, or downed in single combat,
but these were murders you would catch your breath at:
think of us fallen, all our throats cut, winebowl
brimming, tables laden on every side,
while blood ran smoking over the whole floor.
In my extremity I heard Kassandra,
Priam's daughter, piteously crying
as the traitress Klytaimnestra made to kill her
along with me. I heaved up from the ground
and got my hands around the blade, but she
eluded me, that whore. Nor would she close
my two eyes as my soul swam to the underworld
or shut my lips. There is no being more fell,
more bestial than a wife in such an action,
and what an action that one planned!
The murder of her husband and her lord.
Great god, I thought my children and my slaves
at least would give me welcome. But that woman,
plotting a thing so low, defiled herself
and all her sex, all women yet to come,
even those few who may be virtuous.' "

AGAMEMNON TALKS TO AMPHIMEDON

HOMER, *Odyssey*, Book 24. 191-202 (Fitzgerald)

In the Underworld Agamemnon talks with one of the slain suitors of Penelope.

But Agamemnon's

tall shade when he heard this cried aloud:
"O fortunate Odysseus, master mariner
and soldier, blessed son of old Laertes!
The girl you brought home made a valiant wife!
True to her husband's honor and her own,
Penelope, Ikarios' faithful daughter!
The very gods themselves will sing her story
for men on earth—mistress of her own heart,
Penelope!
Tyndareus' daughter waited, too—how differently!
Klytaimnestra, the adulteress,
waited to stab her lord and king. That song
will be forever hateful. A bad name
she gave to womankind, even the best."

AEGISTHUS

AESCHYLUS, *Agamemnon*, 1583-1611 (Morshead)

Aegisthus claims credit for the murder of Agamemnon and recounts the family history leading up to it.

"Dawn of the day of rightful vengeance, hail!
I dare at length aver that gods above
Have care of men and heed of earthly wrongs.
I, I who stand and thus exult to see
This man lie wound in robes the Furies wove,

Slain in the requital of his father's craft.
Take ye the truth, that Atreus, this man's sire,
The lord and monarch of this land of old,
Held with my sire Thyestes deep dispute,
Brother with brother, for the prize of sway,
And drove him from his home to banishment.
Thereafter, the lorn exile homeward stole
And clung a suppliant to the hearth divine,
And for himself won this immunity—
Not with his own blood to defile the land
That gave him birth. But Atreus, godless sire
Of him who here lies dead, this welcome planned—
With zeal that was not love he feigned to hold
In loyal joy a day of festal cheer,
And bade my father to his board, and set
Before him flesh that was his children once.
First, sitting at the upper board alone,
He hid the fingers and the feet, but gave
The rest—and readily Thyestes took
What to his ignorance no semblance wore
Of human flesh, and ate: behold what curse
That eating brought upon our race and name!
For when he knew what all unhallowed thing
He thus had wrought, with horror's bitter cry
Back-starting, spewing forth the fragments foul,
On Pelops' house a deadly curse he spoke—
As darkly as I spurn this damned food,
So perish all the race of Pleisthenes!
Thus by that curse fell he whom here ye see,
And I—who else?—this murder wove and planned:
For me, an infant yet in swaddling bands,
Of the three children youngest, Atreus sent
To banishment by my sad father's side:
But Justice brought me home once more, grown now
To manhood's years; and stranger tho' I was,
My right hand reached unto the chieftain's life,
Plotting and planning all that malice bade.
And death itself were honor now to me,
Beholding him in Justice' ambush taken."

AIAS

SOPHOCLES, *Ajax*, 815-865 (Trevelyan)

Aias, defeated by Odysseus in the contest for the arms of Achilles, went mad and killed a flock of sheep, thinking them his Greek enemies. With the return of sanity he prepares to commit suicide.

"The slayer stands so that his edge may cleave
Most surely (if there be leisure for such thought),
Being the gift of Hector, of all friends
Most unloved, and most hateful to my sight.
Then it is planted in Troy's hostile soil,
New-sharpened on the iron-biting whet.
And heedfully have I planted it, that so
With a swift death it prove to me most kind.
Thus have I made all ready. Next be thou
The first, O Zeus, to aid me, as is right.
It is no mighty boon that I shall crave.
Send some announcer of the evil news
To Teucer, that he first may lift me up,
When I have fallen upon this reeking sword,
Lest ere he come some enemy should espy me
And cast me forth to dogs and birds a prey.
This, O Zeus, I entreat thee, and likewise call
On Hermes, guide to the underworld, to lay me
Asleep without a struggle, at one swift bound,
When I have thrust my heart through with this sword.
Next I call on those maidens ever-living
And ever watchful of all human miseries,
The dread swift-striding Erinyes, that they mark
How by the Atreidae I have been destroyed:
And these vile men by a vile doom utterly
May they cut off, even as they see me here.
Come, O ye swift avenging Erinyes,
Spare not, touch with affliction the whole host.
And thou, whose chariot mounts up the steep sky,

Thou Sun, when on the land where I was born
Thou shalt look down, check thy gold-spangled rein,
And announce my disasters and my doom
To my aged sire and her who nurtured me.
She, woeful woman, when she hears these tidings
Will wail out a loud dirge through all the town.
But I waste labor with this idle moan.
The act must now be done, and that with speed.
O Death, Death, come now and look upon me.—
No, 'tis there I shall meet and speak to thee.
But thee, bright daylight which I now behold,
And Helios in his chariot I accost
For this last time of all, and then no more.
O sunlight! O thou hallowed soil, my own
Salamis, stablished seat of my sire's hearth,
And famous Athens, with thy kindred race,
And you, ye springs and streams, and Trojan plains,
Farewell, all ye who have sustained my life.
This is the last word Ajax speaks to you.
All else in Hades to the dead will I say."

CASTOR AND POLYDEUKES

PINDAR, *Nemean,* 10. 55-90 (Lattimore)

In the Iliad *Homer portrays Castor and Polydeukes as mortals; in Roman times they became the gods of seafarers. Pindar, however, tells the myth in its most popular form, that of alternating divinity.*

They with life changing to and fro dwell one day beside their
    father beloved,
Zeus, and the day that follows under the secret places of the earth
    in the hollows of Therapne.
The destiny they fulfil is the same; such
was the choice of Polydeukes rather than be god indeed
and dwell in the sky, when Kastor fell in the fighting,
whom Idas, angered over some driving of cattle, stabbed with the
    bronze spearhead.

Lynkeus, staring from Taygetos, saw them hiding
in an oak tree, for beyond all mortals else his eye
was sharpest. And in ravening speed of their feet
they came down and devised at once a monstrous act,
and terribly did these sons of Aphareus suffer at the hands of Zeus;
    for straightway
Leda's son, Polydeukes, came pursuing, and they stood at bay by
    their father's tomb.

Ripping aloft the dedication of death, the smoothed gravestone,
they cast it at Polydeukes' chest, but availed not to shatter
nor drive him back. He, leaping with quick spear,
buried the bronze in Lynkeus' side,
and Zeus on Idas crashed the flame of the smoking thunderbolt.
These two burned, forlorn. Men find strife bitter when they under-
    take those who are stronger.

With speed Tyndareus' son ran back to his mighty brother,
and found him not dead, drawing yet some shuddering breath of
    life.
In grief, letting fall hot tears,
he cried aloud: "Kronion, my father, what release
shall there be from sorrow? Grant death also to me with this man,
    my lord.
Bereft of his friends a man's honor is gone. Few mortals are stead-
    fast in distress

"to endure hardship." He spoke, and Zeus came near
and answered: "You are my son; but thereafter her lord, a hero,
embracing your mother, shed seed that is mortal:
this man. Behold: of these two things I give you choice
entire; if you would escape death and age that all men hate,
to dwell beside me on Olympos with Athene and Ares of the black
    spear,

"that right is yours. But if all your endeavor is for
your twin, and you would have in all things shares alike,
half the time you may breathe under the earth,
half the time in the golden houses of the sky."
He spoke, and no twofold counsel divided the hero's heart,
but he set free from darkness the eyes of Kastor of the brazen belt,
    and his voice thereafter.

PHILOCTETES

SOPHOCLES, *Philoctetes*, 261-284 (Grene)

Philoctetes, whose bow and arrows are essential to the cap-
ture of Troy, tells Neoptolemus, the son of Achilles, how
he was abandoned on Lemnos.

"My boy,
you are Achilles' son. I that stand here
am one you may have heard of, as the master
of Heracles' arms. I am Philoctetes
the son of Poias. Those two generals
and Prince Odysseus of the Cephallenians
cast me ashore here to their shame, as lonely
as you can see me now, wasting with my sickness
as cruel as it is, caused by the murderous bite
of a viper mortally dangerous.
I was already bitten when we put in here
on my way from sea-encircled Chryse.
I tell you, boy, those men cast me away here
and ran and left me helpless. They were happy
when they saw that I had fallen asleep on the shore
in a rocky cave, after a rough passage.
They went away and left me with such rags—
and few enough of them—as one might give
an unfortunate beggar and a handful of food.
May God give them the like!"

DIOMEDE

HOMER, *Iliad*, Book 9. 32-49 (Derby)

Diomede is a leading hero during the absence of Achilles from the battlefield. Here is his reply to Agamemnon who has just proposed, for the second time, to give up the siege.

"Atrides, I your folly must confront,
As is my right, in council; you, O King!
Be not offended: once, among the Greeks
You held my prowess light, and with the name
Of coward branded me; how justly so
Is known to all the Greeks, both young and old.
On you the deep-designing Saturn's son
In differing measure has his gifts bestowed:
A throne he gives you, higher far than all;
But valor, noblest boon of Heaven, denies.
How can you hope the sons of Greece shall prove
Such heartless dastards as your words suppose?
If homeward to return thy mind be fixed,
Depart; the way is open, and the ships,
Which from Mycenae followed you in crowds,
Are close at hand, and ready to be launched.
Yet will the other long-haired Greeks remain
Till Priam's city fall: nay, though the rest
Betake them to their ships, and sail for home,
Yet I and Sthenelus, we two, will fight
Till Troy be ours; for Heaven is on our side."

2. The Wanderings of Odysseus

THE PLOT OF THE *ODYSSEY*

ARISTOTLE, *Poetics*, 17.5 (Butcher)

Thus the story of the Odyssey can be stated briefly. A certain man is absent from home for many years; he is jealously watched by Poseidon, and left desolate. Meanwhile his home is in a wretched plight—suitors are wasting his substance and plotting against his son. At length, tempest-tost, he himself arrives; he makes certain persons acquainted with him; he attacks the suitors with his own hand, and is himself preserved while he destroys them. This is the essence of the plot; the rest is episode.

ODYSSEUS' CHARACTER

HOMER, *Iliad*, Book 10. 241-253 (Derby)

Diomede, about to go on a night scouting expedition, chooses a companion.

> Then answer'd valiant Diomede, and said;
> "If my companion I may freely choose,
> How can I pass the sage Ulysses by?
> Of ready wit, and dauntless courage, proved
> In every danger; and to Pallas dear.
> I should not fear, by him accompanied,
> To pass through fire, and safely both return;

So far in prudence he surpasses all."
    Whom answered thus Ulysses, stout of heart:
"Tydides, no exaggerated praise
Bestow on me, nor censure; for you speak
To those who know me all for what I am.
But go we; night wanes fast, the morn is near:
The stars are high in Heaven; and of the night
Two thirds are spent, one third alone remains."

PENELOPE

HOMER, *Odyssey*, Book 2. 87-145 (Fitzgerald)

After the Trojan War several years passed with no sign of Odysseus' return. In Ithaca a large band of suitors for Penelope assembled. One of them, Antinoos, tells Telemachus of Penelope's trick to postpone choosing a new husband.

"For three years now—and it will soon be four—
she has been breaking the hearts of the Akhaians,
holding out hope to all, and sending promises
to each man privately—but thinking otherwise.
    Here is an instance of her trickery:
she had her great loom standing in the hall
and the fine warp of some vast fabric on it;
we were attending her, and she said to us:
'Young men, my suitors, now my lord is dead,
let me finish my weaving before I marry,
or else my thread will have been spun in vain.
It is a shroud I weave for Lord Laërtes,
when cold death comes to lay him on his bier.
The country wives would hold me in dishonor
if he, with all his fortune, lay unshrouded.'
We have men's hearts; she touched them; we agreed.
So every day she wove on the great loom—
but every night by torchlight she unwove it;
and so for three years she deceived the Akhaians.
But when the seasons brought the fourth around,
one of her maids, who knew the secret, told us;

we found her unraveling the splendid shroud.
She had to finish then, although she hated it.
   Now here is the suitors' answer—
you and all the Akhaians, mark it well:
dismiss your mother from the house, or make her marry
the man her father names and she prefers.
Does she intend to keep us dangling forever?
She may rely too long on Athena's gifts—
talent in handicraft and a clever mind;
so cunning—history cannot show the like
among the ringleted ladies of Akhaia,
Mykene with her coronet, Alkmene, Tyro.
Wits like Penelope's never were before,
but this time—well, she made poor use of them.
For here are suitors eating up your property
as long as she holds out—a plan some god
put in her mind. She makes a name for herself,
but you can feel the loss it means for you.
Our own affairs can wait; we'll never go anywhere else,
Until she takes an Akhaian to her liking."
   But clear-headed Telémakhos replied:
"Antinoos, can I banish against her will
the mother who bore me and took care of me?
My father is either dead or far away,
but dearly I should pay for this
at Ikários' hands, if ever I sent her back.
The powers of darkness would requite it, too,
my mother's parting curse would call hell's furies
to punish me, along with the scorn of men.
No: I can never give the word for this.
But if your hearts are capable of shame,
leave my great hall, and take your dinner elsewhere,
consume your own stores. Turn and turn about,
use one another's houses. If you choose
to slaughter one man's livestock and pay nothing,
this is rapine; and by the eternal gods
I beg Zeus you shall get what you deserve:
a slaughter here, and nothing paid for it!"
   Now Zeus who views the wide world sent a sign to him,
launching a pair of eagles from a mountain crest
in gliding flight down the soft blowing wind,
wing-tip to wing-tip quivering taut, companions,

till high above the assembly of many voices
they wheeled, their dense wings beating, and in havoc
dropped on the heads of the crowd—a deathly omen—
wielding their talons, tearing cheeks and throats;
then veered away on the right hand through the city.
Astonished, gaping after the birds, the men
felt their hearts flood, foreboding things to come.

TELEMACHUS

HOMER, *Odyssey*, Book 2. 36-74 (Butler)

*The youthful and immature Telemachus calls a meeting and
addresses the assembly.*

Telemachus rose at once, for he was bursting with what he had to
say. He stood in the middle of the assembly and the good herald
Pisenor brought him his staff. Then, turning to Aegyptius, "Sir,"
said he, "it is I, as you will shortly learn, who have convened you,
for it is I who am the most aggrieved. I have not got wind of any
host approaching about which I would warn you, nor is there any
matter of public moment on which I would speak. My grievance
is purely personal, and turns on two great misfortunes which have
fallen upon my house. The first of these is the loss of my excellent
father, who was chief among all you here present, and was like a
father to every one of you; the second is much more serious, and
ere long will be the utter ruin of my estate. The sons of all the
chief men among you are pestering my mother to marry them
against her will. They are afraid to go to her father Icarius, asking him to choose the one he likes best, and to provide marriage
gifts for his daughter, but day by day they keep hanging about
my father's house, sacrificing our oxen, sheep, and fat goats for
their banquets, and never giving so much as a thought to the quantity of wine they drink. No estate can stand such recklessness. We
have now no Odysseus to ward off harm from our doors, and I
cannot hold my own against them. I shall never all my days be
as good a man as he was; still I would indeed defend myself if I
had power to do so, for I cannot stand such treatment any longer;
my house is being disgraced and ruined. Have respect, therefore,

to your own consciences and to public opinion. Fear, too, the wrath of heaven, lest the gods should be displeased and turn upon you. I pray you by Zeus and Themis, who is the beginning and the end of councils, do not hold back, my friends, and leave me singlehanded—unless it be that my brave father Odysseus did some wrong to the Achaeans which you would now avenge on me, by aiding and abetting these suitors. Moreover, if I am to be eaten out of house and home at all, I had rather you did the eating yourselves, for I could then take action against you to some purpose, and serve you with notices from house to house till I got paid in full, whereas now I have no remedy."

With this Telemachus dashed his staff to the ground and burst into tears.

TELEMACHUS VISITS NESTOR

HOMER, *Odyssey*, Book 3. 65-101 (Palmer)

Telemachus goes to Pylos hoping to learn about Odysseus from Nestor.

But when they had roasted the outer flesh and drawn it off, dividing the portions, they held a glorious feast. And after they had stayed desire for drink and food, then thus began the Gerenian horseman Nestor:

"Now, then, it is more suitable to prove our guests and ask them who they are, since they are refreshed with food. Strangers, who are you? Where do you come from, sailing the watery ways? Are you upon some business? Or do you rove at random, as the pirates roam the seas, risking their lives and bringing ill to strangers?"

Then answered him discreet Telemachus, plucking up courage; for Athene herself put courage in his heart to ask about his absent father and to win a good report among mankind:

"O Nestor, son of Neleus, great glory of the Achaeans, you ask me whence we are, and I will tell you. We are of Ithaca, under Mount Neïon. Our business is our own, no public thing, as I will show. I come afar to seek some tidings of my father, royal hardy

Odysseus, who once, they say, fought side by side with you and sacked the Trojan town. For as to all the others who were in the war at Troy we have already learned where each man met his mournful death; but this man's death the son of Kronos left unknown. No one can surely say where he has died; whether he was borne down on land by foes, or on the sea among the waves of Amphitrite. Therefore I now come hither to your knees to ask if you will tell me of my father's mournful death, in case you saw it for yourself with your own eyes, or from some other heard the story of his wanderings; for to exceeding grief his mother bore him. Use no mild word nor yield to pity from regard for me, but tell me fully all you chanced to see. I do entreat you, if ever my father, good Odysseus, in word or deed kept covenant with you there in the Trojan land where you Achaeans suffered, be mindful of it now; tell me the very truth."

THE CICONES

HOMER, *Odyssey*, Book 9. 39-61 (Pope)

While Telemachus is away from Ithaca seeking news of him, Odysseus at the court of the Phaeacian king, Alcinous, gives an account of his adventures from the time he left Troy with his ships and men. Homer has attached a series of folk tales to the famous wanderer.

"Hear, then, the woes which mighty Jove ordain'd
To wait my passage from the Trojan land.
The winds from Ilion to the Cicons' shore,
Beneath cold Ismarus, our vessels bore.
We boldly landed on the hostile place,
And sack'd the city, and destroy'd the race,
Their wives made captive, their possessions shared,
And ev'ry soldier found a like reward.
I then advised to fly; not so the rest,
Who stay'd to revel, and prolong the feast:
The fatted sheep and sable bulls they slay,
And bowls flow round, and riot wastes the day.
Meantime the Cicons, to their holds retired,

Call on the Cicons, with new fury fired;
With early morn the gather'd country swarms
And all the continent is bright with arms;
Thick as the budding leaves or rising flowers
O'erspread the land, when spring descends in showers:
All expert soldiers, skill'd on foot to dare,
Or from the bounding courser urge the war.
Now fortune changes (so the Fates ordain);
Our hour was come to taste our share of pain.
Close at the ships the bloody fight began,
Wounded they wound, and man expires on man.
Long as the morning sun increasing bright
O'er Heav'n's pure azure spread the growing light,
Promiscuous death the form of war confounds,
Each adverse battle gor'd with equal wounds;
But when his ev'ning wheels o'erhung the main,
Then conquest crown'd the fierce Ciconian train.
Six brave companions from each ship we lost,
The rest escape in haste, and quit the coast.
With sails outspread we fly th' unequal strife,
Sad for their loss, but joyful of our life.
Yet as we fled, our fellows' rites we paid,
And thrice we call'd on each unhappy shade."

THE LOTOS-EATERS

HOMER, *Odyssey*, Book 9. 83-102 (Pope)

"Nine days our fleet th' uncertain tempest bore
Far in wide ocean, and from sight of shore:
The tenth we touch'd, by various errors toss'd,
The land of Lotus, and the flow'ry coast.
We climb'd the beach, and springs of water found,
Then spread our hasty banquet on the ground.
Three men were sent, deputed from the crew
(A herald one) the dubious coast to view,
And learn what habitants possess'd the place.
They went, and found a hospitable race:
Not prone to ill, nor strange to foreign guest,

They eat, they drink, and Nature gives the feast:
The trees around them all their food produce;
Lotus the name: divine, nectareous juice
(Thence called Lotophagi); which whoso tastes,
Insatiate riots in the sweet repasts,
Nor other home nor other care intends,
But quits his house, his country, and his friends.
The three we sent, from off th' enchanting ground
We dragged reluctant, and by force we bound:
The rest in haste forsook the pleasing shore,
Or, the charm tasted, had return'd no more.
Now placed in order on their banks, they sweep
The sea's smooth face, and cleave the hoary deep;
With heavy hearts we labor thro' the tide,
To coasts unknown, and oceans yet untried."

~~~

POLYPHEMUS, THE CYCLOPS

APOLLODORUS, *Epitome,* 7. 4-9 (Frazer)

Apollodorus collected and retold a great many myths and legends from a wide range of earlier Greek authors. This is his account of the Cyclops.

And having left the rest of the ships in the neighbouring island, he stood in for the land of the Cyclopes with a single ship, and landed with twelve companions. And near the sea was a cave which he entered, taking with him the skin of wine that had been given him by Maro. Now the cave belonged to Polyphemus, who was a son of Poseidon and the nymph Thoosa, a huge, wild, cannibal man, with one eye on his forehead. And having lit a fire and sacrificed some of the kids, they feasted. But the Cyclops came, and when he had driven in his flocks, he put a huge stone to the door, and perceiving the men he ate some of them. But Ulysses gave him of Maro's wine to drink, and when he had drunk, he asked for another draught, and when he had drunk the second, he inquired his name: and when Ulysses said that he was called Nobody, he threatened to devour Nobody last and the others first, and that was the token of friendship which he promised to give

him in return. And being overcome by wine, he fell asleep. But
Ulysses found a club lying there, and with the help of four comrades he sharpened it, and, having heated it in the fire, he blinded
him. And when Polyphemus cried to the Cyclopes round about
for help, they came and asked who was hurting him, and when he
said, "Nobody," they thought he meant that he was being hurt
by nobody, and so they retired. And when the flocks sought
their usual pasture, he opened the cave, and standing at the doorway spread out his hands and felt the sheep. But Ulysses tied
three rams together, and himself getting under the bigger, and hiding under its belly, he passed out with the sheep. And having released his comrades from the sheep, he drove the animals to the
ships, and sailing away shouted to the Cyclops that he was Ulysses
and that he had escaped out of his hands. Now the Cyclops had
been forewarned by a soothsayer that he should be blinded by
Ulysses; and when he learned the name, he tore away rocks and
hurled them into the sea, and hardly did the ship evade the rocks.
From that time Poseidon was wroth with Ulysses.

~~~~~

AEOLUS AND THE WINDS

HOMER, *Odyssey*, Book 10. 1-75 (Cotterill)

"Now did we come to the isle Aeolian, home of the monarch
Aeolus, Hippotas' son, by the gods everlasting beloved.
This is an island that floats, and a rampart is builded about it
Bronzen, unbroken; and sheer from the water the precipice rises.
Now to the monarch had been twelve children born in the
    palace,
Six were daughters and six were sons in the bloom of their man-
    hood.
Therefore to each of the sons he had given a daughter in marriage.
These in the halls of their father beloved and excellent mother
Ever do feast; for at hand are ever unfailing provisions;
Filled is the house and the court with the odors and noises of
    feasting
All of the day, but at night at the side of their honor'd consorts
Covered with wrappers they slumber on bedsteads with beautiful
    carvings.

Now when at last we arrived at the city and home of the mon-
   arch,
One whole month he entreated me well, and of all he inquired,
Troy and the Argive fleet and the homeward return of the Gre-
   cians.
Then, when the whole of the story in order was duly related,
I too uttered request concerning my journey, and begged him
Speed my return, and he made not refusal, but furnished an
   escort,
Flaying me also the skin of a nine-year ox for a wallet,
Where fast-bound he imprisoned the ways of the blustering storm-
   blasts,
Seeing that him as the Keeper of winds hath elected Cronion,
Either to lull them to rest or to raise whichever he listeth.
This in my hollow ship with a cord resplendent of silver
Firmly he bound, to allow not a breath to escape, not the faint-
   est,
Letting alone fare forth with its favoring breezes the Zephyr
Homeward to carry the vessels and us; yet fated he was not
This to accomplish, because our own mad folly destroyed us.

Nine days long did we sail, and the nights no less than the day-
   time;
Till, on the tenth, in the even, we sighted the fields of the home-
   land,
Ay and beheld quite near us the folk as they tended the beacons.
Now sweet sleep came creeping upon me, outworn with my
   labors,
Seeing that ever I managed the sheet and to none of my com-
   rades
Trusted it, hoping the quicker to come to the land of my fathers.
Meanwhile thus did my mates hold converse one with another,
Saying that home I was bringing a treasure of gold and of silver,
Presents by Hippotas' son, the munificent Aeolus, given:
So did they secretly talk as they looked each man at his neighbor:
'Lo, how dear, how honored this fellow is ever with all men,
Every mortal the land or the city of whom he arriveth!
Many a treasure he bringeth from Troy, magnificent prizes
Out of the booty; but we, who the selfsame journey have ended,
Homeward return nought having withal sane hands that are empty.
This too sure is a gift which lately hath lavished in friendship
Aeolus. Come now, quick let us spy what is here and discover

How great treasure of gold and of silver is stowed in the wallet.'
Thus did they speak, and the men were won by the counsel of
    mischief.
Loosing the bag they untied it—and out rushed every storm-wind,
Seized them with might of a tempest and carried them suddenly
    seaward
Wailing and weeping, afar from the land of their fathers; whereat I
Waked from my slumber, and straight with my spirit unerring I
    communed
Whether to leap from the ship and to seek for my death in the
    waters
Or to endure it in silence and still to remain with the living.
Well—I endured and remained, and wrapt in my cloak on the
    vessel
Lay, as the ships swept on, by the terrible blast of the storm-wind
Back to the isle Aeolian borne, midst groans of my comrades.

Here on the shore disembarking we drew from a fountain of
    water;
Hastily then did my mates make midday meal by the vessels.
Now when of meat and of drink we had all of us fully partaken,
Then did I, taking as escort a herald and one of my shipmates,
Go to the glorious palace, and here King Aeolus found I
Feasting, and near him was seated his queen, and beside her the
    children.
Entering therefore the house, on the threshold anigh to the door-
    posts
Sat we adown, while all were filled with amazement, and asked
    me:
'Why art thou hither returned? What deity harmed thee, Odys-
    seus?
Surely a speeding we gave thee enow, sufficing to bring thee
Back to thy land and thy home, or whither thy soul desireth.'
Thus did they speak; whereat with a heart right heavy I answered:
'Harmed have evil companions, and pitiless slumber hath harmed
    me,
Woe to it!—Nay now, heal us, my friends, since yours is the
    power.'
So did I speak, and besought them with gentlest words of per-
    suasion;
Yet all silent they sat. Then answered the father in anger:
'Hence from the Isle forthwith, most infamous mortal that liveth!

Wicked I hold it to treat as a guest or to speed on his journey
One whom thus pursueth the hate of the deities blessed.
Hence and begone! since hated of gods everlasting thou camest.'
Spake—and away from his palace he ordered me grievously groaning."

CIRCE

HOMER, *Odyssey*, Book 10. 135-495 (Bryant)

"And now we landed at an isle,—
Aeaea, where the fair-haired Circe dwelt,
A goddess high in rank and skilled in song,
Own sister of the wise Aeaetes. Both
Were children of the source of light, the Sun,
And Perse, Ocean's daughter, brought them forth.
We found a haven here, where ships might lie;
And guided by some deity we brought
Our galley silently against the shore,
And disembarked, and gave two days and nights
To rest, unmanned with hardship and with grief.
"When bright-haired Morning brought the third day round,
I took my spear and my good sword, and left
The ship, and climbed a height, in hope to spy
Some trace of human toil, or hear some voice.
On a steep precipice I stood, and saw
From the broad earth below a rising smoke,
Where midst the thickets and the forest-ground
Stood Circe's palace. Seeing that dark smoke,
The thought arose within my mind that there
I should inquire. I pondered till at last
This seemed the wisest,—to return at once
To my good ship upon the ocean side,
And give my crew their meal, and send them forth
To view the region. Coming to the spot
Where lay my well-oared bark, some pitying god
Beneath whose eye I wandered forth alone
Sent a huge stag into my very path,
High-horned, which from his pasture in the wood

Descended to the river-side to drink,
For grievously he felt the hot sun's power.
Him as he ran I smote; the weapon pierced,
Just at the spine, the middle of his back.
The brazen blade passed through, and with a moan
He fell amid the dust, and yielded up
His life. I went to him, and set my foot
Against him, and plucked forth the brazen spear,
And left it leaning there. And then I broke
Lithe osiers from the shrubs, and twined of these
A rope, which, doubled, was an ell in length.
With that I tied the enormous creature's feet,
And slung him on my neck, and brought him thus
To my black ship. I used the spear to prop
My steps, since he no longer could be borne
Upon the shoulder, aided by the hand,
Such was the animal's bulk. I flung him down
Before the ship, encouraging my men
With cheerful words, and thus I said to each:—
    " 'My friends, we will not, wretched as we are,
Go down to Pluto's realm before our time.
While food and wine are yet within the hold
Of our good galley, let us not forget
Our daily meals, and famine-stricken pine.'
    "I spake; they all obeyed, and at my word
Came forth, and standing by the barren deep
Admired the stag, for he was huge of bulk;
And when their eyes were tired with wondering,
My people washed their hands, and soon had made
A noble banquet ready. All that day
Till set of sun we sat and feasted there
Upon the abundant meat and delicate wine;
And when the sun went down, and darkness came,
We slept upon the shore. But when the Morn,
The rosy-fingered child of Dawn, looked forth,
I called a council of my men and spake:—
    " 'Give ear, my friends, amid your sufferings,
To words that I shall say. We cannot here
Know which way lies the west, nor where the east,
Nor where the sun, that shines for all mankind,
Descends below the earth, nor where again
He rises from it. Yet will we consult,

If room there be for counsel,—which I doubt,
For when I climbed that height I overlooked
An isle surrounded by the boundless deep,—
An isle low lying. In the midst I saw
Smoke rising from a thicket of the wood.'
    "I spake; their courage died within their hearts
As they remembered what Antiphates,
The Laestrigon, had done, and what foul deeds
The cannibal Cyclops, and they wept aloud.
Tears flowed abundantly, but tears were now
Of no avail to our unhappy band.
    "Numbering my well-armed men, I made of them
Two equal parties, giving each its chief.
Myself commanded one; Eurylochus,
The hero, took the other in his charge.
    "Then in a brazen helm we shook the lots;
The lot of brave Eurylochus leaped forth,
And he with two-and-twenty of our men
Went forward with quick steps, and yet in tears,
While we as sorrowful were left behind.
    "They found the fair abode where Circe dwelt,
A palace of hewn stone within the vale,
Yet nobly seated. There were mountain wolves
And lions round it, which herself had tamed
With powerful drugs; yet these assaulted not
The visitors, but, wagging their long tails,
Stood on their hinder feet, and fawned on them,
Like mastiffs on their master when he comes
From banqueting and brings them food. So fawned
The strong-clawed wolves and lions on my men.
With fear my men beheld those beasts of prey,
Yet went, and, standing in the portico
Of the bright-haired divinity, they heard
Her sweet voice singing, as within she threw
The shuttle through the wide immortal web,
Such as is woven by the goddesses,—
Delicate, bright of hue, and beautiful.
    "Polites then, a chief the most beloved
And most discreet of all my comrades, spake:—
    " 'Some one is here, my friends, who sweetly sings,
Weaving an ample web, and all the floor
Rings to her voice. Whoever she may be,

Woman or goddess, let us call to her.'
  "He spake; aloud they called, and forth she came
And threw at once the shining doors apart,
And bade my comrades enter. Without thought
They followed her. Eurylochus alone
Remained without, for he suspected guile.
She led them in and seated them on thrones.
Then mingling for them Pramnian wine with cheese,
Meal, and fresh honey, and infusing drugs
Into the mixture,—drugs which made them lose
The memory of their home,—she handed them
The beverage and they drank. Then instantly
She touched them with a wand, and shut them up
In sties, transformed to swine in head and voice,
Bristles and shape, though still the human mind
Remained to them. Thus sorrowing they were driven
Into their cells, where Circe flung to them
Acorns of oak and ilex, and the fruit
Of cornel, such as nourish wallowing swine.
  "Back came Eurylochus to our good ship
With news of our poor comrades and their fate.
He strove to speak, but could not; he was stunned
By that calamity; his eyes were filled
With tears, and his whole soul was given to grief.
We marvelled greatly; long we questioned him,
And thus he spake of our lost friends at last:—
  " 'Through yonder thickets, as thou gav'st command,
Illustrious chief! we went, until we reached
A stately palace of hewn stones, within
A vale, yet nobly seated. Some one there,
Goddess or woman, weaving busily
An ample web, sang sweetly as she wrought.
My comrades called aloud, and forth she came,
And threw at once the shining doors apart,
And bade us enter. Without thought the rest
Followed, while I alone, suspecting guile,
Remained without. My comrades, from that hour,
Were seen no more; not one of them again
Came forth, though long I sat and watched for them.'
  "He spake; I slung my silver-studded sword
Upon my shoulders,—a huge blade of brass,—
And my bow with it, and commanded him

To lead the way. He seized and clasped my knees
With both his hands in attitude of prayer,
And sorrowfully said these winged words:—
  " 'Take me not thither; force me not to go,
O foster-child of Jove! but leave me here;
For thou wilt not return, I know, nor yet
Deliver one of our lost friends. Our part
Is to betake ourselves to instant flight
With these who yet remain, and so escape.'
  "He spake, and I replied: 'Eurylochus,
Remain thou here, beside our roomy ship,
Eating and drinking. I shall surely go.
A strong necessity is laid on me.'
  "I spake, and from the ship and shore went up
Into the isle; and when I found myself
Within that awful valley, and not far
From the great palace in which Circe dwelt,
Hermes, there met me on my way
A youth; he seemed in manhood's early prime,
When youth has most of grace. He took my hand
And held it, and, accosting me, began:—
  " 'Rash mortal! whither art thou wandering thus
Alone among the hills, where every place
Is strange to thee? Thy comrades are shut up
In Circe's palace in close cells like swine.
Com'st thou to set them free? Nay, thou like them
Wilt rather find thyself constrained to stay.
Let me bestow the means to make thee safe
Against that mischief. Take this potent herb,
And bear it with thee to the palace-halls
Of Circe, and it shall avert from thee
The threatened evil. I will now reveal
The treacherous arts of Circe. She will bring
A mingled draught to thee, and drug the bowl,
But will not harm thee thus; the virtuous plant
I gave thee will prevent it. Hear yet more:
When she shall smite thee with her wand, draw forth
Thy good sword from thy thigh and rush at her
As if to take her life, and she will crouch
In fear, and will solicit thine embrace.
Refuse her not, that so she may release
Thy comrades, and may send thee also back

To thine own land: but first exact of her
The solemn oath which binds the blessed gods,
That she will meditate no other harm
To thee, nor strip thee of thy manly strength.'
   "The Argus-queller spake, and plucked from earth
The potent plant and handed it to me,
And taught me all its powers. The root is black.
The blossom white as milk. Among the gods
Its name is Moly; hard it is for men
To dig it up; the gods find nothing hard.
   "Back through the woody island Hermes went
Toward high Olympus, while I took my way
To Circe's halls, yet with a beating heart.
There, as I stood beneath the portico
Of that bright-haired divinity, I called
Aloud; the goddess heard my voice and came,
And threw at once the shining doors apart,
And prayed me to come in. I followed her,
Yet grieving still. She led me in and gave
A seat upon a silver-studded throne,
Beautiful, nobly wrought, and placed beneath
A footstool, and prepared a mingled draught
Within a golden chalice, and infused
A drug with mischievous intent. She gave
The cup; I drank it off; the charm wrought not,
And then she smote me with her wand and said:—
'Go to the sty, and with thy fellows sprawl.'
   "She spake; but drawing forth the trusty sword
Upon my thigh, I rushed at her as if
To take her life. She shrieked and, stooping low,
Ran underneath my arm and clasped my knees,
And uttered piteously these winged words:—
   " 'Who art thou? of what race and of what land,
And who thy parents? I am wonder-struck
To see that thou couldst drink that magic juice
And yield not to its power. No living man,
Whoever he might be, that tasted once
Those drugs, or passed them o'er his lips, has yet
Withstood them. In thy breast a spirit dwells
Not to be thus subdued. Art thou not then
Ulysses, master of wise stratagems,
Whose coming hither, on his way from Troy,

In his black galley, oft has been foretold
By Hermes of the golden wand? But sheathe
Thy sword and share my couch, that, joined in love,
Each may hereafter trust the other's faith.'

   "She spake, and I replied: 'How canst thou ask,
O Circe, that I gently deal with thee,
Since thou, in thine own palace, hast transformed
My friends to swine, and plottest even now
To keep me with thee, luring me to pass
Into thy chamber and to share thy couch,
That thou mayst strip me of my manly strength.
I come not to thy couch till thou engage,
O goddess, by a solemn oath, that thou
Wilt never seek to do me further harm.'

   "I spake; she straightway took the oath required,
And, after it was uttered and confirmed,
Up to her sumptuous couch I went. Meanwhile
Four diligent maidens ministered within
The palace,—servants of the household they,
Who had their birth from fountains and from groves,
And sacred rivers flowing to the sea.
One spread the thrones with gorgeous coverings;
Above was purple arras, and beneath
Were linen webs; another, setting forth
The silver tables just before the thrones,
Placed on them canisters of gold; a third
Mingled the rich wines in a silver bowl,
And placed the golden cups; and, last, the fourth
Brought water from the fountain, and beneath
A massive tripod kindled a great fire
And warmed the water. When it boiled within
The shining brass, she led me to the bath,
And washed me from the tripod. On my head
And shoulders pleasantly she shed the streams
That from my members took away the sense
Of weariness, unmanning body and mind.
And when she thus had bathed me and with oil
Anointed me, she put a princely cloak
And tunic on me, led me in, and showed
My seat,—a stately silver-studded throne,
High-wrought,—and placed a footstool for my feet.
Then came a handmaid with a golden ewer,

And from it poured pure water for my hands
Into a silver laver. Next she placed
A polished table near to me, on which
The matron of the palace laid the feast,
With many delicacies from her store,
And bade me eat. The banquet pleased me not.
My thoughts were elsewhere; dark imaginings
Were in my mind. When Circe marked my mood,
As in a gloomy revery I sat,
And put not forth my hands to touch the feast,
She came to me and spake these winged words:—
  " 'Why sittest thou like one who has no power
Of speech, Ulysses, wrapt in thoughts that gnaw
Thy heart, and tasting neither food nor wine?
Still dost thou dream of fraud? It is not well
That thou shouldst fear it longer, since I pledged
Myself against it with a mighty oath.'
  "She spake, and I replied: 'What man whose heart
Is faithful could endure to taste of food
Or wine till he should see his captive friends
Once more at large? If with a kind intent
Thou bidst me eat and drink, let me behold
With mine own eyes my dear companions free.'
  "I spake; and Circe took her wand and went
Forth from her halls, and, opening the gate
That closed the sty, drove forth what seemed a herd
Of swine in their ninth year. They ranged themselves
Before her, and she went from each to each
And shed on them another drug. Forthwith
Fell from their limbs the bristles which had grown
All over them, when mighty Circe gave
At first the baleful potion. Now again
My friends were men, and younger than before,
And of a nobler mien and statelier growth.
They knew me all; and each one pressed my hand
In his, and there were tears and sobs of joy
That sounded through the palace. Circe too
Was moved, the mighty goddess; she drew near
And stood by me, and spake these winged words:—
  " 'Son of Laertes, nobly born and wise,
Ulysses! go to thy good ship beside
The sea and draw it up the beach, and hide

The goods and weapons in the caverns there,
And come thou back and bring with thee thy friends.'
   "She spake, and easily my generous mind
Was moved by what she said. Forthwith I went
To my good ship beside the sea, and found
My friends in tears, lamenting bitterly.
As in some grange the calves come leaping round
A herd of kine returning to the stall
From grassy fields where they have grazed their fill,
Nor can the stall contain the young which spring
Around their mothers with continual bleat;
So when my comrades saw me through their tears,
They sprang to meet me, and their joy was such
As if they were in their own native land
And their own city, on the rugged coast
Of Ithaca, where they were born and reared;
And as they wept they spake these winged words:—
   " 'O foster-child of Jove! we welcome thee
On thy return with a delight as great
As if we all had reached again the land
That gave us birth, our Ithaca. And now
Tell by what death our other friends have died.'
   "They spake; I answered with consoling words:—
'First draw our galley up the beach, and hide
Our goods and all our weapons in the caves,
And then let all make haste to follow me,
And see our friends in Circe's sacred halls,
Eating and drinking at the plenteous board.'
   "I spake; and cheerfully my men obeyed,
Save that Eurylochus alone essayed
To hold them back, and spake these winged words:—
   " 'Ah, whither are we going, wretched ones?
Are ye so eager for an evil fate,
That ye must go where Circe dwells, who waits
To turn us into lions, swine, or wolves,
Forced to remain and guard her spacious house?
So was it with the Cyclops, when our friends
Went with this daring chief to his abode,
And perished there through his foolhardiness.'
   "He spake; and then I thought to draw my sword
From my stout thigh, and with the trenchant blade
Strike off his head and let it fall to earth,

Though he were my near kinsman; yet the rest
Restrained me, each one speaking kindly words:—
    " 'Nay, foster-child of Jove! if thou consent,
This man shall stay behind and with the ship,
And he shall guard the ship, but lead us thou
To where the sacred halls of Circe stand.'
    "They spake, and from the ship and shore went up
Into the land, nor was Eurylochus
Left with the ship; he followed, for he feared
My terrible threat. Meantime had Circe bathed
My comrades at the palace, and with oil
Anointed them, and robed them in fair cloaks
And tunics. There we found them banqueting.
When they and those who came with me beheld
Each other, and the memory of the past
Came back to them, they wept abundantly,
And all the palace echoed with their sobs.
And then the mighty goddess came and said:—
    " 'Son of Laertes, nobly born and wise,
Prolong thou not these sorrows. Well I know
What ye have suffered on the fishy deep,
And all the evil that malignant men
Have done to you on land. Now take the food
Before you, drink the wine, till ye receive
Into your hearts the courage that was yours
When long ago ye left your fatherland,
The rugged Ithaca. Ye are unnerved
And spiritless with thinking constantly
On your long wanderings, and your minds allow
No space for mirth, for ye have suffered much.'
    "She spake; her words persuaded easily
Our generous minds, and there from day to day
We lingered a full year, and banqueted
Nobly on plenteous meats and delicate wines.
But when the year was ended, and the hours
Renewed their circle, my beloved friends
From Circe's palace called me forth and said:—
    " 'Good chief, do not forget thy native land,
If fate indeed permit that ever thou
Return in safety to that lofty pile
Thy palace in the country of thy birth.'
    "So spake they, and my generous mind was moved.

All that day long until the set of sun
We sat and feasted on the abundant meats
And delicate wines; and when the sun went down
They took their rest within the darkened halls,
While I to Circe's sumptuous couch went up,
A suppliant at her knees. The goddess heard
My prayer, as thus in winged words I said:—
   " 'O Circe! make, I pray, the promise good
Which thou hast given, to send me to my home.
My heart is pining for it, and the hearts
Of all my friends, who weary out my life
Lamenting round me when thou art not nigh.'
   "I spake; the mighty goddess thus replied:—
'Son of Laertes, nobly born and wise,
Ulysses! ye must not remain with me
Unwillingly; but ye have yet to make
Another voyage, and must visit first
The abode of Pluto, and of Proserpine
His dreaded queen, and there consult the soul
Of the blind seer Tiresias,—him of Thebes,—
Whose intellect was spared; for Proserpine
Gave back to him in death the power of mind,
That only he might know of things to come.
The rest are shades that flit from place to place.' "

ELPENOR

HOMER, *Odyssey*, Book 11. 51-78 (Palmer)

"First came the spirit of my man, Elpenor. He had not yet been buried under the broad earth; for we left his body at the hall of Circe, unwept, unburied, since other tasks were urgent. I wept to see him and pitied him from my heart, and speaking in winged words I said:

   " 'Elpenor, how came you in this murky gloom? Faster you came on foot than I in my black ship.'

"So I spoke, and with a groan he answered: 'High-born son of Laertes, ready Odysseus, Heaven's cruel doom destroyed me, and excess of wine. After I went to sleep on Circe's house, I did not notice how to go down again by the long ladder, but I fell headlong from the roof; my neck was broken in its socket, and my soul came down to the house of Hades. Now I entreat you by those left behind, not present here, by your wife, and by the father who cared for you when little, and by Telemachus whom you left at home alone,—for I know, as you go hence out of the house of Hades, you will touch with your stanch ship the island of Aeaea,—there then, my master, I charge you, think of me. Do not, in going, leave me behind, unwept, unburied, deserting me, lest I become a cause of anger to the gods against you; but burn me in the armor that was mine, and on the shore of the foaming sea erect the mound of an unhappy man, that future times may know. Do this for me, and fix upon my grave the oar with which in life I rowed among my comrades.' "

THE SIRENS

HOMER, *Odyssey*, Book 12. 154-200 (Rees)

"Friends, it's not right
That only one or two of us should know
The divine predictions that the beautiful goddess Circe
Made known to me. I'm going to tell all of you,
That thus informed we may die, or escape this fate
And live on. First she bade me avoid the song
Of the Sirens, who sing so divinely in their flowery meadow.
I alone, she said, might hear their voices,
But you must bind me fast with ropes so tight
They cut, upright on the thwart supporting the mast
And lash me securely to the mast itself, and if
I implore and command you to release me, tie me
Still tighter with even more ropes.
   "While I was repeating
What Circe had told me, our sturdy ship, rapidly
Running before the fine breeze, bore down on the island
Where the two Sirens live. Soon the wind died down
To a calm, and the waves were lulled by a god. My comrades
Got up, furled the sail, and stowed it away
In the hollow ship. Then they sat down at their oars

Of polished fir and churned the water white,
While I took a large round of wax and with my sharp sword
Cut it up in small pieces. These I kneaded with my powerful
Hands, and soon the wax grew warm, what with
The kneading and the rays of that ruler, Hyperion the Sun.
So with it I plugged the ears of all my comrades,
And they bound me hand and foot in the ship, upright
On the thwart supporting the mast and lashed me securely
To the mast itself. Then, sitting down at their oars,
They smote the gray sea. But no sooner were we within call
Of the island, moving on at a goodly clip, than the Sirens
Saw the swift ship approaching and began their sweet song:
  " 'Here on your way, O great glory of all the Achaeans,
Most famous Odysseus, linger awhile. Stay your ship
And listen as we two blend our voices. Never yet
Has any man rowed his black ship by this spot without hearing
The honeyed tones of our song. Such listeners enjoy
What they hear and go on all the wiser. For we know all
The suffering and hardship that Argives and Trojans endured
By will of the gods at wide Troy, and we know all
That will happen on the bountiful earth.'
  "Thus they sang
With their beautiful voices, and I, more than willing to do
As they wished, ordered my men to release me, frowning
And nodding my head. But they bent to their oars and rowed on,
And soon Perimedes and Eurylochus got up and drew
My bonds tighter and added still more. But when they had rowed
By the Sirens far enough not to hear their singing, my loyal
Companions took out the wax I had put in their ears
And untied the ropes that held me."

SCYLLA AND CHARYBDIS

HOMER, *Odyssey*, Book 12. 202-259 (Palmer)

"I observed a smoke, I saw high waves and heard a plunging
sound. From the hands of my frightened men down fell the oars,
and splashed against the current. There the ship stayed, for they

worked the tapering oars no more. Along the ship I passed, inspiriting my men with cheering words, standing by each in turn:

"'Friends, hitherto we have not been untried in danger. Here is no greater danger than when the Cyclops penned us with brutal might in the deep cave. Yet out of that, through energy of mine, through will and wisdom, we escaped. These dangers, too, I think some day we shall remember. Come then, and what I say let us all follow. You with your oars strike the deep breakers of the sea, while sitting at the pins, and see if Zeus will set us free from present death and let us go in safety. And, helmsman, these are my commands for you; lay them to heart, for you control the rudders of our hollow ship: keep the ship off that smoke and surf and hug the crags, or else, before you know it, she may veer off that way, and you will bring us into danger.'

"So I spoke, and my words they quickly heeded. But Scylla I did not name,—that hopeless horror,—for fear through fright my men might cease to row, and huddle all together in the hold. I disregarded too the hard behest of Circe, when she had said I must by no means arm. Putting on my glittering armor and taking in my hands my two long spears, I went upon the ship's fore-deck, for thence I looked for the first sight of Scylla of the rock, who brought my men disaster. Nowhere could I descry her; I tired my eyes with searching up and down the dusky cliff.

"So up the strait we sailed in sadness; for here lay Scylla, and there divine Charybdis fearfully sucked the salt sea-water down. Whenever she belched it forth, like a kettle in fierce flame all would foam swirling up, and overhead spray fell upon the tops of both the crags. But when she gulped the salt sea-water down, then all within seemed in a whirl; the rock around roared fearfully, and down below the bottom showed, dark with the sand. Pale terror seized my men; on her we looked and feared to die.

"And now it was that Scylla snatched from the hollow ship six of my comrades who were best in skill and strength. Turning my eyes toward my swift ship to seek my men, I saw their feet and hands already in the air as they were carried up. They screamed aloud and called my name for the last time, in agony of heart. As when a fisher, on a jutting rock, with long rod throws a bait to lure the little fishes, casting into the deep the horn of stall-fed ox; then, catching a fish, flings it ashore writhing; even so were these drawn writhing up the rocks. There at her door she ate them, loudly shrieking and stretching forth their hands in mortal pangs toward me. That was the saddest sight my eyes have ever seen, in all my toils, searching the ocean pathways."

THE CATTLE OF HELIOS

HOMER, *Odyssey*, Book 12. 127-141 (Chapman)

Circe warns Odysseus not to touch the cattle of Helios. In his absence his companions slaughter some of the cattle, and, in punishment, they fail to return.

"Thou shalt ascend the isle triangular,
Where many oxen of the Sun are fed,
And fatted flocks. Of oxen fifty head
In ev'ry herd feed, and their herds are seven;
And of his fat flocks is their number even.
Increase they yield not, for they never die.
There ev'ry shepherdess a Deity.
Fair Phaethusa, and Lampetie,
The lovely Nymphs are that their guardians be,
Who to the daylight's lofty-going Flame
Had gracious birthright from the heav'nly Dame,
Still young Neaera; who (brought forth and bred)
Far off dismiss'd them, to see duly fed
Their father's herds and flocks in Sicily.
These herds and flocks if to the Deity
Ye leave, as sacred things, untouch'd, and on
Go with all fit care of your home, alone,
(Though through some suff'rance) you yet safe shall land
In wished Ithaca. But if impious hand
You lay on those herds to their hurts, I then
Presage sure ruin to thy ship and men.
If thou escap'st thyself, extending home
Thy long'd-for landing, thou shalt loaded come
With store of losses, most exceeding late,
And not consorted with a saved mate."

~~~~~

CALYPSO

HOMER, *Odyssey*, Book 5. 75-147 (Butler)

*Athene persuades Zeus that Odysseus should be allowed to
return home after his seven-year stay with Calypso. Hermes
takes the message to her.*

Hermes flew and flew over many a weary wave, but when at last
he got to the island which was his journey's end, he left the sea
and went on by land till he came to the cave where the nymph
Calypso lived.

He found her at home. There was a large fire burning on the
hearth, and one could smell from far the fragrant reek of burning
cedar and sandalwood. As for herself, she was busy at her loom,
shooting her golden shuttle through the warp and singing beautifully. Round her cave there was a thick wood of alder, poplar,
and sweet-smelling cypress trees, wherein all kinds of great birds
had built their nests—owls, hawks, and chattering sea crows that
occupy their business in the waters. A vine loaded with grapes
was trained and grew luxuriantly about the mouth of the cave;
there were also four running rills of water in channels cut pretty
close together, and turned hither and thither so as to irrigate
the beds of violets and luscious herbage over which they flowed.
Even a god could not help being charmed with such a lovely spot,
so Hermes stood still and looked at it; but when he had admired
it sufficiently he went inside the cave.

Calypso knew him at once—for the gods all know each other,
no matter how far they live from one another—but Odysseus was
not within; he was on the seashore as usual, looking out upon the
barren ocean with tears in his eyes, groaning and breaking his
heart for sorrow. Calypso gaves Hermes a seat and said: "Why
have you come to see me, Hermes—honored, and ever welcome
—for you do not visit me often? Say what you want; I will do it
for you at once if I can, and if it can be done at all. But come inside, and let me set refreshment before you."

As she spoke she drew a table loaded with ambrosia beside

him and mixed him some red nectar, so Hermes ate and drank till he had had enough, and then said:

"We are speaking god and goddess to one another, and you ask me why I have come here, and I will tell you truly as you would have me do. Zeus sent me; it was no doing of mine. Who could possibly want to come all this way over the sea where there are no cities full of people to offer me sacrifices or choice hecatombs? Nevertheless, I had to come, for none of us other gods can cross Zeus, or transgress his orders. He says that you have here the most ill-starred of all those who fought nine years before the city of King Priam and sailed home in the tenth year after having sacked it. On their way home they sinned against Athene, who raised both wind and waves against them, so that all his brave companions perished, and he alone was carried hither by wind and tide. Zeus says that you are to let this man go at once, for it is decreed that he shall not perish here, far from his own people, but shall return to his house and country and see his friends again."

Calypso trembled with rage when she heard this. "You gods," she exclaimed, "ought to be ashamed of yourselves! You are always jealous, and hate seeing a goddess take a fancy to a mortal man, and live with him in open matrimony. So when rosy-fingered Dawn made love to Orion, you precious gods were all of you furious till Artemis went and killed him in Ortygia. So again when Demeter fell in love with Iasion, and yielded to him in a thrice-ploughed fallow field, Zeus came to hear of it before so very long and killed Iasion with his thunderbolts. And now you are angry with me too because I have a man here. I found the poor creature sitting all alone astride of a keel, for Zeus had struck his ship with lightning and sunk it in mid-ocean, so that all his crew were drowned, while he himself was driven by wind and waves on to my island. I got fond of him and cherished him, and had set my heart on making him immortal, so that he should never grow old all his days. Still I cannot cross Zeus, or bring his counsels t nothing; therefore, if he insists upon it, let the man go beyonc the seas again. But I cannot send him anywhere myself, for I have neither ships nor men who can take him. Nevertheless, I will readily give him such advice, in all good faith, as will be likely to bring him safely to his own country."

"Then send him away," said Hermes, "or Zeus will be angry with you and punish you."

CALYPSO

HOMER, *Odyssey*, Book 5. 202-224 (Butler)

Calypso promises to send Odysseus home.

"Odysseus, noble son of Laertes, so you would start home to your own land at once? Good luck go with you, but if you could only know how much suffering is in store for you before you get back to your own country, you would stay where you are, keep house along with me, and let me make you immortal, no matter how anxious you may be to see this wife of yours, of whom you are thinking all the time day after day. Yet I flatter myself that I am no whit less tall or well-looking than she is, for it is not to be expected that a mortal woman should compare in beauty with an immortal."

"Goddess," replied Odysseus, "do not be angry with me about this. I am quite aware that my wife Penelope is nothing like so tall or so beautiful as yourself. She is only a woman, whereas you are an immortal. Nevertheless, I want to get home, and can think of nothing else. If some god wrecks me when I am on the sea, I will bear it and make the best of it. I have had infinite trouble both by land and sea already, so let this go with the rest."

Presently the sun set and it became dark, whereon the pair retired into the inner part of the cave and went to bed.

NAUSICAA

HOMER, *Odyssey*, Book 6. 1-331 (Butler)

After leaving Calypso, Odysseus is shipwrecked and finally comes ashore on the island of Phaeacia.

So here Odysseus slept, overcome by sleep and toil; but Athene went off to the country and city of the Phaeacians, a people who used to live in the fair town of Hypereia, near the lawless Cyclopes. Now the Cyclopes were stronger than they and plundered them, so their king Nausithous moved them thence and settled them in Scheria, far from all other people. He surrounded the city with a wall, built houses and temples, and divided the lands among his people; but he was dead and gone to the house of Hades, and King Alcinous, whose counsels were inspired of heaven, was now reigning. To his house, then, did Athene hie in further-ance of the return of Odysseus.

She went straight to the beautifully decorated bedroom in which there slept a girl who was as lovely as a goddess, Nausicaa, daughter to King Alcinous. Two maidservants were sleeping near her, both very pretty, one on either side of the doorway, which was closed with well-made folding doors. Athene took the form of the famous sea captain Dymas' daughter, who was a bosom friend of Nausicaa and just her own age; then, coming up to the girl's bedside like a breath of wind, she hovered over her head and said:

"Nausicaa, what can your mother have been about, to have such a lazy daughter? Here are your clothes all lying in disorder, yet you are going to be married almost immediately, and should not only be well dressed yourself, but should find good clothes for those who attend you. This is the way to get yourself a good name, and to make your father and mother proud of you. Sup-pose, then, that we make tomorrow a washing day, and start at daybreak. I will come and help you so that you may have every-thing ready as soon as possible, for all the best young men among your own people are courting you, and you are not going to remain a maid much longer. Ask your father, therefore, to have a wagon and mules ready for us at daybreak, to take the rugs, robes, and girdles; and you can ride, too, which will be much pleasanter for you than walking, for the washing cisterns are some way from the town."

When she had said this Athene went away to Olympus, which they say is the everlasting home of the gods. Here no wind beats roughly, and neither rain nor snow can fall; but it abides in everlasting sunshine and in a great peacefulness of light, wherein the blessed gods are illumined for ever and ever. This was the place to which the goddess went when she had given instructions to the girl.

By and by morning came and woke Nausicaa, who began wondering about her dream; she therefore went to the other end of the house to tell her father and mother all about it, and found them in their own room. Her mother was sitting by the fireside spinning her purple yarn with her maids around her, and she happened to catch her father just as he was going out to attend a meeting of the town council, which the Phaeacian aldermen had convened. She stopped him and said:

"Papa dear, could you manage to let me have a good big wagon? I want to take all our dirty clothes to the river and wash them. You are the chief man here, so it is only right that you should have a clean shirt when you attend meetings of the council. Moreover, you have five sons at home, two of them married, while the other three are good-looking bachelors; you know they always like to have clean linen when they go to a dance, and I have been thinking about all this."

She did not say a word about her own wedding, for she did not like to, but her father knew and said, "You shall have the mules, my love, and whatever else you have a mind for. Be off with you, and the men shall get you a good strong wagon with a body to it that will hold all your clothes."

On this he gave his orders to the servants, who got the wagon out, harnessed the mules, and put them to, while the girl brought the clothes down from the linen room and placed them on the wagon. Her mother prepared her a basket of provisions with all sorts of good things, and a goatskin full of wine. The girl now got into the wagon, and her mother gave her also a golden cruse of oil, that she and her women might anoint themselves. Then she took the whip and reins and lashed the mules on, whereon they set off, and their hoofs clattered on the road. They pulled without flagging, and carried not only Nausicaa and her wash of clothes but the maids also who were with her.

When they reached the water side they went to the washing cisterns, through which there ran at all times enough pure water to wash any quantity of linen, no matter how dirty. Here they unharnessed the mules and turned them out to feed on the sweet juicy herbage that grew by the water side. They took the clothes out of the wagon, put them in the water, and vied with one another in treading them in the pits to get the dirt out. After they had washed them and got them quite clean, they laid them out by the seaside, where the waves had raised a high beach of shingle, and set about washing themselves and anointing themselves with olive oil. Then they got their dinner by the side of the stream, and waited for the sun to finish drying the clothes. When they had done dinner they threw off the veils that covered their heads and began to play at ball, while Nausicaa sang for them. As the huntress Artemis goes forth upon the mountains of Taygetus or Erymanthus to hunt wild boars or deer, and the woodnymphs, daughters of aegis-bearing Zeus, take their sport along with her (then is Leto proud at seeing her daughter stand a full head taller than the others, and eclipse the loveliest amid a whole bevy of beauties), even so did the girl outshine her handmaids.

When it was time for them to start home, and they were folding the clothes and putting them into the wagon, Athene began to consider how Odysseus should wake up and see the handsome girl who was to conduct him to the city of the Phaeacians. The girl, therefore, threw a ball at one of the maids, which missed her and fell into deep water. On this they all shouted, and the noise they made woke Odysseus, who sat up in his bed of leaves and began to wonder what it might all be.

"Alas," said he to himself, "what kind of people have I come amongst? Are they cruel, savage, and uncivilized, or hospitable and humane? I seem to hear the voices of young women, and they sound like those of the nymphs that haunt mountain tops, or springs of rivers and meadows of green grass. At any rate I am among a race of men and women. Let me try if I cannot manage to get a look at them."

As he said this he crept from under his bush, and broke off a bough covered with thick leaves to hide his nakedness. He looked like some lion of the wilderness that stalks about exulting in his strength and defying both wind and rain; his eyes glare as he prowls in quest of oxen, sheep, or deer, for he is famished, and will dare break even into a well-fenced homestead, trying to get at the sheep—even such did Odysseus seem to the young women, as he drew near to them all naked as he was, for he was in great want. On seeing one so unkempt and so begrimed with salt water, the others scampered off along the spits that jutted out into the sea, but the daughter of Alcinous stood firm, for Athene put courage into her heart and took away all fear from her. She stood right in front of Odysseus, and he doubted whether he should go up to her, throw himself at her feet, and embrace her knees as a suppliant, or stay where he was and entreat her to give him some clothes and show him the way to the town. In the end he deemed it best to entreat her from a distance, in case the girl should take offense at his coming near enough to clasp her knees, so he addressed her in honeyed and persuasive language.

"O queen," he said, "I implore your aid—but tell me, are

you a goddess or are you a mortal woman? If you are a goddess and dwell in heaven, I can only conjecture that you are Zeus' daughter Artemis, for your face and figure resemble none but hers; if, on the other hand, you are a mortal and live on earth, thrice happy are your father and mother—thrice happy, too, are your brothers and sisters. How proud and delighted they must feel when they see so fair a scion as yourself going out to a dance! Most happy, however, of all will he be whose wedding gifts have been the richest, and who takes you to his own home. I never yet saw anyone so beautiful, neither man nor woman, and am lost in admiration as I behold you. I can only compare you to a young palm tree which I saw when I was at Delos growing near the altar of Apollo—for I was there, too, with much people after me, when I was on that journey which has been the source of all my troubles. Never yet did such a young plant shoot out of the ground as that was, and I admired and wondered at it exactly as I now admire and wonder at yourself. I dare not clasp your knees, but I am in great distress; yesterday made the twentieth day that I had been tossing about upon the sea. The winds and waves have taken me all the way from the Ogygian island, and now fate has flung me upon this coast that I may endure still further suffering; for I do not think that I have yet come to the end of it, but rather that heaven has still much evil in store for me.

"And now, O queen, have pity upon me, for you are the first person I have met, and I know no one else in this country. Show me the way to your town, and let me have anything that you may have brought hither to wrap your clothes in. May heaven grant you in all things your heart's desire—husband, house, and a happy, peaceful home; for there is nothing better in this world than that man and wife should be of one mind in a house. It discomfits their enemies, makes the hearts of their friends glad, and they themselves know more about it than anyone."

To this Nausicaa answered: "Stranger, you appear to be a sensible, well-disposed person. There is no accounting for luck; Zeus gives prosperity to rich and poor just as he chooses, so you must take what he has seen fit to send you, and make the best of it. Now, however, that you have come to this our country, you shall not want for clothes or for anything else that a foreigner in distress may reasonably look for. I will show you the way to the town, and will tell you the name of our people. We are called Phaeacians, and I am daughter to Alcinous, in whom the whole power of the state is vested."

Then she called her maids and said: "Stay where you are, you girls. Can you not see a man without running away from him? Do you take him for a robber or a murderer? Neither he nor anyone else can come here to do us Phaeacians any harm, for we are dear to the gods, and live apart on a land's end that juts into the sounding sea, and have nothing to do with any other people. This is only some poor man who has lost his way, and we must be kind to him, for strangers and foreigners in distress are under Zeus' protection, and will take what they can get and be thankful. So, girls, give the poor fellow something to eat and drink, and wash him in the stream at some place that is sheltered from the wind."

On this the maids left off running away and began calling one another back. They made Odysseus sit down in the shelter as Nausicaa had told them, and brought him a shirt and cloak. They also brought him the little golden cruse of oil, and told him to go and wash in the stream. But Odysseus said, "Young women, please to stand a little on one side that I may wash the brine from my shoulders and anoint myself with oil, for it is long enough since my skin has had a drop of oil upon it. I cannot wash as long as you all keep standing there. I am ashamed to strip before a number of good-looking young women."

Then they stood on one side and went to tell the girl, while Odysseus washed himself in the stream and scrubbed the brine from his back and from his broad shoulders. When he had thoroughly washed himself, and had got the brine out of his hair, he anointed himself with oil, and put on the clothes which the girl had given him. Athene then made him look taller and stronger than before; she also made the hair grow thick on the top of his head, and flow down in curls like hyacinth blossoms. She glorified him about the head and shoulders as a skillful workman who has studied art of all kinds under Hephaestus and Athene enriches a piece of silver plate by gilding it—and his work is full of beauty. Then he went and sat down a little way off upon the beach, looking quite young and handsome, and the girl gazed on him with admiration; then she said to her maids:

"Hush, my dears, for I want to say something. I believe the gods who live in heaven have sent this man to the Phaeacians. When I first saw him I thought him plain, but now his appearance is like that of the gods who dwell in heaven. I should like my future husband to be just such another as he is, if he would only stay here and not want to go away. However, give him something to eat and drink."

They did as they were told, and set food before Odysseus, who ate and drank ravenously, for it was long since he had had food of any kind. Meanwhile, Nausicaa bethought her of another matter. She got the linen folded and placed in the wagon, she then yoked the mules, and, as she took her seat, she called Odysseus:

"Stranger," said she, "rise and let us be going back to the town; I will introduce you at the house of my excellent father, where I can tell you that you will meet all the best people among the Phaeacians. But be sure and do as I bid you, for you seem to be a sensible person. As long as we are going past the fields and farm lands, follow briskly behind the wagon along with the maids and I will lead the way myself. Presently, however, we shall come to the town, where you will find a high wall running all round it, and a good harbor on either side with a narrow entrance into the city, and the ships will be drawn up by the roadside, for everyone has a place where his own ship can lie. You will see the market place with a temple of Poseidon in the middle of it, and paved with large stones bedded in the earth. Here people deal in ship's gear of all kinds, such as cables and sails, and here, too, are the places where oars are made; for the Phaeacians are not a nation of archers—they know nothing about bows and arrows, but are a seafaring folk, and pride themselves on their masts, oars, and ships, with which they travel far over the sea.

"I am afraid of the gossip and scandal that may be set on foot against me later on; for the people here are very ill-natured, and some low fellow, if he met us, might say, 'Who is this fine-looking stranger that is going about with Nausicaa? Where did she find him? I suppose she is going to marry him. Perhaps he is a vagabond sailor whom she has taken from some foreign vessel, for we have no neighbors; or some god has at last come down from heaven in answer to her prayers, and she is going to live with him all the rest of her life. It would be a good thing if she would take herself off and find a husband somewhere else, for she will not look at one of the many excellent young Phaeacians who are in love with her.' This is the kind of disparaging remark that would be made about me, and I could not complain, for I should myself be scandalized at seeing any other girl do the like, and go about with men in spite of everybody, while her father and mother were still alive, and without having been married in the face of all the world.

"If, therefore, you want my father to give you an escort and to help you home, do as I bid you. You will see a beautiful grove of poplars by the roadside dedicated to Athene; it has a well in it and a meadow all round it. Here my father has a field of rich garden ground, about as far from the town as a man's voice will carry. Sit down there and wait for a while till the rest of us can get into the town and reach my father's house. Then, when you think we must have done this, come into the town and ask the way to the house of my father Alcinous. You will have no difficulty in finding it; any child will point it out to you, for no one else in the whole town has anything like such a fine house as he has. When you have got past the gates and through the outer court, go right across the inner court till you come to my mother. You will find her sitting by the fire and spinning her purple wool by firelight. It is a fine sight to see her as she leans back against one of the bearing-posts with her maids all ranged behind her. Close to her seat stands that of my father, on which he sits and topes like an immortal god. Never mind him, but go up to my mother and lay your hands upon her knees, if you would get home quickly. If you can gain her over, you may hope to see your own country again, no matter how distant it may be."

So saying she lashed the mules with her whip and they left the river. The mules drew well, and their hoofs went up and down upon the road. She was careful not to go too fast for Odysseus and the maids who were following on foot along with the wagon, so she plied her whip with judgment. As the sun was going down they came to the sacred grove of Athene, and there Odysseus sat down and prayed to the mighty daughter of Zeus.

"Hear me," he cried, "daughter of aegis-bearing Zeus, unweariable, hear me now, for you gave no heed to my prayers when Poseidon was wrecking me. Now, therefore, have pity upon me and grant that I may find friends and be hospitably received by the Phaeacians."

Thus did he pray, and Athene heard his prayer, but she would not show herself to him openly, for she was afraid of her uncle Poseidon, who was still furious in his endeavors to prevent Odysseus from getting home.

~~~

ODYSSEUS AND NAUSICAA

HOMER, *Odyssey*, Book 8. 454-468 (Butler)

After a hospitable reception by Alcinous and his wife, Odysseus goes to the bath.

When the servants had done washing and anointing him with oil and had given him a clean cloak and shirt, he left the bathroom and joined the guests who were sitting over their wine. Lovely Nausicaa stood by one of the bearing-posts supporting the roof of the cloister, and admired him as she saw him pass. "Farewell stranger," said she, "do not forget me when you are safe at home again, for it is to me first that you owe a ransom for having saved your life."

And Odysseus said, "Nausicaa, daughter of great Alcinous, may Zeus the mighty husband of Hera grant that I may reach my home; so shall I bless you as my guardian angel all my days, for it was you who saved me."

~~~

ODYSSEUS AND PENELOPE

HOMER, *Odyssey*, Book 19. 559-587 (Palmer)

The Phaeacians return Odysseus to Ithaca and leave him in a hidden place. He goes to the hut of Eumaeus, his faithful swineherd, who receives him cordially despite his beggarly appearance. Presently Telemachus, escaping an ambush of the suitors, reaches the hut. Odysseus discloses his identity and plans vengeance on the suitors. In disguise he goes to the palace, where Penelope tells him her plan to subject the suitors to the trial of the bow.

But heedful Penelope said to him once more: "Stranger, in truth dreams do arise perplexed and hard to tell, dreams which come not, in men's experience, to their full issue. Two gates there are

for unsubstantial dreams, one made of horn and one of ivory.
The dreams that pass through the carved ivory delude and bring
us tales that turn to naught; those that come forth through polished horn accomplish real things, whenever seen. Yet through
this gate came not I think my own strange dream. Ah, welcome,
were it so, to me and to my child! But this I will say farther; mark
it well. This is the fatal dawn which parts me from Odysseus'
home; for now I shall propose a contest with the axes which when
at home he used to set in line, like trestles, twelve in all; then he
would stand a great way off and send an arrow through. This contest I shall now propose to all the suitors. And whoever with his
hands shall lightliest bend the bow and shoot through all twelve
axes, him I will follow and forsake this home, this bridal home,
so very beautiful and full of wealth, a place I think I ever shall remember even in my dreams."

Then wise Odysseus answered her and said: "O honored wife
of Laërtes' son, Odysseus, delay no longer this contest at the hall;
for wise Odysseus will be here before the suitors, handling the polished bow, can stretch the string and shoot an arrow through the
iron."

~~~~

ARGUS, THE HOUND

HOMER, *Odyssey*, Book 17. 291-327 (Rees)

Odysseus talks with Eumaeus outside the palace.

As they were talking, a hound
Lying there lifted his head and pricked up his ears—
Argus, the very dog that stalwart Odysseus
Had raised from a pup but had never got to hunt,
Since before there was time he had to leave for Troy.
Time was when Argus was the constant companion of young men
In the field, hunting the wild deer, goat, and hare.
But now, with his master gone, he lay neglected
On one of the many large piles of mule and cattle
Manure which lay in front of the doors till the slaves
Of Odysseus could take it away to fertilize great fields.
There lay Argus the hound, crawling with fleas

And dog-wrecking lice. Even so, when he knew Odysseus
Was near, he wagged his tail and dropped his ears,
But hadn't the strength to move any nearer his master.
Looking away, Odysseus wiped a tear,
Easily hiding his grief from Eumaeus, whom quickly
He questioned thus:
 "Eumaeus, isn't it odd
That so noble a hound should be lying out here in the dung?
Handsome he is, though I really can't be sure
Whether he was equally gifted with speed, or merely
One of those table-dogs men keep for their proud appearance."
 Then, Eumaeus, this was your reply:
"Surely the man died far from home who owned
This dog. If he were in brawn and performance what he was
When Odysseus left him for Troy, believe me you
Would marvel at his splendid speed and endurance. No beast
Whose trail he followed through the depths of the forest ever
Escaped him, so keen was he on the scent. But he is
In bad shape now. His master died far from home,
And the slovenly women pay him no mind at all.
Servants who lose their masters are no longer inclined
To do a very good job, for Zeus, who sees all,
Takes half a man's worth away on the day he becomes
A slave."
 Then Eumaeus entered the stately palace
And went straight to the hall where the lordly wooers were feast-
  ing.
But Argus now, after nineteen long years, no sooner
Saw Odysseus again, than he gave in to fate
And lay still in the grip of black death.

TELEMACHUS SPEAKS OUT

HOMER, *Odyssey*, Book 20. 299-337 (Palmer)

*Telemachus shows his increased maturity by his rebuke to
Ctesippus.*

So saying, he flung with his strong hand an ox-hoof which lay near,
taking it from the basket. Odysseus with a quick turning of the

head avoided it, and in his heart smiled grimly. It struck the massive wall. But Telemachus rebuked Ctesippus thus:

"Surely, Ctesippus, that was lucky for your life. You missed our guest. He shunned your missile. Else I had run you through the middle with my pointed spear, and in the place of wedding-feast your father had been busied with a funeral here. Let no man in this house henceforth show rudeness; for I now mark and understand each deed, good deeds as well as bad. Before, I was a child. And even yet we bear what nevertheless we see,—sheep slain, wine drunk, bread wasted,—for hard it is for one to cope with many. Nay then, do me no more deliberate wrong. But if you seek to slay me with the sword, that I would choose; and better far were death than constantly behold disgraceful deeds, strangers abused, and damsels dragged to shame through the fair palace."

So he spoke and all were hushed to silence; but by and by said Agelaüs, son of Damastor: "Friends, in answering what is fairly said, none should be angry and retort with spiteful words. Let none abuse the stranger nor any of the servants in great Odysseus' hall. But to Telemachus and his mother I would say one friendly word; perhaps it may find favor in the mind of each. So long as your hearts hoped wise Odysseus would return to his own home, it was no harm to wait and hold the suitors at the palace. That was the better way, if but Odysseus had returned and reached his home once more. Now it is plain that he will never come. Go then, sit down beside your mother and plainly tell her this, to marry the man who is the best and offers most. So shall you keep in peace all that your father left, to eat and drink your fill, and she shall guide the household of another."

THE TRIAL OF THE BOW

HOMER, *Odyssey*, Book 21. 404-423 (Fitzgerald)

After the suitors all fail to string the bow, Odysseus obtains it.

The man skilled in all ways of contending,
satisfied by the great bow's look and heft,
like a musician, like a harper, when

with quiet hand upon his instrument
he draws between his thumb and forefinger
a sweet new string upon a peg: so effortlessly
Odysseus in one motion strung the bow.
Then slid his right hand down the cord and plucked it,
so the taut gut vibrating hummed and sang
a swallow's note.

          In the hushed hall it smote the suitors
and all their faces changed. Then Zeus thundered
overhead, one loud crack for a sign.
And Odysseus laughed within him that the son
of crooked-minded Kronos had flung that omen down.
He picked one ready arrow from his table
where it lay bare: the rest were waiting still
in the quiver for the young men's turn to come.
He nocked it, let it rest across the handgrip,
and drew the string and grooved butt of the arrow,
aiming from where he sat upon the stool.

                      Now flashed
arrow from twanging bow clean as a whistle
through every socket ring, and grazed not one,
to thud with heavy brazen head beyond.

DEATH OF THE SUITORS

HOMER, *Odyssey*, Book 22. 381-389 (Fitzgerald)

*Odysseus, aided by Telemachus, Eumaeus, and the herds-
man Philoetius, kills all the suitors except the herald Medon
and Phemius the harper.*

At this the two men stirred and picked their way
to the door and out, and sat down at the altar,
looking around with wincing eyes
as though the sword's edge hovered still.
And Odysseus looked around him, narrow-eyed,
for any others who had lain hidden
while death's black fury passed.

                  In blood and dust
he saw that crowd all fallen, many and many slain.

Think of a catch that fishermen haul in to a halfmoon bay
in a fine-meshed net from the white-caps of the sea:
how all are poured out on the sand, in throes for the salt sea,
twitching their cold lives away in Helios' fiery air:
so lay the suitors heaped on one another.

ODYSSEUS AND PENELOPE:
THE FINAL TEST

HOMER, *Odyssey*, Book 23. 153-204 (Fitzgerald)

*After the killing of the suitors Penelope is stunned and in-
credulous. She subjects Odysseus to a final test.*

Greathearted Odysseus, home at last,
was being bathed now by Eurynome
and rubbed with golden oil, and clothed again
in a fresh tunic and a cloak. Athena
lent him beauty, head to foot. She made him
taller, and massive, too, with crisping hair
in curls like petals of wild hyacinth
but all red-golden. Think of gold infused
on silver by a craftsman, whose fine art
Hephaistos taught him, or Athena: one
whose work moves to delight: just so she lavished
beauty over Odysseus' head and shoulders.
He sat then in the same chair by the pillar,
facing his silent wife, and said:
                                        "Strange woman,
the immortals of Olympos made you hard,
harder than any. Who else in the world
would keep aloof as you do from her husband
if he returned to her from years of trouble,
cast on his own land in the twentieth year?

Nurse, make up a bed for me to sleep on.
Her heart is iron in her breast."
                                        Penelope

spoke to Odysseus now. She said:

                                    "Strange man,
if man you are . . . This is no pride on my part
nor scorn for you—not even wonder, merely.
I know so well how you—how he—appeared
boarding the ship for Troy. But all the same . . .

Make up his bed for him, Eurykleia.
Place it outside the bedchamber my lord
built with his own hands. Pile the big bed
with fleeces, rugs, and sheets of purest linen."

With this she tried him to the breaking point,
and he turned on her in a flash raging:

"Woman, by heaven you've stung me now!
Who dared to move my bed?
No builder had the skill for that—unless
a god came down to turn the trick. No mortal
in his best days could budge it with a crowbar.
There is our pact and pledge, our secret sign,
built into that bed—my handiwork
and no one else's!
                          An old trunk of olive
grew like a pillar on the building plot,
and I laid out our bedroom round that tree,
lined up the stone walls, built the walls and roof,
gave it a doorway and smooth-fitting doors.
Then I lopped off the silvery leaves and branches,
hewed and shaped that stump from the roots up
into a bedpost, drilled it, let it serve
as model for the rest. I planed them all,
inlaid them all with silver, gold and ivory,
and stretched a bed between—a pliant web
of oxhide thongs dyed crimson.
                                    There's our sign!
I know no more. Could someone's else's hand
have sawn that trunk and dragged the frame away?"

THE END OF THE *ODYSSEY*

HOMER, *Odyssey*, Book 24. 539-548 (Rees)

*Hermes leads the spirits of the suitors to the Underworld;
their families seek to avenge their deaths in battle, and
finally Athene intervenes.*

    Cronos' son hurled down
A flaming bolt of thunder that landed directly
In front of the mighty Father's bright-eyed daughter.
Then Athena, her blue eyes blazing, spoke thus to Odysseus:
    "Son of Laertes, Zeus-born, resourceful man,
Hold back! and end the brawling of war, disastrous
To all, before you offend far-thundering Zeus."
    She spoke, and the heart of Odysseus was glad to obey.
Then Pallas Athena, daughter of aegis-bearing Zeus,
She who appeared like Mentor in form and voice,
Made a sacred and lasting covenant of peace between them.

3. Aeneas and Rome

Aeneas is a minor figure in the action of Homer's Iliad, but the Romans, especially Vergil, brought him to full stature as a representative of the Heroic Age.

~~~~~

THE PLOT OF THE *AENEID*

VERGIL, *Aeneid*, Book 1. 1-7 (Mackail)

The Romans generally were not creators of myths. Vergil is, above all, the shaper of what is significant in Roman myth and saga. Therefore, I have concentrated on him, since it is his treatment which has so largely determined what portions of Rome's story became the mythology of Rome for later generations.

I sing of arms and the man who came of old, a fated wanderer, from the coasts of Troy to Italy and the shore of Lavinium; hard driven on land and on the deep by the violence of heaven, by reason of cruel Juno's unforgetful anger, and hard bestead in war also, ere he might found a city and carry his gods into Latium; from whom is the Latin race, the lords of Alba, and high-embattled Rome.

~~~~

ROME'S DESTINY

VERGIL, *Aeneid*, Book 1. 257-294 (Mackail)

After Aeneas and his followers have been rescued from the violent storm brought on by the malice of Juno and have safely reached Africa, Jupiter tells Venus the destiny which awaits the descendants of Aeneas.

"Spare thy fear, Cytherean; thy people's destiny abides unshaken. Thine eyes shall see the city Lavinium, their promised fortress; thou shalt exalt to the starry heaven thy noble Aeneas; nor is my decree reversed. He whom thou lovest (for I will speak, since this care keeps torturing thee, and will unroll further the secret records of fate) shall wage a great war in Italy, and crush warrior nations; he shall appoint his people a law and a city; till the third summer see him reigning in Latium, and three winters' camps are overpast among the conquered Rutulians. But the boy Ascanius, whose surname is now Iülus—Ilus he was while the Ilian state stood sovereign—thirty great circles of rolling months shall he fulfil in government; he shall carry the kingdom from its seat in Lavinium, and make a strong fortress of Alba the Long. Here the full space of thrice an hundred years shall the kingdom endure under the race of Hector's kin, till the royal priestess Ilia from Mars' embrace shall give birth to a twin progeny. Thence shall Romulus, gay in the tawny hide of the she-wolf that nursed him, take up their line, and name them Romans after his own name. To these I ordain neither period nor boundary of empire: I have given them dominion without end. Nay, harsh Juno, who in her fear now troubles earth and sea and sky, shall change to better counsels, and with me shall cherish the lords of the world, the gowned race of Rome. Thus is it willed. A day will come in the lapse of cycles, when the house of Assaracus shall lay Phthia and famed Mycenae in bondage, and reign over conquered Argos. From the fair line of Troy a Caesar shall arise, who shall limit his empire with ocean, his glory with the firmament, Julius, inheritor of great Iülus' name. Him one day, thy care done, thou shalt welcome to heaven loaded with Eastern spoils; to him too shall vows be addressed. Then shall war cease, and the iron ages soften. Hoar Faith and Vesta, Quirinus and Remus brothers again, shall deliver statutes. The dreadful steel-clenched gates of War shall be shut fast; inhuman Fury, his hands bound behind him with an hundred rivets of brass, shall sit within on murderous weapons, shrieking with ghastly blood-stained lips."

AENEAS AND DIDO

VERGIL, *Aeneid*, Book 1. 340-368 (Mackail)

As Aeneas and Achates explore the strange country where they have landed, Venus in disguise meets them and tells Aeneas Dido's history.

"Punic is the realm thou seest, Tyrian the people, and the city of Agenor's kin; but their borders are Libyan, a race untameable in war. Dido sways the scepter, who flying her brother set sail from the Tyrian town. Long is the tale of crime, long and intricate; but I will follow its argument in brief. Her husband was Sychaeus, wealthiest in lands of the Phoenicians, and loved of her with ill-fated passion; to whom with virgin rites her father had given her maidenhood in wedlock. But the kingdom of Tyre was in her brother Pygmalion's hands, a monster of guilt unparalleled. Between these madness came; the unnatural brother, blind with lust of gold, and reckless of his sister's love, lays Sychaeus low before the altars with stealthy unsuspected weapon; and for long he hid the deed, and by many a crafty pretence cheated her love-sickness with hollow hope. But in slumber came the very ghost of her unburied husband, lifting up a face pale in wonderful wise; he exposed the cruel altars and his breast stabbed through with steel, and unwove all the blind web of household guilt. Then he counsels hasty flight and abandonment of her country, and to aid her passage discloses treasures long hidden underground, an untold mass of silver and gold. Stirred thereby, Dido gathered a company for flight. All assemble in whom hatred of the tyrant was relentless or terror keen; they seize on ships that chanced to lie ready, and load them with the gold. Pygmalion's hoarded wealth is borne overseas; a woman guides the enterprise. They came at last to the land where thou wilt descry a city now great, New Carthage, and her rising citadel, and bought ground, called thence Byrsa, as much as a bull's hide would encircle."

~~~~~~

AENEAS SEES DIDO

VERGIL, *Aeneid*, Book 1. 588-656 (Mackail)

Aeneas, concealed in a mist, is encouraged to discover that the temple in Carthage has scenes from the Trojan war on the walls. He sees Dido ruling her people and is delighted when his lost companions appear. The cloud suddenly parts.

Aeneas stood discovered in sheen of brilliant light, like a god in face and shoulders; for his mother's self had shed on her son the grace of clustered locks, the radiant light of youth, and the luster of joyous eyes; as when ivory takes beauty under the artist's hand, or when silver or Parian stone is inlaid in gold. Then breaking in on all with unexpected speech he thus addresses the queen:

"I whom you seek am here before you, Aeneas of Troy, snatched from the Libyan waves. O thou who alone hast pitied Troy's untold agonies, thou who with us, a remnant of the Grecian foe, the cup of misfortune drained on land and sea, with us in our utter want dost share thy city and home! to render meet recompense is not possible for us, O Dido, nor for all who scattered over the wide world are left of our Dardanian race. The gods grant thee worthy reward, if their deity turn any regard on goodness, if aught avails justice and conscious purity of soul. What happy ages bore thee? what mighty parents gave birth to a soul like thine? While rivers run into the sea, while the mountain shadows move across their slopes, while the stars feed in the fields of heaven, ever shall thine honor, thy name and praises endure in whatsoever lands may summon me." With these words he advances his right hand to dear Ilioneus, his left to Serestus; then to the rest, brave Gyas and brave Cloanthus.

Dido the Sidonian stood astonished, first at the sight of him, then at his strange fortunes, and thus broke into speech:

"What fate follows thee, goddess-born, through perilous ways? what violence throws thee on this evil coast? Art thou that

Aeneas whom Venus the bountiful bore to Dardanian Anchises by the wave of Phrygian Simoïs? And well I remember how Teucer came to Sidon, when exiled from his native land he sought Belus' aid to gain new realms; Belus my father even then ravaged rich Cyprus and held it under his conquering sway. From that time forth have I known the fall of the Trojan city, known thy name and the Pelasgian princes. Their very foe would extol the Teucrians with highest praises, and boasted himself a branch of the ancient Teucrian stem. Come therefore, O men, and enter our house. Me too has a like fortune driven through many a woe, and willed at last to find my rest in this land. Not ignorant of ill I learn to succor the afflicted."

With such tale she leads Aeneas into the royal house, and orders sacrifice in the gods' temples. Therewith she sends to his crews on the shore twenty bulls, an hundred great bristly-backed swine, an hundred fat lambs and their mothers with them, gifts of the day's gladness. . . . But the palace within is decked with splendor of royal state, and a banquet made ready amid the halls. The coverings are curiously wrought in splendid purple; on the tables is massy silver and deeds of ancestral valor graven in gold, all the long course of history drawn through many a heroic name from the nation's primal antiquity.

Aeneas—for a father's affection let not his spirit rest—sends Achates speeding to his ships, to carry this news to Ascanius, and lead him to the town: in Ascanius is fixed all the parent's loving care. Presents likewise he bids him bring saved from the wreck of Ilium, a mantle stiff with gold embroidery, and a veil with woven border of yellow acanthus-flower, that once decked Helen of Argos, her mother Leda's wondrous gift; Helen had borne them from Mycenae, when she sought Troy towers and a lawless bridal; the scepter too that Ilione, Priam's eldest daughter, once had worn, a beaded necklace, and a double circlet of jewelled gold. Achates, hasting on his message, bent his way towards the ships.

DIDO IN LOVE

VERGIL, *Aeneid*, Book 4. 65-85 (Humphries)

Aeneas fascinates Dido with accounts of the fall of Troy and his long wandering before he reached Carthage. At the command of Venus, Cupid causes Dido to fall in love with Aeneas.

Alas, poor blind interpreters! What woman
In love is helped by offerings or altars?
Soft fire consumes the marrow-bones, the silent
Wound grows, deep in the heart.
Unhappy Dido burns, and wanders, burning,
All up and down the city, the way a deer
With a hunter's careless arrow in her flank
Ranges the uplands, with the shaft still clinging
To the hurt side. She takes Aeneas with her
All through the town, displays the wealth of Sidon,
Buildings projected; she starts to speak, and falters,
And at the end of the day renews the banquet,
Is wild to hear the story, over and over,
Hangs on each word, until the late moon, sinking,
Sends them all home. The stars die out, but Dido
Lies brooding in the empty hall, alone,
Abandoned on a lonely couch. She hears him,
Sees him, or sees and hears him in Iulus,
Fondles the boy, as if that ruse might fool her,
Deceived by his resemblance to his father.

THE HUNT

VERGIL, *Aeneid*, Book 4. 151-172 (Humphries)

Juno, in an effort to advance the fortunes of her city of Carthage and to prevent the rise of Rome, conspires with Venus to bring Dido and Aeneas together during a hunt.

They reach the mountain heights, the hiding-places
Where no trail runs; wild goats from the rocks are started,
Run down the ridges; elsewhere, in the open
Deer cross the dusty plain, away from the mountains.
The boy Ascanius, in the midst of the valley,
Is glad he has so good a horse, rides, dashing
Past one group or another: deer are cowards
And wild goats tame; he prays for some excitement,
A tawny lion coming down the mountain
Or a great boar with foaming mouth.
                                        The heaven
Darkens, and thunder rolls, and rain and hail
Come down in torrents. The hunt is all for shelter,
Trojans and Tyrians and Ascanius dashing
Wherever they can; the streams pour down the mountains.
To the same cave go Dido and Aeneas,
Where Juno, as a bridesmaid, gives the signal,
And mountain nymphs wail high their incantations,
First day of death, first cause of evil. Dido
Is unconcerned with fame, with reputation,
With how it seems to others. This is marriage
For her, not hole-and-corner guilt; she covers
Her folly with this name.

MERCURY WARNS AENEAS

VERGIL, *Aeneid*, Book 4. 256-276 (Humphries)

When Iarbas, a Numidian rival of Aeneas, learns of Dido's infatuation, he prays to Jupiter to send Aeneas away. Mercury is sent on the mission.

So Mercury darted between earth and heaven
To Libya's sandy shore, cutting the wind
From the home of Maia's father.
Soon as the winged sandals skim the rooftops,
He sees Aeneas founding towers, building
New homes for Tyrians; his sword is studded
With yellow jasper; he wears across his shoulders
A cloak of burning crimson, and golden threads
Run through it, the royal gift of the rich queen.
Mercury wastes no time:—"What are you doing,
Forgetful of your kingdom and your fortunes,
Building for Carthage? Woman-crazy fellow,
The ruler of the gods, the great compeller
Of heaven and earth, has sent me from Olympus
With no more word than this: what are you doing,
With what ambition wasting time in Libya?
If your own fame and fortune count as nothing,
Think of Ascanius at least, whose kingdom
In Italy, whose Roman land, are waiting
As promise justly due."

DIDO ADDRESSES AENEAS

VERGIL, *Aeneid*, Book 4. 305-387 (Humphries)

Dido suspects that Aeneas is about to leave her and addresses him.

"And so, betrayer,
You hoped to hide your wickedness, go sneaking
Out of my land without a word? Our love
Means nothing to you, our exchange of vows,
And even the death of Dido could not hold you.
The season is dead of winter, and you labor
Over the fleet; the northern gales are nothing—
You must be cruel, must you not? Why, even,
If ancient Troy remained, and you were seeking
Not unknown homes and lands, but Troy again,
Would you be venturing Troyward in this weather?
I am the one you flee from: true? I beg you
By my own tears, and your right hand—(I have nothing
Else left my wretchedness)—by the beginnings
Of marriage, wedlock, what we had, if ever
I served you well, if anything of mine
Was ever sweet to you, I beg you, pity
A falling house; if there is room for pleading
As late as this, I plead, put off that purpose.
You are the reason I am hated; Libyans,
Numidians, Tyrians, hate me; and my honor
Is lost, and the fame I had, that almost brought me
High as the stars, is gone. To whom, O guest—
I must not call you husband any longer—
To whom do you leave me? I am a dying woman;
Why do I linger on? Until Pygmalion,
My brother, brings destruction to this city?
Until the prince Iarbas leads me captive?
At least if there had been some hope of children
Before your flight, a little Aeneas playing
Around my courts, to bring you back, in feature

At least, I would seem less taken and deserted."
    There was nothing he could say. Jove bade him keep
Affection from his eyes, and grief in his heart
With never a sign. At last, he managed something:—
"Never, O Queen, will I deny you merit
Whatever you have strength to claim; I will not
Regret remembering Dido, while I have
Breath in my body, or consciousness of spirit.
I have a point or two to make. I did not,
Believe me, hope to hide my flight by cunning;
I did not, ever, claim to be a husband,
Made no such vows. If I had fate's permission
To live my life my way, to settle my troubles
At my own will, I would be watching over
The city of Troy, and caring for my people,
Those whom the Greeks had spared, and Priam's palace
Would still be standing; for the vanquished people
I would have built the town again. But now
It is Italy I must seek, great Italy,
Apollo orders, and his oracles
Call me to Italy. There is my love,
There is my country. If the towers of Carthage,
The Libyan citadels, can please a woman
Who came from Tyre, why must you grudge the Trojans
Ausonian land? It is proper for us also
To seek a foreign kingdom. I am warned
Of this in dreams: when the earth is veiled in shadow
And the fiery stars are burning, I see my father,
Anchises, or his ghost, and I am frightened;
I am troubled for the wrong I do my son,
Cheating him out of his kingdom in the west,
And lands that fate assigns him. And a herald,
Jove's messenger—I call them both to witness—
Has brought me, through the rush of air, his orders;
I saw the god myself, in the full daylight,
Enter these walls, I heard the words he brought me.
Cease to inflame us both with your complainings;
I follow Italy not because I want to."
    Out of the corner of her eye she watched him
During the first of this, and her gaze was turning
Now here, now there; and then, in bitter silence,
She looked him up and down; then blazed out at him:—

"You treacherous liar! No goddess was your mother,
No Dardanus the founder of your tribe,
Son of the stony mountain-crags, begotten
On cruel rocks, with a tigress for a wet-nurse!
Why fool myself, why make pretense? what is there
To save myself for now? When I was weeping
Did he so much as sigh? Did he turn his eyes,
Ever so little, toward me? Did he break at all,
Or weep, or give his lover a word of pity?
What first, what next? Neither Jupiter nor Juno
Looks at these things with any sense of fairness.
Faith has no haven anywhere in the world.
He was an outcast on my shore, a beggar,
I took him in, and, like a fool, I gave him
Part of my kingdom; his fleet was lost, I found it,
His comrades dying, I brought them back to life.
I am maddened, burning, burning: now Apollo
The prophesying god, the oracles
Of Lycia, and Jove's herald, sent from heaven,
Come flying through the air with fearful orders,—
Fine business for the gods, the kind of trouble
That keeps them from their sleep. I do not hold you,
I do not argue, either. Go. And follow
Italy on the wind, and seek the kingdom
Across the water. But if any gods
Who care for decency have any power,
They will land you on the rocks; I hope for vengeance,
I hope to hear you calling the name of Dido
Over and over, in vain. Oh, I will follow
In blackest fire, and when cold death has taken
Spirit from body, I will be there to haunt you,
A shade, all over the world. I will have vengeance,
And hear about it; the news will be my comfort
In the deep world below." She broke it off,
Leaving the words unfinished; even light
Was unendurable; sick at heart, she turned
And left him, stammering, afraid, attempting
To make some kind of answer. And her servants
Support her to her room, that bower of marble,
A marriage-chamber once; here they attend her,
Help her lie down.
                              And good Aeneas, longing

To ease her grief with comfort, to say something
To turn her pain and hurt away, sighs often,
His heart being moved by this great love, most deeply,
And still—the gods give orders, he obeys them;
He goes back to the fleet.

MERCURY AGAIN WARNS AENEAS

VERGIL, *Aeneid*, Book 4. 554-570 (Humphries)

Aeneas prepares his ships for departure. Dido builds a funeral-pyre, ostensibly to burn everything connected with her love for Aeneas. He sleeps on shipboard.

Meanwhile Aeneas, on the lofty stern,
All things prepared, sure of his going, slumbers
As Mercury comes down once more to warn him,
Familiar blond young god: "O son of Venus,
Is this a time for sleep? The wind blows fair,
And danger rises all around you. Dido,
Certain to die, however else uncertain,
Plots treachery, harbors evil. Seize the moment
While it can still be seized, and hurry, hurry!
The sea will swarm with ships, the fiery torches
Blaze, and the shore rankle with fire by morning.
Shove off, be gone! A shifty, fickle object
Is woman, always."

DIDO SEES THE SHIPS LEAVING THE HARBOR

VERGIL, *Aeneid*, Book 4. 584-624 (Humphries)

Aurora
Came from Tithonus' saffron couch to freshen
The world with rising light, and from her watch-tower

The queen saw day grow whiter, and the fleet
Go moving over the sea, keep pace together
To the even spread of the sail; she knew the harbors
Were empty of sailors now; she struck her breast
Three times, four times; she tore her golden hair,
Crying, "God help me, will he go, this stranger,
Treating our kingdom as a joke? Bring arms,
Bring arms, and hurry! follow from all the city,
Haul the ships off the ways, some of you! Others,
Get fire as fast as you can, give out the weapons,
Pull oars! What am I saying? Or where am I?
I must be going mad. Unhappy Dido,
Is it only now your wickedness strikes home?
The time it should have was when you gave him power.
Well, here it is, look at it now, the honor,
The faith of the hero who, they tell me, carries
With him his household gods, who bore on his shoulders
His aged father! Could I not have seized him,
Torn him to pieces, scattered him over the waves?
What was the matter? Could I not have murdered
His comrades, and Iulus, and served the son
For a dainty at the table of his father?
But fight would have a doubtful fortune. It might have,
What then? I was going to die; whom did I fear?
I would have, should have, set his camp on fire,
Filled everything with flame, choked off the father,
The son, the accursed race, and myself with them.
Great Sun, surveyor of all the works of earth,
Juno, to whom my sorrows are committed,
Hecate, whom the cross-roads of the cities
Wail to by night, avenging Furies, hear me,
Grant me divine protection, take my prayer.
If he must come to harbor, then he must,
If Jove ordains it, however vile he is,
False, and unspeakable. If Jove ordains,
The goal is fixed. So be it. Take my prayer.
Let him be driven by arms and war, an exile,
Let him be taken from his son Iulus,
Let him beg for aid, let him see his people dying
Unworthy death, let him accept surrender
On unfair terms, let him never enjoy the kingdom,
The hoped-for light, let him fall and die, untimely,

Let him lie unburied on the sand. Oh, hear me,
Hear the last prayer, poured out with my last blood!
Are you, O Tyrians, hate, and hate forever
The Trojan stock. Offer my dust this homage.
No love, no peace, between these nations, ever!"

DIDO'S LAST WORDS

VERGIL, *Aeneid*, Book 4. 642-665 (Humphries)

Dido, trembling,
Wild with her project, the blood-shot eyeballs rolling,
Pale at the death to come, and hectic color
Burning the quivering cheeks, broke into the court,
Mounted the pyre in madness, drew the sword,
The Trojan gift, bestowed for no such purpose,
And she saw the Trojan garments, and the bed
She knew so well, and paused a little, weeping,
Weeping, and thinking, and flung herself down on it,
Uttering her last words:—
"Spoils that were sweet while gods and fate permitted,
Receive my spirit, set me free from suffering.
I have lived, I have run the course that fortune gave me,
And now my shade, a great one, will be going
Below the earth. I have built a noble city,
I have seen my walls, I have avenged a husband,
Punished a hostile brother. I have been
Happy, I might have been too happy, only
The Trojans made their landing." She broke off,
Pressed her face to the couch, cried:—"So, we shall die,
Die unavenged; but let us die. So, so,—
I am glad to meet the darkness. Let his eyes
Behold this fire across the sea, an omen
Of my death going with him."

As she spoke,
Her handmaids saw her, fallen on the sword,
The foam of blood on the blade, and blood on the hands.

~~~~~

THE DEATH OF DIDO

VERGIL, *Aeneid*, Book 4. 693-705 (Humphries)

At last all-powerful Juno, taking pity,
Sent Iris from Olympus, in compassion
For the long racking agony, to free her
From the limbs' writhing and the struggle of spirit.
She had not earned this death, she had only sought it
Before her time, driven by sudden madness,
Therefore, the queen of Hades had not taken
The golden lock, consigning her to Orcus.
So Iris, dewy on saffron wings, descending,
Trailing a thousand colors through the brightness
Comes down the sky, poises above her, saying,
"This lock I take as bidden, and from the body
Release the soul," and cuts the lock; and cold
Takes over, and the winds receive the spirit.

~~~~~

MYTHS OF EARLY ROME

VERGIL, *Aeneid*, Book 8. 626-674 (Mackail)

After he leaves Carthage Aeneas returns to Sicily, where he holds funeral games in memory of his father Anchises. He finally reaches Italy and visits the Underworld. His long conflict with the native inhabitants begins. Aeneas enters into friendly relations with King Latinus, is opposed by a confederation of Italic peoples, obtains Etruscan allies, and is aided by Evander, the Arcadian king of a colony on the site of Rome. Venus gives Aeneas a shield made for him by Vulcan on which are depicted the most famous of Rome's myths.

There the Lord of Fire had fashioned the story of Italy and the triumphs of the Romans, not witless of prophecy or ignorant of the age to be; there all the race of Ascanius' future seed and their wars fought one after one. Likewise had he fashioned the she-wolf couched after the birth in the green cave of Mars; round her teats the twin boys hung playing, and fearlessly mouthed their foster-mother; she, with sleek neck bent back, stroked them by turns and shaped their bodies with her tongue. Thereto not far from this he had set Rome and the lawless rape of the Sabines in the concourse of the theater when the great Circensian games were held, and a fresh war suddenly arising between the people of Romulus and aged Tatius and austere Cures. Next these same kings laid down their mutual strife and stood armed before Jove's altar with cup in hand, and joined treaty over a slain sow. Not far from there four-hourse chariots driven apart had torn Mettus asunder (but thou, O Alban, shouldst have kept by thy words!), and Tullus tore the flesh of the liar through the forest, his splashed blood dripping from the briars. Therewithal Porsena commanded to admit the exiled Tarquin, and held the city in the grasp of a strong blockade; the Aeneadae rushed on the sword for liberty. Him thou couldst espy like one who chafes and like one who threatens, because Cocles dared to tear down the bridge, and Cloelia broke her bonds and swam the river. Highest of all Manlius, warder of the Tarpeian fortress, stood with the temple behind him and held the high Capitoline; and Romulus' palace stood fresh in its crisp thatch. And here the silver goose, fluttering in the gilded colonnades, cried that the Gauls were there on the threshold. The Gauls were there among the brushwood, hard on the fortress, secure in the darkness and the dower of dim night. Their clustering locks are of gold, and of gold their attire; their striped cloaks glitter, and their milk-white necks are entwined with gold. Two Alpine pikes sparkle in the hand of each, and long shields guard their bodies. Here he had embossed the dancing Salii and the naked Luperci, the miters wreathed in wool, and the sacred shields that fell from heaven; in cushioned cars the virtuous matrons led on their rites through the city. Far hence he adds the habitations of hell also, the high gates of Dis and the dooms of guilt; and thee, O Catiline, clinging on the beetling rock and shuddering at the faces of the Furies; and far apart the good, Cato delivering them statutes. Amidst it all flows wide the likeness of the swelling sea, wrought in gold, though the foam surged gray upon blue water; and round about dolphins, in shining silver, swept the seas with their tails in circle as they cleft through the tide.

~~~~~

THE DEATH OF PALLAS

VERGIL, *Aeneid*, Book 10. 453-509 (Mackail)

Evander sends his son Pallas to the war. He is killed by Turnus, the leader of the enemy and Aeneas' rival for the hand of the native princess Lavinia.

Turnus leaps from his chariot and prepares to close with Pallas. And as a lion sees from some lofty outlook a bull stand far off on the plain revolving battle, and flies at him, even such to see is Turnus' coming. When Pallas deemed him within reach of a spear-throw, he advances, if so chance may assist the daring of his overmatched strength, and thus cries into the depth of sky: "By my father's hospitality and the board whereto thou camest a wanderer, on thee I call, Alcides; be favorable to my high emprise; let Turnus even in death discern me stripping his blood-stained armor, and his swooning eyes endure the sight of his conqueror." Alcides heard him, and deep in his heart he stifled a heavy sigh, and let idle tears fall. Then with kindly words the father accosts his son: "Each has his own appointed day; short and irrecoverable is the span of life for all: but to spread renown by deeds is the task of valor. Under high Troy town many and many a god's son fell; nay, mine own child Sarpedon likewise perished. Turnus too his own fate summons, and his allotted period has reached the goal." So speaks he, and turns his eyes away from the Rutulian fields. But Pallas hurls his spear with all his strength, and pulls his sword flashing out of the hollow scabbard. The flying spear lights where the armor rises high above the shoulder, and, forcing a way through the shield's rim, stayed not till it drew blood from mighty Turnus. At this Turnus long poises the spearshaft with its sharp steel head, and hurls it on Pallas with these words: "See thou if our weapon have not a keener point." He ended; but for all the shield's plating of iron and brass, for all the bull-hide that covers it round about, the quivering spear-head smashes it fair through and through, passes the guard of the corslet, and pierces the breast with a gaping hole. He tears the warm weapon from the wound; in vain; together and at once life-blood and sense follow it.

He falls heavily on the ground, his armor clashes over him, and his bloodstained face sinks in death on the hostile soil. And Turnus standing over him . . . : "Arcadians," he cries, "remember these my words, and bear them to Evander. I send him back his Pallas as was due. All the meed of the tomb, all the solace of sepulture, I give freely. Dearly must he pay his welcome to Aeneas." And with these words, planting his left foot on the dead, he tore away the broad heavy sword-belt engraven with a tale of crime, the array of grooms foully slain together on their bridal night, and the nuptial chambers dabbled with blood, which Clonus, son of Eurytus, had wrought richly in gold. Now Turnus exults in spoiling him of it, and rejoices at his prize. Ah spirit of man, ignorant of fate and the allotted future, or to keep bounds when elate with prosperity!—the day will come when Turnus shall desire to have bought Pallas' safety at a great ransom, and curse the spoils of this fatal day. But with many moans and tears Pallas' comrades lay him on his shield and bear him away amid their ranks. O grief and glory and grace of the father to whom thou shalt return! This one day sent thee first to war, this one day takes thee away, while yet thou leavest heaped high thy Rutulian dead.

THE DEATH OF TURNUS

VERGIL, *Aeneid*, Book 12. 924-952 (Mackail)

The long conflict ends with Aeneas the victor over Turnus.

Carrying grim death with it, Aeneas' spear flies in fashion of some dark whirlwind, and opens the rim of the corslet and the utmost circles of the sevenfold shield. Right through the thigh it passes hurtling on; under the blow Turnus falls huge to earth with his leg doubled under him. The Rutulians start up with a groan, and all the hill echoes round about, and the width of high woodland returns their cry. Lifting up beseechingly his humbled eyes and suppliant hand: "I have deserved it," he says, "nor do I ask for mercy; use thy fortune. If an unhappy parent's distress may at all touch thee, this I pray; even such a father was Anchises to thee; pity Daunus' old age, and restore to my kindred which thou wilt, me or my body bereft of day. Thou art conqueror, and the Ausonians have seen me stretch conquered hands. Lavinia is thine in marriage; press not hatred farther."

Aeneas stood wrathful in arms, with rolling eyes, and lowered his hand; and now and now yet more the speech began to bend him to waver: when high on his shoulder appeared the sword-belt with the shining bosses that he knew, the luckless belt of the boy Pallas, whom Turnus had struck down with mastering wound, and wore on his shoulders the fatal ornament. The other, as his eyes drank in the plundered record of his fierce grief, kindles to fury, and cries terrible in anger: "Mayest thou, clad in the spoils of my dearest, be snatched from me now? Pallas it is, Pallas who strikes the deathblow, and exacts vengeance in thy guilty blood." So saying, he fiercely plunges the steel full in his breast. But his limbs grow slack and chill, and the life with a moan flies indignant into the dark.

I V

INDIVIDUAL
MYTHS

BELLEROPHON

PINDAR, *Olympian*, 13. 60-90 (Lattimore)

The Danaans shook before Glaukos, who came from Lykia. Be-
    fore them
he vaunted that in the city of Peirene the power abode
and the deep domain and the house of Bellerophon, his fore-
    father,

who beside the Springs, striving to break the serpent Gorgon's
    child,
Pegasos, endured much hardship
until the maiden Pallas gave him
the bridle gold-covered. Out of dream
there was waking, and she spoke: "Do you sleep, king descended
    of Aiolos?
Behold, take this magic for the horse
and dedicate to the father who tames
beasts, a shining bull in sacrifice."

To his dream in darkness
the girl of the black shield seemed to speak
such things, and he sprang upright on his feet.
Gathering up the strange thing that lay beside him,
he sought out, delighted, the prophet in the land
and showed Koiranides all the ending of the matter, how he had
    slept
that night, at his behest, by the goddesses' altar. How the very
    child

of Zeus of the thunder-spear had given into
his hands the conquering gold.
The seer bade him obey
in speed the dream; and, when he had immolated
a bull to him who grips the earth in his wide strength,
to found straightway an altar of Athene of the horses.
God's power makes light possession of things beyond oath or
  hope.
Strong Bellerophon, pondering, caught
with the quiet device drawn to the jaw

the winged horse. Riding, he made weapon play in full armor of
  bronze.
So mounted, out of the cold gulfs
of the high air forlorn, he smote
the archered host of women, the Amazons;
and the Chimaira, breathing flame; and the Solymoi, and slew
  them.
On his fate at the last I will keep silence.

BELLEROPHON

HOMER, *Iliad*, Book 6. 152-202 (Derby)

There is a city, in the deep recess
Of pastoral Argos, Ephyre by name:
There Sisyphus of old his dwelling had,
Of mortal men the craftiest; Sisyphus,
The son of Aeolus; to him was born
Glaucus; and Glaucus in his turn begot
Bellerophon, on whom the Gods bestowed
The gifts of beauty and of manly grace.
But Proetus sought his death; and, mightier far,
From all the coasts of Argos drove him forth,
To Proetus subjected by Jove's decree.
For him the monarch's wife, Antaea, nursed
A maddening passion, and to guilty love
Would fain have tempted him; but failed to move
The upright soul of chaste Bellerophon.

With lying words she then address'd the King:
"Die, Proetus, thou, or slay Bellerophon,
Who basely sought my honor to assail."
The King with anger listened to her words;
Slay him he would not; that his soul abhorred;
But to the father of his wife, the King
Of Lycia, sent him forth, with tokens charged
Of dire import, on folded tablets traced,
Poisoning the monarch's mind, to work his death.
To Lycia, guarded by the Gods, he went;
But when he came to Lycia, and the streams
Of Xanthus, there with hospitable rites
The King of wide-spread Lycia welcomed him.
Nine days he feasted him, nine oxen slew;
But with the tenth return of rosy morn
He questioned him, and for the tokens asked
He from his son-in-law, from Proetus, bore.
The tokens' fatal import understood,
He bade him first the dread Chimaera slay;
A monster, sent from Heaven, not human born,
With head of lion, and a serpent's tail,
And body of a goat; and from her mouth
There issued flames of fiercely-burning fire:
Yet her, confiding in the Gods, he slew.
Next, with the valiant Solymi he fought,
The fiercest fight that e'er he undertook.
Thirdly, the women-warriors he o'erthrew,
The Amazons; from whom returning home,
The King another stratagem devised;
For, choosing out the best of Lycia's sons,
He set an ambush; they returned not home,
For all by brave Bellerophon were slain.
But, by his valor when the King perceived
His heavenly birth, he entertained him well;
Gave him his daughter; and with her the hall
Of all his royal honors he bestowed:
A portion too the Lycians meted out,
Fertile in corn and wine, of all the state
The choicest land, to be his heritage.
Three children there to brave Bellerophon
Were born; Isander, and Hippolochus,
Laodamia last, beloved of Jove,

The Lord of counsel; and to him she bore
Godlike Sarpedon of the brazen helm.
Bellerophon at length the wrath incurred
Of all the Gods; and to the Aleian plain
Alone he wandered; there he wore away
His soul, and shunned the busy haunts of men.

CADMUS

OVID, *Metamorphoses*, Book 3. 1-137 (Gregory)

Even now Jove shed the image of a bull,
Confessed himself a god, and stepped ashore
On the beached mountainside of Crete,
This while Europa's father, ignorant
Of what fate fell upon his ravished daughter,
Sent his son Cadmus out to look for her,
Saying if he did not find her, exile
Would be his doom, a warning that was both
Pious and cursed. After Agenor's son
Went up and down the world (who can discover
A secret Jove conceals?) the boy, distraught,
Fearful of Father's anger, strayed from home
To be a stranger everywhere he turned.
Cadmus, a pilgrim, came to Phoebus' shrine
To ask Apollo's spirit where to live,
And Phoebus said, "Go to the countryside,
Where lonely in a field a white ox wanders,
One who has never led the crooked plough
Nor carried the bent yoke across her shoulders.
Go with her till she falls to rest in grass,
And in this place erect your city's walls,
Then to her honor call it Boeotia."
As soon as Cadmus stepped down from Parnassus
He saw the wandering ox who strolled alone
Unmarked by plough or halter. Thoughtfully
He kept in step behind her, singing praise
Beneath his breath to Phoebus who had shown
Him where to go. Meanwhile the beast had led him
Through shoals of Cephisus and past deserted

Plains of Panope, where she stood still and
Lifted her fair head up with wide-spread horns
As though they pierced the very veils of heaven,
Then filled the air with her deep cries; she turned
To look behind to see who followed her,
Then kneeled, then sank to rest upon sweet grasses.
Cadmus thanked heaven and bent to kiss the earth,
Such was his praise of unknown fields and mountains.

    With piety in mind Cadmus prepared
Duties to Jove and sent his men to look
For running waters, sacred springs and rills.
The men arrived upon a trackless forest
And deep within it, fast with underbrush,
A cave. There, through a rock-hung arc rushed its
Welled waters; and the place was shared by Mars'
Serpent who wore a golden plume, who as
He rolled his body thick with bile poured fire
From his eyes; flashed from his triple teeth
His three-pronged tongue. When the misfortunate
Tyrians stumbled here, they dipped their pitchers
Into the cave's well; the silence then became‾
A plangent darkness and a hissing terror
As sea-blue snake's long head rose from the cave
And into outer air. Water jugs and pitchers
Slipped from men's hands and blood ran chill and limbs
Were taken with cold palsy. Then as the serpent
Wheeled in glittering knots, at once he
Had become a great arc, swung more than half
His length in air, as though his eyes looked down
Over the forest. If it were possible
To see him at a glance, he was as high,
As long, as sky's snake that shines at night
Between twin bears. Nor did he waste his time,
But fell on the Phoenicians, whether they
Ran or showed fight, stilled or held back by fear.
Some he killed outright with his forked tongue,
And some were crushed within his knotted tail,
Some lost their lives within his tainted breath.

    When sun at noon had narrowed shade on earth,
Cadmus began to miss his men and set out

To find where they had gone, or if they'd strayed:
His shield a lion's carcass, his arms a javelin
And iron-tipped spear—and better yet than these,
A hardy spirit—fit to enter deepest woods,
To see about him the poor bodies of his men,
And above them their victorious enemy,
Gorged with their entrails, eating at their wounds
With blood-wet tongue. Then Cadmus cried aloud,
"O naked dead, all friends grown true to me,
Your vengeance mine, or I shall die with you."
And as he spoke, his body swayed with weight
Of the great stone he hurled with his right hand—
A shot (that would have made thick walls collapse
And towers fall) struck the shrewd serpent, yet
The beast rose unharmed; his scales and dark skin
Were like sheets of iron. But these could not
Endure the javelin-thrust that pierced mid-length
His back, its iron shaft deep-bedded
In his side. The creature, wild with pain, reared
Up his head, saw where he suffered, bit at
The shaft, and, writhing as he eased the folds
Around it, drew it out, yet the sharp spear-
Head held fast within his spine, while greater
Heat waked fires in his rage. His throat grew large
With flooded veins, and white foam gushed and bubbled
At his black jaws. And as his scales scraped earth
A tearing sound grew everywhere, and foul
Dark odors like the breath of Hell through air.
The serpent wheeled in green and yellow rings
As high as trees, then rolling into floods
Like springtide rivers, his heavy breast tore down
The forest as he moved. Cadmus stepped back,
Took up the serpent's rushes at his shield,
The lion's skin, but thrust his spear into
The serpent's mouth; the beast in rage clamped down
The iron bit between his teeth, yet could not
Break it, then his black throat began to bleed
And green grass at his feet grew red with blood.
Because the beast retreated at each spear-
Thrust the wound was shallow, yet hardy Cadmus
Kept the spear forward at the serpent's throat
Until an oak stood at its back; then with

A last lunge Cadmus followed his stroke home
Through beast and oak. The tree swayed double
With the serpent's weight, its great sides moaned
As the spent monster lashed them with his tail.

While Cadmus, victor, stared at his great prize,
The conquered beast, a voice came to his ears,
From where he did not know, but heard it say,
"O son of Agenor, why look at ruins
Of monsters you've destroyed? You too shall be
A serpent in men's eyes!" Cold terror came
At him, he pale and trembling stood with hair
As stiff as frost. But look! His good friend Pallas,
Slipped down beside him from the vault of heaven,
Told him to salt the earth with serpent's teeth
Which were to be the seeds of a new people.
At her command, he steered his deep-forked plough
And sowed the earth with teeth of the dead creature,
The seeds of mortal being. Then (as by magic)
The field began to break and from its furrows
First came a line of lances, then gay plumes,
Fluttering in air, then helmets, iron shoulders,
Breastplates, swords, javelins, shields, till earth
Grew heavy with its crowds of men at arms.
As on a feast day when theaters are thrown open
The curtains part and men rise up from trapdoors
Of the stage—first seen are faces, then slowly
The actors in full dress, their feet in line
Behind the curtain's margin—so was the rise
Of the armed charging army Cadmus saw.

In terror at what seemed new enemies,
Cadmus picked up his javelin and shield;
"Hands up," one of the earth's progeny called out,
"You have no business in our civil war."
With this his broad sword slashed his earth-born brother,
And as he closed with him he fell, struck by
A javelin thrown from another quarter,
And as his slayer turned, he too was killed,
All dying in the same breath and spirit,
The give and take of war, they spent on each.
These brothers of mutual madness and disaster

Died by their common wounds; the young,
Whose lives were all too short, lay groaning
In warm heart's blood on earth which gave them birth—
All except five, and one was Echion,
Who at Minerva's orders dropped his sword
And made a truce with his surviving brothers.
These were the friends that homeless Cadmus had
To build the city of Phoebus' oracle.

Now Thebes arose, and Cadmus, though exiled,
Would've seemed to be the happiest of men,
His wife the child of Venus and of Mars,
His children worthy of their heritage,
O many sons and daughters at his side!
And grandsons grown to men. Yet no man
Is called happy till his death, and all
The taxes at his wake and funeral paid.

DAEDALUS

OVID, *Metamorphoses*, 8. 153-235 (Humphries)

Minos duly paid his vows to Jove,
A hundred bulls, on landing, and in the palace
Hung up the spoils of war, but in his household
Shame had grown big, and the hybrid monster-offspring
Revealed his queen's adultery, and Minos
Contrived to hide this specimen in a maze,
A labyrinth built by Daedalus, an artist
Famous in building, who could set in stone
Confusion and conflict, and deceive the eye
With devious aisles and passages. As Maeander
Plays in the Phyrygian fields, a doubtful river,
Flowing and looping back and sends its waters
Either to source or sea, so Daedalus
Made those innumerable windings wander,
And hardly found his own way out again,
Through the deceptive twistings of that prison.
Here Minos shut the Minotaur, and fed him

Twice, each nine years, on tribute claimed from Athens,
Blood of that city's youth. But the third tribute
Ended the rite forever. Ariadne,
For Theseus' sake, supplied the clue, the thread
Of gold, to unwind the maze which no one ever
Had entered and left, and Theseus took her with him,
Spreading his sails for Dia, and there he left her,
Fine thanks for her devotion, but Bacchus brought her
His loving aid, and that she might be shining
In the immortal stars, he took the chaplet
She wore, and sent it spinning high, its jewels
Changing to gleaming fire, a coronal
Still visible, a heavenly constellation
Between the Kneeler and the Serpent-Holder.

Homesick for homeland, Daedalus hated Crete
And his long exile there, but the sea held him.
"Though Minos blocks escape by land or water,"
Daedalus said, "surely the sky is open,
And that's the way we'll go. Minos' dominion
Does not include the air." He turned his thinking
Toward unknown arts, changing the laws of nature.
He laid out feathers in order, first the smallest,
A little larger next it, and so continued,
The way that pan-pipes rise in gradual sequence.
He fastened them with twine and wax, at middle,
At bottom, so, and bent them, gently curving,
So that they looked like wings of birds, most surely.
And Icarus, his son, stood by and watched him,
Not knowing he was dealing with his downfall,
Stood by and watched, and raised his shiny face
To let a feather, light as down, fall on it,
Or stuck his thumb into the yellow wax,
Fooling around, the way a boy will, always,
Whenever a father tries to get some work done.
Still, it was done at last, and the father hovered,
Poised, in the moving air, and taught his son:
"I warn you, Icarus, fly a middle course:
Don't go too low, or water will weigh the wings down;
Don't go too high, or the sun's fire will burn them.
Keep to the middle way. And one more thing,
No fancy steering by star or constellation,

Follow my lead!" That was the flying lesson,
And now to fit the wings to the boy's shoulders.
Between the work and warning the father found
His cheeks were wet with tears, and his hands trembled.
He kissed his son (*Good-bye,* if he had known it),
Rose on his wings, flew on ahead, as fearful
As any bird launching the little nestlings
Out of high nest into thin air. *Keep on,*
Keep on, he signals, *follow me!* He guides him
In flight—O fatal art!—and the wings move
And the father looks back to see the son's wings moving.
Far off, far down, some fisherman is watching
As the rod dips and trembles over the water,
Some shepherd rests his weight upon his crook,
Some ploughman on the handles of the ploughshare,
And all look up, in absolute amazement,
At those air-borne above. They must be gods!
They were over Samos, Juno's sacred island,
Delos and Paros toward the left, Lebinthus
Visible to the right, and another island,
Calymne, rich in honey. And the boy
Thought *This is wonderful!* and left his father,
Soared higher, higher, drawn to the vast heaven,
Nearer the sun, and the wax that held the wings
Melted in that fierce heat, and the bare arms
Beat up and down in air, and lacking oarage
Took hold of nothing. *Father!* he cried, and *Father!*
Until the blue sea hushed him, the dark water
Men call the Icarian now. And Daedalus,
Father no more, called "Icarus, where are you!
Where are you, Icarus? Tell me where to find you!"
And saw the wings on the waves, and cursed his talents,
Buried the body in a tomb, and the land
Was named for Icarus.

IO

BACCHYLIDES, *Complete Poems*, 19 (Fagles)

Rife are the roads
Of immortal song—
If Pierian Muses
Grant you gifts,
And winners of wreaths,
The Graces whose eyelids
Bloom to black,
Bind honor
Around your hymns:
So weave my lines
In a fresh design
For lovestruck Athens
Dear to the gods,
Genius of Ceos
Charged with fame.
Your flight soars high
On Calliope's prize
That climbs esteem.

Why did the Limitless Lord
Direct that Inachus' Io
With fresh hands,
The peerless calfgirl
Race out of foaling Argos?
Hera, superb Queen
With the golden robes,
Commanded Argus
Whose glances bristle
Out through the world,
To manage a close
And sleepless watch
On her spiral horns,
And Hermes could not
Outwit him in mornings

Rinsed by the sun
Or the rapt nights.
But if in struggle
The Master's herald
Pounced on the spawn
Of prolific Earth,
Argus proud in arms,
Or his menacing eyes
Fell limp from his stint of work,
Or sleep slipped in on Pierian song,
Dissolving his endless cares—
No matter:
Mine is the road
That leaps time,
Till Io distract
From the gadfly's sting,
Came where the Nile teems,
Her belly quick
With the touch of Zeus;
Birthing Epaphus,
Prince alive
With eminent honor,
King of a land
Of linen stoles,
She gave to light
Man's greatest line,
The roots of Cadmus,
Agenor's son
Who in Thebes
Of the Seven Gates,
Sired Semele, mother
Of frenzy-incensing Dionysus,
Lord of delightful rites
And the chorus that wins wreaths.

~~~~~

NIOBE

HOMER, *Iliad*, Book 24. 602-617 (Bryant)

For even Niobe, the golden-haired,
Refrained not from her food, though children twelve
Perished within her palace,—six young sons
And six fair daughters. Phoebus slew the sons
With arrows from his silver bow, incensed
At Niobe, while Dian, archer-queen,
Struck down the daughters; for the mother dared
To make herself the peer of rosy-cheeked
Latona, who, she boastfully proclaimed,
Had borne two children only, while herself
Had brought forth many. Yet, though only two,
The children of Latona took the lives
Of all her own. Nine days the corses lay
In blood, and there was none to bury them,
For Jove had changed the dwellers of the place
To stone; but on the tenth the gods of heaven
Gave burial to the dead. Yet Niobe,
Though spent with weeping long, did not refrain
From food. And now forever mid the rocks
And desert hills of Sipylus, where lie,
Fame says, the couches of the goddess-nymphs,
Who lead the dance where Acheloüs flows,
Although she be transformed to stone, she broods
Over the woes inflicted by the gods.

~~~~~

PROCNE

OVID, *Metamorphoses*, Book 6. 422-673 (Gregory)

Athens sent no word;
For war had severed diplomatic ties—

Barbarians from across the seas were storming
Its walls once fortified by Mopsopius.
Tereus fought them back with his battalion
That raised the siege which gave him greater fame.
Since he was rich and had his own stout army,
And fortunate also in having noble blood
From Mars himself—King Pandion of Athens
Took him as son-in-law, husband of Procne.
But Juno, chosen as the bride's own goddess,
Hymen, and the three Graces were not there
To bless the wedding—and the Furies came
With torches stolen from a funeral pyre;
They made the bridal bed, and a scritch owl
Howled from the rafters of the wedding room:
And with these blessings Procne took Tereus
And in their presence they conceived a child.
All Thrace joined in a general celebration
And praised the gods: first when King Pandion's
Daughter received her lord and their great tyrant,
And second on that day Itys was born—
So are the fortunes of our lives concealed.

Now through five autumns Titan turned the years,
Then Procne, as she flirted with her husband,
Said, "Dear, if I am sweet to give you pleasure,
Let me go home to visit with my sister.
Or rather, bring her here to visit us;
Promise my father that her stay is short—
For if I see her, that is my reward."
Swiftly Tereus mounted sail and oar;
Steering through Cerops' harbor he set foot
On Piraeus and took the king's right hand:
Good cheer and welcome!—then began to talk
Of why he came, his wife's desire, and said her
Sister would be returned almost at once
To her own home—when look! the girl walked in,
Young Philomela, dressed like any queen
But richer underneath her clothes her beauty;
So as one hears of water nymphs and dryads
Moving among the green shades of the forest,
It was the way she seemed—that is, if they
Were dressed as fine as she. With one look at her

Tereus was in flames—the kind of fire
That sweeps through corn, dry leaves, or autumn hay
Heaped in a barn. Of course the girl was worth it,
But all his natural passions drove him on;
Men of his country were well known for heat—
Their fire took root within him as his own.
His impulse was to bribe her maids, her nurse,
Or with his riches make the girl a whore,
Even at the price of losing all he ruled,
Or rape her at the cost of war and terror.
Stormed by the heat of love, nothing could stop him,
Nor heart hold back the flames within his body.
Nor could he wait: he made his wishes seem
Procne's desire; love made him quick of speech,
And when he talked too fast, too eagerly,
He said he took instructions from his wife
And at her inspiration begged and wept.
Great gods! What darkness fills the human heart!
As he built up his plans Tereus got
Credit for being kind, soft, pious; he
Was loudly praised for criminal intentions,
And more than that, unwary Philomela
Shared his impatience; with her soothing arms
Around her father's neck, she begged to go,
To see her sister for her own good health—
But, if she knew, against it; still she pleaded.
As Tereus looked at her, he had a vision:
The girl was in his arms. Then as she glided
Her arms around her father's neck and kissed him
All this increased his fire; he saw himself
Taking her father's place—if he had done so,
His flushed desires were none the less unholy.
King Pandion at last gave way to both;
Tereus' wishes were no less obscene,
His hopes were no less evil. Then the King
Gave way to them. His daughter danced with joy
And thanked her father for herself and Procne,
Unlucky fool!—which brought despair for both.

Day's journey of the Sun had nearly ended,
Westward his horses steered behind Olympus.
Royal supper served, red wine in golden vessels,

Feasted and drunk, the palace fell asleep,
But not Tereus—though he went to bed,
His mind still boiled with thoughts of Philomela,
Her glance, how she moved her feet and hands—
And what he had not seen he well imagined,
Which fed his furnace high and drove off sleep.
Daylight arrived and Pandion wrung his hand,
And weeping gave his daughter to his care:
"My loving son, benevolence has won me;
Since both my daughters wish to see each other
(And that is your desire, my Tereus)
I trust this girl to you; and by your faith,
Our kinship and gods' will, take charge of her
As with a father's love, and in brief season
(Which is long to me!) send the girl home again,
For she's the last delight of my old age.
And as you think of me, my Philomela
Come back to me at once (even your sister
Is far away)." These were his last instructions:
He kissed his child with swelling tears, then asked
The two to keep their promises by taking
His right hand, and joined theirs to seal the contract,
Not to forget to bring from him warm greetings
To Procne and her son; at this his voice
Gave way; he shook with weeping and thick tears
Through his good-byes. He feared what was to come.

With Philomela on his painted galley,
Waves curled and toiling under its swift oars,
Land falling out of sight, then stout Tereus
Cried, "Now, I've won the answer to my prayers!"
His barbarous heart held cheers, and he could barely
Hold back his naked gladness; his eyes shone at her
Never to leave her face; he, like Jove's eagle
When the bird has clawed then dropped a shrinking
Rabbit in a high nest and the spent creature
Has no chance of an escape—Tereus gazed,
And gloried at the prospect of his feast.

The wave-tossed ship soon struck the shores of Thrace,
Then the barbarian king seized Pandion's daughter,
And where old forests hid a small stone cottage

He thrust her in and turned to lock the door;
The girl, pale, frightened, shaken with tears, asked where
Her sister was, while he disclosed his need
And mounted her. Like any helpless girl,
Trapped and alone, she cried out for her father,
Then her sister, but, more than these, she called
The names of gods. She trembled like a lamb,
Which, torn and fearful, clipped by a gray wolf
Does not believe itself alive, or as a pigeon
Blood-winged and throbbing from the claws that pierced it,
Still fears the tearing of its beating veins.
When her mind cleared she plucked her hanging hair,
Tore at her arms like one who had seen death,
Then with her hands reached out she said,
"What have you done to me? O beast, O savage horror!
Have you undone my father's will, his words,
His tears, my sister's love, my innocence,
The laws of marriage? And all changed to madness!
I am a whore that turns against her sister,
And you are married to us both; now even Procne
Is my enemy; why don't you kill me?
O liar, liar, false! I wish you had,
Even before this happened; I'd be a ghost,
Bloodless and pure among the shades. If those
Who live above the earth look down, if there are gods
Who see and know this room, my fate, my terror,
If all things have not perished where I turn,
The day will come, or late or very soon
When you shall find just payment for your crimes.
I'll tell the world how you have ravished me,
And if you keep me here within the forest,
I'll make each rock, each stone weep with my story,
And if God lives, heaven and He shall hear it."

At which the tyrant's anger rose in flames,
No less his fear; quickened by both, he drew
Sword from its scabbard at his side, and seized
His mistress by her hair and pinned her arms
Behind her as he bound them. Philomela
Saw the sword flash before her eyes and gave
Her neck to meet the blow, to welcome death;
Instead he thrust sharp tongs between her teeth

Her tongue still crying out her father's name.
Then as the forceps caught the tongue, his steel
Sliced through it, its roots still beating while the rest
Turned, moaning on black earth; as the bruised tail
Of a dying serpent lashes, so her tongue
Crept, throbbed, and whimpered at her feet. This done
The tyrant (it was said; we scarce accept it)
Renewed his pleasure on her wounded body.

Carrying his guilt he entered Procne's rooms,
And when his wife asked where her sister was,
He lied and sobbed, spoke of her sister's death:
His very tears made what he said seem true.
Then she ripped off her gold-embroidered cloak
And dressed in black. She raised a sepulcher
In memory of her sister and the false image
Of an absent spirit took prayers and lentils.
It was not proper that her sister's fate
Received this kind of honor or its grief.

Twice six times in the courses of the year
Phoebus rode through the wheeling Zodiac.
And how could Philomela spend her days?
A spy was kept in arms outside her door;
Around the cottage was a stout stone wall;
Her silent lips could not tell tales of loss.
Deep sadness turns to help from mother wit,
And misery generates a subtle shrewdness.
She strung crude country wool across a loom
(The purple threads pricked out against the white);
She wove a tapestry of her sad story.
When it was done she gave it to her servant,
The one poor maid she had, and with dumb show,
Begged her to take a present to the queen.
Not knowing what it was, the frail old woman
Delivered the rolled gift to Procne's hands
And when the monster's wife undid the package,
She read the fearful story of her betrayal.
Then she was silent (which was a miracle!);
Grief closed her lips, held back the words that stormed
To speak her anger; and there were no tears,

No thought of right or wrong—only her fury
With all her being speeded toward revenge.

   This was the time, once every other year,
When Thracian women held a feast to Bacchus
(Night joined their mysteries: at night Rhodope
Clanged, and all air trembled with the noise of brass).
It was at night the queen slipped from her house:
She wore the dress of Frenzy; vines that hung
Down from her hair, the deerskin flying at her
Left side, the light spear carried on her shoulder.
There with her retinue, like one gone mad with grief,
She raced the forest (O the perfect actress
Of your passion, great God Bacchus). She had come
To Philomela's hidden cottage door,
Crying the name of Bacchus, smashed its bars,
And decked her sister as a wild Bacchante,
Her face green-draped in ivy and ripe vines,
Swept her half-dazed into her own apartments.

   When Philomela saw where she had come,
The house of curses and of nameless sins,
The luckless girl went white with shock and horror
Then Procne found a room to quiet her,
Unwound the vines that hid her guilty face,
And held her in her arms. The trembling girl
Could not look at her sister; she felt shy
At being cause of Procne's injury.
Face turned to earth she wept and longed to call
Gods down to prove her sins were not her will;
Speechless, she raised her hands to speak her prayers.
But, turned to fire, Procne scolded her
And cried, "Now is no time for tears; we need
Good steel, something that has a bolder strength
Than iron, and with a keener edge, my dear.
This is my day for crime, to take a torch
To all rooms of the palace, to push Tereus,
Who made us what we are, into its flames,
Or clip away his tongue, tear out his eyes,
Cut off the genitals that injured you—
And then still gaping with a thousand wounds

Whip from that body breath of its damned soul.
My heart is fixed upon some major plan,
But what or where I'm still of several minds."

As Procne spoke, young Itys sauntered by;
The sight of him became an inspiration;
She glanced down at him with unfeeling eyes:
"How much," said she, "the boy looks like his father,"
And said no more, yet her blood boiled with rage—
Then she began to plot her new design.
But when he came to throw his arms around her
And kissed her with a sweet, curt boyishness,
Her anger vanished; she became all mother.
Though she resisted them, tears filled her eyes;
Then when she saw her plan less clear and shaken,
And she herself becoming more maternal,
She stared back at her sister, then her son,
And looked at both: "Why does one speak so sweetly,
While the other's lost tongue cannot say a word?
Why can't she call me sister? He cries mother.
I am the child of Pandion, a king,
Must I recall whose wife I am? Tereus?
Honor his bed? Such honor is perversion
In my blood!" And no more words—she caught up
Itys, and as a tigress carries off
A poor teat-sucking fawn down the deep forests
Of the Ganges' side, so she took Itys,
Far to a lonely room of the huge palace.
The boy saw death within his mother's face
And screamed, "O mother, mother!" reached his hands
As though to throw his arms around her neck,
And Procne, with no change of eyes or feature,
Ran a quick knife below his beating breast.
The boy died with one thrust, but Philomela
Stabbed through his throat; the body warm, still breathing,
Was cut and pared: some pieces turned on spits,
Others boiled in a pot. The room ran blood.

This was the preparation Procne made
For the high supper served to bold Tereus
Who in his ignorance took each dish from her hands,
She saying it was his ancient privilege

To eat the feast alone, servants and slaves
Dismissed—and she his maid in waiting. So
He sat as on a throne for a state banquet
And eagerly ate flesh of his own flesh;
Blind as he was to what his wife had done,
"Bring Itys here," he called; and she, bright with
Mad joy to be the first to let him know
His fate, cried out, "You have the boy inside."
Again he turned to ask her where he was,
And as he called a third time, Philomela,
Spotted with blood of Itys, her wild hair
Flying, leaped up to him, tossing the boy's
Blood-dabbled head into his face: at no time
Had she the greater need for words of joy
She felt at serving him. Then with a cry
The Thracian tyrant kicked away the table,
And hailed the snakehaired Furies from Hell's pit.
Now, if he could, he'd cut his breast in two
And from it tear the body of his son.
Weeping he called himself his son's sad tomb;
Then with a naked steel he paced the floor
To trap, to strike down both of Pandion's daughters—
Who flew, as if on wings, ahead of him.
In truth, they were on wings: one took to forest,
The other fluttered to the roof. Even now
Such birds have stains of murder on their breasts
In flickering drops of blood among their feathers.
And he himself in flight, spurred by hot grief
Changed to a bird, his crown spiked quills, his beak
A long spear pointed toward revenge, slow-winged,
He was a red-eyed plover, armed for war.

PHAETHON

OVID, *Metamorphoses*, Book 2. 1-331, with omissions (Humphries)

The royal palace of the Sun rose high
On lofty columns, bright with flashing gold,
With bronze that glowed like fire, and ivory crowned

The gables, and the double folding-doors
Were radiant with silver.

    .   .   .   .

And here Clymene's son
Came climbing, up the stairway to the palace,
Entered the palace which might be his father's,
Turned toward the face that might have been his father's,
And stopped, far off; he could not bear that radiance.
Clothed in a robe of crimson, there was Phoebus
High on the throne, with brightest emeralds gleaming,
To left and right the Days, the Months, the Years,
The Centuries, stood, and the Hours, at even spaces,
Young Spring was there, wearing a crown of flowers,
And naked Summer, carrying sheaves of grain,
And Autumn, stained with trodden grapes, and Winter,
Icy, with hoary hair.
                    And from their center
The all-seeing Sun saw this young man, who trembled
At all the strangeness. "Phaethon," he said,
"What have you come here for, to this high dwelling?
What do you seek, O Phaethon, my son,
Undoubtedly my son?" And the boy answered:
"O common light of the great universe,
Phoebus, my father, if I have the right
To use that name, and my mother is not lying
To hide some guilt with false pretense, my father,
Give me a proof, so people will believe me,
Know me for what I am, and let my mind
Be free from doubting!" As he spoke, the Sun-god
Put off his diadem of light, and called him
Closer and held him fast, and said, "My son,
You are worthy of acknowledgment; your mother
Has told no lies about your birth. To prove it,
To make you doubt the less, ask any favor,
Whatever you will; it surely will be granted,
I swear by Styx. I have never seen that river,
But no god takes his name in vain, so let him
Be witness of my promise."
                    As he ended,
Or even before, the boy asked for the chariot,
Control, for one day, over the winged horses.
Too late to take the oath back, but the father

Repented having sworn it; over and over
He shook his shining head. "Your words," he said,
"Have made mine rash: could I take back the promise,
This is the only thing I would deny you.
So, let me try persuasion. What you want,
My son, is dangerous; you ask for power
Beyond your strength and years: your lot is mortal,
But what you ask beyond the lot of mortals.
Poor ignorant boy, you ask for more than gods
Have any claim on. Each of them may do
Much as he will, but none of them has power,
With one exception, your father, to hold the reins
Riding that fiery car. Not even Jove,
Hurler of thunderbolts, could drive this chariot,
And who is greater than Jove? The road at first
Is steep, up-hill, and the horses hardly make it
With all their morning ardor fresh upon them.
Then it runs very high across mid-Heaven,
So very high that I myself am frightened
Sometimes, to see the world so far below me.
Last it descends as steeply as it rises,
Needing the tightest kind of rein: the goddess,
Tethys, who takes me to her ocean waters,
Has often feared for me in that downward plunging.
To make bad matters worse, the sky is always
Whirling with dizzy motion, and the stars
Wheel with its speed. I make my way against it,
I drive against the turning systems, safely,
But you—suppose you had my chariot, could you
Keep the wheels steady, fight the spin of the world?
Do you think there are cities there, and lovely woodlands,
And temples rich with gifts? No, no, my son!
That highway runs through every lurking danger,
Past fearful monsters. Even on the course,
Even with no mistake at all, you must
Pass the Bull's lowered horns, the savage Archer,
The Lion, open-mouthed, the wicked Scorpion
Curving the sweep of his arms in one direction,
The Crab another. And it is not easy
To hold these horses, hot with fire, and snorting
From mouth and nostrils. I can hardly hold them
When they warm up for the work and fight the bridle.

Beware, my son! I do not want to give you
The gift of death; there is time to change your prayer.
Of course you want the most convincing proof
I am your father. That I give you, surely,
By fearing as I do. I am proved a father
By a father's fear. Look at me! You see my face;
Would you could see my heart and all the cares
Held there for you, my son. Or look about you,
Ask something, anything, from all those riches
Of Heaven, earth, and ocean: you shall have it!
Only this one thing do not ask, I beg you;
A punishment, not a favor. Silly boy,
Why put those pleading arms around me? Doubt not,
It will be given, whatever you choose. I swore it.
But choose more wisely!"

          So his warning ended,
And did no good, as Phaethon insisted
On what he first had asked, to drive the chariot.
All that the father could do was keep him waiting,
But he finally consented, led him down
To where the chariot stood, the work of Vulcan,
Axle and pole of gold, and tires of gold,
And spokes of silver, and along the yoke
Chrysolites shone, and every kind of jewel
Gave back the bright reflection. And the boy
Was marveling at the craftsmanship, when, look you,
Aurora, watcher of the rosy morning,
Opened the crimson portals and the courtways
All full of roses, and the stars were gone,
Whom Lucifer, last of all to leave the heaven,
Marshalled along their way.

          The Sun-god saw him,
Saw the world redden, and the moon's thin crescent
Vanish from sight, and bade the speedy Hours
To yoke the horses, and they did so, quickly,
Leading them from the lofty stalls, with fire
Breathed from the nostrils, and well-fed, on juices
Of rich ambrosial fodder. Then the harness
Was put in place, and the Sun-god, for protection,
Touched his son's face with holy medication,
Put on the radiant diadem, and sighed
From his foreboding heart, and said: "At least,

My son, perhaps you can obey a father's warning:
Go easy on the whip, hard on the reins;
They need no urging, the trouble is, to hold them.
Do not cut straight through the five zones of Heaven:
The course runs on a slant, a middle pathway
Missing the north and south. Follow the wheel-tracks,
You will see them clearly. Sky and earth both need
Equal degrees of heat: too low, you burn
The one, too high the other. The middle is safest.
Beware, on the right, the writhing of the Serpent,
Beware, on the left, the dangerous sunken Altar:
Keep between both. The rest I leave to Fortune
To help you, and to give you, or I hope so,
Better direction than you give yourself.
And now, while I am talking, dewy night
Has reached her goal in the West. We cannot linger.
Our call is on us. Look! The dawn is glowing,
The shadows gone. Here, take the reins, and hold them.
Or better still—there still is time—be taking
My counsel, not my chariot. Let me light
The world, and you stand there, on solid ground,
And watch in safety."
                              But while he was talking
The boy was in the car, and stood there proudly,
Holding the reins, all happiness, and thanking
His father for the gift he gave unwilling.
Meanwhile the horses, Pyrois, Eous,
Aethon, and Phlegon, filled the air with neighing,
Snorting, and pawing at their bars. And Tethys,
Ignorant of her grandson's fate, let fall
The barriers: they had their chance at Heaven,
The horses, now, and took it, and their hoofs
Cut through the clouds before them, and their wings
Bore them aloft, and they overtook the winds
That rose from the same east. But the weight was light,
Not such as they were used to, and the yoke
Without its usual pressure; so, as schooners,
Unballasted, career and roll and yaw
Out of the proper course, so the bright chariot
Tosses and bounds, as if there were no driver.
It did not take the horses long to know it,
To run away, beyond control; the driver,

In panic, does not know in which direction
To turn the reins, does not know where the road is,
And even if he knew, he could do nothing
With those wild plunging animals. The Bear,
For the first time in all his life, grew hot
And tried, in vain, to seek forbidden oceans
For coolness, and the Serpent, near the pole,
Torpid and harmless with the chill upon him,
Burned into angry fury, and the Plow-Ox,
Clumsy and tame in the shafts of his heavy wagon,
Went dashing off in terror.
                                    From the Heaven
The unhappy boy looked down. Far, far below him
He saw the lands, and he grew pale; his knees
Trembled beneath him, and the darkness came
Into his eyes from too much light. He wishes
He had never touched those horses of his father.
To have learned his birth was nothing, to have gained
By pleading now seems worse than loss; he might be
The son of Merops, he would be even eager
To have them call him so. But he is borne
Like a ship before a gale, unsteered, unmastered,
Abandoned to the gods and useless praying.
What should he do? Much of the sky behind him,
Much more is still ahead. Imagination
Measures them both, and his eyes, at times look forward
To the West he will not reach, again look back
Eastward, and he is dazed and stunned and dazzled,
And neither drops the reins or really holds them.
He does not know the horses' names. And terror
Is doubled, tripled, as he sees around him
Strange figures in the sky and savage beasts.

                    .   .   .   .

Out of his senses, with cold fear upon him,
Phaethon dropped the reins.
                                    And when the horses
Feel them across their backs, and none to check them,
Bolting, they charge the air of unknown regions,
Wherever impulse hurls them, lawless, crashing
Against high stars; they keep the chariot bounding
Through pathless ways, now high, now low, toward Heaven
Or plunging sheer toward earth. The Moon, in wonder,

Watches her brother's horses running lower
Than her own steeds. The scorched clouds smoke. The
    mountains
Of earth catch fire, the prairies crack, the rivers
Dry up, the meadows are white-hot, the trees,
The leaves, burn to a crisp, the crops are tinder.
I grieve at minor losses. The great cities
Perish, and their great walls; and nations perish
With all their people: everything is ashes.

. . . .

And Mount Olympus . . .
The Alps, the cloud-topped Apennines, are burning.
And Phaethon sees the earth on fire; he cannot
Endure this heat, the blast of some great furnace.
Under his feet he feels the chariot glowing
White-hot; he cannot bear the sparks, the ashes,
The soot, the smoke, the blindness. He is going
Somewhere, that much he knows, but where he is
He does not know. They have their way, the horses.
And that was when, or so men think, the people
Of Africa turned black, since the blood was driven
By that fierce heat to the surface of their bodies,
And Libya was desert, and the nymphs
Mourned for their pools and fountains. And the rivers,
Wide though they might have been, had no more safety.

. . . .

The earth gapes open and the light goes down
Deep to the underworld, whose king and queen
Blink in their terror of it. Even the ocean
Shrinks to a plain of sand; the hidden mountains
Emerge to join the Cyclades; the dolphins
Dare leap and curve in the high air no longer;
The fish dive deep, and the dead seals are floating,
White-bellied, on the surface. The story has it
That Nereus and Doris and their daughters
Found even their deep-sea caverns hot and stifling.
Neptune, with scowling countenance, dared lift
His arms, three times, above the waves; three times
He could not bear the fiery air.
                And Earth,
Our mother, circled by the ocean,
Amid the waters and the shrinking fountains

Contracting into her darkness, parched by heat,
Raised up her stifled face, and put a hand
To shield her forehead, and her trembling made
Everything shudder. She sank down again,
Lower than ever before, and then she spoke:
"O greatest of the gods, if this is pleasing
And I deserve it, why hold back the lightning?
If I must die by fire, then let me perish
By fire you send, and lighten the destruction
Because you are its author. I can hardly"—
The smoke was suffocating—"open my lips to speak;
Look at my hair, burned crisp; look at the ashes
In eyes and face! Is this what I am given
For being fruitful, dutiful? for bearing
The wounds of harrow and plowshare, year on year?
Is this my due reward for giving fodder
To flocks and herds, and corn to men, and incense
For the gods' altars? Maybe I deserve it,
But what about the ocean, and your brother?
Neptune's allotted waters ebb and vanish,
Farther and farther from Heaven. Well; never mind him,
Never mind me, but have a little pity
For your own skies. Look! On both sides the poles
Are smoking. If that fire corrupts the heavens
Your palaces will topple. Even Atlas
Strains and can hardly bear his white-hot burden.
If sea and land and sky are lost, we are hurled
Into the ancient chaos. Save us, father;
Preserve this residue; take thought, take counsel
For the sum of things."

                      The Earth could say no more,
So fierce the smothering heat, and she sank deeper
Into the caverns nearer the world below us.
But the almighty father called for witness
All of the gods, and most of all the Sun-god
Who had given his son the chariot, that all things
Would perish if he did not help, and quickly.
And then he sought the citadel of Heaven,
Its very peak and pinnacle, whence he spreads
Clouds over the world and sets his thunder rolling
And hurls his lightning-bolts. But now he has
No clouds to veil the earth with, and no rainfall:

But he makes thunder sound, and poises lightning
Head-high in his right hand, and flings it from him,
Striking the charioteer, and the bolt smashes
His car, his life. So fire extinguished fire,
And the mad horses leapt, tore loose the yoke,
Broke from the broken reins. The axle lies
Far from the pole, the spokes and wheels are shattered,
The wreckage scatters far.
                                        And Phaethon,
His ruddy hair on fire, falls streaming down
The long trail of the air. A star, sometimes,
Falls from clear heaven, so, or seems to fall.
And far from home, a river-god receives him,
Bathes his poor burning face, and the Western Naiads
Give burial to the broken body, smoking
With the fire of that forked bolt, and on the stone
They carve an epitaph:
                                Here Phaethon lies,
Who drove his father's chariot: if he did not
Hold it, at least he fell in splendid daring.
And his poor father, sick at heart, refused
To show his countenance, and one whole day,
Or so men say, went by without the sun.

⁓⁓⁓

ASKLEPIOS

PINDAR, *Pythian*, 3. 1-68 (Lattimore)

I could wish that Chiron, Philyra's son
(if such word of prayer from my lips could be published),
the departed, were living yet,
child wide-minded of Uranian Kronos, and ruled the Pelian
        glades, that beast of the hills
with the heart kindly to men, as of old when he reared
the gentle smith of pain's ease to heal bodies, Asklepios,
the hero who warded sickness of every kind.

Koronis, daughter of Phlegyas the rider,
before with the ministration of Eleithyia she brought her child to
        birth, was stricken

by the golden bow of Artemis
and went down into the house of death from her chamber, by
    design of Apollo. No slight thing
is the anger of the children of Zeus. She, forgetting him
in her confused heart, accepted a second marriage, in secrecy from
    her father,
she who had lain before with Phoibos of the loose hair

and carried the immaculate seed of the god.
She could not stay for the coming of the bride-feast,
not for hymen cry in many voices, such things
as the maiden companions of youth are accustomed to sing
at nightfall, using the old names of endearment. No.
She was in love with what was not there; it has happened to
    many.
There is a mortal breed most full of futility.
In contempt of what is at hand, they strain into the future,
hunting impossibilities on the wings of ineffectual hopes.

The will of delicately robed Koronis held
this sin of pride. For she lay in bed with a stranger
that came from Arkadia, nor escaped
the Watcher. In his temple at Pytho, where the sheep are offered,
    King Loxias knew,
persuading his heart to the sheerest witness, his own
mind that knows all; he has no traffic with lies, nor god
nor man escapes him in purpose or deed of the hand.

Knowing the hospitality of bed given Ischys,
Eilatos' son, and the graceless treachery, he sent his sister, in-
    flamed
with anger that brooked no bar,
to Lakereia, for the girl lived by Boibias under the pendulous
    cliffs; her angel
shifted to evil and struck her down; and many a neighbor
shared, and was smitten together. Fire on a mountain leaping
from one seed will obliterate a great forest.

But when her kinsmen had laid the girl in the wall
of wood, and Hephaistos' greedy flame
ran high, then spoke Apollo: "No longer
will I endure in my heart the destruction of my own child

by death in agony for the weight of his mother's punish-
    ment."
He spoke, and in the first stride was there and caught the boy
from the body, and the blaze of the pyre was divided before him.
Carrying him to the centaur in Magnesia, he gave him to be per-
    fected
in the healing of sickness that brings many pains to men.

They came to him with ulcers the flesh had grown,
or their limbs mangled with the gray bronze, or bruised
with the stone flung from afar,
or the body stormed with summer fever, or chill; and he released
    each man and led him
from his individual grief. Some he treated with guile of incanta-
    tions,
some with healing potions to drink; or he tended the limbs with
    salves
from near and far; and some by the knife he set on their feet
    again.

But even genius is tied to profit. Someone
turned even Asklepios with a winning price, showing the gold in
    his hand,
to bring back from death a man
already gone. But Kronion, with a cast of his hand, tore life from
    the hearts of both men
instantly, and the shining thunder dashed them to death.
With our mortal minds we should seek from the gods that which
    becomes us,
knowing the way of the destiny ever at our feet.

—⟁—

PROTEUS

VERGIL, *Georgics*, Book 4. 387-414 (Bovie)

The nymph Cyrene advises her son Aristaeus.

"A sea-blue prophet dwells in the Aegean,
Proteus, who rides the mighty deep behind

A string of fish and brace of water-horses.
At present, he is looking in on ports
In Thessaly and his native land, Pallene.
We nymphs and ancient Nereus praise this seer
For, as a prophet, he knows everything,
What is, what has been, what is soon to come.
It pleased Neptune to grant the gift to him,
For Proteus tends the monsters of the deep
And feeds the ugly seals beneath the waves.
Now, son, first capture Proteus and chain him,
That he divulge the reason for your plague
And show its cure. But he will not give counsel
Until forced: for words he'll not relent.
So bind him fast with force and chains, and then
His tricks will clash against their bonds in vain.
I'll lead you to the place the old man hides
When the sun enkindles flaming heat at noon,
When grass is parched and cattle seek the shade.
You'll steal upon him as he lies asleep,
Tired from his morning's journey with the waves.
But when you have him anchored down with chains,
He'll alter into various forms of beast:
First to savage boar, then to jet-black tiger,
To scaly dragon, tawny lioness;
Or, hissing like greedy flame, he slips the bounds
Or dissolves into vaporous flood and so makes off.
But all the more the shapes that he assumes
Hold on, my son, and draw the chains more tight,
Until once more he turns back to the form
He had at first when sleep obscured his sight."

MIDAS

OVID, *Metamorphoses*, Book 11. 101-193 (Gregory)

Satyrs and happy drunken naked women
Surrounded Bacchus—all there except Silenus,
For the old man weighed half a ton with wine;
His years had made him heavy with his drinking.

The Spartan peasants tripped him up and caught him,
Twined vine leaves round his head and carried him
Before their famous king, unwary Midas.
Not many years ago Orpheus had taught
The joys of Bacchus to the Spartan king,
And in like fashion pleased the King of Athens.
When Midas saw the old man was Silenus—
They had been filthy drunken good old friends—
He ordered up a dozen rounds of drinks,
Then more and more, and drank ten days and nights.
When the eleventh dawn streaked hills with red
And drove reluctant stars behind the sky,
Midas, still cheerful-drunk, took gay Silenus
The road to Lydia, nor did he stop till he delivered
The old man to the ruler he loved best,
His foster child in drink, the young God Bacchus.

Then Bacchus, glad to see the old man home,
And like a good adopted son, thanked Midas,
Gave him the choice of making a wish come true:
What would he have? Midas was always sure
To make the worst of every good occasion—
Of turning glory into desperate ill—
So Midas said, "Make everything I touch turn gold."
Bacchus gave him the golden touch, yet thought
"What foolishness; it almost makes me sad." Meanwhile
The Hero Midas danced on his way, and touched all things
That flashed before his eyes. Could he believe this?
Yes! He plucked a green shoot from a tree—
It was all gold, pure gold, had the right weight and color;
Then a handful of wet clay—he had but to touch it
And it was gold. His trembling fingers plucked
A head of wheat—it might have been the promise
Of golden harvest—and next he took an apple from a tree,
And in his hand it shone as though it were a gift
Transported to him from the Hesperides.
He touched a standing beam that held the roof;
Look sharply now! It was a pillar of gold.
And as he dipped his hands in running water,
A stream of gold rushed out that could have raped Danae.
Midas' imagination, his hopes, his dreams grew big with gold:
He called his slaves to bring a feast before him,

From wine to meat to bread to fruits to wine.
And as he broke bread, that rich gift of Ceres,
It did not break but was of gold itself,
Beautifully hard, not stale, and as his teeth
Ate into meat, the meat was gold, too
And he could not close his jaws. As he poured
Water into wine (Bacchus' own wine) red, sunset colour,
And raised them to his lips, both turned to gold.
Dazed, damned by gold, a golden terror took him,
Midas began to hate his wealth, tried to escape
The very riches that he prayed for. However large
The feast laid out before him, he went hungry,
And though his throat burned dry, no drink could wet it.
By his own choice gold had become his torture.
He lifted glittering hands and arms to heaven:
"O Bacchus, Father of your unlucky son!
I have done wrong, wrong from the start, wrong, wrong forever,
But take away your gift that shines in gold.
It's damned—it curses me." Because he seemed to learn
His way was error, the gods took pity on him.
Bacchus reversed him to what he was before;
He said, "Through your own foolishness you wear
A golden coffin, your very body is a tomb of gold;
Go to the river that winds past Sardis city,
Walk up the Lydian hills to its high source,
In that pure font be birthday naked, head to foot
To wash your guilt away." The king obeyed;
And gold fell from him to the waters that ran gold.
Even now the golden touch has stained the river,
And the soil it waters is as hard as gold.

Midas, no longer lured by dreams of riches,
Took to the woods, became a nature-lover;
He worshipped Pan, uphill then down to caves
Under the mountains. His wits did not improve;
His mind was fated to undo new masters.
He lived where tall Mount Tmolus looked out far
Above the sea, one side a deep cleft down
To Sardis city, the other to Hypaepae.
As Pan sang to the country girls around him
(The girls were young, wide-eyed, and ignorant)

He held the tune by piping on his reeds.
During intermissions, he would tell them how
Much better his voice was than Apollo's;
Nor could Apollo whistle on his lyre.
In this way, with Mount Tmolus as the judge,
He entered an unequal competition.

Tmolus, both judge and mountain, was an ancient
Who took his seat on high, shaking his head
To free his ears of leaves from tallest trees;
An oak wreath held his dark green hair in order,
While acorns dangled round his cloud-white forehead.
Down, down he glanced at shaggy, goat-heeled Pan,
Then coughed. "Your judge is here," was all he said,
And Pan began to whistle country airs
Which Midas overheard and stood enchanted
Hearing them rock and roll and scream and moan.
The noise was of a kind that pierced the head
And Pan was done. Then Tmolus quickly turned
His face to Phoebus, and with him all the forest
Faced the god. Apollo's golden head shone through his laurels,
His cloak swung from his shoulders to the earth,
And 'gainst the purple folds the ivory lyre,
Flashing with diamonds, was held in his left hand,
The plectrum in his right. He was the very image
Of the artist, all poise and pose;
He touched the string and Tmolus gazed down at him;
He then told Pan to throw his pipes away.
The show was over: only echoes filled the air;
Tmolus had spoken and the lyre won.

Tmolus was cheered by everyone who heard—
And who would have his say against a mountain?
Only poor foolish Midas raised his voice
To speak for Pan. Apollo Delius
Knew well enough that Midas' ears were not
The kind of ears that human creatures wore—
So he enlarged them, made them grow gray hair,
And as they twitched, they wheeled for better hearing.
Midas looked like a man, except for ears—
Which were the property of mules and asses.

Even Midas felt a loss of dignity
And wrapped a purple turban round his head,
Which spared his vanity and held his secret.
Only the slave who trimmed King Midas' hair
Knew what another slave would love to know.
The story burned his lips—where could he tell it?
He kneeled as if to pray and with quick fingers
Thrust hand in earth, his lips above it whispered,
"King Midas has ass ears," then closed his voice
Within the hole he made, covering it up
With large handfuls of moist earth. Then frightened,
He ran away. But whispering reeds grew up
Around that spot and through the earth beneath them
The imprisoned voice came whispering to the wind,
Then all the world learned of King Midas' ears.

HIPPOLYTUS

VERGIL, *Aeneid*, Book 7. 761-782 (Mackail)

*Vergil tells the story of Hippolytus and Phaedra, with a
sequel to connect Hippolytus with Italy.*

Likewise the seed of Hippolytus marched to war, Virbius most
excellent in beauty, sent by his mother Aricia. The groves of
Egeria nursed him round the spongy shore where Diana's altar
stands rich and gracious. For they say in story that Hippolytus,
after he fell by his stepmother's treachery, torn asunder by his
frightened horses to fulfil in blood a father's revenge, came again
to the daylight and heaven's upper air, recalled by Diana's love
and the drugs of the Healer. Then the Lord omnipotent, indignant
that any mortal should rise from the nether shades to the light of
life, launched his thunder and hurled down to the Stygian water
the Phoebus-born, the discoverer of such craft and cure. But Trivia
the bountiful hides Hippolytus in a secret habitation, and sends
him away to the nymph Egeria and the woodland's keeping,
where, solitary in Italian forests, he should spend an inglorious
life, and have Virbius for his altered name. Whence also hoofed

horses are kept away from Trivia's temple and consecrated groves, because, affrighted at the portents of the sea, they overset the chariot and flung him out upon the shore. Notwithstanding did his son train his fiery steeds on the level plain, and sped charioted to war.

V

LOVERS,
IMMORTAL
AND MORTAL

Ideas of love among the ancients are best understood by bringing together some of their stories of the loves of the gods with the myths about mortal lovers. The poets who tell these stories lived in quite different societies over a period of about one thousand years, but their attitudes and sympathies cannot necessarily be related directly either to the nature of the story or to the environment of the author.

ZEUS AND HERA

HOMER, *Iliad*, Book 14. 153-353 (Pope)

Meantime Saturnia from Olympus' brow,
High-throned in gold, beheld the fields below;
With joy the glorious conflict she survey'd,
Where her great brother gave the Grecians aid.
But placed aloft, on Ida's shady height
She sees her Jove, and trembles at the sight.
Jove to deceive, what methods shall she try,
What arts, to blind his all-beholding eye?
At length she trusts her power; resolv'd to prove
The old, yet still successful, cheat of love;
Against his wisdom to oppose her charms,
And lull the Lord of Thunders in her arms.

Swift to her bright apartment she repairs,
Sacred to dress, and beauty's pleasing cares:
With skill divine had Vulcan form'd the bower,
Safe from access of each intruding power.
Touch'd with her secret key, the doors unfold
Self-closed, behind her shut the valves of gold.
Here first she bathes; and round her body pours
Soft oils of fragrance, and ambrosial showers:

The winds, perfumed, the balmy gale convey
Thro' Heav'n, thro' earth, and all th' aërial way;
Spirit divine! whose exhalation greets
The sense of Gods with more than mortal sweets.
Thus while she breathed of Heav'n, with decent pride
Her artful hands the radiant tresses tied;
Part on her head in shining ringlets roll'd,
Part o'er her shoulders waved like melted gold.
Around her next a heav'nly mantle flow'd,
That rich with Pallas' labor'd colors glow'd;
Large clasps of gold the foldings gather'd round,
A golden zone her swelling bosom bound.
Far-beaming pendants tremble in her ear,
Each gem illumin'd with a triple star.
Then o'er her head she cast a veil more white
Than new-fall'n snow, and dazzling as the light.
Last her fair feet celestial sandals grace.
Thus issuing radiant, with majestic pace,
Forth from the dome th' imperial Goddess moves,
And calls the mother of the smiles and loves.
    "How long" (to Venus thus apart she cried)
"Shall human strife celestial minds divide?
Ah yet, will Venus aid Saturnia's joy,
And set aside the cause of Greece and Troy?"
"Let Heav'n's dread Empress" (Cytherea said)
"Speak her request, and deem her will obey'd."
    "Then grant me" (said the Queen) "those conquering charms,
That Power, which mortals and immortals warms,
That love, which melts mankind in fierce desires,
And burns the sons of Heav'n with sacred fires!
For lo! I haste to those remote abodes,
Where the great parents (sacred source of Gods!)
Ocean and Tethys their old empire keep,
On the last limits of the land and deep.
In their kind arms my tender years were pass'd;
What time old Saturn, from Olympus cast,
Of upper Heav'n to Jove resign'd the reign,
Whelm'd under the huge mass of earth and main.
For strife, I hear, has made the union cease,
Which held so long that ancient pair in peace.
What honor, and what love, shall I obtain,
If I compose those fatal feuds again?

Once more their minds in mutual ties engage,
And what my youth has owed, repay their age."
   She said. With awe divine the Queen of Love
Obey'd the sister and the wife of Jove;
And from her fragrant breast the zone unbraced,
With various skill and high embroid'ry graced.
In this was ev'ry art, and ev'ry charm,
To win the wisest, and the coldest warm:
Fond love, the gentle vow, the gay desire,
The kind deceit, the still reviving fire;
Persuasive speech, and more persuasive sighs,
Silence that spoke, and eloquence of eyes.
This on her hand the Cyprian Goddess laid;
"Take this, and with it all thy wish," she said:
With smiles she took the charm; and smiling press'd
The powerful cestus to her snowy breast.
   Then Venus to the courts of Jove withdrew;
Whilst from Olympus pleas'd Saturnia flew.
O'er high Pieria thence her course she bore,
O'er fair Emathia's ever-pleasing shore,
O'er Haemus' hills with snows eternal crown'd:
Nor once her flying foot approach'd the ground.
Then taking wing from Athos' lofty steep,
She speeds to Lemnos o'er the rolling deep,
And seeks the cave of Death's half-brother, Sleep.
   "Sweet pleasing Sleep!" (Saturnia thus began)
"Who spread'st thy empire o'er each God and man;
If e'er obsequious to thy Juno's will,
O Power of Slumbers! hear, and favor still.
Shed thy soft dews on Jove's immortal eyes,
While sunk in love's entrancing joys he lies.
A splendid footstool, and a throne, that shine
With gold unfading, Somnus, shall be thine;
The work of Vulcan, to indulge thy ease,
When wine and feasts thy golden humors please."
   "Imperial Dame" (the balmy Power replies),
"Great Saturn's heir, and Empress of the Skies!
O'er other Gods I spread my easy chain;
The sire of all, old Ocean, owns my reign,
And his hush'd waves lie silent on the main.
But how, unbidden, shall I dare to steep
Jove's awful temples in the dew of sleep?

Long since, too venturous, at thy bold command,
On those eternal lids I laid my hand;
What time, deserting Ilion's wasted plain,
His conquering son, Alcides, plough'd the main:
When lo! the deeps arise, the tempests roar,
And drive the hero to the Coan shore;
Great Jove, awaking, shook the bless'd abodes
With rising wrath, and tumbled Gods on Gods;
Me chief he sought, and from the realms on high
Had hurl'd indignant to the nether sky,
But gentle Night, to whom I fled for aid
(The friend of Earth and Heav'n), her wings display'd;
Empower'd the wrath of Gods and men to tame,
Ev'n Jove revered the venerable dame."

"Vain are thy fears" (the Queen of Heav'n replies,
And, speaking, rolls her large majestic eyes);
"Think'st thou that Troy has Jove's high favor won,
Like great Alcides, his all-conquering son?
Hear, and obey the Mistress of the Skies,
Nor for the deed expect a vulgar prize:
For know, thy lov'd-one shall be ever thine,
The youngest Grace, Pasithaë the divine."

"Swear then" (he said) "by those tremendous floods,
That roar thro' Hell, and bind th' invoking Gods:
Let the great parent earth one hand sustain,
And stretch the other o'er the sacred main:
Call the black Titans that with Cronos dwell,
To hear and witness from the depths of Hell;
That she, my lov'd-one, shall be ever mine,
The youngest Grace, Pasithaë the divine."

The Queen assents, and from th' infernal bowers
Invokes the sable subtartarean powers,
And those who rule th' inviolable floods,
Whom mortals name the dread Titanian Gods.

Then, swift as wind, o'er Lemnos' smoky isle,
They wing their way, and Imbrus' sea-beat soil,
Thro' air, unseen, involv'd in darkness glide,
And light on Lectos, on the point of Ide
(Mother of savages, whose echoing hills
Are heard resounding with a hundred rills);
Fair Ida trembles underneath the God;
Hush'd are her mountains, and her forests nod.

There, on a fir, whose spiry branches rise
To join its summit to the neighb'ring skies,
Dark in embow'ring shade, conceal'd from sight,
Sat Sleep, in likeness of the bird of night
(Chalcis his name with those of heav'nly birth,
But called Cymindis by the race of earth).
   To Ida's top successful Juno flies;
Great Jove surveys her with desiring eyes:
The God, whose lightning sets the Heav'ns on fire,
Thro' all his bosom feels the fierce desire;
Fierce as when first by stealth he seiz'd her charms,
Mix'd with her soul, and melted in her arms.
Fix'd on her eyes he fed his eager look,
Then press'd her hand, and then with transport spoke:
"Why comes my Goddess from th' ethereal sky,
And not her steeds and flaming chariot nigh!"
   Then she—"I haste to those remote abodes,
Where the great parents of the deathless Gods,
The rev'rend Ocean and great Tethys reign,
On the last limits of the land and main.
I visit these, to whose indulgent cares
I owe the nursing of my tender years.
For strife, I hear, has made that union cease,
Which held so long this ancient pair in peace.
The steeds, prepared my chariot to convey
O'er earth and seas, and thro' th' aerial way,
Wait under Ide: of thy superior power
To ask consent, I leave th' Olympian bower;
Nor seek, unknown to thee, the sacred cells
Deep under seas, where hoary Ocean dwells."
   "For that" (said Jove) "suffice another day;
But eager love denies the least delay.
Let softer cares the present hour employ,
And be these moments sacred all to joy.
Ne'er did my soul so strong a passion prove,
Or for an earthly, or a heav'nly love;
Not when I press'd Ixion's matchless dame,
Whence rose Pirithous, like the Gods in fame.
Not when fair Danae felt the shower of gold
Stream into life, whence Perseus brave and bold.
Not thus I burn'd for either Theban dame
(Bacchus from this, from that Alcides came),

Not Phoenix' daughter, beautiful and young,
Whence Godlike Rhadamanth and Minos sprung;
Not thus I burn'd for fair Latona's face,
Nor comelier Ceres' more majestic grace.
Not thus ev'n for thyself I felt desire,
As now my veins receive the pleasing fire."
  He spoke; the Goddess with the charming eyes
Glows with celestial red, and thus replies:
"Is this a scene for love? On Ida's height,
Exposed to mortal and immortal sight;
Our joys profaned by each familiar eye;
The sport of Heav'n, and fable of the sky!
How shall I e'er review the bless'd abodes,
Or mix among the Senate of the Gods?
Shall I not think, that, with disorder'd charms,
All Heav'n beholds me recent from thy arms?
With skill divine has Vulcan form'd thy bower,
Sacred to love and to the genial hour;
If such thy will, to that recess retire,
And secret there indulge thy soft desire."
  She ceas'd: and smiling with superior love,
Thus answer'd mild the cloud-compelling Jove:
"Not God nor mortal shall our joys behold,
Shaded with clouds, and circumfused in gold;
Not ev'n the sun, who darts thro' Heav'n his rays,
And whose broad eye th' extended earth surveys."
  Gazing he spoke, and, kindling at the view,
His eager arms around the Goddess threw.
Glad Earth perceives, and from her bosom pours
Unbidden herbs, and voluntary flowers;
Thick new-born violets a soft carpet spread,
And clust'ring lotos swell'd the rising bed,
And sudden hyacinths the turf bestrow,
And flamy crocus made the mountain glow.
There golden clouds conceal the heav'nly pair,
Steep'd in soft joys, and circumfused with air;
Celestial dews, descending o'er the ground,
Perfume the mount, and breathe ambrosia round.
At length with Love and Sleep's soft power oppress'd,
The panting Thund'rer nods, and sinks to rest.

EUROPA

MOSCHUS, *Idyl*, 2. 1-166, with omissions (Lang)

To Europa, once on a time, a sweet dream was sent by Cypris, when the third watch of the night sets in, and near is the dawning; when sleep more sweet than honey rests on the eyelids, limb-loosening sleep, that binds the eyes with his soft bond, when the flock of truthful dreams fares wandering.

At that hour she was sleeping, beneath the roof-tree of her home, Europa, the daughter of Phoenix, being still a maid unwed. Then she beheld two Continents at strife for her sake, Asia, and the farther shore, both in the shape of women. Of these one had the guise of a stranger, the other of a lady of that land, and closer still she clung about her maiden, and kept saying how "she was her mother, and herself had nursed Europa." But that other with mighty hands, and forcefully, kept haling the maiden, nothing loth; declaring that, by the will of Aegis-bearing Zeus, Europa was destined to be her prize.

But Europa leaped forth from her strown bed in terror, with beating heart, in such clear vision had she beheld the dream. Then she sat upon her bed, and long was silent, still beholding the two women, albeit with waking eyes; and at last the maiden raised her timorous voice:—

"Who of the gods of heaven has sent forth to me these phantoms? What manner of dreams have scared me when right sweetly slumbering on my strown bed, within my bower? Ah, and who was the alien woman that I beheld in my sleep? How strange a longing for her seized my heart, yea, and how graciously she herself did welcome me, and regard me as it had been her own child.

"Ye blessed gods, I pray you, prosper the fulfilment of the dream."

Therewith she arose, and began to seek the dear maidens of her company, girls of like age with herself, born in the same year, beloved of her heart, the daughters of noble sires, with whom she was always wont to sport, when she was arrayed for the dance, or when she would bathe her bright body at the mouths of the rivers, or would gather fragrant lilies on the leas.

And soon she found them, each bearing in her hand a basket to fill with flowers, and to the meadows near the salt sea they set forth, where always they were wont to gather in their company, delighting in the roses, and the sound of the waves. But Europa herself bore a basket of gold, a marvel well worth gazing on, a choice work of Hephaestus.

Now the girls, so soon as they were come to the flowering meadows, took great delight in various sorts of flowers, whereof one would pluck sweet-breathed narcissus, another the hyacinth, another the violet, a fourth the creeping thyme, and on the ground there fell many petals of the meadows rich with spring. Others again were emulously gathering the fragrant tresses of the yellow crocus; but in the midst of them all the princess culled with her hand the splendor of the crimson rose, and shone pre-eminent among them all like the foam-born goddess among the Graces. Verily she was not for long to set her heart's delight upon the flowers, nay, nor long to keep untouched her maiden girdle. For of a truth, the son of Cronos, so soon as he beheld her, was troubled, and his heart was subdued by the sudden shafts of Cypris, who alone can conquer even Zeus. Therefore, both to avoid the wrath of jealous Hera, and being eager to beguile the maiden's tender heart, he concealed his godhead, and changed his shape, and became a bull. Not such a one as feeds in the stall nor such as cleaves the furrow, and drags the curved plough, nor such as grazes on the grass, nor such a bull as is subdued beneath the yoke, and draws the burdened cart. Nay, but while all the rest of his body was bright chestnut, a silver circle shone between his brows, and his eyes gleamed softly, and ever sent forth lightning of desire. From his brow branched horns of even length, like the crescent of the horned moon, when her disk is cloven in twain. He came into the meadow, and his coming terrified not the maidens, nay, within them all wakened desire to draw near the lovely bull, and to touch him, and his heavenly fragrance was scattered afar, exceeding even the sweet perfume of the meadows. And he stood before the feet of fair Europa, and kept licking her neck, and cast his spell over the maiden. And she still caressed him, and gently with her hands she wiped away the deep foam from his lips, and kissed the bull. Then he lowed so gently, you would think you heard the Mygdonian flute uttering a dulcet sound.

He bowed himself before her feet, and, bending back his neck, he gazed on Europa, and showed her his broad back. Then she spoke among her deep-tressed maidens, saying—

"Come, dear playmates, maidens of like age with me, let us mount the bull here and take our pastime, for truly, he will bear us on his back, and carry all of us; and how mild he is, and dear, and gentle to behold, and no whit like other bulls. A mind as honest as a man's possesses him, and he lacks nothing but speech."

So she spoke, and smiling, she sat down on the back of the bull, and the others were about to follow her. But the bull leaped up immediately, now he had gotten her that he desired, and swiftly he sped to the deep. The maiden turned, and called again and again to her dear playmates, stretching out her hands, but they could not reach her. The strand he gained, and forward he sped like a dolphin, faring with unwetted hooves over the wide waves. And the sea, as he came, grew smooth, and the sea-monsters gamboled around, before the feet of Zeus, and the dolphin rejoiced, and rising from the deeps, he tumbled on the swell of the sea. The Nereids arose out of the salt water, and all of them came on in orderly array, riding on the backs of sea-beasts. And himself, the thund'rous Shaker of the World, appeared above the sea, and made smooth the wave, and guided his brother on the salt sea path; and round him were gathered the Tritons, these hoarse trumpeters of the deep, blowing from their long conches a bridal melody.

Meanwhile Europa, riding on the back of the divine bull, with one hand clasped the beast's great horn, and with the other caught up the purple fold of her garment, lest it might trail and be wet in the hoar sea's infinite spray. And her deep robe was swelled out by the winds, like the sail of a ship, and lightly still did waft the maiden onward. But when she was now far off from her own country, and neither sea-beat headland nor steep hill could now be seen, but above, the air, and beneath, the limitless deep, timidly she looked around and uttered her voice, saying—

"Where do you bear me, bull-god? What are you? how do you fare on your feet through the path of the sea-beasts, nor fear the sea? The sea is a path for swift ships that traverse the brine, but bulls dread the salt sea-ways. What drink is sweet to you, what food shall you find from the deep? Nay, are you then some god, for godlike are these deeds of yours? Lo, neither do dolphins of the brine fare on land, nor bulls on the deep, but dreadless do you rush o'er land and sea alike, your hooves serving you for oars.

"Perhaps you will rise above the gray air, and flee on high, like the swift birds. Alas for me, and alas again, for my exceeding evil fortune, alas for me that have left my father's house, and following this bull, on a strange sea-faring I go, and wander lonely. But I pray you that rule the gray salt sea, Shaker of the Earth, propitious meet me, and I think I see you smoothing this path of mine before me. For surely it is not without a god to aid, that I pass through these paths of waters!"

So spoke she, and the horned bull made answer to her again—

"Take courage, maiden, and dread not the swell of the deep. Behold I am Zeus, even I, though, closely beheld, I wear the form of a bull, for I can put on the semblance of what thing I will. But 'tis love of you that has compelled me to measure out so great a space of the salt sea, in a bull's shape. Lo, Crete shall presently receive you, Crete that was my own foster-mother, where your bridal chamber shall be. Yea, and from me shall you bear glorious sons to be scepter-swaying kings over earthly men."

So spoke he, and all he spoke was fulfilled. And Crete appeared, and Zeus took his own shape again, and he loosed her girdle, and the Hours arrayed their bridal bed. She that before was a maiden straightway became the bride of Zeus, and she bore children to Zeus, yea, soon she was a mother.

APOLLO AND DAPHNE

OVID, *Metamorphoses*, Book 1. 452-567 (Dryden)

The first and fairest of his loves was she,
Whom not blind fortune, but the dire decree
Of angry Cupid forc'd him to desire:
Daphne her name, and Peneus was her sire,
Swell'd with the pride, that new success attends,
He sees the stripling, while his bow he bends,

And thus insults him: "Thou lascivious boy,
Are arms like these, for children to employ?
Know, such achievements are my proper claim:
Due to my vigor and unerring aim:
Restless are my shafts, and Python late,
In such a feather'd death, has found his fate.
Take up thy torch, (and lay my weapons by;)
With that the feeble souls of lovers fry."
To whom the son of Venus thus reply'd:
"Phoebus, thy shafts are sure on all beside;
But mine on Phoebus, mine the fame shall be
Of all thy conquests, when I conquer thee."

He said, and soaring swiftly wing'd his flight;
Nor stopt but on Parnassus' airy height.
Two diff'rent shafts he from his quiver draws;
One to repel desire, and one to cause.
One shaft is pointed with refulgent gold,
To bribe the love, and make the lover bold:
One blunt, and tipped with lead, whose base allay
Provokes disdain, and drives desire away.
The blunted bolt against the nymph he drest:
But with the sharp, transfixed Apollo's breast.

Th' enamor'd deity pursues the chase;
The scornful damsel shuns his loath'd embrace;
In hunting beasts of prey her youth employs;
And Phoebe rivals in her rural joys.
With naked neck she goes, and shoulders bare,
And with a fillet binds her flowing hair.
By many suitors sought, she mocks their pains,
And still her vow'd virginity maintains.
Impatient of a yoke, the name of bride
She shuns, and hates the joys she never try'd.
On wilds and woods she fixes her desire:
Nor knows what youth and kindly love inspire.
Her father chides her oft: "Thou ow'st," says he,
"A husband to thy self, a son to me."
She, like a crime, abhors the nuptial bed:
She glows with blushes, and she hangs her head.
Then, casting round his neck her tender arms,
Soothes him with blandishments, and filial charms:
"Give me, my lord," she said, "to live and die
A spotless maid, without the marriage tie.

'Tis but a small request; I beg no more
Than what Diana's father gave before."
The good old sire was softn'd to consent;
But said her wish wou'd prove her punishment:
For so much youth, and so much beauty join'd,
Oppos'd the state, which her desires design'd.
   The god of light, aspiring to her bed,
Hopes what he seeks, with flattering fancies fed:
And is, by his own oracles mis-led.
And as in empty fields, the stubble burns,
Or nightly travellers, when day returns,
Their useless torches on dry hedges throw,
That catch the flames, and kindle all the row;
So burns the God, consuming in desire,
And feeding in his breast a fruitless fire:
Her well-turn'd neck he view'd (her neck was bare)
And on her shoulders her dishevel'd hair:
Oh were it comb'd, said he, with what a grace
Wou'd every waving curl become her face!
He view'd her eyes, like heavenly lamps that shone;
He view'd her lips, too sweet to view alone,
Her taper fingers, and her panting breast;
He praises all he sees, and for the rest,
Believes the beauties yet unseen are best:
Swift as the wind, the damsel fled away,
Nor did for these alluring speeches stay:
"Stay, nymph," he cry'd, "I follow not a foe:
Thus from the lion trips the trembling doe:
Thus from the wolf the frightn'd lamb removes,
And, from pursuing falcons, fearful doves;
Thou shunn'st a god, and shunn'st a god that loves.
Ah lest some thorn shou'd pierce thy tender foot,
Or thou shou'd'st fall in flying my pursuit!
To sharp uneven ways thy steps decline;
Abate thy speed, and I will bate of mine.
Yet think from whom thou dost so rashly fly;
Nor basely born, nor shepherd's swain am I.
Perhaps thou know'st not my superior state;
And from that ignorance proceeds thy hate.
Me Claros, Delphos, Tenedos obey,
These hands the Patareian scepter sway.
The King of Gods begot me: what shall be,

Or is, or ever was, in Fate, I see.
Mine is th' invention of the charming lyre;
Sweet notes, and heav'nly numbers I inspire.
Sure is my bow, unerring is my dart;
But ah more deadly his, who pierc'd my heart.
Med'cine is mine, what herbs and simples grow
In fields and forests, all their pow'rs I know;
And am the great physician call'd, below.
Alas that fields and forests can afford
No remedies to heal their love-sick lord!
To cure the pains of love, no plant avails;
And his own physic the physician fails."

    She heard not half; so furiously she flies,
And on her ear th' imperfect accent dies.
Fear gave her wings; and as she fled, the wind
Increasing spread her flowing hair behind;
And left her legs and thighs expos'd to view;
Which made the God more eager to pursue.
The God was young, and was too hotly bent
To lose his time in empty compliment:
But led by love, and fir'd with such a sight,
Impetuously pursu'd his near delight.

    As when th' impatient greyhound slipt from far,
Bounds o'er the glebe, to course the fearful hare,
She in her speed does all her safety lay;
And he with double speed pursues the prey;
O'er-runs her at the sitting turn, and licks
His chaps in vain, and blows upon the flix,
She scapes, and for the neighb'ring covert strives,
And gaining shelter, doubts if yet she lives:
If little things with great we may compare,
Such was the God, and such the flying fair:
She urg'd by fear, her feet did swiftly move,
But he more swiftly, who was urg'd by love.
He gathers ground upon her in the chase:
Now breaths upon her hair, with nearer pace;
And just is fast'ning on the wish'd embrace.
The nymph grew pale, and in a mortal fright,
Spent with the labor of so long a flight;
And now despairing, cast a mournful look,
Upon the streams of her paternal brook:
"Oh help," she cry'd, "in this extremest need,

If water gods are deities indeed:
Gape, earth and this unhappy wretch intomb:
Or change my form whence all my sorrows come."
Scarce had she finish'd, when her feet she found
Benumb'd with cold, and fasten'd to the ground:
A filmy rind about her body grows,
Her hair to leaves, her arms extend to boughs:
The nymph is all into a laurel gone,
The smoothness of her skin remains alone.
Yet Phoebus loves her still, and, casting round
Her bole, his arms, some little warmth he found.
The tree still panted in the unfinish'd part,
Not wholly vegetive, and heav'd her heart.
He fix'd his lips upon the trembling rind;
It swerv'd aside, and his embrace declin'd.
To whom the God: "Because thou canst not be
My mistress, I espouse thee for my tree:
Be thou the prize of honor and renown;
The deathless poet, and the poem crown.
Thou shalt the Roman festivals adorn,
And, after poets, be by victors worn.
Thou shalt returning Caesar's triumph grace;
When pomps shall in a long procession pass:
Wreath'd on the posts before his palace wait;
And be the sacred guardian of the gate:
Secure from thunder, and unharm'd by Jove,
Unfading as th' immortal pow'rs above:
And as the locks of Phoebus are unshorn,
So shall perpetual green thy boughs adorn."
The grateful tree was pleas'd with what he said,
And shook the shady honors of her head.

HYACINTHUS

OVID, *Metamorphoses*, Book 10. 162-219 (More)

Orpheus touches the homosexual theme in telling the story
of Hyacinthus.

You also, Hyacinthus, would have been
Set in the sky! if Phoebus had been given
Time which the cruel fates denied for you.
But in a way you are immortal too.
Though you have died.—Always when warm spring
Drives winter out, and Aries (the Ram)
Succeeds to Pisces (watery Fish), you rise
And blossom on the green turf. And the love
My father had for you was deeper than he felt
For others. Delphi center of the world,
Had no presiding guardian, while the God
Frequented the Eurotas and the land
Of Sparta, never fortified with walls.
His zither and his bow no longer fill
His eager mind; and now without a thought
Of dignity, he carried nets and held
The dogs in leash, and did not hesitate
To go with Hyacinthus on the rough,
Steep mountain ridges; and by all of such
Associations, his love was increased.

Now Titan was about midway, betwixt
The coming and the banished night, and stood
At equal distance from those two extremes.
Then, when the youth and Phoebus were well stripped,
And gleaming with rich olive oil, they tried
A friendly contest with the discus. First
Phoebus, well-poised, sent it awhirl through air,
And cleft the clouds beyond with its broad weight;
From which at length it fell down to the earth,
A certain evidence of strength and skill.

Heedless of danger Hyacinthus rushed
For eager glory of the game, resolved
To get the discus. But it bounded back
From off the hard earth, and struck full against
Your face, O Hyacinthus! Deadly pale
The God's face went—as pallid as the boy's.
With care he lifted the sad huddled form.

The kind God tries to warm you back to life,
And next endeavors to attend your wound,
And stay your parting soul with healing herbs.
His skill is no advantage, for the wound
Is past all art of cure. As if someone,
When in a garden, breaks off violets,
Poppies, or lilies hung from golden stems,
Then drooping they must hang their withered heads,
And gaze down towards the earth beneath them; so,
The dying boy's face droops, and his bent neck,
A burden to itself, falls back upon
His shoulder: "You are fallen in your prime
Defrauded of your youth, O Hyacinthus!"
Moaned Apollo. "I can see in your sad wound
My own guilt, and you are my cause of grief
And self-reproach. My own hand gave you death
Unmerited—I only can be charged
With your destruction.—What have I done wrong?"
Can it be called a fault to play with you?
Should loving you be called a fault? And oh,
That I might now give up my life for you!
Or die with you! But since our destinies
Prevent us, you shall always be with me,
And you shall dwell upon my care-filled lips.
The lyre struck by my hand, and my true songs
Will always celebrate you. A new flower
You shall arise, with markings on your petals,
Close imitation of my constant moans:
And there shall come another to be linked
With this new flower, a valiant hero shall
Be known by the same marks upon its petals."

And while Phoebus, Apollo, sang these words
With his truth-telling lips, behold the blood

Of Hyacinthus, which had poured out on
The ground beside him and there stained the grass,
Was changed from blood; and in its place a flower,
More beautiful than Tyrian dye, sprang up.
It almost seemed a lily, were it not
That one was purple and the other white.

But Phoebus was not satisfied with this.
For it was he who worked the miracle
Of his sad words inscribed on flower leaves.
These letters AI, AI, are inscribed
On them. And Sparta certainly is proud
To honor Hyacinthus as her son;
And his loved fame endures; and every year
They celebrate his solemn festival.

APHRODITE AND ARES

HOMER, *Odyssey*, Book 8. 266-366 (Cowper)

Then, tuning his sweet chords, Demodocus
A jocund strain began, his theme, the loves
Of Mars and Cytherea chaplet-crown'd;
How first, clandestine, they embraced beneath
The roof of Vulcan, her, by many a gift
Seduced, Mars won, and with adult'rous lust
The bed dishonor'd of the King of fire.
The sun, a witness of their amorous sport,
Bore swift the tale to Vulcan; he, apprized
Of that foul deed, at once his smithy sought,
In secret darkness of his inmost soul
Contriving vengeance; to the stock he heav'd
His anvil huge, on which he forged a snare
Of bands indissoluble, by no art
To be untied, durance for ever firm.
The net prepared, he bore it, fiery-wroth,
To his own chamber and his nuptial couch,
Where, stretching them from post to post, he wrapp'd
With those fine meshes all his bed around,

And hung them num'rous from the roof, diffused
Like spiders' filaments, which not the Gods
Themselves could see, so subtle were the toils.
When thus he had encircled all his bed
On ev'ry side, he feign'd a journey thence
To Lemnos, of all cities that adorn
The earth, the city that he favors most.
Nor kept the God of the resplendent reins
Mars, drowsy watch, but seeing that the famed
Artificer of heav'n had left his home,
Flew to the house of Vulcan, hot to enjoy
The Goddess with the wreath-encircled brows.
She, newly from her potent Sire return'd
The son of Saturn, sat. Mars, ent'ring, seiz'd
Her hand, hung on it, and thus urg'd his suit.

  To bed, my fair, and let us love! for lo!
Thine husband is from home, to Lemnos gone,
And to the Sintians, men of barb'rous speech.

  He spake, nor she was loth, but bedward too
Like him inclined; so then, to bed they went,
And as they lay'd them down, down stream'd the net
Around them, labor exquisite of hands
By ingenuity divine inform'd.
Small room they found, so prison'd; not a limb
Could either lift, or move, but felt at once
Entanglement from which was no escape.
And now the glorious artist, ere he yet
Had reach'd the Lemnian isle, limping, return'd
From his feign'd journey, for his spy the sun
Had told him all. With aching heart he sought
His home, and, standing in the vestibule,
Frantic with indignation roar'd to heav'n,
And roar'd again, summoning all the Gods.—
Oh Jove! and all ye Pow'rs for ever blest!
Here; hither look, that ye may view a sight
Ludicrous, yet too monstrous to be borne,
How Venus always with dishonor loads
Her cripple spouse, doting on fiery Mars!
And wherefore? for that he is fair in form
And sound of foot, I ricket-boned and weak.
Whose fault is this? Their fault, and theirs alone
Who gave me being; ill-employ'd were they

Begetting me, one, better far unborn.
See where they couch together on my bed
Lascivious! ah, sight hateful to my eyes!
Yet cooler wishes will they feel, I ween,
To press my bed hereafter; here to sleep
Will little please them, fondly as they love.
But these my toils and tangles will suffice
To hold them here, till Jove shall yield me back
Complete, the sum of all my nuptial gifts
Paid to him for the shameless strumpet's sake
His daughter, as incontinent as fair.

    He said, and in the brazen-floor'd abode
Of Jove the Gods assembled. Neptune came
Earth-circling Pow'r; came Hermes friend of man,
And, regent of the far-commanding bow,
Apollo also came; but chaste reserve
Bashful kept all the Goddesses at home.
The Gods, by whose beneficence all live,
Stood in the portal; infinite arose
The laugh of heav'n, all looking down intent
On that shrewd project of the smith divine,
And, turning to each other, thus they said.

    Bad works speed ill. The slow o'ertakes the swift.
So Vulcan, tardy as he is, by craft
Hath outstript Mars, although the fleetest far
Of all who dwell in heav'n, and the light-heel'd
Must pay the adult'rer's forfeit to the lame.

    So spake the Pow'rs immortal; then the King
Of radiant shafts thus question'd Mercury.

    Jove's son, heaven's herald, Hermes, bounteous God!
Would'st *thou* such stricture close of bands endure
For golden Venus lying at thy side?

    Whom answer'd thus the messenger of heav'n.
Archer divine! yea, and with all my heart;
And be the bands which wind us round about
Thrice these innumerable, and let all
The Gods and Goddesses in heav'n look on,
So I may clasp Vulcan's fair spouse the while.

    He spake; then laugh'd the Immortal Pow'rs again.
But not so Neptune; he with earnest suit
The glorious artist urged to the release
Of Mars, and thus in accents wing'd he said.

Loose him; accept my promise; he shall pay
Full recompense in presence of us all.
 Then thus the limping smith far-famed replied.
Earth-circler Neptune, spare me that request.
Lame suitor, lame security. What bands
Could I devise for thee among the Gods,
Should Mars, emancipated once, escape,
Leaving both debt and durance, far behind?
 Him answer'd then the Shaker of the shores.
I tell thee, Vulcan, that if Mars by flight
Shun payment, I will pay, myself, the fine.
 To whom the glorious artist of the skies.
Thou must not, canst not, shalt not be refused.
 So saying, the might of Vulcan loos'd the snare,
And they, detain'd by those coercive bands
No longer, from the couch upstarting, flew,
Mars into Thrace, and to her Paphian home
The Queen of smiles, where deep in myrtle groves
Her incense-breathing altar stands embow'r'd.
Her there, the Graces laved, and oils diffused
O'er all her form, ambrosial, such as add
Fresh beauty to the Gods for ever young,
And cloth'd her in the loveliest robes of heav'n.

～～

VENUS AND ADONIS

OVID, *Metamorphoses*, Book 10. 519-599; 706-739 (Humphries)

*Adonis was the child of the incestuous passion of Myrrha
for her father Cinyras.*

Time, in its stealthy gliding, cheats us all
Without our notice; nothing goes more swiftly
Than do the years. That little boy, whose sister
Became his mother, his grandfather's son,
Is now a youth, and now a man, more handsome
Than he had ever been, exciting even
The goddess Venus, and thereby avenging
His mother's passion. Cupid, it seems, was playing,

Quiver on shoulder, when he kissed his mother,
And one barb grazed her breast; she pushed him away,
But the wound was deeper than she knew; deceived,
Charmed by Adonis' beauty, she cared no more
For Cythera's shores nor Paphos' sea-ringed island,
Nor Cnidos, where fish teem, nor high Amathus,
Rich in its precious ores. She stays away
Even from Heaven, Adonis is better than Heaven.
She is beside him always; she has always,
Before this time, preferred the shadowy places,
Preferred her ease, preferred to improve her beauty
By careful tending, but now, across the ridges,
Through woods, through rocky places thick with brambles,
She goes, more like Diana than like Venus,
Bare-kneed and robes tucked up. She cheers the hounds,
Hunts animals, at least such timid creatures
As deer and rabbits; no wild boars for her,
No wolves, no bears, no lions. And she warns him
To fear them too, as if there might be good
In giving him warnings. "Be bold against the timid,
The running creatures, but against the bold ones
Boldness is dangerous. Do not be reckless.
I share whatever risk you take; be careful!
Do not attack those animals which Nature
Has given weapons, lest your thirst for glory
May cost me dear. Beauty and youth and love
Make no impression on bristling boars and lions,
On animal eyes and minds. The force of lightning
Is in the wild boar's tusks, and tawny lions
Are worse than thunderbolts. I hate and fear them."
He asks her why. She answers, "I will tell you,
And you will wonder at the way old crime
Leads to monstrosities. I will tell you sometime,
Not now, for I am weary, all this hunting
Is not what I am used to. Here's a couch
Of grassy turf and a canopy of poplar,
I would like to lie there with you." And she lay there,
Making a pillow for him of her breast,
And kisses for her story's punctuation.

. . . .

"Adonis, let all beasts alone, which offer
Breasts to the fight, not backs, or else your daring

Will be the ruin of us both." Her warning
Was given, and the goddess took her way,
Drawn by her swans through air. But the young hunter
Scorned all such warnings, and one day, it happened,
His hounds, hard on the trail, roused a wild boar,
And as he rushed from the wood, Adonis struck him
A glancing blow, and the boar turned, and shaking
The spear from the side, came charging at the hunter,
Who feared, and ran, and fell, and the tusk entered
Deep in the groin, and the youth lay there dying
On the yellow sand, and Venus, borne through air
In her light swan-guided chariot, still was far
From Cyprus when she heard his groans, and, turning
The white swans from their course, came back to him,
Saw, from high air, the body lying lifeless
In its own blood, and tore her hair and garments,
Beat her fair breasts with cruel hands, came down
Reproaching Fate. "They shall not have it always
Their way," she mourned, "Adonis, for my sorrow,
Shall have a lasting monument: each year
Your death will be my sorrow, but your blood
Shall be a flower. If Persephone
Could change to fragrant mint the girl called Mentha,
Cinyras' son, my hero, surely also
Can be my flower." Over the blood she sprinkled
Sweet-smelling nectar, and as bubbles rise
In rainy weather, so it stirred, and blossomed,
Before an hour, as crimson in its color
As pomegranates are, as briefly clinging
To life as did Adonis, for the winds
Which gave a name to the flower, anemone,
The wind-flower, shake the petals off, too early,
Doomed all too swift and soon.

PAN AND SYRINX

OVID, *Metamorphoses*, Book 1. 689-712 (Dryden)

Then Hermes thus; a nymph of late there was,
Whose heav'nly form her fellows did surpass.
The pride and joy of fair Arcadia's plains;
Belov'd by deities, ador'd by swains:
Syrinx her name, by Sylvans oft pursu'd,
As oft she did the lustful gods delude:
The rural, and the woodland pow'rs disdain'd;
With Cynthia hunted, and her rites maintain'd;
Like Phoebe clad, even Phoebe's self she seems,
So tall, so straight, such well-proportion'd limbs:
The nicest eye did no distinction know,
But that the goddess bore a golden bow:
Distinguish'd thus, the sight she cheated too.
Descending from Lycaeus, Pan admires
The matchless nymph, and burns with new desires.
A crown of pine upon his head he wore;
And thus began her pity to implore.
But e're he thus began, she took her flight
So swift, she was already out of sight.
Nor staid to hear the courtship of the god;
But bent her course to Ladon's gentle flood:
There by the river stopped, and, tir'd before,
Relief from water nymphs her pray'rs implore.

Now while the lustful god, with speedy pace,
Just thought to strain her in strict embrace,
He fills his arms with reeds, new rising on the place.
And while he sighs his ill-success to find,
The tender canes were shaken by the wind;
And breath'd a mournful air, unhear'd before;
That much surprising Pan, yet pleas'd him more.
Admiring this new music, thou, he said,
Who can'st not be the partner of my bed,
At least shalt be the consort of my mind;
And often, often, to my lips be join'd.

He form'd the reeds, proportion'd as they are:
Unequal in their length, and wax'd with care,
They still retain the name of his ungrateful fair.

ORPHEUS AND EURYDICE

VERGIL, *Georgics*, Book 4. 454-527 (Bovie)

Vergil motivates the death of Eurydice by her flight from Aristaeus to whom Proteus tells this story.

"Unhappy Orpheus roused this punishment,
Who rages still with grief for his stolen bride.
Headlong past a stream, the fated girl
In fleeing your advances, failed to see
The monstrous serpent lurking on the shore.
Her Dryads filled the mountain heights with moans;
Summits wept in Thrace and Macedon,
And in Rhesus' martial land; the Hebrus wept,
The Danube, and the fair princess of Athens.
Orpheus soothed his love with the hollow lyre,
Singing to thee, sweet bride, along the strand
Alone, with rising day and falling night.
He breached the jaws of Hell, the home of Dis,
The pitch-black groves of fear; approached the dead,
To win the frightful king, and all the hearts
That know not how to answer human prayer.
At his song, from Hell's deep places rustled forth
The slender shades of those whose light has failed,
Like birds that flock by thousands to the leaves
When Winter rain or nightfall sends them down
From mountainsides: the mothers and their husbands,
Noble heroes' bodies void of life,
Boys, unwedded girls, and youthful sons
Consigned to fire before their parents' eyes.
Around them wind Cocytus' twisted reeds
And grisly mud; the sluggish, hateful swamp
Confines them, as the ninefold swirling Styx
Encompasses them about. The very halls

Of Hell and inmost Tartarus stand open
In surprise; the Furies are astounded,
Their bluish tresses intertwined with snakes.
Cerberus, in amazement, holds his three
Months open, and even the wind subsides;
Ixion's wheel stands still. Now Orpheus had
Retraced his steps, avoiding all mischance,
Eurydice approached the upper air
Behind him (as Proserpina had ruled),
When all at once a mad desire possessed
The unwise lover—pardonable, indeed,
If Hell knew how to pardon. Overcome
By love, he stopped and—oh, forgetful man!—
Looked back at his, his own, Eurydice,
As they were drawing near the upper light.
That instant, all his labor went to waste,
His pact with the cruel tyrant fell apart,
And three times thunder rocked Avernus' swamps.
She cried out, 'What wild fury ruins us,
My pitiable self, and you, my Orpheus?
See, once again the cruel fates call me back
And once more sleep seals closed my swimming eyes.
Farewell: prodigious darkness bears me off,
Still reaching out to you these helpless hands
That you may never claim.' And with her words
She vanished from his sight like smoke in air,
Not seeing him clutch wildly after shadows
And yearning still to speak. Hell's ferryman
Refused him further passage through the swamp
That intervened. What could he do? Where turn,
A second time bereft of her? What tears
Might sway the dead, what human voice might alter
Heaven's will? Her body, stiff and cold,
Reposed long since adrift in the Stygian bark.
Seven continuous months, they say, he wept
By Strymon's lonely wave under soaring cliffs,
Unfolding his tragic song to the frozen stars,
Enchanting tigers, moving oaks with his theme:
Like a nightingale concealed in the poplar's shade,
Who sings a sad lament for her stolen brood
Some stony-hearted ploughman saw and dragged
Still naked from the nest: she weeps all night

And, perching on the bough, renews her song
Of elegiac woe; her grave complaint
Fills places far and wide. No thought of love
Or wedding rites could bend his inflexible will.
He wandered lonely through the icy North,
Past the snow-encrusted Don, through mountain fields
Of unadulterated frost, conveyed the grief
At Hell's ironic offerings, and rapt
Eurydice. By such unwavering faith
The Thracian women felt themselves outraged,
And at their sacred exercise, nocturnal
Bacchanals, they tore the youth apart,
And scattered his limbs around the spacious fields.
But even then his voice, within the head
Torn from its marble neck, and spinning down
The tide of his paternal River Hebrus,
The cold-tongued voice itself, as life fled away,
Called out 'Oh, my forlorn Eurydice!
Eurydice!' and the shoreline answered back
Along the river's breadth, 'Eurydice!' "

ARETHUSA

ovid, *Metamorphoses*, Book 5. 572-641 (Gregory)

Then Ceres, all at ease and generous,
Asked why the lady Arethusa came
To be the spirit of a sacred fountain;
And while their goddess rose from her deep streams,
Wringing green hair with her pale hands, the waters
Fell to quiet murmuring, so the old
Legend of River Elis' love could be
Distinctly heard. "I was a nymph," she said,
"Of Achaia; none were more active in the chase
At beating thickets or at laying traps
Than I. Though I was bold enough I never
Tried to excel among the local beauties,
Yet I was known for being beautiful.
My looks, though praised, refused to give me pleasure;

Most girls would find them a sufficient dowry—
I blushed as red as any farmer's daughter
To get that kind of praise; I felt it wrong
To tempt and then allure. After a day
(If I remember rightly) tired and spent
With chasing through a tangled Thracian forest,
The heat was fearful and a full day's work
Had made it twice as hot. I saw a brook
So clear it seemed to run without a ripple,
Nor was there any murmuring, so clear
That one could count the smallest stones that lay
Beneath the brook that scarcely seemed to stir.
Willow and poplar, shaking silver leaves
Whose roots drank at the stream on either side,
Rose from the green and gentle banks below them,
The river stilled as if in nature's shade.
At first my feet slipped in, then up to knees;
Nor this enough, I tossed all I was wearing
On yielding willow boughs, naked I dived
Curving a thousand rings within the waters.
And as I thrashed my arms I seemed to feel
A voice beneath the stream. Then terror took me,
And I had climbed the near bank; from his waters
Alpheus cried, 'Where are you, Arethusa?'
I climbed the nearest bank while Alpheus
Himself called from the waves, 'Where are you running,
Arethusa, so fast, so fast, where do you run
Away?' So echoes of his deep sea voice
Came at me, while I, my shift, my dresses
Left across the stream, ran naked as if ripe
For him to overtake me. I ran, I fluttered
As the dove runs and shakes its wings; he hot
And racing as the hawk, flew after me
Cross field and brake, past Orchomenus,
Psophis, Cyllene, and the gulf Maenalus
And frost-tipped Erymanthus and far Elis,
Nor could he show more speed than I, yet I,
Less hardy than his strength, began to fail
While he could hold the pace of a long track.
Through prairies and hilled forests, down cliffs and rocks,
Beyond known trails I ran, the sun behind me,
My follower's shadow growing with each step longer

Before my eyes—my eyes, or fear's. I heard
His foot-beat sound like terror in my veins,
And felt his lung-deep breath sweep through my hair.
Half dead with running, I called out, 'O goddess
Of the hunting snare, I am trapped, sunk, bound,
Unless you save me; it was I who carried
Your bow, your arrows; you must save me now!'
The goddess heard me; then a dense white cloud
Of dew—no eye could pierce it—fell over me.
The river god paced round me through the fog,
Blind in white darkness, crying, 'Arethusa,
Arethusa,' twice near around me stepping
Close, then nearer. And how did I, sad creature,
Feel or care? Was I a lamb who hears the baying
Wolf cry round the herd? Or a stilled hare sheltered
Under the thorns, who fears to tremble when
It sees the fatal jaws of dogs clip near?
Nor did he leave me, for he saw no footprints
Beyond the cloud; he stood and stared at it.
Then freezing sweat poured down my thighs and knees
A darkening moisture fell from all my body
And where I stepped a stream ran down; from hair
To foot it flowed, faster than words can tell.
I had been changed into a pool, a river;
Yet in these streams Alpheus saw and knew
The one he loved, and slipped from man's disguise
To water flowing toward me as I moved.
My Delian goddess opened up the earth,
And I, a cataract, poured down to darkness
Until I came to island Ortygia
Blessed by my goddess' name and which I love,
And here I first returned to living air."

ATALANTA

OVID, *Metamorphoses*, Book 10. 560-707 (More)

Venus tells the story to Adonis.

Perhaps you may have heard of a swift maid,
Who ran much faster than swift-footed men
Contesting in the race. What they have told
Is not an idle tale.—She did excel
Them all—and you could not have said
Whether her swift speed or her beauty was
More worthy of your praise. When this maid once
Consulted with an oracle, of her
Fate after marriage, the God answered her:
"You, Atalanta, never will have need
Of husband, who will only be your harm.
For your best good you should avoid the tie;
But surely you will not avoid your harm;
And while yet living you will lose yourself."

She was so frightened by the oracle,
She lived unwedded in far shaded woods;
And with harsh terms repulsed insistent throngs
Of suitors. "I will not be won," she said,
"Till I am conquered first in speed. Contest
The race with me. A wife and couch shall both
Be given to reward the swift, but death
Must recompense the one who lags behind.
This must be the condition of a race."
Indeed she was that pitiless, but such
The power of beauty, a rash multitude
Agreed to her harsh terms.

                    Hippomenes
Had come, a stranger, to the cruel race,
With condemnation in his heart against
The racing young men for their headstrong love;

And said, "Why seek a wife at such a risk?"
But when he saw her face, and perfect form
Disrobed for perfect running, such a form
As mine, Adonis, or as yours—if you
Were woman—he was so astonished he
Raised up his hands and said, "Oh pardon me
Brave men whom I was blaming, I could not
Then realize the value of the prize
You strove for." And as he is praising her,
His own heart leaping with love's fire, he hopes
No young man may outstrip her in the race;
And, full of envy, fears for the result.

"But why," he cries, "is my chance in the race
Untried? Divinity helps those who dare."
But while the hero weighed it in his mind
The virgin flew as if her feet had wings.
Although she seemed to him in flight as swift
As any Scythian arrow, he admired
Her beauty more; and her swift speed appeared
In her most beautiful. The breeze bore back
The streamers on her flying ankles, while
Her hair was tossed back over her white shoulders;
The bright trimmed ribbons at her knees were fluttering,
And over her white girlish body came
A pink flush, just as when a purple awning
Across a marble hall gives it a wealth
Of borrowed hues. And while Hippomenes
In wonder gazed at her, the goal was reached;
And Atalanta crowned victorious
With festal wreath.—But all the vanquished youths
Paid the death-penalty with sighs and groans,
According to the stipulated bond.

Not frightened by the fate of those young men,
He stood up boldly in the midst of all;
And fixing his strong eyes upon the maiden, said:
"Where is the glory in an easy victory
Over such weaklings? Try your fate with me!
If fortune fail to favor you, how could
It shame you to be conquered by a *man?*
Megareus of Onchestus is my father,

His grandsire, Neptune, God of all the seas.
I am descendant of the King of Waves:
And add to this, my name for manly worth
Has not disgraced the fame of my descent.
If you should prove victorious against
This combination, you will have achieved
A great enduring name—the only one
Who ever bested great Hippomenes."

While he was speaking, Atalanta's gaze
Grew softer, in her vacillating hopes
To conquer and be conquered; till at last,
Her heart, unbalanced, argued in this way:

"It must be some God envious of youth,
Wishing to spoil this one prompts him to seek
Wedlock with me and risk his own dear life.
I am not worth the price, if I may judge.
His beauty does not touch me—but I could
Be moved by it—I must consider he
Is but a boy. It is not he himself
Who moves me, but his youth. Sufficient cause
For thought are his great courage and his soul
Fearless of death. What of his high descent;—
Great grandson of the King of all the seas?
What of his love for me that has such great
Importance, he would perish if his fate
Denied my marriage to him? O strange boy,
Go from me while you can; abandon hope
Of this alliance stained with blood—A match
With me is fatal. Other maids will not
Refuse to wed you, and a wiser girl
Will gladly seek your love.—But what concern
Is it of mine, when I but think of those
Who have already perished! Let him look
To it himself; and let him die. Since he
Is not warned by his knowledge of the fate
Of many other suitors, he declares
Quite plainly, he is weary of his life.—

"Shall he then die, because it must be his
One hope to live with me? And suffer death

Though undeserved, for me because he loves?
My victory will not ward off the hate,
The odium of the deed! But it is not
A fault of mine.—Oh fond, fond man, I would
That you had never seen me! But you are
So madly set upon it, I could wish
You may prove much the swifter! Oh how dear,
How lovable is his young girlish face!—
Ah, doomed Hippomenes, I only wish
Mischance had never let you see me! You
Are truly worthy of a life on earth.
If I had been more fortunate, and not
Denied a happy marriage day; I would
Not share my bed with any man but you."

All this the virgin Atalanta said;
And knowing nothing of the power of love,
She is so ignorant of what she does,
She loves and does not know she is in love.

Meanwhile her father and the people, all
Loudly demanded the accustomed race.
A suppliant, the young Hippomenes
Invoked me with his anxious voice, "I pray
To you, O Venus, Queen of Love, be near
And help my daring—smile upon the love
You have inspired!" The breeze, not envious,
Wafted this prayer to me; and I confess,
It was so tender it did move my heart—
I had but little time to give him aid.

There is a field there which the natives call
The Field Tamasus—the most prized of all
The fertile lands of Cyprus. This rich field,
In ancient days, was set apart for me,
By chosen elders who decreed it should
Enrich my temples yearly. In this field
There grows a tree, with gleaming golden leaves,
And all its branches crackle with bright gold.
Since I was coming from there, by some chance,
I had three golden apples in my hand,
Which I had plucked. With them I planned to aid

Hippomenes. While quite invisible
To all but him, I taught him how to use
Those golden apples for his benefit.

The trumpet soon gave signal for the race
And both of them crouching flashed quickly forth
And skimmed the surface of the sandy course
With flying feet. You might even think those two
Could graze the sea with unwet feet and pass
Over the ripened heads of standing grain.

Shouts of applause gave courage to the youth:
The cheering multitude cried out to him:
"Now is the time to use your strength. Go on!
Hippomenes! Bend to the work! You're sure
To win!" It must be doubted who was most
Rejoiced by those brave words, Megareus' son,
Or Schoeneus' daughter. Oh, how often, when
She could have passed him, she delayed her speed;
And after gazing long upon his face
Reluctantly again would pass him! Now
Dry panting breath came from his weary throat—
The goal still far away.—Then Neptune's scion
Threw one of three gold apples. Atalanta
With wonder saw it—eager to possess
The shining fruit, she turned out of her course,
Picked up the rolling gold. Hippomenes
Passed by her, while spectators roared applause.
Increasing speed, she overcame delay,
Made up for time lost, and again she left
The youth behind. She was delayed again
Because he tossed another golden apple.
She followed him, and passed him in the race.

The last part of the course remained. He cried
"Be near me, Goddess, while I use your gift."
With youthful might he threw the shining gold,
In an oblique direction to the side,
So that pursuit would mean a slow return.
The virgin seemed to hesitate, in doubt
Whether to follow after this third prize.

I forced her to turn for it; take it up;
And, adding weight to the gold fruit, she held,
Impeded her with weight and loss of time.
For fear my narrative may stretch beyond
The race itself,—the maiden was outstripped;
Hippomenes then led his prize away.

Adonis, did I not deserve his thanks
With tribute of sweet incense? But he was
Ungrateful, and, forgetful of my help,
He gave me neither frankincense nor thanks.
Such conduct threw me into sudden wrath,
And, fretting at the slight, I felt I must
Not be despised at any future time.
I told myself 'twas only right to make
A just example of them. They were near
A temple, hidden in the forest, which
Glorious Echion in remembered time
Had built to Rhea, Mother of the gods,
In payment of a vow. So, wearied from
The distance traveled, they were glad to have
A needed rest. Hippomenes while there,
Was seized with love his heart could not control.—
A passion caused by my divinity.

Quite near the temple was a cave-like place,
Covered with pumice. It was hallowed by
Religious veneration of the past.
Within the shadows of that place, a priest
Had stationed many wooden images
Of olden gods. The lovers entered there
And desecrated it. The images
Were scandalized, and turned their eyes away.
The tower-crowned Mother, Cybele, at first
Prepared to plunge the guilty pair beneath
The waves of Styx, but such a punishment
Seemed light. And so their necks, that had been smooth,
Were covered instantly with tawny manes;
Their fingers bent to claws; their arms were changed
To fore-legs; and their bosoms held their weight;
And with their tails they swept the sandy ground.

Their casual glance is anger, and instead
Of words they utter growls. They haunt the woods,
A bridal-room to their ferocious taste.
And now fierce lions they are terrible
To all of life; except to Cybele;
Whose harness has subdued their champing jaws.

My dear Adonis, keep away from all
Such savage animals; avoid all those
Which do not turn their fearful backs in flight
But offer their bold breasts to your attack,
Lest courage should be fatal to us both.

BOREAS AND ORITHYIA

OVID, *Metamorphoses*, Book 6. 677-721 (More)

Erechtheus, next in line, with mighty sway
And justice, ruled all Athens on the throne
Left vacant by the good Pandion's death.
Four daughters and four sons were granted him;
And of his daughters, two were beautiful,
And one of these was wed to Cephalus,
Grandson of Æolus.—But mighty Boreas
Desired the hand of Orithyia, fair
And lovable.—King Tereus and the Thracians
Were then such obstacles to Boreas
The God was long kept from his dear beloved.
Although the great king (who compels the cold
North-wind) had sought with prayers to win her hand,
And urged his love in gentleness, not force.

When quite aware his wishes were disdained,
He roughly said, with customary rage
And violence: "Away with sentimental talk!
My prayers and kind intentions are despised,
But I should blame nobody but myself;

Then why should I, despising my great strength,
Debase myself to weakness and soft prayers?—
Might is my right, and violence my strength!—
By force I drive the force of gloomy clouds.

"Tremendous actions are the wine of life!—
Monarch of Violence, rolling on clouds,
I toss wide waters, and I fell huge trees—
Knotted old oaks—and whirled upon ice-wings,
I scatter the light snow, and pelt the Earth
With sleet and hail! I rush through boundless voids,
My thunders rumble in the hollow clouds—
And crash upon my brothers—fire to fire!

"Possessed of daemon-rage, I penetrate,
Sheer to the utmost caverns of old Earth;
And straining, up from those unfathomed deeps,
Scatter the terror-stricken shades of hell;
And hurl death-dealing earthquakes through the world!

"Such are the fateful powers I should use,
And never trust entreaties to prevail,
Or win my bride—Force is the law of life!"

And now impetuous Boreas, having howled
Resounding words, unrolled his rushing wings—
That fan the earth and ruffle the wide sea—
And, swiftly wrapping untrod mountain peaks
In whirling mantles of far-woven dust,
Thence downward hovered to the darkened world;
And, canopied in artificial night
Of swarthy overshadowing wings, caught up
The trembling Orithyia to his breast:
Nor did he hesitate in airy course
Until his huge wings fanned the chilling winds
Around Ciconian Walls.

                           There, she was pledged
The wife of that cold, northern king of storms;
And unto him she gave those hero twins,
Endowed with wings of their immortal sire,
And graceful in their mother's form and face.

Their bird-like wings were not fledged at their birth
And those twin boys, Zetes and Calais,
At first were void of feathers and soft down.
But when their golden hair and beards were grown,
Wings like an eagle's came;—and feather-down
Grew golden on their cheeks: and when from youth
They entered manhood, quick they were to join
The Argonauts, who for the Golden Fleece,
Sought in that first ship, ventured on the sea.

~~~

CEPHALUS AND PROCRIS

OVID, *Metamorphoses*, Book 7. 694-862 (More)

"My sweet wife, Procris!—if you could compare
Her beauty with her sister's—Orithyia's,
(Ravished by the blustering Boreas)
You would declare my wife more beautiful.

" 'Tis she her sire Erechtheus joined to me,
'Tis she the God Love also joined to me.
They called me happy, and in truth I was,
And all pronounced us so until the Gods
Decreed it otherwise. Two joyful months
Of our united love were almost passed,
When, as the gray light of the dawn dispelled,
Upon the summit of Hymettus green,
Aurora, glorious in her golden robes,
Observed me busy with encircling nets,
Trapping the antlered deer.

                              "Against my will
Incited by desire, she carried me
Away with her. Oh, let me not increase
Her anger, for I tell you what is true,
I found no comfort in her lovely face!
And, though she is the very queen of light,
And reigns upon the edge of shadowy space,
Where she is nourished on rich nectar-wine,

Adding delight to beauty, I could give
No heed to her entreaties, for the thought
Of my beloved Procris intervened;
And only her sweet name was on my lips.

"I told Aurora of our wedding joys
And all refreshing joys of love—and my
First union of my couch deserted now:

"Enraged against me, then the Goddess said:
'Keep to your Procris, I but trouble you,
Ungrateful clown! but, if you can be warned,
You will no longer wish for her!' And so,
In anger, she returned me to my wife.

"Alas, as I retraced the weary way,
Long-brooding over all Aurora said,
Suspicion made me doubtful of my wife,
So faithful and so fair.—But many things
Reminding me of steadfast virtue, I
Suppressed all doubts; until the dreadful thought
Of my long absence filled my jealous mind:
From which I argued to the criminal
Advances of Aurora; for if she,
So lovely in appearance, did conceal
Such passion in the garb of innocence
Until the moment of temptation, how
Could I be certain of the purity
Of even the strongest when the best are frail?

"So brooding—every effort I devised
To cause my own undoing. By the means
Of bribing presents, favored by disguise,
I sought to win her guarded chastity.
Aurora had disguised me, and her guile
Determined me to work in subtle snares.

"Unknown to all my friends, I paced the streets
Of sacred Athens till I reached my home.
I hoped to search out evidence of guilt:
But everything seemed waiting my return;
And all the household breathed an air of grief.

"With difficulty I, disguised, obtained
An entrance to her presence by the use
Of artifices many: and when I
There saw her, silent in her grief,—amazed,
My heart no longer prompted me to test
Such constant love. An infinite desire
Took hold upon me. I could scarce restrain
An impulse to caress and kiss her. Pale
With grief that I was gone, her lovely face
In sorrow was more beautiful—the world
Has not another so divinely fair.

"Ah, Phocus, it is wonderful to think
Of beauty so surpassing fair it seems
More lovable in sorrow! Why relate
To you how often she repulsed my feigned
Attempts upon her virtue? To each plea
She said: 'I serve one man: no matter where
He may be I will keep my love for one.'

"Who but a man insane with jealousy,
Would doubt the virtue of a loving wife,
When tempted by the most insidious wiles,
Whose hallowed honor was her husband's love?
But I, not satisfied with proof complete,
Would not abandon my depraved desire
To poison the pure fountain I should guard;—
Increasing my temptations, I caused her
To hesitate, and covet a rich gift.

"Then, angered at my own success I said,
Discarding all disguise, 'Behold the man
Whose lavish promise has established proof,
The witness of your shameful treachery;
Your absent husband has returned to this!'

"Unable to endure a ruined home,
Where desecration held her sin to view,
Despairing and in silent shame she fled;
And I, the author of that wickedness
Ran after: but enraged at my deceit

And hating all mankind, she wandered far
In wildest mountains; hunting the wild game.

"I grieved at her desertion; and the fires
Of my neglected love consumed my health;
With greater violence my love increased,
Until unable to endure such pain,
I begged forgiveness and acknowledged fault:
Nor hesitated to declare that I
Might yield, the same way tempted, if such great
Gifts had been offered to me. When I had made
Abject confession and she had avenged
Her outraged feelings, she came back to me
And we spent golden years in harmony.

"She gave to me the hound she fondly loved,
The very one Diana gave to her
When lovingly the Goddess had declared,
'This hound all others shall excel in speed.'
Nor was that gift the only one was given
By kind Diana when my wife was hers,
As you may guess—this javelin I hold forth,
No other but a Goddess could bestow.

"Would you be told the story of both gifts?
Attend my words and you shall be amazed,
For never such another sad event
Has added sorrow to the grieving world.

"After the son of Laius,—Oedipus,—
Had solved the riddle of the monster-sphinx,
So often baffling to the wits of men,
And after she had fallen from her hill,
Mangled, forgetful of her riddling craft;
Not unrevenged the mighty Themis brooked
Her loss. Without delay that Goddess raised
Another savage beast to ravage Thebes,
By which the farmer's cattle were devoured,
The land was ruined and its people slain.

"Then all the valiant young men of the realm,
With whom I also went, enclosed the field

(Where lurked the monster) in a mesh
Of many tangled nets: but not a strand
Could stay its onrush, and it leaped the crest
Of every barrier where the toils were set.

"Already they had urged their eager dogs,
Which swiftly as a bird it left behind,
Eluding all the hunters as it fled.

"At last all begged me to let slip the leash
Of straining Tempest; such I called the hound,
My dear wife's present. As he tugged and pulled
Upon the tightened cords, I let them slip:
No sooner done, then he was lost to sight;
Although, wherever struck his rapid feet
The hot dust whirled. Not swifter flies the spear,
Nor whizzing bullet from the twisted sling,
Nor feathered arrow from the twanging bow!

"A high hill jutted from a rolling plain,
On which I mounted to enjoy the sight
Of that unequalled chase. One moment caught,
The next as surely free, the wild beast seemed
Now here now there, elusive in its flight;
Swiftly sped onward, or with sudden turn
Doubled in circles to deceive or gain.
With equal speed pursuing at each turn,
The rapid hound could neither gain nor lose.
Now springing forward and now doubling back,
His great speed foiled, he snapped at empty air.

"I then turned to my javelin's aid; and while
I poised it in my right hand, turned away
My gaze a moment as I sought to twine
My practiced fingers in the guiding thongs;
But when again I lifted up my eyes,
To cast the javelin where the monster sped,
I saw two marble statues standing there,
Transformed upon the plain. One statue seemed
To strain in attitude of rapid flight,
The other with wide-open jaws was changed,
Just in the act of barking and pursuit.

Surely some God—if any God controls—
Decreed both equal, neither could succeed."

Now after these miraculous events,
It seemed he wished to stop, but Phocus said,
"What charge have you against the javelin?"

And Cephalus rejoined; "I must relate
My sorrows last; for I would tell you first
The story of my joys—'Tis sweet to think,
Upon the gliding tide of those few years
Of married life, when my dear wife and I
Were happy in our love and confidence.
No woman could allure me then from her;
And even Venus could not tempt my love;
All my great passion for my dearest wife
Was equalled by the passion she returned.

"As early as the sun, when golden rays
First glittered on the mountains, I would rise
In youthful ardor, to explore the fields
In search of game. With no companions, hounds,
Nor steeds nor nets, this javelin was alone
My safety and companion in my sport.
"And often when my right hand felt its weight,
A-wearied of the slaughter it had caused,
I would come back to rest in the cool shade,
And breezes from cool vales—the breeze I wooed,
Blowing so gently on me in the heat;
The breeze I waited for; she was my rest
From labor. I remember, 'Aura come,'
I used to say, 'Come soothe me, come into
My breast most welcome one, and yes indeed,
You do relieve the heat with which I burn.'

"And as I felt the sweet breeze of the morn,
As if in answer to my song, my fate impelled
Me further to declare my joy in song;

" 'You are my comfort, you are my delight!
Refresh me, cherish me, breathe on my face!
I love you child of lonely haunts and trees!"

"Such words I once was singing, not aware
Of some one spying on me from the trees,
Who thought I sang to some beloved Nymph,
Or Goddess by the name of Aura—so
I always called the breeze.—Unhappy man!
The meddling tell-tale went to Procris with
A story of supposed unfaithfulness,
And slyly told in whispers all he heard.
True love is credulous (and as I heard
The story) Procris in a swoon fell down.
When she awakened from her bitter swoon,
She ceased not wailing her unhappy fate,
And, wretched, moaned for an imagined woe.

"So she lamented what was never done!
Her woe incited by a whispered tale,
She feared the fiction of a harmless name!
But hope returning soothed her wretched state;
And now, no longer willing to believe
Such wrong, unless her own eyes saw it, she
Refused to think her husband sinned.

                                    "When dawn
Had banished night, and I, rejoicing, ranged
The breathing woods, victorious in the hunt
Paused and said, 'Come Aura—lovely breeze—
Relieve my panting breast!' It seemed I heard
The smothered moans of sorrow as I spoke:
But not conceiving harm, I said again;

" 'Come here, oh my delight!' And as those words
Fell from my lips, I thought I heard a soft
Sound in the thickets, as of moving leaves;
And thinking surely 'twas a hidden beast,
I threw this winged javelin at the spot.—

"It was my own wife, Procris, and the shaft
Was buried in her breast—'Ah, wretched me!'
She cried; and when I heard her well-known voice,
Distracted I ran towards her,—only to find
Her bathed in blood, and dying from the wound
Of that same javelin she had given to me:

And in her agony she drew it forth,—
Ah me! alas! from her dear tender side.

"I lifted her limp body to my own,
In these bloody-guilty arms, and wrapped the wound
With fragments of my tunic, that I tore
In haste to staunch her blood; and all the while
I moaned, 'Oh, do not now forsake me—slain
By these accursed hands!'

                              "Weak with the loss
Of blood, and dying, she compelled herself
To utter these few words, 'It is my death;
But let my eyes not close upon this life
Before I plead with you!—By the dear ties
Of sacred marriage; by your God and mine;
And if my love for you can move your heart;
And even by the cause of my sad death,—
My love for you increasing as I die,—
Ah, put away that Aura you have called,
That she may never separate your soul,—
Your love from me.'

                        "So, by those dying words
I knew that she had heard me call the name
Of Aura, when I wished the cooling breeze,
And thought I called a Goddess,—cause of all
Her jealous sorrow and my bitter woe.

"Alas, too late, I told her the sad truth;
But she was sinking, and her little strength
Swiftly was ebbing with her flowing blood.
As long as life remained her loving gaze
Was fixed on mine; and her unhappy life
At last was breathed out on my grieving face.
It seemed to me a look of sweet content
Was in her face, as if she feared not death."

CEYX AND ALCYONE

OVID, *Metamorphoses*, Book 11. 410-748, with omissions (More)

King Ceyx, disturbed by his loved brother's fate
And prodigies which happened since that time,
Prepared to venture to the Clarian god,
That he might there consult the oracle,
So sanctified to consolation of distress:
For then the way to Delphi was unsafe
Because of Phorbas and his Phlegyans.
Before he went he told his faithful queen,
His dear Alcyone. She felt at once
Terror creep through the marrow of her bones,
Pallor of boxwood overspread her face,
And her two cheeks were wet with gushing tears.
Three times she tried to speak while tears and sobs
Delayed her voice, until at last she said:—

"What fault of mine, my dearest, has so changed
Your usual thoughts? Where is that care for me
That always has stood first? Can you leave me
For this long journey with no anxious fear—
Alcyone, forsaken in these halls?
Will this long journey be a pleasant change
Because far from you I should be more dear?
Perhaps you think you will go there by land,
And I shall only grieve, and shall not fear.
The sea affrights me with its tragic face.
Just lately I observed some broken planks
Upon our seashore, and I've read and read
The names of seamen on their empty tombs!

"Oh, let no false assurance fill your mind
Because your father-in-law is Aeolus,
Who in a dungeon shuts the stormful winds
And smoothes at will the troubled ocean waves.
Soon as the winds get freedom from his power,

They take entire possession of the deep,
And nothing is forbidden their attack;
And all the rights of every land and sea
Are disregarded by them. They insult
Even the clouds of heaven and their wild
Concussions urge the lightnings to strike fires.
The more I know of them, for I knew
Them in my childhood and I often saw
Them from my father's home, the more I fear.

"But, O dear husband! if this new resolve
Can not be altered by my prayers and fears,
And if you are determined, take me, too:
Some comfort may be gained, if in the storms
We may be tossed together. I shall fear
Only the ills that really come to us,
Together we can certainly endure
Discomforts till we gain that distant land."

Such words and tears of the daughter of Aeolus
Gave Ceyx, famed son of the Morning Star,
Much thought and sorrow; for the flame of love
Burned in his heart as strongly as in hers.

Reluctant to give up the voyage, even more
To make Alcyone his partner on
The dangerous sea, he answered her complaints
In many ways to pacify her breast,
But could not comfort her until at last
He said, "This separation from your love
Will be most sorrowful; and so I swear
To you, as witnessed by the sacred fire
Of my Star-father, if the fates permit
My safe return, I will come back to you
Before the moon has rounded twice her orb."
These promises gave hope of his return.
Without delay he ordered a ship should
Be drawn forth from the dock, launched in the sea,
And properly supplied against the needs
Of travel.—Seeing this, Alcyone,
As if aware of future woe, shuddered,

Wept, and embraced him, and in extreme woe
Said with a sad voice, "Ah—Farewell!" and then,
Her nerveless body sank down to the ground.

While Ceyx longed for some pretext to delay,
The youthful oarsmen, chosen for their strength,
In double rows began to draw the oars
Back towards their hardy breasts, cutting the waves
With equal strokes. She raised her weeping eyes
And saw her husband on the high-curved stern.
He by his waving hand made signs to her,
And she returned his signals. Then the ship
Moved farther from the shore until her eyes
Could not distinguish his loved countenance.
Still, while she could, she followed with her gaze
The fading hull; and, when that too was lost
Far in the distance, she remained and gazed
At the white topsails, waving from the mast.
But, when she could no longer see the sails,
With anxious heart she sought her lonely couch
And laid herself upon it. Couch and room
Renewed her sorrow and reminded her
How much of life was absent on the sea.

. . . .

Perhaps the ship had not sailed half her course,
On every side the land was out of sight
In fact at a great distance, when, towards dark
The sea grew white with its increasing waves,
While boisterous east winds blew with violence.—
Prompt in his duty, the captain warns his crew,
"Lower the top sails—quick—furl all the sails
Tight to the yards!"—He ordered, but the storm
Bore all his words away, his voice could not
Be heard above the roaring of the sea.

. . . .

The ship was tossed about in the wild storm:
Aloft as from a mountain peak it seemed
To look down on the valley and the depth
Of Acheron; and, when sunk down in a trough
Of waves engulfing, it appeared to look
Up at the zenith from infernal seas.

Often the waves fell on the sides with crash
As terrible as when a flying stone
Or iron ram shatters a citadel.

. . . .

King Ceyx thinks only of Alcyone,
No other name is on his lips but hers:
And though he longs for her, yet he is glad
That she is safe at home. Ah, how he tried
To look back to the shore of his loved land,
To turn his last gaze towards his wife and home.
But he has lost direction.—The tossed sea
Is raging in a hurricane so vast,
And all the sky is hidden by the gloom
Of thickened storm-clouds, doubled in pitch-black.

The mast is shattered by the violence
Of drenching tempests, and the useless helm
Is broken. One undaunted giant wave
Stands over wreck and spoil, and looks down like
A conqueror upon the other waves:
Then falls as heavily as if some god
Should hurl Mount Athos or Mount Pindus, torn
From rock foundations, into that wide sea:
So, with down-rushing weight and violence
It struck and plunged the ship to the lowest deeps.
And as the ship sank, many of the crew
Sank overwhelmed in deep surrounding waves,
Never to rise from suffocating death:
But some in desperation, clung for life
To broken timbers and escaped that fate.

King Ceyx clung to a fragment of the wreck
With that majestic hand which often before
Had proudly swayed the scepter. And in vain,
Alas, he called upon his father's name,
Alas, he begged his father-in-law's support.
But, while he swam, his lips most frequently
Pronounced that dearest name, Alcyone!
He longs to have his body carried by waves
To her dear gaze and have at last,
Entombment by the hands of his loved friends.
Swimming, he called Alcyone—far off,

As often as the billows would allow
His lips to open, and among the waves
His darling's name was murmured, till at last
A night-black arch of water swept above
The highest waves and buried him beneath
Engulfing billows.

              Lucifer was dim
Past recognition when the dawn appeared
And, since he never could depart from heaven,
Soon hid his grieving countenance in clouds.
   Meanwhile, Alcyone, all unaware
Of his sad wreck, counts off the passing nights
And hastens to prepare for him his clothes
That he may wear as soon as he returns to her;
And she is choosing what to wear herself,
And vainly promises his safe return—
All this indeed, while she in hallowed prayer
Is giving frankincense to please the gods:
And first of loving adorations, she
Paid at the shrine of Juno. There she prayed
For Ceyx—after he had suffered death,
That he might journey safely and return
And might love her above all other women,
This one last prayer alone was granted to her.

   But Juno could not long accept as hers
These supplications on behalf of one
Then dead; and that she might persuade Alcyone
To turn her death-polluted hands away
From hallowed altars, Juno said in haste,
"O, Iris, best of all my messengers,
Go quickly to the dreadful court of Sleep,
And in my name command him to despatch
A dream in the shape of Ceyx, who is dead,
And tell Alcyone the woeful truth."

   So she commanded.—Iris instantly
Assumed a garment of a thousand tints;
And as she marked the high skies with her arch,
Went swiftly thence as ordered, to the place
Where Sleep was then concealed beneath a rock.

Near the Cimmerian Land there is a cave,
With a long entrance, in a hallowed mountain,
The home of slothful Sleep. To that dark cave
The Sun, when rising or in middle skies,
Or setting, never can approach with light.
There dense fogs, mingled with the dark, exhale
Darkness from the black soil—and all that place
Is shadowed in a deep mysterious gloom.

As soon as Iris entered that dread gloom,
She pushed aside the visions in her way
With her fair glowing hands; and instantly,
That sacred cavern of the God of Sleep
Was all illuminated with the glow
And splendor of her garment.—Out of himself
The god with difficulty lifted up
His languid eyes. From this small sign of life
Relapsing many times to languid sloth,
While nodding, with his chin he struck his breast
Again and again. At last he roused himself
From gloom and slumber; and, while raised upon
His elbow, he enquired of Iris why
She came to him.—He knew her by her name.

She answered him, "O, Sleep, divine repose
Of all things! Gentlest of the deities!
Peace to the troubled mind, from which you drive
The cares of life, restorer of men's strength
When wearied with the toils of day, command
A vision that shall seem the actual form
Of royal Ceyx to visit Trachis famed
For Hercules and tell Alcyone
His death by shipwreck. It is Juno's wish."

Morpheus at once flew through the night
Of darkness, on his wings that make no sound,
And in brief space of intervening time,
Arrived at the Haemonian city walls;
And there he laid aside his wings, and took
The face and form of Ceyx. In that form
As one deprived of life, devoid of clothes,
Wan and ghastly, he stood beside the bed

Of the sad wife. The hero's beard seemed dripping,
Sea water streamed down from his drenching hair.

Then leaning on the bed, while dropping tears
Were running down his cheeks, he said these words:
"Most wretched wife, can you still recognize
Your own loved Ceyx, or have my looks changed
So much with death you can not?—Look at me,
And you will be assured I am your own:
But here instead of your dear husband, you
Will find only his ghost. Your faithful prayers
Did not avail, Alcyone, and I
Have perished. Give up all deluding hopes
Of my return. The stormy Southwind caught
My ship while sailing the Aegean sea;
And there, tossed by the mighty wind, my ship
Was dashed to pieces. While I vainly called
Upon your name, the angry waters closed
Above my drowning head and it is no
Uncertain messenger that tells you this
And nothing from vague rumors has been told.
But it is I myself, come from the wreck,
Now telling you my fate. Come then, arise,
Shed tears, and put on mourning; do not send
Me unlamented, down to Tartarus."

And Morpheus added to these words a voice
Which she would certainly believe was her
Beloved husband's; and he seemed to be
Shedding fond human tears; and even his hands
Were moved in gestures that Ceyx often used.

Alcyone shed tears and groaned aloud,
And, as she moved her arms and caught at his
Dear body, she embraced the vacant air,
She cried out loudly, "Stay, oh stay with me!
Why do you hurry from me? We will go
Together!" Agitated by her own
Excited voice; and by what seemed to be
Her own dear husband, she awoke from sleep.
And first looked all about her to persuade
Herself that he whom she had lately seen

Must yet be with her, for she had aroused
The servants who in haste brought lights desired.

When she could find him nowhere, in despair
She struck her face and tore her garment from
Her breast and beat her breast with mourning hands.
She did not wait to loosen her long hair;
But tore it with her hands and to her nurse,
Who asked the cause of her wild grief, she cried:
"Alas, Alcyone is no more! no more!
With her own Ceyx she is dead! is dead!
Away with words of comfort, he is lost
By shipwreck! I have seen him, and I knew
Him surely—as a ghost he came to me;
And when desirous to detain him, I
Stretched forth my arms to him, his ghost left me—
It vanished from me; but it surely was
The ghost of my dead husband. If you ask
Description of it, I must truly say
He did not have his well-known features—he
Was not so cheerful as he was in life!
Alas, I saw him pale and naked, with
His hair still dripping—his ghost from the waves
Stood on this very spot:" and while she moaned
She sought his footprints on the floor. "Alas,
This was my fear, and this is what my mind
Shuddered to think of, when I begged that you
Would not desert me for the wind's control.
But how I wish, since you were sailing forth
To perish, that you had but taken me
With you. If I had gone with you, it would
Have been advantage to me, for I should
Have shared the whole course of my life with you
And you would not have met a separate death.
I linger here but I have met my death,
I toss on waves, and drift upon the sea.

"My heart would be more cruel than the waves,
If it should ask me to endure this life—
If I should struggle to survive such grief.
I will not strive nor leave you so forlorn,
At least I'll follow you to death. If not

The urn, at least the lettered stone
Shall keep us still together. If your bones
Are not united with my bones, 'tis sure
Our names must be united." Overcome
With grief, she could not say another word—
But she continued wailing, and her groans
Were heaved up from her sorrow-stricken breast.

At early dawn, she went from her abode
Down to the seashore, where most wretchedly,
She stood upon the spot from which he sailed,
And sadly said: "He lingered here while he
Was loosening the cables, and he kissed
Me on this seashore when he left me here."
And while she called to recollection all
That she had seen when standing there, and while
She looked far out on flowing waves from there,
She noticed floating on the distant sea—
What shall I say? At first even she could not
Be sure of what she saw. But presently
Although still distant—it was certainly
A floating corpse. She could not see what man
He might be, but because it seemed to her
It surely was a shipwrecked body, she
Was moved as at an omen and began
To weep; and, moaning as she stood there, said:– ·
"Ah, wretched one, whoever it may be,
Ah, wretched is the wife whom you have left!"

As driven by the waves the body came
Still nearer to her, she was less and less
The mistress of herself, the more she looked
Upon it; and, when it was close enough
For her to see its features, she beheld
Her husband. "It is he," she cried and then
She tore her face, her hair, her royal robe
And then, extending both her trembling hands
Towards Ceyx, "So dearest one! So do you come
To me again?" She cried, "O luckless mate."

A mole, made by the craft of man, adjoins
The sea and breaks the shoreward rush of waves.

To this she leaped—it seemed impossible—
And then, while beating the light air with wings
That instant formed upon her, she flew on,
A mourning bird, and skimmed above the waves.
And while she lightly flew across the sea
Her clacking mouth with its long slender bill,
Full of complaining, uttered moaning sounds:
But when she touched the still and pallid form,
Embracing his dear limbs with her new wings,
She gave cold kisses with her hardened bill.

All those who saw it doubted whether Ceyx
Could feel her kisses; and it seemed to them
The moving waves had raised his countenance.
But he was truly conscious of her grief;
And through the pity of the gods above,
At last they both were changed to flying birds,
Together in their fate. Their love lived on,
Nor in these birds were marriage bonds dissolved,
And they soon coupled and were parent birds.
Each winter during seven full days of calm
Alcyone broods on her floating nest—
Her nest that sails upon a halcyon sea:
The passage of the deep is free from storms,
Throughout those seven full days; and Aeolus
Restraining harmful winds, within their cave,
For his descendants' sake gives halcyon seas.

ECHO AND NARCISSUS

OVID, *Metamorphoses*, Book 3. 339-509, with omissions
(Humphries)

                                    And so Tiresias,
Famous through all Aonian towns and cities,
Gave irreproachable answers to all comers
Who sought his guidance. One of the first who tested
The truths he told was a naiad of the river,
Liriope, whom the river-god Cephisus,

Embraced and ravished in his watery dwelling.
In time she bore a child, most beautiful
Even as child, gave him the name Narcissus,
And asked Tiresias if the boy would ever
Live to a ripe old age. Tiresias answered:
"Yes, if he never knows himself." How silly
Those words seemed, for how long! But as it happened,
Time proved them true—the way he died, the strangeness
Of his infatuation.
            Now Narcissus
Was sixteen years of age, and could be taken
Either for boy or man, and boys and girls
Both sought his love, but in that slender stripling
Was pride so fierce no boy, no girl, could touch him.
He was out hunting one day, driving deer
Into the nets, when a nymph named Echo saw him,
A nymph whose way of talking was peculiar
In that she could not start a conversation
Nor fail to answer other people talking.

. . . .

She saw Narcissus roaming through the country,
Saw him, and burned, and followed him in secret,
Burning the more she followed, as when sulphur
Smeared on the rim of torches, catches fire
When other fire comes near it. Oh, how often
She wanted to come near with coaxing speeches,
Make soft entreaties to him! But her nature
Sternly forbids; the one thing not forbidden
Is to make answers. She is more than ready
For words she can give back. By chance Narcissus
Lost track of his companions, started calling
"Is anybody here?" and "Here!" said Echo.
He looked around in wonderment, called louder
"Come to me!" "Come to me!" came back the answer.
He looked behind him, and saw no one coming;
"Why do you run from me?" and heard his question
Repeated in the woods. "Let us get together!"
There was nothing Echo would ever say more gladly,
"Let us get together!" And, to help her words,
Out of the woods she came, with arms all ready
To fling around his neck. But he retreated:
"Keep your hands off," he cried, "and do not touch me!

I would die before I give you a chance at me."
"I give you a chance at me," and that was all
She ever said thereafter, spurned and hiding,
Ashamed, in the leafy forests, in lonely caverns.
But still her love clings to her and increases
And grows on suffering; she cannot sleep,
She frets and pines, becomes all gaunt and haggard,
Her body dries and shrivels till voice only
And bones remain, and then she is voice only
For the bones are turned to stone. She hides in woods
And no one sees her now along the mountains,
But all may hear her, for her voice is living.

She was not the only one on whom Narcissus
Had visited frustration; there were others,
Naiads or Oreads, and young men also
Till finally one rejected youth, in prayer,
Raised up his hands to Heaven: "May Narcissus
Love one day, so, himself, and not win over
The creature whom he loves!" Nemesis heard him,
Goddess of Vengeance, and judged the plea was righteous.
There was a pool, silver with shining water,
To which no shepherds came, no goats, no cattle,
Whose glass no bird, no beast, no falling leaf
Had ever troubled. Grass grew all around it,
Green from the nearby water, and with shadow
No sun burned hotly down on. Here Narcissus,
Worn from the heat of hunting, came to rest
Finding the place delightful, and the spring
Refreshing for the thirsty. As he tried
To quench his thirst, inside him, deep within him,
Another thirst was growing, for he saw
An image in the pool, and fell in love
With that unbodied hope, and found a substance
In what was only shadow. He looks in wonder,
Charmed by himself, spell-bound, and no more moving
Than any marble statue. Lying prone
He sees his eyes, twin stars, and locks as comely
As those of Bacchus or the god Apollo,
Smooth cheeks, and ivory neck, and the bright beauty
Of countenance, and a flush of color rising
In the fair whiteness. Everything attracts him

That makes him so attractive. Foolish boy,
He wants himself; the loved becomes the lover,
The seeker sought, the kindler burns. How often
He tries to kiss the image in the water,
Dips in his arms to embrace the boy he sees there,
And finds the boy, himself, elusive always,
Not knowing what he sees, but burning for it,
The same delusion mocking his eyes and teasing.
Why try to catch an always fleeing image,
Poor credulous youngster? What you seek is nowhere,
And if you turn away, you will take with you
The boy you love. The vision is only shadow,
Only reflection, lacking any substance.
It comes with you, it stays with you, it goes
Away with you, if you can go away.
No thought of food, no thought of rest, can make him
Forsake the place. Stretched on the grass, in shadow,
He watches, all unsatisfied, that image
Vain and illusive, and he almost drowns
In his own watching eyes. He rises, just a little,
Enough to lift his arms in supplication
To the trees around him, crying to the forest:
"What love, whose love, has ever been more cruel?
You woods should know: you have given many lovers
Places to meet and hide in; has there ever,
Through the long centuries, been anyone
Who has pined away as I do? He is charming,
I see him, but the charm and sight escape me.
I love him and I cannot seem to find him!
To make it worse, no sea, no road, no mountain,
No city-wall, no gate, no barrier, parts us
But a thin film of water. He is eager
For me to hold him. When my lips go down
To kiss the pool, his rise, he reaches toward me.
You would think that I could touch him—almost nothing
Keeps us apart. Come out, whoever you are!
Why do you tease me so? Where do you go
When I am reaching for you? I am surely
Neither so old or ugly as to scare you,
And nymphs have been in love with me. You promise,
I think, some hope with a look of more than friendship.
You reach out arms when I do, and your smile

Follows my smiling; I have seen your tears
When I was tearful; you nod and beckon when I do;
Your lips, it seems, answer when I am talking
Though what you say I cannot hear. I know
The truth at last. He is myself! I feel it,
I know my image now. I burn with love
Of my own self; I start the fire I suffer.
What shall I do? Shall I give or take the asking?
What shall I ask for? What I want is with me,
My riches make me poor. If I could only
Escape from my own body! if I could only—
How curious a prayer from any lover—
Be parted from my love! And now my sorrow
Is taking all my strength away; I know
I have not long to live, I shall die early,
And death is not so terrible, since it takes
My trouble from me; I am sorry only
The boy I love must die: we die together."
He turned again to the image in the water,
Seeing it blur through tears, and the vision fading,
And as he saw it vanish, he called after:
"Where are you going? Stay: do not desert me,
I love you so. I cannot touch you; let me
Keep looking at you always, and in looking
Nourish my wretched passion!" In his grief
He tore his garment from the upper margin,
Beat his bare breast with hands as pale as marble,
And the breast took on a glow, a rosy color,
As apples are white and red, sometimes, or grapes
Can be both green and purple. The water clears,
He sees it all once more, and cannot bear it.
As yellow wax dissolves with warmth around it,
As the white frost is gone in morning sunshine,
Narcissus, in the hidden fire of passion,
Wanes slowly, with the ruddy color going,
The strength and hardihood and comeliness,
Fading away, and even the very body
Echo had loved. She was sorry for him now,
Though angry still, remembering; you could hear her
Answer "Alas!" in pity, when Narcissus
Cried out "Alas!" You could hear her own hands beating
Her breast when he beat his. "Farewell, dear boy,

Beloved in vain!" were his last words, and Echo
Called the same words to him. His weary head
Sank to the greensward, and death closed the eyes
That once had marveled at their owner's beauty.
And even in Hell, he found a pool to gaze in,
Watching his image in the Stygian water.
While in the world above, his naiad sisters
Mourned him, and dryads wept for him, and Echo
Mourned as they did, and wept with them, preparing
The funeral pile, the bier, the brandished torches,
But when they sought his body, they found nothing,
Only a flower with a yellow center
Surrounded with white petals.

SALMACIS AND HERMAPHRODITUS

OVID, *Metamorphoses*, Book 4. 285-388 (Gregory)

Alcithoe tells her sisters a story.

"The waters of the fountain Salmacis
Have earned an evil name: the men who take them
Become effeminate or merely zero—
Certainly less than men, which is well known.
The reason why has been a guarded secret.
The infant son of Mercury and Venus
Was nursed by naiads in Mount Ida's caves;
His pretty face showed who his parents were,
Even his name combined their names in Greek.
When he had reached the age of three-times-five
He left the pastures of stepmother Ida
To visit hills and streams of foreign lands;
Boyish delight made rough foot-travel easy
And pleasure came with each strange thing he saw;
He drifted toward the cities of Lycia
Where the Carians settled near their gates,
And there he found a tempting pool of water
So clear that one could read its sandy depth.
No swamps grew there, rank grasses, nor black weeds;

Only the purest water flowed, and round it
Neat turf and dainty ferns as though they were
Eternal greenery. A nymph lived there
Who never stirred abroad, nor followed deer,
Nor entered friendly races with the girls,
Nor took out hunting license with Diana.
Her sisters, it was said, made fun of her,
Or scolded, 'Salmacis, pick up your spear,'
Or, 'Have you lost your pretty painted quiver?'
'Why not take turns at getting exercise;
A life of ease gives pleasure to the chase.'
But Salmacis refused; she took a bath,
Gazed at her lovely arms and legs in water,
And found her private pool a likely mirror
To show her how to rearrange her hair
Even with a boxwood comb. Then, lightly dressed,
She sank upon the turf, or sometimes wandered
To pick a garland of sweet-smelling flowers
Which grew nearby—and that day saw the boy;
O how she yearned to take him in her arms!

"Yet she held off a while in coming near him;
Stood still a moment till her blood ran cool,
Plucked at her dress and calmly fixed her eyes;
When she was certain that she looked her best,
She chose her words and spoke: 'O lovely boy,
If you are not a god, then you should be one,
Cupid himself—and if your birth was human
How proud, how pleased your parents should have been.
What happy brothers, if you had them, doting
Sisters, and O, the nurse who held you close
To reach her breast. But gladder than all these,
Your lucky bride. If she exists, then let
Our love take shelter in the shade; if not,
Then let us find our wedding bed.' She paused;
The boy flushed red, half innocent of love,
Yet red and white increased his fragile beauty:
As apples ripen in a sun-swept meadow,
Or ivory brushed with paint, or the gray moon,
When brass urns sounding beat for her release
At hour of her eclipse, red under white,
Such were the colors that played across his face.
As the girl asked him for a sister's kiss

And was about to stroke his snow-white neck,
He cried, 'Leave me or I must run away—
Get out of here.' Salmacis, shaken, said,
'This place is yours, but stay, O darling stranger!'
Then turned as if to leave him alone,
Walked slowly, cautiously beyond his view,
Looked back, dropped to her knees behind a hedge.
Meanwhile the boy as though he were unseen
Strolled the green turf and stepping near its waters
Tested the rippling surface with his toes,
Then dipped his feet and, charmed by flowing coolness
Of the stream, stripped off his clothes; and when she saw
Him naked, the girl was dazzled; her eyes shone
With blazing blinding light that Phoebus' face
Poured in a looking-glass, nor could she wait
To hold him naked in her arms. Striking
His arms against his sides, he leaped and dived
Overhand stroke, into the pool; his glittering body
Flashed and turned within clear waters, as if
It were of ivory or of white lilies seen
Through walls of glass. 'I've won, for he is mine,'
She cried, clothes torn away and naked, as she
Leaped to follow him, her arms about him fast,
Where, though he tried to shake her off, she clung,
Fastening his lips to hers, stroking his breast,
Surrounding him with arms, legs, lips, and hands
As though she were a snake caught by an eagle,
Who leaping from his claws wound her tall body
Around his head, and lashed his wings with her
Long tail, as though she were quick ivy tossing
Her vines round the thick body of a tree,
Or as the cuttlefish at deep sea's bottom
Captures its enemy—so she held to him.
The heir of Atlas struggled as he could
Against the pleasure that the girl desired,
But she clung to him as though their flesh were one,
'Dear, naughty boy,' she said, 'to torture me;
But you won't get away. O gods in heaven,
Give me this blessing; clip him within my arms
Like this forever.' At which the gods agreed:
They grew one body, one face, one pair of arms
And legs, as one might graft branches upon

A tree, so two became nor boy nor girl,
Neither yet both within a single body.

"When tamed Hermaphroditus learned his fate,
Knew that his bath had sent him to his doom,
To weakened members and a girlish voice,
He raised his hands and prayed, 'O Father, Mother,
Hear your poor son who carried both your names:
Make all who swim these waters impotent,
Half men, half women.' Which his parents heard
And gave the fountained pool its weird magic."

PYGMALION

OVID, *Metamorphoses*, Book 10. 243-297 (Humphries)

*The story of Pygmalion begins with the sculptor's disgust
with the evil sexuality of the women about him and ends
with Venus in a benign mood. Galatea is not named in the
ancient sources.*

One man, Pygmalion, who had seen these women
Leading their shameful lives, shocked at the vices
Nature has given the female disposition
Only too often, chose to live alone,
To have no woman in his bed. But meanwhile
He made, with marvelous art, an ivory statue,
As white as snow, and gave it greater beauty
Than any girl could have, and fell in love
With his own workmanship. The image seemed
That of a virgin, truly, almost living,
And willing, save that modesty prevented,
To take on movement. The best art, they say,
Is that which conceals art, and so Pygmalion
Marvels, and loves the body he has fashioned.
He would often move his hands to test and touch it,
Could this be flesh, or was it ivory only?
No, it could not be ivory. His kisses,
He fancies, she returns; he speaks to her,

Holds her, believes his fingers almost leave
An imprint on her limbs, and fears to bruise her.
He pays her compliments, and brings her presents
Such as girls love, smooth pebbles, winding shells,
Little pet birds, flowers with a thousand colors,
Lilies, and painted balls, and lumps of amber.
He decks her limbs with dresses, and her fingers
Wear rings which he puts on, and he brings a necklace,
And earrings, and a ribbon for her bosom,
And all of these become her, but she seems
Even more lovely naked, and he spreads
A crimson coverlet for her to lie on,
Takes her to bed, puts a soft pillow under
Her head, as if she felt it, calls her *Darling,*
My darling love!
                    And Venus' holiday
Came round, and all the people of the island
Were holding festival, and snow-white heifers,
Their horns all tipped with gold, stood at the altars,
Where incense burned, and, timidly, Pygmalion
Made offering, and prayed: "If you can give
All things, O gods, I pray my wife may be—
(He almost said, *My ivory girl,* but dared not)—
One like my ivory girl." And golden Venus
Was there, and understood the prayer's intention,
And showed her presence, with the bright flame leaping
Thrice on the altar, and Pygmalion came
Back where the maiden lay, and lay beside her,
And kissed her, and she seemed to glow, and kissed her,
And stroked her breast, and felt the ivory soften
Under his fingers, as wax grows soft in sunshine,
Made pliable by handling. And Pygmalion
Wonders, and doubts, is dubious and happy,
Plays lover again, and over and over touches
The body with his hand. It is a body!
The veins throb under the thumb. And oh, Pygmalion
Is lavish in his prayer and praise to Venus,
No words are good enough. The lips he kisses
Are real indeed, the ivory girl can feel them,
And blushes and responds, and the eyes open
At once on lover and heaven, and Venus blesses
The marriage she has made. The crescent moon

Fills to full orb, nine times, and wanes again,
And then a daughter is born, a girl named Paphos,
From whom the island later takes its name.

SCYLLA AND MINOS

OVID, *Metamorphoses*, Book 8. 6-151, with omissions (More)

King Minos, while the fair wind moved their ship,
Was laying waste the land of Megara.
He gathered a great army round the walls
Built by Alcathous, where reigned in splendor
King Nisus—mighty and renowned in war—
Upon the center of whose hoary head
A lock of purple hair was growing.—Its
Proved virtue gave protection to his throne.

Six times the horns of rising Phoebe grew,
And still the changing fortune of the war
Was in suspense; so, Victory day by day
Between them hovered on uncertain wings.

Within that city was a regal tower
On tuneful walls; where once Apollo laid
His golden harp; and in the throbbing stone
The sounds remained. And there, in times of peace
The daughter of king Nisus loved to mount
The walls and strike the sounding stone with pebbles:
So, when the war began, she often viewed
The dreadful contest from that height;
Until, so long the hostile camp remained,
She had become acquainted with the names,
And knew the habits, horses and the arms
Of many a chief, and could discern the signs
Of their Cydonean quivers.

More than all,
The features of King Minos were engraved
Upon the tablets of her mind. And when

He wore his helmet, crested with gay plumes,
She deemed it glorious; when he held his shield
Shining with gold, no other seemed so grand;
And when he poised to hurl the tough spear home,
She praised his skill and strength; and when he bent
His curving bow with arrow on the cord,
She pictured him as Phoebus taking aim,—
But when, arrayed in purple, and upon
The back of his white war horse, proudly decked
With richly broidered housings, he reined in
The nervous steed, and took his helmet off,
Showing his fearless features, then the maid,
Daughter of Nisus, could control herself
No longer; and a frenzy seized her mind.

    She called the javelin happy which he touched,
And blessed were the reins within his hand.
    She had an impulse to direct her steps,
A tender virgin, through the hostile ranks,
Or cast her body from the topmost towers
Into the Gnossian camp. She had a wild
Desire to open to the enemy
The heavy brass-bound gates, or anything
That Minos could desire.

                  .And as she sat
Beholding the white tents, she cried, "Alas!
Should I rejoice or grieve to see this war?
I grieve that Minos is the enemy
Of her who loves him; but unless the war
Had brought him, how could he be known to me?
But should he take me for a hostage? That
Might end the war—a pledge of peace, he might
Keep me for his companion.

                  "O, supreme
Of mankind! she who bore you must have been
As beautiful as you are; ample cause
For Jove to lose his heart.

                  "O, happy hour!
If moving upon wings through yielding air,

I could alight within the hostile camp
In front of Minos, and declare to him
My name and passion!

        "Then would I implore
What dowry he could wish, and would provide
Whatever he might ask, except alone
The city of my father. Perish all
My secret hopes before one act of mine
Should offer treason to accomplish it.
And yet, the kindness of a conqueror
Has often proved a blessing, manifest
To those who were defeated. Certainly
The war he carries on is justified
By his slain son.

        "He is a mighty king,
Thrice strengthened in his cause. Undoubtedly
We shall be conquered, and, if such a fate
Awaits our city, why should he by force
Instead of my consuming love, prevail
To open the strong gates? Without delay
And dreadful slaughter, it is best for him
To conquer and decide this savage war.

    "Ah, Minos, how I fear the bitter fate
Should any warrior hurl his cruel spear
And pierce you by mischance, for surely none
Can be so hardened to transfix your breast
With purpose known."

        O, let her love prevail
To open for his army the great gates.
Only the thought of it, has filled her soul;
She is determined to deliver up
Her country as a dowry with herself,
And so decide the war! But what avails
This idle talk.

    "A guard surrounds the gates,
My father keeps the keys, and he alone

Is my obstruction, and the innocent
Account of my despair. Would to the Gods
I had no father! Is not man the God
Of his own fortune, though his idle prayers
Avail not to compel his destiny?

"Another woman crazed with passionate desires,
Which now inflame me, would not hesitate,
But with a fierce abandon would destroy
Whatever checked her passion. Who is there
With love to equal mine? I dare to go
Through flames and swords; but swords and flames
Are not now needed, for I only need
My royal father's lock of purple hair.
More precious than fine gold, it has a power
To give my heart all that it may desire."

While Scylla said this, night that heals our cares
Came on, and she grew bolder in the dark.
And now it is the late and silent hour
When slumber takes possession of the breast,
Outwearied with the cares of busy day;
Then as her father slept, with stealthy tread
She entered his abode, and there despoiled,
And clipped his fatal lock of purple hair.

Concealing in her bosom the sad prize
Of crime degenerate, she at once went forth
A gate unguarded, and with shameless haste
Sped through the hostile army to the tent
Of Minos, whom, astonished, she addressed:

"Only my love has led me to this deed.
The daughter of King Nisus, I am called
The maiden Scylla. Unto you I come
And offer up a power that will prevail
Against my country, and I stipulate
No recompense except yourself. Take then
This purple hair, a token of my love.—
Deem it not lightly as a lock of hair
Held idly forth to you; it is in truth

My father's life." And as she spoke
She held out in her guilty hand the prize,
And begged him to accept it with her love.

Shocked at the thought of such a heinous crime,
Minos refused, and said, "O execrable thing!
Despised abomination of our time!
May all the Gods forever banish you
From their wide universe, and may the earth
And the deep ocean be denied to you!
So great a monster shall not be allowed
To desecrate the sacred Isle of Crete,
Where Jupiter was born." So Minos spoke.

Nevertheless he conquered Megara,
(So aided by the damsel's wicked deed)
And as a just and mighty king imposed
His own conditions on the vanquished land.

He ordered his great fleet to tarry not;
The hawsers were let loose, and the long oars
Quickly propelled his brazen-pointed ships.—

. . . .

She leaped into the waves,
And followed the receding ships—for strength
From passion came to her. And soon she clung
Unwelcome, to the sailing Gnossian ship.

Meanwhile, the Gods had changed her father's form
And now he hovered over the salt deep,
A hawk with tawny wings. So when he saw
His daughter clinging to the hostile ship
He would have torn her with his rending beak;—
He darted towards her through the yielding air.
In terror she let go, but as she fell
The light air held her from the ocean spray;
Her feather-weight supported by the breeze;
She spread her wings, and changed into a bird.
They called her "Ciris" when she cut the wind,
And "Ciris"—cut-the-lock—remains her name.

ALCESTIS AND ADMETUS

PLATO, *Symposium*, 179B,C. (Jowett)

Plato has the young man Phaedrus give an account of Alcestis' devotion to her husband Admetus, a story best known from the Alcestis *of Euripides.*

Love will make men dare to die for their beloved; and women as well as men. Of this, Alcestis the daughter of Pelias is a monument to all Hellas; for she was willing to lay down her life on behalf of her husband, when no one else would, although he had a father and mother; but the tenderness of her love so far exceeded theirs, that they seemed to be as strangers to their own son, having no concern with him; and so noble did this action of hers appear, not only to men but also to the gods, that among the many who have done virtuously she was one of the very few to whom the gods have granted the privilege of returning to earth, in admiration of her virtue; such exceeding honor is paid by them to the devotion and virtue of love.

LAODAMIA AND PROTESILAUS

CATULLUS, 68. 73-108, with omissions (Lamb)

Thus erst, while love warmed every tender thought,
Her husband's home Laodamia sought.
Too eager bride! No victim led to die
Had yet propitious made the gods on high—
Thy power, dread Nemesis, hath e'er suppressed
All hopes unsanctioned by the heavens' behest:
Hapless, who grasp, unless the gods approve,
The proffered gift of glory, wealth, or love!—
Soon did she learn how keen the thirsty fane
Desires the sacred blood of victims slain,

Forced from her parting husband's neck to tear
The close embrace that longed to linger there;
Ere yet two winters in their length of nights
Had glutted passion with its own delights,
Or taught the bride a strength, how hard to give,
To lose the mate she loved and yet to live.
The Fates knew well his doom not distant far
If the bold chieftain sought the Trojan war.

. . . .

To Troy then hastening the assembled band
Of Grecian youths had left their native land,
To burst on Paris in fair Helen's bower
And rouse him from beside his paramour,
Nor let his crime its lawless rapture shed
On days of quiet or a peaceful bed.
'Twas in that hour that he, beloved too well,
Thine heart-dear spouse Laodamia, fell:
And wild despair with overwhelming flow
Hurried thee down the deep abyss of woe.

———

PROTESILAUS AND LAODAMIA

HYGINUS, *Myths*, 103, 104 (Grant)

An oracle warned the Achaeans that the man who first reached
the shore of the Trojans would perish. When the Greek fleet had
neared shore, and the others were delaying, Iolaus, son of Iphiclus
and Diomedia, was first to leap from his ship, and was promptly
killed by Hector. All called him Protesilaus, since he was first of all
to die. When his wife Laodamia, daughter of Acastus, heard that
he had died, she wept and begged the gods that she be allowed
to speak with him for three hours. It was granted, and when he
was led back by Mercury, she spoke with him for three hours. But
when Protesilaus died a second time, Laodamia could not endure
her grief.

. . . .

And so she made a bronze likeness of her husband Protesilaus,
put it in her room under pretense of sacred rites, and devoted
herself to it. When a servant early in the morning had brought

fruit for the offerings, he looked through a crack in the door and saw her folding the image of Protesilaus in her embrace and kissing it. Thinking she had a lover he told her father Acastus. When he came and burst into the room, he saw the statue of Protesilaus. To put an end to her torture he had the statue and the sacred offerings burned on a pyre he had made, but Laodamia, not enduring her grief, threw herself on it and was burned to death.

PYRAMUS AND THISBE

OVID, *Metamorphoses*, Book 4. 55-166 (Gregory)

Ovid apparently took this story from an Oriental source. Although it is otherwise unknown in Classical literature, Ovid's telling has made it one of the best-known myths.

"Pyramus and Thisbe: both the best-looking
Of young people in the East were next-door
Neighbors; they lived within a high-walled, brick-built
City made (so it was said) by Queen Semiramis.
Proximity was the first reason why
They came to know each other; as time passed
Love flourished, and if their parents had
Not come between them, then they would have shared
A happy wedding bed. And yet no parent
Can check the heat of love, therefore, the lovers
Burned with mutual flames. Nor friend nor servant
Spoke for them; their speech was in the gesture
Of a nod, a smile; the more they banked the flames
The more they smouldered with a deeper heat.
There was a fissure in the wall between
Their homes, a small, thin crevice that no one
Had seen. What eyes are sharper than the eyes
Of love? The lovers found the slit and made it
The hidden mouthpiece of their voices where
Love's subtle words in sweetest whispers came
And charmed the ear. And as they took their places,
Thisbe on one side, Pyramus on his,

Both waited, listening for the other's breath.
'O cold and bitter wall,' they said, 'why stand
Between two lovers at your side? Let limbs
And bodies join; at least open your gate
To take our kisses. Yet we do not show
Ingratitude, nor shall we, nor forget
The way through which our words met lovers' ears.'
Divided as they were, each futile day
Was spent in whispers, closing with 'Good night.'
Both pressed their lips against the silent wall.
Next day when dawn outshone the lamps of night
And Sun had dried the dew on frost-white grasses,
The lovers took their places at the wall
And in soft cries complained of heartless fate.
But as they talked they came to a decision:
Under the quiet darkness of the night
To glide from eyes that watched them out of doors,
To leave the town behind them; to prevent
The chance of being led astray they chose
The site of Ninus' tomb to meet each other,
There in the shadow of a famous tree,
The white tall mulberry that waved its branches
Not far from a bright flashing stream of water;
The plot delighted them, but from that moment
The day seemed all too long; the quick Sun lagged,
Then dove into the sea where Night came up.

"No sooner dark than Thisbe, veiled, unseen,
Slipped out of doors, a shade among the shadows,
Ran to the tomb, and took her place beneath
The appointed tree. For love had given her
Audacity. But look! A lioness!
And through the moonlit distance Thisbe saw her
With bloody lamb-fed jaws came up the road
And headed toward well waters for a drink
Where through the moonlit distance Thisbe saw her.
The Babylonian girl, trembling yet swift,
Turned to the recess of a darkening cave,
And as she ran dropped her white cloak behind her.
Meanwhile the beast had had her fill of drinking
And as she wandered back between the trees
She stepped across the cloak that Thisbe wore,

Now empty of its mistress, worried it
Between her teeth and left it stained with blood.
A moment later Pyramus arrived
Who saw the footprints of the beast in dust;
Then turned death-pale, but when he found the torn
Blood-tinted cloak, he said, 'One night shall be
The killing of two lovers. She whom I love
Deserves the longer life; on me all guilt
Should fall, for it was I who sent her out
Through deepest night into this evil place
Where I arrived too late. May all the lions
Who breed beneath this rocky cliff come at me,
Tear at my body and eat its guilt away—
But only cowards merely ask for death.'
At which he gathered up his Thisbe's cloak
And walked within the shadow of the tree,
There where he kissed the cloak and covered it
With tears. 'Now drink my blood,' he said aloud
And thrust the sword he wore into his side
Then in death's frenzy quickly drew it out,
Torn from warm flesh, and straightway fell
Backward to earth. And as a split lead joint
Shoots hissing sprays of water into air,
So his blood streamed above him to the tree,
Staining white fruit to darkest red, coloring
Tree's roots and growing fruit with purple dye.

"Then Thisbe came from shelter, fearful, shaken,
Thinking perhaps her lover had misplaced her,
Looked for him with her eyes, her soul, her heart,
Trembling to tell him dangers she escaped.
And though she knew the landmarks, the tall tree,
She wondered at the color of its fruit,
Doubting if it was the same tree she saw,
And while she wavered, glanced where something moved,
Arms, legs it had, stirring on blood-soaked ground,
Then she stepped back; her face had turned as pale
As the green boxwood leaf, her body tremulous
As fair lake waters rippling in the wind.
But when she saw that it was he, her lover,
She tore her hair and clasped her arms with grief,
Then fondled him, tears poured in wounds and blood.

And as she kissed his death-cold lips she cried,
'Pyramus, what misfortune takes you from me?
And O, Pyramus, speak to answer me.
It is your darling Thisbe calling you.
Listen, my dear, raise up your lazy head.'
At Thisbe's name, Pyramus raised an eyelid,
Weighted with death; her face seen in a vision,
And then his eyes had closed forever more.

"When she discovered her own cloak, the empty
Ivory sheath that held his sword, she said,
'By your own hand even your love has killed you,
Unlucky boy. Like yours my hand has courage,
My heart, love for the last act. I have the strength
To share your death and some shall say I was
The unhappy cause, the partner of your fate;
Only Lord Death had power to take you from me,
Yet even he cannot divorce us now.
O twice unhappy parents, his as mine,
Come, take our prayers, nor think the worse of us
Whom true love and death's hour have made one
And we shall sleep in the same bed, our tomb.
And you, O tree whose branches weave their shadows
Dark over the pitiful body of one lover
Shall soon bear shade for two; O fateful tree
Be the memorial of our twin deaths,
And your dark fruit the color of our mourning.'
Then Thisbe placed sword's point beneath her breast
The blade still warm with blood from her love's heart,
And leaned upon it till she sank to earth.
Her prayers had reached the gods, had moved both parents:
The ripe fruit of the tree turned deep rose color;
And they who loved sleep in a single urn."

CYCLOPS AND GALATEA

THEOCRITUS, *Idylls*, 11. 19-66 (Lang)

The savage monster of the Odyssey *becomes a lovelorn swain when the pastoral poet puts a song in his mouth.*

"O milk-white Galatea, why cast off him that loves thee? More white than is pressed milk to look upon, more delicate than the lamb art thou, than the young calf wantoner, more sleek than the unripened grape! Here dost thou resort, even so, when sweet sleep possesses me, and home straightway dost thou depart when sweet sleep lets me go, fleeing me like an ewe that has seen the gray wolf.

"I fell in love with thee, maiden, I, on the day when first thou camest, with my mother, and didst wish to pluck the hyacinths from the hill, and I was thy guide on the way. But to leave loving thee, when once I had seen thee, neither afterward, nor now at all, have I the strength, even from that hour. But to thee all this is as nothing, by Zeus, nay, nothing at all!

"I know, thou gracious maiden, why it is that thou dost shun me. It is all for the shaggy brow that spans all my forehead, from this to the other ear, one long unbroken eyebrow. And but one eye is on my forehead, and broad is the nose that overhangs my lip. Yet I (even such as thou seest me) feed a thousand cattle, and from these I draw and drink the best milk in the world. And cheese I never lack, in summer time or autumn, nay, nor in the dead of winter, but my baskets are always overladen.

"Also I am skilled in piping, as none other of the Cyclopes here, and of thee, my love, my sweet-apple, and of myself too I sing, many a time, deep in the night. And for thee I tend eleven fawns, all crescent-browed, and four young whelps of the bear.

"Nay, come thou to me, and thou shalt lack nothing that now thou hast. Leave the gray sea to roll against the land; more sweetly, in this cavern, shalt thou fleet the night with me! Thereby the laurels grow, and there the slender cypresses, there is the ivy dun, and the sweet clustered grapes; there is chill water, that for me deep-wooded Aetna sends down from the white snow, a draught divine! Ah who, in place of these, would chose the sea to dwell in, or the waves of the sea?

"But if thou dost refuse because my body seems shaggy and rough, well, I have faggots of oakwood, and beneath the ashes is fire unwearied, and I would endure to let thee burn my very soul, and this my one eye, the dearest thing that is mine.

"Ah me, that my mother bore me not a finny thing, so would I have gone down to thee, and kissed thy hand, if thy lips thou would not suffer me to kiss! And I would have brought thee either white lilies, or the soft poppy with its scarlet petals. Nay, these are summer's flowers, and those are flowers of winter, so I could not have brought thee them all at one time.

"Now, verily, maiden, now and here will I learn to swim, if perchance some stranger come hither, sailing with his ship, that I may see why it is so dear to thee, to have thy dwelling in the deep.

"Come forth, Galatea, and forget as thou comest, even as I that sit here have forgotten, the homeward way! Nay, choose with me to go shepherding, with me to milk the flocks, and to pour the sharp rennet in, and to fix the cheeses."

HERO AND LEANDER

VERGIL, *Georgics*, Book 3. 258-263 (Bovie)

In a few lines, without naming Hero, Vergil presents the essence of the famous myth. Ovid develops the theme in poetic epistles; further expansion by the late poet Musaeus seems to have been the immediate inspiration of Marlowe and Chapman.

What of cruel love's consuming fire
That fans the flames deep in Leander's heart?
He swims the storm-tossed straits in blackest night
And above him thunder splits the ports of sky
While the waters crash and plunge on the cliff-lined shore.
His heartsick parents cannot call him back,
Nor can his maiden, spared for her cruel end.

BAUCIS AND PHILEMON

OVID, *Metamorphoses*, Book 8. 620-724 (Humphries)

This account of Ovid's is notable both for his re-handling of the story of the Flood and for his picture of conjugal felicity.

"An oak-tree stands
Beside a linden, in the Phrygian hills.
There's a low wall around them. I have seen
The place myself; a prince once sent me there
To land ruled by his father. Not far off
A great marsh lies, once habitable land,
But now a playground full of coots and divers.
Jupiter came here, once upon a time,
Disguised as mortal man, and Mercury,
His son, came with him, having laid aside
Both wand and wings. They tried a thousand houses,
Looking for rest; they found a thousand houses
Shut in their face. But one at last received them,
A humble cottage, thatched with straw and reeds.
A good old woman, Baucis, and her husband,
A good old man, Philemon, used to live there.
They had married young, they had grown old together
In the same cottage; they were very poor,
But faced their poverty with cheerful spirit
And made its burden light by not complaining.
It would do you little good to ask for servants
Or masters in that household, for the couple
Were all the house; both gave and followed orders.
So, when the gods came to this little cottage,
Ducking their heads to enter, the old man
Pulled out a rustic bench for them to rest on,
As Baucis spread a homespun cover for it.
And then she poked the ashes around a little,
Still warm from last night's fire, and got them going
With leaves and bark, and blew at them a little,
Without much breath to spare, and added kindling,

The wood split fine, and the dry twigs, made smaller
By breaking them over the knee, and put them under
A copper kettle, and then she took the cabbage
Her man had brought from the well-watered garden,
And stripped the outer leaves off. And Philemon
Reached up, with a forked stick, for the side of bacon,
That hung below the smoky beam, and cut it,
Saved up so long, a fair-sized chunk, and dumped it
In the boiling water. They made conversation
To keep the time from being too long, and brought
A couch with willow frame and feet, and on it
They put a sedge-grass mattress, and above it
Such drapery as they had, and did not use
Except on great occasions. Even so,
It was pretty worn, it had only cost a little
When purchased new, but it went well enough
With a willow couch. And so the gods reclined.
Baucis, her skirts tucked up, was setting the table
With trembling hands. One table-leg was wobbly;
A piece of shell fixed that. She scoured the table,
Made level now, with a handful of green mint,
Put on the olives, black or green, and cherries
Preserved in dregs of wine, endive and radish,
And cottage cheese, and eggs, turned over lightly
In the warm ash, with shells unbroken. The dishes,
Of course, were earthenware, and the mixing-bowl
For wine was the same silver, and the goblets
Were beech, the inside coated with yellow wax.
No time at all, and the warm food was ready,
And wine brought out, of no particular vintage,
And pretty soon they had to clear the table
For the second course: here there were nuts and figs
And dates and plums and apples in wide baskets—
Remember how apples smell?—and purple grapes
Fresh from the vines, and a white honeycomb
As centerpiece, and all around the table
Shone kindly faces, nothing mean or poor
Or skimpy in good will.
                              "The mixing-bowl,
As often as it was drained, kept filling up
All by itself, and the wine was never lower.
And this was strange, and scared them when they saw it.

They raised their hands and prayed, a little shaky—
'Forgive us, please, our lack of preparation,
Our meager fare!' They had one goose, a guardian,
Watchdog, he might be called, of their estate,
And now decided they had better kill him
To make their offering better. But the goose
Was swift of wing, too swift for slow old people
To catch, and they were weary from the effort,
And could not catch the bird, who fled for refuge,
Or so it seemed, to the presence of the strangers.
'Don't kill him,' said the gods, and then continued:
'We are gods, you know: this wicked neighborhood
Will pay as it deserves to; do not worry,
You will not be hurt, but leave the house, come with us,
Both of you, to the mountain-top!' Obeying,
With staff and cane, they made the long climb, slowly
And painfully, and rested, where a bowman
Could reach the top with a long shot, looked down,
Saw water everywhere, only their cottage
Standing above the flood. And while they wondered
And wept a little for their neighbors' trouble,
The house they used to live in, the poor quarters
Small for the two of them, became a temple:
Forked wooden props turned into marble columns;
The thatch grew brighter yellow; the roof was golden;
The doors were gates, most wonderfully carved;
The floor that used to be of earth was marble.
Jupiter, calm and grave, was speaking to them:
'You are good people, worthy of each other,
Good man, good wife—ask us for any favor,
And you shall have it.' And they hesitated,
Asked, 'Could we talk it over, just a little?'
And talked together, apart, and then Philemon
Spoke for them both: 'What we would like to be
Is to be priests of yours, and guard the temple,
And since we have spent our happy years together,
May one hour take us both away; let neither
Outlive the other, that I may never see
The burial of my wife, nor she perform
That office for me.' And the prayer was granted.
As long as life was given, they watched the temple,
And one day, as they stood before the portals,

Both very old, talking the old days over,
Each saw the other put forth leaves, Philemon
Watched Baucis changing, Baucis watched Philemon,
And as the foliage spread, they still had time
To say 'Farewell, my dear!' and the bark closed over
Sealing their mouths. And even to this day
The peasants in that district show the stranger
The two trees close together, and the union
Of oak and linden in one. The ones who told me
The story, sober ancients, were no liars,
Why should they be? And my own eyes have seen
The garlands people bring there; I brought new ones,
Myself, and said a verse: *The gods look after
Good people still, and cherishers are cherished.*"

APPENDIX

1. The Cyclic Epics

PROCLUS, *Chrestomathy*, i-ii (Evelyn-White)

The Iliad *and the* Odyssey *were supplemented by a number of epics of uncertain authorship which provided a considerable body of material about the actions and persons connected with the Trojan War. The dramatists and other ancient authors seem to have used a good deal of this mythological material. Although the epics are lost, fortunately Photius has preserved a summary of the prose paraphrases made by Proclus.*

THE CYPRIA

The epic called *Cypria* is current in eleven books. Its contents are as follows.

Zeus plans with Themis to bring about the Trojan War. Strife arrives while the gods are feasting at the marriage of Peleus and starts a dispute between Hera, Athena, and Aphrodite as to which of them is fairest. The three are led by Hermes at the command of Zeus to Alexandrus [Paris] on Mount Ida for his decision, and Alexandrus, lured by his promised marriage with Helen, decides in favour of Aphrodite.

Then Alexandrus builds his ships at Aphrodite's suggestion, and Helenus foretells the future to him, and Aphrodite orders Aeneas to sail with him, while Cassandra prophesies as to what will happen afterwards. Alexandrus next lands in Lacedaemon and is entertained by the sons of Tyndareus, and afterwards by

Menelaus in Sparta, where in the course of a feast he gives gifts to Helen.

After this, Menelaus sets sail for Crete, ordering Helen to furnish the guests with all they require until they depart. Meanwhile, Aphrodite brings Helen and Alexandrus together, and they, after their union, put very great treasures on board and sail away by night. Hera stirs up a storm against them and they are carried to Sidon, where Alexandrus takes the city. From there he sailed to Troy and celebrated his marriage with Helen.

In the meantime Castor and Polydeuces, while stealing the cattle of Idas and Lynceus, were caught in the act, and Castor was killed by Idas, and Lynceus and Idas by Polydeuces. Zeus gave them immortality every other day.

Iris next informs Menelaus of what has happened at his home. Menelaus returns and plans an expedition against Ilium with his brother, and then goes on to Nestor. Nestor in a digression tells him how Epopeus was utterly destroyed after seducing the daughter of Lycus, and the story of Oedipus, the madness of Heracles, and the story of Theseus and Ariadne. Then they travel over Hellas and gather the leaders, detecting Odysseus when he pretends to be mad, not wishing to join the expedition, by seizing his son Telemachus for punishment at the suggestion of Palamedes.

All the leaders then meet together at Aulis and sacrifice. The incident of the serpent and the sparrows takes place before them, and Calchas foretells what is going to befall. After this, they put out to sea, and reach Teuthrania and sack it, taking it for Ilium. Telephus comes out to the rescue and kills Thersander the son of Polyneices, and is himself wounded by Achilles. As they put out from Mysia a storm comes on them and scatters them, and Achilles first puts in at Scyros and marries Deïdameia, the daughter of Lycomedes, and then heals Telephus, who had been led by an oracle to go to Argos, so that he might be their guide on the voyage to Ilium.

When the expedition had mustered a second time at Aulis, Agamemnon, while at the chase, shot a stag and boasted that he surpassed even Artemis. At this the goddess was so angry that she sent stormy winds and prevented them from sailing. Calchas then told them of the anger of the goddess and bade them sacrifice Iphigeneia to Artemis. This they attempt to do, sending to fetch Iphigeneia as though for marriage with Achilles. Artemis, however, snatched her away and transported her to the Tauri, making her immortal, and putting a stag in place of the girl upon the altar.

Next they sail as far as Tenedos: and while they are feasting, Philoctetes is bitten by a snake and is left behind in Lemnos because of the stench of his sore. Here, too, Achilles quarrels with Agamemnon because he is invited late. Then the Greeks tried to land at Ilium, but the Trojans prevent them, and Protesilaus is killed by Hector. Achilles then kills Cycnus, the son of Poseidon, and drives the Trojans back. The Greeks take up their dead and send envoys to the Trojans demanding the surrender of Helen and the treasure with her. The Trojans refusing, they first assault the city, and then go out and lay waste the country and cities round about. After this, Achilles desires to see Helen, and Aphrodite and Thetis contrive a meeting between them. The Achaeans next desire to return home, but are restrained by Achilles, who afterwards drives off the cattle of Aeneas, and sacks Lyrnessus and Pedasus and many of the neighboring cities, and kills Troïlus. Patroclus carries away Lycaon to Lemnos and sells him as a slave, and out of the spoils Achilles receives Briseïs as a prize, and Agamemnon Chryseis. Then follows the death of Palamedes, the plan of Zeus to relieve the Trojans by detaching Achilles from the Hellenic confederacy, and a catalogue of the Trojan allies.

THE AETHIOPIS

The *Cypria*, described in the preceding book, has its sequel in the *Iliad* of Homer, which is followed in turn by the five books of the *Aethiopis*, the work of Arctinus of Miletus. Their contents are as follows. The Amazon Penthesileia, the daughter of Ares and of Thracian race, comes to aid the Trojans, and after showing great prowess, is killed by Achilles and buried by the Trojans. Achilles then slays Thersites for abusing and reviling him for his supposed love for Penthesileia. As a result a dispute arises amongst the Achaeans over the killing of Thersites, and Achilles sails to Lesbos and after sacrificing to Apollo, Artemis, and Leto, is purified by Odysseus from bloodshed.

Then Memnon, the son of Eos, wearing armor made by Hephaestus, comes to help the Trojans, and Thetis tells her son about Memnon. A battle takes place in which Antilochus is slain by Memnon and Memnon by Achilles. Eos then obtains of Zeus and bestows upon her son immortality; but Achilles routs the Trojans, and, rushing into the city with them, is killed by Paris and Apollo. A great struggle for the body then follows, Aias taking up the body and carrying it to the ships, while Odysseus drives off the Trojans behind. The Achaeans then bury Antilochus and lay out the body of Achilles, while Thetis, arriving with the Muses and her sisters, bewails her son, whom she afterwards catches away from the pyre and transports to the White Island. After this, the Achaeans pile him a cairn and hold games in his honor. Lastly a dispute arises between Odysseus and Aias over the arms of Achilles.

THE LITTLE ILIAD

Next comes the Little Iliad in four books by Lesches of Mitylene: its contents are as follows. The adjudging of the arms of Achilles takes place, and Odysseus, by the contriving of Athena, gains them. Aias then becomes mad and destroys the herd of the Achaeans and kills himself. Next Odysseus lies in wait and catches Helenus, who prophesies as to the taking of Troy, and Diomedes accordingly brings Philoctetes from Lemnos. Philoctetes is healed by Machaon, fights in single combat with Alexandrus and kills him: the dead body is outraged by Menelaus, but the Trojans recover and bury it. After this Deïphobus marries Helen, Odysseus brings Neoptolemus from Scyros and gives him his father's arms, and the ghost of Achilles appears to him.

Eurypylus the son of Telephus arrives to aid the Trojans, shows his prowess and is killed by Neoptolemus. The Trojans are now closely besieged, and Epeius, by Athena's instruction, builds the wooden horse. Odysseus disfigures himself and goes in to Ilium as a spy, and there being recognized by Helen, plots with her for the taking of the city; after killing certain of the Trojans, he returns to the ships. Next he carries the Palladium out of Troy with the help of Diomedes. Then after putting their best men in the wooden horse and burning their huts, the main body of the

Hellenes sail to Tenedos. The Trojans, supposing their troubles over, destroy a part of their city wall and take the wooden horse into their city and feast as though they had conquered the Hellenes.

THE SACK OF ILIUM

Next come two books of the *Sack of Ilium*, by Arctinus of Miletus with the following contents. The Trojans were suspicious of the wooden horse and standing round it debated what they ought to do. Some thought they ought to hurl it down from the rocks, others to burn it up, while others said they ought to dedicate it to Athena. At last this third opinion prevailed. Then they turned to mirth and feasting believing the war was at an end. But at this very time two serpents appeared and destroyed Laocöon and one of his two sons, a portent which so alarmed the followers of Aeneas that they withdrew to Ida. Sinon then raised the fire-signal to the Achaeans, having previously got into the city by pretense. The Greeks then sailed in from Tenedos, and those in the wooden horse came out and fell upon their enemies, killing many and storming the city. Neoptolemus kills Priam who had fled to the altar of Zeus Herceius; Menelaus finds Helen and takes her to the ships, after killing Deiphobus; and Aias the son of Ileus, while trying to drag Cassandra away by force, tears away with her the image of Athena. At this the Greeks are so enraged that they determine to stone Aias, who only escapes from the danger threatening him by taking refuge at the altar of Athena. The Greeks, after burning the city, sacrifice Polyxena at the tomb of Achilles: Odysseus murders Astyanax; Neoptolemus takes Andromache as his prize, and the remaining spoils are divided. Demophon and Acamas find Aethra and take her with them. Lastly the Greeks sail away and Athena plans to destroy them on the high seas.

THE RETURNS

After the *Sack of Ilium* follow the *Returns* in five books by Agias of Troezen. Their contents are as follows. Athena causes a quarrel between Agamemnon and Menelaus about the voyage from Troy. Agamemnon then stays on to appease the anger of Athena. Diomedes and Nestor put out to sea and get safely home. After them Menelaus sets out and reaches Egypt with five ships, the rest having been destroyed on the high seas. Those with Calchas, Leontes, and Polypoetes go by land to Colophon and bury Teiresias who died there. When Agamemnon and his followers were sailing away, the ghost of Achilles appeared and tried to prevent them by foretelling what should befall them. The storm at the rocks called Capherides is then described, with the end of Locrian Aias. Neoptolemus, warned by Thetis, journeys overland and, coming into Thrace, meets Odysseus at Maronea, and then finishes the rest of his journey after burying Phoenix who dies on the way. He himself is recognized by Peleus on reaching the Molossi. Then comes the murder of Agamemnon by Aegisthus and Clytaemnestra, followed by the vengeance of Orestes and Pylades. Finally, Menelaus returns home.

THE TELEGONY

After the *Returns* comes the *Odyssey* of Homer, and then the *Telegony* in two books by Eugammon of Cyrene, which contain the following matters. The suitors of Penelope are buried by their kinsmen, and Odysseus, after sacrificing to the Nymphs, sails to Elis to inspect his herds. He is entertained there by Polyxenus and receives a mixing bowl as a gift; the story of Trophonius and Agamedes and Augeas then follows. He next sails back to Ithaca and performs the sacrifices ordered by Teiresias, and then goes to Thesprotis where he marries Callidice, queen of the Thesprotians.

A war then breaks out between the Thesprotians, led by Odysseus, and the Brygi. Ares routs the army of Odysseus and Athena engages with Ares, until Apollo separates them. After the death of Callidice Polypoetes, the son of Odysseus, succeeds to the kingdom, while Odysseus himself returns to Ithaca. In the meantime Telegonus, while traveling in search of his father, lands on Ithaca and ravages the island: Odysseus comes out to defend his country, but is killed by his son unwittingly. Telegonus, on learning his mistake, transports his father's body with Penelope and Telemachus to his mother's island, where Circe makes them immortal, and Telegonus marries Penelope, and Telemachus Circe.

2. Poetical History in Herodotus

HERODOTUS, *The Persian Wars* (Rawlinson)

*Many accounts in Herodotus are clearly poetical or mytho-
logical in their presentation and treatment, even though the
persons involved are historical. I have included four examples
of the method for their own sake and because later writers
found them congenial.*

SOLON AND CROESUS

HERODOTUS, *The Persian Wars*, Book 1. 30-33

On this account, as well as to see the world, Solon set out upon
his travels, in the course of which he went to Egypt to the court
of Amasis, and also came on a visit to Croesus at Sardis. Croesus
received him as his guest, and lodged him in the royal palace. On
the third or fourth day after, he bade his servants conduct Solon
over his treasuries, and show him all their greatness and magnifi-
cence. When he had seen them all, and, so far as time allowed, inspected them, Croesus addressed this question to him,
"Stranger of Athens, we have heard much of your wisdom and of
your travels through many lands, from love of knowledge and a
wish to see the world. I am curious therefore to inquire of you,
whom, of all the men that you have seen, you consider the most
happy?" This he asked because he thought himself the happiest
of mortals: but Solon answered him without flattery, according to
his true sentiments, "Tellus of Athens, sire." Full of astonishment

at what he heard, Croesus demanded sharply, "And wherefore do you deem Tellus happiest?" To which the other replied, "First, because his country was flourishing in his days, and he himself had sons both beautiful and good, and he lived to see children born to each of them, and these children all grew up; and further because, after a life spent in what our people look upon as comfort, his end was surpassingly glorious. In a battle between the Athenians and their neighbors near Eleusis, he came to the assistance of his countrymen, routed the foe, and died upon the field most gallantly. The Athenians gave him a public funeral on the spot where he fell, and paid him the highest honors."

Thus did Solon admonish Croesus by the example of Tellus, enumerating the manifold particulars of his happiness. When he had ended, Croesus inquired a second time, who after Tellus seemed to him the happiest, expecting that, at any rate, he would be given the second place. "Cleobis and Bito," Solon answered, "they were of Argive race: their fortune was enough for their wants, and they were besides endowed with so much bodily strength that they had both gained prizes at the Games. Also this tale is told of them: There was a great festival in honor of the goddess Hera at Argos, to which their mother must needs be taken in a car. Now the oxen did not come home from the field in time: so the youths, fearful of being too late, put the yoke on their own necks, and themselves drew the car in which their mother rode. Five miles they drew her, and stopped before the temple. This deed of theirs was witnessed by the whole assembly of worshippers, and then their life closed in the best possible way. Herein, too, God showed forth most evidently, how much better a thing for man death is than life. For the Argive men stood thick around the car and extolled the vast strength of the youths; and the Argive women extolled the mother who was blessed with such a pair of sons; and the mother herself, overjoyed at the deed and at the praises it had won, standing straight before the image, besought the goddess to bestow on Cleobis and Bito, the sons who had so mightily honored her, the highest blessing to which mortals can attain. Her prayer ended, they offered sacrifice, and partook of the holy banquet, after which the two youths fell asleep in the temple. They never woke more, but so passed from the earth. The Argives, looking on them as among the best of men, caused statues of them to be made, which they gave to the shrine at Delphi."

When Solon had thus assigned these youths the second place.

Croesus broke in angrily, "What, stranger of Athens, is my happiness, then, valued so little by you, that you do not even put me on a level with private men?"

"Croesus," replied the other, "you asked a question concerning the condition of man, of one who knows that the power above us is full of jealousy, and fond of troubling our lot. A long life gives one to witness much, and experience much oneself, that one would not choose. Seventy years I regard as the limit of the life of man. In these seventy years are contained, without reckoning intercalary months, 25,200 days. Add an intercalary month to every other year, that the seasons may come round at the right time, and there will be, besides the seventy years, thirty-five such months, making an addition of 1,050 days. The whole number of the days contained in the seventy years will thus be 26,250, whereof not one but will produce events unlike the rest. Hence man is wholly accident. For yourself, Croesus, I see that you are wonderfully rich, and the lord of many nations; but with respect to your question, I have no answer to give, until I hear that you have closed your life happily. For assuredly he who possesses great store of riches is no nearer happiness than he who has what suffices for his daily needs, unless luck attend upon him, and so he continue in the enjoyment of all his good things to the end of life. For many of the wealthiest men have been unfavored of fortune, and many whose means were moderate, have had excellent luck. Men of the former class excel those of the latter but in two respects; these last excel the former in many. The wealthy man is better able to content his desires, and to bear up against a sudden buffet of calamity. The other has less ability to withstand these evils (from which, however, his good luck keeps him clear), but he enjoys all these following blessings: he is whole of limb, a stranger to disease, free from misfortune, happy in his children, and comely to look upon. If, in addition to all this, he end his life well, he is of a truth the man of whom you are in search, the man who may rightly be termed happy. Call him, however, until he die, not happy but fortunate. Scarcely, indeed, can any man unite all these advantages: as there is no country which contains within it all that it needs, but each, while it possesses some things, lacks others, and the best country is that which contains the most; so no single human being is complete in every respect—something is always lacking. He who unites the greatest number of advantages, and retaining them to the day of his death, then dies peaceably, that man alone, sire, is, in my judgment, entitled to bear the name of 'happy.' But in every matter we must mark well the end; for oftentimes God gives men a gleam of happiness, and then plunges them into ruin."

Such was the speech which Solon addressed to Croesus, a speech which brought him neither largess nor honor. The king saw him depart with much indifference, since he thought that a man must be an arrant fool who made no account of present good, but bade men always wait and mark the end.

ARION

HERODOTUS, *The Persian Wars*, Book 1. 24

They relate that Arion of Methymna, who as a player on the harp was second to no man living at that time, and who was, so far as we know, the first to invent the dithyrambic measure, to give it its name, and to recite in it at Corinth, was carried to Taenarum on the back of a dolphin.

He had lived for many years at the court of Periander, when a longing came upon him to sail across to Italy and Sicily. Having made rich profits in those parts, he wanted to recross the seas to Corinth. He therefore hired a vessel, the crew of which were Corinthians, thinking that there was no people in whom he could more safely confide; and, going on board, he set sail from Tarentum. The sailors, however, when they reached the open sea, formed a plot to throw him overboard and seize upon his riches. Discovering their design, he fell on his knees, beseeching them to spare his life, and making them welcome to his money. But they refused; and required him either to kill himself outright, if he wished for a grave on the dry land, or without loss of time, to leap overboard into the sea. In this strait Arion begged them, since such was their pleasure, to allow him to mount upon the quarterdeck, dressed in his full costume, and there to play and sing, promising that, as soon as his song was ended, he would destroy himself. Delighted at the prospect of hearing the very best harper in the world, they consented, and withdrew from the stern to the middle of the vessel: while Arion dressed himself in the full costume of his calling, took his harp, and standing on the quarterdeck, chanted the Orthian. His strain ended, he flung himself, fully attired as he was, headlong into the sea. The Corinthians then sailed on to Corinth. As for Arion, a dolphin, they say, took him upon his back and carried him to Taenarum, where he went ashore, and thence walked to Corinth in his musician's dress, and told all that had happened to him. Periander, however, disbelieved the story, and put Arion in ward, to prevent his leaving Corinth, while he watched anxiously for the return of the mariners. On their arrival he summoned them before him and asked them if they could give him any tidings of Arion. They returned for answer that he was alive and in good health in Italy, and that they had left him at Tarentum, where he was doing well. Thereupon Arion appeared before them, just as he was when he jumped from the vessel: the men, astonished and detected in falsehood, could no longer deny their guilt. Such is the account which the Corinthians and Lesbians give; and there is to this day at Taenarum, an offering of Arion's at the shrine, which is a small figure in bronze, representing a man seated upon a dolphin.

GYGES AND CANDAULES

HERODOTUS, *The Persian Wars*, Book 1. 8-12

Now it happened that Candaules was in love with his own wife; and not only so, but thought her the fairest woman in the whole world. This fancy had strange consequences. There was in his bodyguard a man whom he specially favored, Gyges, the son of Dascylus. All affairs of greatest moment were entrusted by Candaules to this person, and to him he was wont to extol the surpassing beauty of his wife. So matters went on for a while. At length, one day, Candaules, for he was fated to end ill, thus addressed his follower, "I see you do not credit what I tell you of my lady's loveliness; but come now, since men's ears are less credulous than their eyes, contrive some means whereby you may behold her naked." At this the other loudly exclaimed, saying, "What most unwise speech is this, master, which you have uttered? Would you have me behold my mistress when she is naked? Remember that a woman, with her clothes, puts off her bashfulness. Our fathers, in time past, distinguished right and wrong plainly enough, and it is our wisdom to submit to be taught by them. There is an old say-ing, 'Let each look on his own.' I hold your wife for the fairest of all womankind. Only, I beseech you, ask me not to do wickedly."

Gyges thus endeavored to decline the king's proposal, trem-bling lest some dreadful evil should befall him through it. But the king replied to him, "Courage, friend; suspect me not of the design to prove you by this discourse; nor dread your mistress, lest mischief befall you at her hands. Be sure I will so manage that she shall not even know that you have looked upon her. I will place you behind the open door of the chamber in which we sleep. When I enter to go to rest she will follow me. There stands a chair close to the entrance, on which she will lay her clothes one by one as she takes them off. You will be able thus at your leisure to pe-ruse her person. Then, when she is moving from the chair towards the bed, and her back is turned on you, be it your care that she see you not as you pass through the door-way."

Gyges, unable to escape, could but declare his readiness. Then Candaules, when night came, led Gyges into his sleeping-chamber, and a moment after the queen followed. She came in, and laid her garments on the chair, and Gyges gazed on her. After a while she moved towards the bed, and her back being then turned, he glided stealthily from the apartment. As he was passing out, however, she saw him, and instantly divining what had hap-pened, she neither screamed as her shame impelled her, nor even appeared to have noticed anything, purposing to take vengeance upon the husband who had so affronted her. For among the Lyd-ians, and indeed among the barbarians generally, it is reckoned a deep disgrace, even to a man, to be seen naked.

No sound or sign of intelligence escaped her at the time. But in the morning, as soon as day broke, she hastened to choose from among her retinue, such as she knew to be most faithful to her, and preparing them for what was to ensue, summoned Gyges into her presence. Now it had often happened before that the queen had desired to confer with him, and he was accustomed to come to her at her call. He therefore obeyed the summons, not suspect-ing that she knew what had occurred. Then she addressed these words to him, "Take your choice, Gyges, of two courses which are open to you. Slay Candaules, and thereby become my lord, and obtain the Lydian throne, or die this moment in his room. So you will not again, obeying all behests of your master, behold what is not lawful for you. It must needs be, that either he perish by whose counsel this thing was done, or you, who saw me naked, and so did break our usages." At these words Gyges stood awhile in mute astonishment; recovering after a time, he earnestly besought the queen that she would not compel him to so hard a choice. But finding he implored in vain, and that necessity was indeed laid on him to kill or to be killed, he made choice of life for himself, and replied by this inquiry, "If it must be so, and you compel me against my will to put my lord to death, come, let me hear how you will have me set on him." "Let him be attacked," she answered, "on that spot where I was by him shown naked to you, and let the assault be made when he is asleep."

All was then prepared for the attack, and when night fell, Gyges, seeing that he had no retreat or escape, but must absolutely either slay Candaules, or himself be slain, followed his mistress into the sleeping-room. She placed a dagger in his hand, and hid him carefully behind the self-same door. Then Gyges, when the king was fallen asleep, entered privily into the chamber and struck him dead. Thus did the wife and kingdom of Candaules pass into the possession of his follower Gyges, of whom Archilochus the Parian, who lived about the same time, made mention in a poem written in iambic trimeter verse.

~~~~~

POLYCRATES

HERODOTUS, *The Persian Wars*, Book 3. 40-43

The exceeding good fortune of Polycrates did not escape the notice of Amasis, who was much disturbed thereat. When therefore his successes continued increasing, Amasis wrote him the following letter, and sent it to Samos. "Amasis to Polycrates speaks thus: It is a pleasure to hear of a friend and ally prospering, but your exceeding prosperity does not cause me joy, for as much as I know that the gods are envious. My wish for myself, and for those whom I love, is, to be now successful, and now to meet with a check; thus passing through life amid alternate good and ill, rather than with perpetual good fortune. For never yet did I hear tell of any one succeeding in all his undertakings, who did not meet with calamity at last, and come to utter ruin. Now, therefore, give ear to my words, and meet your good luck in this way. Think which of all your treasures you value most and can least bear to part with; take it, whatsoever it be, and throw it away, so that it may be sure never to come any more into the sight of man. Then, if your good fortune be not thenceforth chequered with ill, save yourself from harm by again doing as I have counselled."

When Polycrates read this letter, and perceived that the advice of Amasis was good, he considered carefully with himself which of the treasures that he had it would grieve him most to lose. After much thought he made up his mind that it was a signet-ring which he wore, an emerald set in gold, the workmanship of Theodore, son of Telecles, a Samian. So he determined to throw this away; and, manning a fifty-oared ship, he went on board, and bade the sailors put out into the open sea. When he was now a long way from the island, he took the ring from his finger, and, in the sight of all those who were on board, flung it into the deep. This done, he returned home, and gave vent to his sorrow.

Now it happened five or six days afterwards that a fisherman caught a fish so large and beautiful, that he thought it well deserved to be made a present of to the king. So he took it with him to the gate of the palace, and said that he wanted to see Polycrates. Then Polycrates allowed him to come in, and the fisherman gave him the fish with these words, "O king, when I took this prize, I thought I would not carry it to market, though I am a poor man who live by my trade. I said to myself, it is worthy of Polycrates and his greatness; and so I brought it here to give it to you." The speech pleased the king; who thus spoke in reply, "You did right well, friend, and I am doubly indebted, both for the gift and for the speech. Come now, and sup with me." So the fisherman went home, esteeming it a high honor that he had been asked to sup with the king. Meanwhile the servants, on cutting open the fish, found the signet of their master in its belly. No sooner did they see it than they seized upon it, and, hastening to Polycrates with great joy, restored it to him, and told him in what way it had been found. The king, who saw something providential in the matter, forthwith wrote a letter to Amasis, telling him all that had happened, what he had himself done, and what had been the upshot—and despatched the letter to Egypt.

When Amasis had read the letter of Polycrates, he perceived that it does not belong to man to save his fellow-man from the fate which is in store for him; likewise he felt certain that Polycrates would end ill, as he prospered in everything, even finding what he had thrown away. So he sent a herald to Samos, and dissolved the contract of friendship. This he did, that when the great and heavy misfortune came, he might escape the grief which he would have felt if the sufferer had been his bond-friend.

3. Philosophic Use of Myth in Plato

Plato found that frequently the method of myth or allegory was suitable to the expression of his insights and convictions, rather than vigorous logical or dialectic exposition.

THE SOUL

PLATO, *Phaedrus*, 253D-254E (Jowett)

As I said at the beginning of this tale, I divided each soul into three parts, two of them having the forms of horses and the third that of a charioteer; and one of the horses was good and the other bad, but I have not yet explained the virtue and vice of either, and to that I will now proceed. The well-conditioned horse is erect and well-formed; he has a lofty neck and an aquiline nose, and his color is white, and he has dark eyes and is a lover of honor and modesty and temperance, and the follower of true glory; he needs not the touch of the whip but is guided by word and admonition only. Whereas the other is a large misshapen animal, put together anyhow; he has a strong short neck; he is flat-faced and of a dark color, gray-eyed and bloodshot, the mate of insolence and pride, shag-eared, deaf, hardly yielding to blow or spur. Now when the charioteer beholds the vision of love, and has his whole soul warmed with sense, and is full of tickling and desire, the obedient steed then as always under the government of shame, refrains himself from leaping on the beloved; but the other, instead of heeding the blows of the whip, prances away and gives all manner of trouble to his companion and to the charioteer and urges them on towards the beloved and reminds them of the joys of love. They at first indignantly oppose him and will not be urged on to do terrible and unlawful deeds; but at last, when there is no end of evil, they yield and suffer themselves to be led on to do as he bids them. And now they are at the spot and behold the flashing beauty of the beloved. But when the charioteer sees that, his memory is carried to the true beauty, and he beholds her in company with Modesty set in her holy place. And when he sees her he is afraid and falls back in adoration, and in falling is compelled to pull back the reins, which he does with such force as to bring both the steeds on their haunches, the one willing and unresisting, the unruly one very unwilling; and when they have gone back a little, the one is overflowing with shame and wonder, and pours forth rivers of perspiration over the entire soul; the other, when the pain is over which the bridle and the fall had given him, having with difficulty taken breath, is full of wrath and reproaches, which he heaps upon the charioteer and his fellow-steed, as though from want of courage and manhood they had been false to their agreement and guilty of desertion. And, when they again decline, he forces them on, and will scarce yield to their request that he would wait until another time. Returning at the appointed hour, they make as if they had forgotten, and he reminds them, fighting and neighing and dragging them, until at length he on the same thoughts intent, forces them to draw near. And when they are near he stoops his head and puts up his tail, and takes the bit in his mouth and pulls shamelessly. Then the charioteer is worse off than ever; he drops at the very start, and with still greater violence draws the bit out of the teeth of the wild steed and covers his abusive tongue and jaws with blood, and forces his legs and haunches to the ground and punishes him sorely. And when this has happened several times and the villain has ceased from his wanton way, he is tamed and humbled, and follows the will of the charioteer, and when he sees the beautiful one he is ready to die of fear. And from that time forward the soul of the lover follows the beloved in modesty and holy fear.

MAN'S NATURE

PLATO, *Symposium*, 189C-191D (Jowett)

Aristophanes professed to open another vein of discourse; he had a mind to praise Love in another way, not like that either of Pausanias or Eryximachus. Mankind, he said, judging by their neglect of him, have never, as I think, at all understood the power of Love. For if they had understood him they would surely have built noble temples and altars, and offered solemn sacrifices in his honor; but this is not done, and certainly ought to be done: for of all the gods he is the best friend of men, the helper and the healer of the ills which are the great obstruction to the happiness of the race. I shall rehearse to you his power, and you may repeat what I say to the rest of the world. And first let me treat of the nature and state of man; for the original human nature was not like the present, but different. In the first place, the sexes were originally three in number, not two as they are now; there was man, woman, and the union of the two, having a name corresponding to this double nature; this once had a real existence, but is now lost, and the name only is preserved as a term of reproach. In the second place, the primeval man was round and had four hands and four feet, back and sides forming a circle, one head with two faces, looking opposite ways, set on a round neck and precisely alike; also four ears, two privy members, and the remainder to correspond. When he had a mind he could walk as men now do, and he could also roll over and over at a great rate, leaning on his four hands and four feet, eight in all, like tumblers going over and over with their legs in the air; this was when he wanted to run fast. Now there were these three sexes, because the sun, moon, and earth are three; and the man was originally the child of the sun, the woman of the earth, and the man-woman of the moon, which is made up of sun and earth, and they were all round and moved round and round like their parents. Terrible was their might and strength, and the thoughts of their hearts were great, and they made an attack upon the gods; and of them is told the tale of Otus and Ephialtes who, as Homer says, dared to scale heaven, and would have laid hands upon the gods. Doubt reigned in the councils of

Zeus and of the gods. Should they kill them and annihilate the race with thunderbolts, as they had done the giants, then there would be an end of the sacrifice and worship which men offered to them; but, on the other hand, the gods could not suffer their insolence to be unrestrained. At last, after a good deal of reflection, Zeus discovered a way. He said: "I have a notion which will humble their pride and mend their manners; they shall continue to exist, but I will cut them in two, and then they will be diminished in strength and increased in numbers; this will have the advantage of making them more profitable to us. They shall walk upright on two legs, and if they continue insolent and won't be quiet, I will split them again and they shall hop about on a single leg." He spoke and cut men in two, like a sorb-apple which is halved for pickling, or as you might divide an egg with a hair; and as he cut them one after another, he bade Apollo give the face and the half of the neck a turn in order that the man might contemplate the section of himself: this would teach him a lesson of humility. He was also to heal their wounds and compose their forms. Apollo twisted the face and pulled the skin all round over that which in our language is called the belly, like the purses which draw in, and he made one mouth in the center, which he fastened in a knot (this is called the navel); he also moulded the breast and took out most of the wrinkles, much as a shoemaker might smooth out leather upon a last; he left a few, however, in the region of the belly and navel, as a memorial of the primeval change. After the division the two parts of man, each desiring his other half, came together, and threw their arms about one another eager to grow into one, and would have perished from hunger without ever making an effort, because they did not like to do anything apart; and when one of the halves died and the other survived, the survivor sought another mate, whether the section of an entire man or of an entire woman, which had usurped the name of man and woman, and clung to that. And this was being the destruction of them, when Zeus in pity invented a new plan: he turned the parts of generation round in front, for this was not always their position, and they sowed the seed no longer as hitherto like grasshoppers in the ground, but in one another; and after the transposition the male generated in the female in order that by the mutual embraces of man and woman they might breed, and the race might continue; or if man came to man they might be satisfied, and rest and go their ways to the business of life: so

ancient is the desire of one another which is implanted in us, re-
uniting our original nature, making one of two, and healing the
state of man. Each of us when separated is but the indenture of a
man, having one side only like a flat fish, and he is always looking
for his other half. Men who are a section of that double nature
which was once called Androgynous are lascivious; adulterers are
generally of this breed, and also adulterous and lascivious women:
the women who are a section of the woman don't care for men,
but have female attachments; the female companions are of this
sort. But the men who are a section of the male follow the male,
and while they are young, being a piece of the man, they hang
about him and embrace him, and they are themselves the best of
boys and youths because they have the most manly nature.

THE ALLEGORY OF THE CAVE

PLATO, *Republic*, Book 7. 514-517 (Jowett)

After this, I said, imagine the enlightenment or ignorance of our
nature in a figure: Behold! human beings living in a sort of
underground den, which has a mouth open towards the light and
reaching all across the den; they have been here from their childhood, and have their legs and necks chained so that they cannot
move, and can only see before them; for the chains are arranged
in such a manner as to prevent them from turning round their
heads. At a distance above and behind them the light of a fire is
blazing, and between the fire and the prisoners there is a raised
way; and you will see, if you look, a low wall built along the way,
like the screen which marionette players have before them, over
which they show the puppets.

I see, he said.

And do you see, I said, men passing along the wall carrying
vessels, which appear over the wall; also figures of men and animals, made of wood and stone and various materials; and some of
the passengers, as you would expect, are talking, and some of
them are silent?

That is a strange image, he said, and they are strange prisoners.

Like ourselves, I replied; and they see only their own shadows, or the shadows of one another, which the fire throws on the opposite wall of the cave?

True, he said; how could they see anything but the shadows if they were never allowed to move their heads?

And of the objects which are being carried in like manner they would only see the shadows?

Yes, he said.

And if they were able to talk with one another, would they not suppose that they were naming what was actuallly before them?

Very true.

And suppose further that the prison had an echo which came from the other side, would they not be sure to fancy that the voice which they heard was that of a passing shadow?

No question, he replied.

There can be no question, I said, that the truth would be to them just nothing but the shadows of the images.

That is certain.

And now look again, and see how they are released and cured of their folly. At first, when any one of them is liberated and compelled suddenly to go up and turn his neck round and walk and look at the light, he will suffer sharp pains; the glare will distress him, and he will be unable to see the realities of which in his former state he had seen the shadows; and then imagine some one saying to him, that what he saw before was an illusion, but that now he is approaching real being and has a truer sight and vision of more real things,—what will be his reply? And you may further imagine that his instructor is pointing to the objects as they pass and requiring him to name them,—will he not be in a difficulty? Will he not fancy that the shadows which he formerly saw are truer than the objects which are now shown to him?

Far truer.

And if he is compelled to look at the light, will he not have a pain in his eyes which will make him turn away to take refuge in the object of vision which he can see, and which he will conceive to be clearer than the things which are now being shown to him?

True, he said.

And suppose once more, that he is reluctantly dragged up a steep and rugged ascent, and held fast and forced into the presence of the sun himself, do you not think that he will be pained and irritated, and when he approaches the light he will have his eyes dazzled, and will not be able to see any of the realities which are now affirmed to be the truth?

Not all in a moment, he said.

He will require to get accustomed to the sight of the upper world. And first he will see the shadows best, next the reflections of men and other objects in the water, and then the objects themselves; next he will gaze upon the light of the moon and the stars; and he will see the sky and the stars by night, better than the sun, or the light of the sun, by day?

Certainly.

And at last he will be able to see the sun, and not mere reflections of him in the water, but he will see him as he is in his own proper place, and not in another, and he will contemplate his nature.

Certainly.

And after this he will reason that the sun is he who gives the seasons and the years, and is the guardian of all that is in the visible world, and in a certain way the cause of all things which he and his fellows have been accustomed to behold?

Clearly, he said, he would come to the other first and to this afterwards.

And when he remembered his old habitation, and the wisdom of the den and his fellow-prisoners, do you not suppose that he would felicitate himself on the change, and pity them?

Certainly, he would.

And if they were in the habit of conferring honors on those who were quickest to observe and remember and foretell which of the shadows went before, and which followed after, and which were together, do you think that he would care for such honors and glories, or envy the possessors of them? Would he not say with Homer,—

"Better to be a poor man, and have a poor master,"

and endure anything, rather than to think and live after their manner?

Yes, he said, I think that he would rather suffer anything than live after their manner.

Imagine once more, I said, that such a one coming suddenly out of the sun were to be replaced in his old situation, is he not certain to have his eyes full of darkness?

Very true, he said.

And if there were a contest, and he had to compete in measuring the shadows with the prisoners who have never moved out of the den, during the time that his sight is weak, and before his eyes are steady (and the time which would be needed to acquire this new habit of sight might be very considerable), would he not be ridiculous? Men would say of him that up he went and down he comes without his eyes; and that there was no use in even thinking of ascending: and if any one tried to loose another and lead him up to the light, let them only catch the offender in the act, and they would put him to death.

No question, he said.

This allegory, I said, you may now append to the previous argument; the prison is the world of sight, the light of the fire is the sun, the ascent and vision of the things above you may truly regard as the upward progress of the soul into the intellectual world; that is my poor belief, to which, at your desire, I have given expression. Whether I am right or not God only knows; but, whether true or false, my opinion is that in the world of knowledge the idea of good appears last of all, and is seen only with an effort; and, when seen, is also inferred to be the universal author of all things beautiful and right, parent of light and the lord of light in this world, and the source of truth and reason in the other: this is the first great cause which he who would act rationally either in public or private life must behold.

THE APOCALYPSE OF ER

PLATO, *Republic*, Book 10. 614B-621B (Jowett)

Well, I said, I will tell you a tale; not one of the tales which Odysseus tells to Alcinous, yet this too is a tale of a brave man, Er the son of Armenius, a Pamphylian by birth. He was slain in battle, and ten days afterwards, when the bodies of the dead were brought in already in a state of corruption, he was brought in with them undecayed, and carried home to be buried. And on the twelfth day, as he was lying on the funeral pile, he returned to life and told them what he had seen in the other world. He said that when his soul departed he went on a journey with a great company, and that they came to a mysterious place at which there were two chasms in the earth; they were near together, and over against them were two other chasms in the heaven above. In the intermediate space there were judges seated, who bade the just, after they had judged them, ascend by the heavenly way on the right hand, having the signs of the judgment bound on their foreheads; and in like manner the unjust were commanded by them to descend by the lower way on the left hand; these also had the symbols of their deeds fastened on their backs. He drew near, and they told him that he was to be the messenger of the other world to men, and they bade him hear and see all that was to be heard and seen in that place. Then he beheld and saw on one side the souls departing at either chasm of heaven and earth when sentence had been given on them; and at the two other openings other souls, some ascending out of the earth dusty and worn with travel, some descending out of heaven clean and bright. And always, on their arrival, they seemed as if they had come from a long journey, and they went out into the meadow with joy and there encamped as at a festival, and those who knew one another embraced and conversed, the souls which came from earth curiously inquiring about the things of heaven, and the souls which came from heaven of the things of earth. And they told one another of what had happened by the way, some weeping and sorrowing at the remembrance of the things which they had endured and seen in their journey beneath the earth (now the journey lasted a thousand years), while others were describing heavenly blessings and visions of inconceivable beauty. There is not time, Glaucon, to tell all; but the sum was this: He said that for every wrong which they had done to any one they suffered tenfold; the thousand years answering to the hundred years which are reckoned as the life of man. If, for example, there were any who had committed murders, or had betrayed or enslaved cities or armies, or been guilty of any other evil behavior, for each and all of these they received punishment ten times over, and the rewards of beneficence and justice and holiness were in the same proportion. Not to repeat what he had to say concerning young children dying almost as soon as they were born; of piety and impiety to gods and parents, and of murderers, there were retributions yet greater which he narrated. He mentioned that he was present when one of the spirits asked another, "Where is Ardiaeus the Great?" (Now this Ardiaeus was the tyrant of some city of Pamphylia, who had murdered his aged father and his elder brother, and had committed many other abominable crimes, and he lived a thousand years before the time of Er.) The answer was: "He comes not hither, and will never come." And, "indeed," he said, "this was one of the terrible sights which was witnessed by us. For we were approaching the mouth of the cave, and having seen all, were about to re-ascend, when of a sudden Ardiaeus appeared and several others, most of whom were tyrants; and there were also besides the tyrants private individuals who had been great criminals; they were just at the mouth, being, as they fancied, about to return into the upper world, but the opening, instead of receiving them, gave a roar, as was the case when any incurable or unpunished sinner tried to ascend; and then wild men of fiery aspect, who knew the meaning of the sound, came up and seized and carried off several of them, and Ardiaeus and others they bound head and foot and hand, and threw them down and flayed them with scourges, and dragged them along the road at the side, carding them on thorns like wool, and declaring to the pilgrims as they passed what were their crimes, and that they were being taken away to be cast into hell. And of all the terrors of the place there was no terror like this of hearing the voice; and when there was silence they ascended with joy." These were the penalties and retributions, and there were blessings as great.

Now when the spirits that were in the meadow had tarried seven days, on the eighth day they were obliged to proceed on their journey, and on the fourth day from that time they came to a place where they looked down from above upon a line of light, like a column extending right through the whole heaven and earth, in color not unlike the rainbow, only brighter and purer; another day's journey brought them to the place, and there, in the midst of the light, they saw reaching from heaven the extremities of the chains of it: for this light is the belt of heaven, and holds together the circle of the universe, like the undergirders of a trireme. And from the extremities of the chains is extended the spindle of Necessity, on which all the revolutions turn. The shaft and hook of this spindle are made of steel, and the whorl is made partly of steel and also partly of other materials. Now the whorl is in form like the whorl used on earth; and you are to suppose, as he described, that there is one large hollow whorl which is scooped out, and into this is fitted another lesser one, and another, and another, and four others, making eight in all, like boxes which fit into one another; their edges are turned upwards, and all together form one continuous whorl. This is pierced by the spindle, which is driven home through the center of the eighth. The first and outermost whorl has the rim broadest, and the seven inner whorls narrow, in the following proportions—the sixth is next to the first in size, the fourth next to the sixth; then comes the eighth; the seventh is fifth, the fifth is sixth, the third is seventh, last and eighth comes the second. The largest [or fixed stars] is spangled, and the seventh [or sun] is brightest; the eighth [or moon] colored by the reflected light of the seventh; the second and fifth [Mercury and Saturn] are like one another, and of a yellower color than the preceding; the third [Venus] has the whitest light; the fourth [Mars] is reddish; the sixth [Jupiter] is in whiteness second. Now the whole spindle has the same motion; but, as the whole revolves in one direction, the seven inner circles move slowly in the other, and of these the swiftest is the eighth; next in swiftness are the seventh, sixth, and fifth, which move together; third in swiftness appeared to them to move in reversed orbit the fourth; the third appeared fourth, and the second fifth. The spindle turns on the knees of Necessity; and on the upper surface of each circle is a siren, who goes round with them, hymning a single sound and note. The eight together form one harmony; and round about, at equal intervals, there is another band, three in number, each sitting upon her throne: these are the Fates, daughters of Necessity, who are clothed in white raiment and have garlands upon their heads, Lachesis and Clotho and Atropos, who accompany with their voices the harmony of the sirens—Lachesis singing of the past, Clotho of the present, Atropos of the future; Clotho now and then assisting with a touch of her right hand the motion of the outer circle or whorl of the spindle, and Atropos with her left hand touching and guiding the inner ones, and Lachesis laying hold of either in turn, first with one hand and then with the other.

Now when the spirits arrived, their duty was to go to Lachesis; but first a prophet came and arranged them in order; then he took from the knees of Lachesis lots and samples of lives, and going up to a high place, spoke as follows: "Hear the word of Lachesis, the daughter of Necessity. Mortal souls, behold a new cycle of mortal life. Your genius will not choose you, but you will choose your genius; and let him who draws the first lot have the first choice of life, which shall be his destiny. Virtue is free, and as a man honors or dishonors her he will have more or less of her; the chooser is answerable—God is justified." When the Interpreter had thus spoken he cast the lots among them, and each one took up the lot which fell near him, all but Er himself (he was not allowed), and each as he took his lot perceived the number which he had drawn. Then the Interpreter placed on the ground before them the samples of life; and there were many more lives than the souls present, and there were all sorts of lives—of every animal and every condition of man. And there were tyrannies among them, some continuing while the tyrant lived, others which broke off in the middle and came to an end in poverty and exile and beggary; and there were lives of famous men, some who were famous for their form and beauty as well as for their strength and success in games, or, again, for their birth and the qualities of their ancestors; and some who were the reverse of famous for the opposite qualities. And of women likewise; there was not, however, any definite character among them, because the soul must of necessity choose another life, and become another. But there were many elements mingling with one another, and also with elements of wealth and poverty, and disease and health; and there were mean states also. And this, my dear Glaucon, is the great danger of man; and therefore the utmost care should be taken. Let each one of us leave every other kind of knowledge and seek and follow one thing only, if peradventure he may be able to learn and find who there is who can and will teach him to distinguish the life of good and evil, and to choose always and everywhere the better life as far as possible. He should consider the bearing of all these things which have been mentioned severally and collectively upon a virtuous life; he should know what the effect of beauty is when compounded with poverty or wealth in a particular soul, and what are the good and evil consequences of noble and humble birth, of private and public station, of strength and weakness, of cleverness and dullness, and of all the natural and acquired gifts of the soul, and study the composition of them; then he will look at the nature of the soul, and from the consideration of all this he will determine which is the better and which is the worse life, and at last he will choose, giving the name of evil to the life which will make his soul more unjust, and good to the life which will make his soul more just; all else he will disregard. For this, as we have seen, is the best choice both for this life and after death. Such an iron sense of truth and right must a man take with him into the world below, that there too he may be undazzled by the desire of wealth or the other allurements of evil, lest, coming upon tyrannies and similar villainies, he do irremediable wrongs to others and suffer yet worse himself; but let him know how to choose the mean and avoid the extremes on either side, as far as in him lies, not only in this life but in all that which is to come. For this is the way of happiness.

And this was what the Interpreter said at the time, as the messenger from the other world reported him to have spoken: "Even for the last comer, if he chooses wisely and will live diligently, there is appointed a happy and not undesirable existence. Let not the first be careless in his choice, and let not the last despair." As he spoke these words he who had the first choice drew near and at once chose the greatest tyranny; his mind, having been darkened by folly and sensuality, he did not well consider, and therefore did not see at first that he was fated, among other evils, to devour his own children. But, when he came to himself and saw what was in the lot, he began to beat his breast and lament over his choice, forgetting the proclamation of the Interpreter; for, instead of blaming himself as the author of his calamity, he accused chance and the gods, and everything rather than himself. Now he was one of those who came from heaven, and in a former life had dwelt in a well-ordered State, but his virtue was a matter of habit only, and he had no philosophy. And this was more often the fortune of those who came from heaven, because they had no experience of life; whereas, in general, the dwellers upon earth, who had seen and known trouble, were not in a hurry to choose. And owing to this inexperience of theirs, and also because the lot was a chance, many of the souls exchanged a good destiny for an evil or an evil for a good. For if a man had always from the first dedicated himself to sound philosophy, and had been moderately fortunate in the number of the lot, he might, as the messenger reported, be happy in this life, and also his passage to another life and return to this, instead of being rugged and underground, would be smooth and heavenly. Most curious, he said, was the spectacle of the election—sad and laughable and strange; the souls generally choosing according to their condition in a previous life. There he saw the soul that was once Orpheus choosing the life of a swan out of enmity to the race of women, hating to be born of a woman because they had been his murderers; he saw also the soul of Thamyris choosing the life of a nightingale; birds, on the other hand, like the swan and other musicians, choosing to be men. The soul which obtained the twentieth lot chose the life of a lion, and this was the soul of Ajax the son of Telamon, who would not be a man, remembering the injustice which was done him in the judgment of the arms. The next was Agamemnon, who took the life of an eagle, because, like Ajax, he hated human nature on account of his sufferings. About the middle was the lot of Atalanta; she, seeing the great fame of an athlete, was unable to resist the temptation; and after her there came the soul of Epeus the son of Panopeus passing into the nature of a woman cunning in the arts; and far away among the last who chose, the soul of the jester Thersites was putting on the form of a monkey. There came also the soul of Odysseus having yet to make a choice, and his lot happened to be the last of them all. Now the recollection of former toils had disenchanted him of ambition, and he went about for a considerable time in search of the life of a private man who had nothing to do; he had some difficulty in finding this which was lying about and had been neglected by everybody else; and when he saw it he said that he would have done the same had he been first instead of last, and that he was delighted at his choice. And not only did men pass into animals, but I must also mention that there were animals tame and wild who changed into one another and into corresponding human natures, the good into the gentle and the evil into the savage, in all sorts of combinations. All the souls had now chosen their lives, and they went in the order of their choice to Lachesis, who sent with them the genius whom they had severally chosen, to be the guardian of their lives and the fulfiller of the choice; this genius led the souls first to Clotho, and drew them within the revolution of the spindle impelled by her hand, thus ratifying the destiny of each; and then, when they were fastened, carried them to Atropos, who spun the threads and made them irreversible; whence without turning round they passed beneath the throne of Necessity; and when they had all passed, they marched on in a scorching heat to the plain of Forgetfulness, which was a barren waste destitute of trees and verdure; and then towards evening they encamped by the river of Negligence, the water of which no vessel can hold; of this they were all obliged to drink a certain quantity, and those who were not saved by wisdom drank more than was necessary; and those who drank forgot all things. Now after they had gone to rest, about the middle of the night there was a thunderstorm and earthquake, and then in an instant they were driven all manner of ways like stars shooting to their birth. He himself was hindered from drinking the water. But in what manner or by what means he returned to the body he could not say; only, in the morning awaking suddenly, he saw himself lying on the pyre.

And thus, Glaucon, the tale has been saved and has not perished, and may be our salvation if we are obedient to the word spoken; and we shall pass safely over the river of Forgetfulness and our soul will not be defiled. Wherefore my counsel is, that we hold fast to the heavenly way and follow after justice and virtue always, considering that the soul is immortal and able to endure every sort of good and every sort of evil. Thus shall we live dear to one another and to the gods, both while remaining here and when, like conquerors in the games who go round to gather gifts, we receive our reward. And it shall be well with us both in this life and in the pilgrimage of a thousand years which we have been reciting.

4. Cupid and Psyche

~

APULEIUS, *The Golden Ass*, 4. 28 to 6. 24, compressed (Pater)

Apuleius' intention in telling the story of Cupid and Psyche was, at least in part, to create a religious allegory, but his sheer delight in the story itself has obscured the initial purpose. Walter Pater in Marius The Epicurean *succeeded remarkably in communicating the tone and color of the original, although he abbreviated and compressed the story.*

In a certain city lived a king and queen who had three daughters exceeding fair. But the beauty of the elder sisters, though pleasant to behold, yet passed not the measure of human praise, while such was the loveliness of the youngest that men's speech was too poor to commend it worthily and could express it not at all. Many of the citizens and of strangers, whom the fame of this excellent vision had gathered thither, confounded by that matchless beauty, could but kiss the finger-tips of their right hands at sight of her, as in adoration to the goddess Venus herself. And soon a rumor passed through the country that she whom the blue deep had borne, forbearing her divine dignity, was even then moving among men, or that by some fresh germination from the stars, not the sea, now, but the earth, had put forth a new Venus, endued with the flower of virginity.

This belief, with the fame of the maiden's loveliness, went daily further into distant lands, so that many people were drawn together to behold that glorious model of the age. Men sailed no longer to Paphos, to Cnidus or Cythera, to the presence of the goddess Venus: her sacred rites were neglected, her images stood uncrowned, the cold ashes were left to disfigure her forsaken altars. It was to a maiden that men's prayers were offered, to a human countenance they looked, in propitiating so great a godhead: when the girl went forth in the morning they strewed flowers on her way, and the victims proper to that unseen goddess were presented as she passed along. This conveyance of divine worship to a mortal kindled meantime the anger of the true Venus. "Lo! now, the ancient parent of nature," she cried, "the fountain of all elements! Behold me, Venus, benign mother of the world, sharing my honors with a mortal maiden, while my name, built up in heaven, is profaned by the mean things of earth! Shall a perishable woman bear my image about with her? In vain did the shepherd of Ida prefer me! Yet shall she have little joy, whosoever she be, of her usurped and unlawful loveliness!" Thereupon she called to her that winged, bold boy, of evil ways, who wanders armed by night through men's houses, spoiling their marriages; and stirring yet more by her speech his inborn wantonness, she led him to the city, and showed him Psyche as she walked.

"I pray thee," she said, "give thy mother a full revenge. Let this maid become the slave of an unworthy love." Then, embracing him closely, she departed to the shore and took her throne upon the crest of the wave. And lo! at her unuttered will, her ocean-servants are in waiting: the daughters of Nereus are there singing their song, and Portunus, and Salacia, and the tiny charioteer of the dolphin, with a host of Tritons leaping through the billows. And one blows softly through his sounding sea shell, another spreads a silken web against the sun, a third presents the mirror to the eyes of his mistress, while the others swim side by side below, drawing her chariot. Such was the escort of Venus as she went upon the sea.

Psyche meantine, aware of her loveliness, had no fruit thereof. All people regarded and admired, but none sought her in marriage. It was but as on the finished work of the craftsman that they gazed upon that divine likeness. Her sisters, less fair than she, were happily wedded. She, even as a widow, sitting at home, wept over her desolation, hating in her heart the beauty in which all men were pleased.

And the king, supposing the gods were angry, inquired of the oracle of Apollo and Apollo answered him thus: "Let the damsel be placed on the top of a certain mountain, adorned as for the bed of marriage and of death. Look not for a son-in-law of mortal birth; but for that evil serpent-thing, by reason of whom even the gods tremble and the shadows of Styx are afraid."

So the king returned home and made known the oracle to his wife. For many days she lamented, but at last the fulfillment of the divine precept is urgent upon her, and the company make ready to conduct the maiden to her deadly bridal. And now the nuptial torch gathers dark smoke and ashes: the pleasant sound of the pipe is changed into a cry: the marriage hymn concludes in a sorrowful wailing: below her yellow wedding-veil the bride shook away her tears; insomuch that the whole city was afflicted together at the ill-luck of the stricken house.

But the mandate of the god impelled the hapless ·Psyche to her fate, and, these solemnities being ended, the funeral of the living soul goes forth, all the people following. Psyche, bitterly weeping, assists not at her marriage but at her own obsequies, and while the parents hesitate to accomplish a thing so unholy the daughter cries to them: "Wherefore torment your luckless age by long weeping? This was the prize of my extraordinary beauty! When all people celebrated us with divine honors, and in one voice named the New Venus, it was then ye should have wept for me as one dead. Now at last I understand that that one name of Venus has been my ruin. Lead me and set me upon the appointed place. I am in haste to submit to that well-omened marriage, to behold that goodly spouse. Why delay the coming of him who was born for the destruction of the whole world?"

She was silent, and with firm step went on the way. And they proceeded to the appointed place on the steep mountain, and left there the maiden alone, and took their way homewards dejectedly. The wretched parents, in their close-shut house, yielded themselves to perpetual night; while to Psyche, fearful and trembling and weeping sore upon the mountain-top, comes the gentle Zephyrus. He lifts her mildly, and, with vesture afloat on either side, bears her by his own soft breathing over the windings of the hills, and sets her lightly among the flowers in the bosom of a valley below.

Psyche, in those delicate grassy places, lying sweetly on her dewy bed, rested from the agitation of her soul and arose in peace. And lo! a grove of mighty trees, with a fount of water, clear as glass, in the midst; and hard by the water, a dwelling-place, built not by human hands but by some divine cunning. One recognized, even at the entering, the delightful hostelry of a god. Golden pillars sustained the roof, arched most curiously in cedar-wood and ivory. The walls were hidden under wrought silver:—all tame and woodland creatures leaping forward to the visitor's gaze. Wonderful indeed was the craftsman, divine or half-divine, who by the subtlety of his art had breathed so wild a soul into the silver! The very pavement was distinct with pictures in goodly stones. In the glow of its precious metal the house is its own daylight, having no need of the sun. Well might it seem a place fashioned for the conversation of gods with men!

Psyche, drawn forward by the delight of it, came near, and, her courage growing, stood within the doorway. One by one, she admired the beautiful things she saw; and, most wonderful of all! no lock, no chain, nor living guardian protected that great treasure-house. But as she gazed there came a voice—a voice, as it were unclothed of bodily vesture—"Mistress!" it said, "all these things are thine. Lie down, and relieve thy weariness, and rise again for the bath when thou wilt. We thy servants, whose voice thou hearest, will be beforehand with our service, and a royal feast shall be ready."

And Psyche understood that some divine care was providing, and, refreshed with sleep and the bath, sat down to the feast. Still she saw no one: only she heard words falling here and there, and had voices alone to serve her. And the feast being ended, one entered the chamber and sang to her unseen, while another struck the chords of a harp, invisible with him who played on it. Afterwards the sound of a company singing together came to her, but still so that none was present to sight; yet it appeared that a great multitude of singers was there.

And the hour of evening inviting her, she climbed into the bed; and as the night was far advanced, behold a sound of a certain clemency approaches her. Then, fearing for her maiden-hood in so great solitude, she trembled, and more than any evil she knew dreaded that she knew not. And now the husband, that unknown husband, drew near, and ascended the couch, and made her his wife; and lo! before the rise of dawn he had departed hastily. And the attendant voices ministered to the needs of the newly married. And so it happened with her for a long season. And as nature has willed, this new thing, by continual use, became a delight to her: the sound of the voice grew to be her solace in that condition of loneliness and uncertainty.

One night the bridegroom spoke thus to his beloved, "O Psyche, most pleasant bride! Fortune is grown stern with us, and threatens thee with mortal peril. Thy sisters, troubled at the report of thy death and seeking some trace of thee, will come to the mountain's top. But if by chance their cries reach thee, answer not, neither look forth at all, lest thou bring sorrow upon me and destruction upon thyself." Then Psyche promised that she would do according to his will. But the bridegroom was fled away again with the night. And all that day she spent in tears, repeating that she was now dead indeed, shut up in that golden prison, powerless to console her sisters sorrowing after her, or to see their faces; and so went to rest weeping.

And after a while came the bridegroom again, and lay down beside her, and embracing her as she wept, complained, "Was this thy promise, my Psyche? What have I to hope from thee? Even in the arms of thy husband thou ceasest not from pain. Do now as thou wilt. Indulge thine own desire, though it seeks what will ruin thee. Yet wilt thou remember my warning, repentant too late." Then, protesting that she is like to die, she obtains from him that he suffer her to see her sisters, and present to them moreover what gifts she would of golden ornaments; but therewith he ofttimes advised her never at any time, yielding to pernicious counsel, to inquire concerning his bodily form, lest she fall, through unholy curiosity, from so great a height of fortune, nor feel ever his embrace again. "I would die a hundred times," she said, cheerful at last, "rather than be deprived of thy most sweet usage. I love thee as my own soul, beyond comparison even with Love himself. Only bid thy servant Zephyrus bring hither my sisters, as he brought me. My honeycomb! My husband! Thy Psyche's breath of life!" So he promised; and after the embraces of the night, ere the light appeared, vanished from the hands of his bride.

And the sisters, coming to the place where Psyche was abandoned, wept loudly among the rocks, and called upon her by name, so that the sound came down to her, and running out of the palace distraught, she cried, "Wherefore afflict your souls with lamentation? I whom you mourn am here." Then, summoning Zephyrus, she reminded him of her husband's bidding; and he bare them down with a gentle blast. "Enter now," she said, "into my house, and relieve your sorrow in the company of Psyche your sister."

And Psyche displayed to them all the treasures of the golden house, and its great family of ministering voices, nursing in them the malice which was already at their hearts. And at last one of them asks curiously who the lord of that celestial array may be, and what manner of man her husband? And Psyche answered dissemblingly, "A young man, handsome and mannerly, with a goodly beard. For the most part he hunts upon the mountains." And lest the secret should slip from her in the way of further speech, loading her sisters with gold and gems, she commanded Zephyrus to bear them away.

And they returned home, on fire with envy. "See now the injustice of fortune!" cried one. "We, the elder children, are given like servants to the wives of strangers, while the youngest is possessed of so great riches, who scarcely knows how to use them. You saw, Sister! what a hoard of wealth lies in the house; what glittering gowns; what splendor of precious gems, besides all that gold trodden under foot. If she indeed hath, as she said, a bridegroom so goodly, then no one in all the world is happier. And it may be that this husband, being of divine nature, will make her too a goddess. Nay! so in truth it is. It was even thus she bore herself. Already she looks aloft and breathes divinity, who, though but a woman, has voices for her handmaidens, and can command the winds." "Think," answered the other, "how arrogantly she dealt with us, grudging us these trifling gifts out of all that store, and when our company became a burden, causing us to be hissed and driven away from her through the air! But I am no woman if she keep her hold on this great fortune; and if the insult done us has touched thee too, take we counsel together. Meanwhile let us hold our peace, and know nought of her, alive or dead. For they are not truly happy of whose happiness other folk are unaware."

And the bridegroom, whom still she knows not, warns her thus a second time, as he talks with her by night: "Seest thou what peril besets thee? Those cunning wolves have made ready for thee their snares, of which the sum is that they persuade thee to search into the fashion of my countenance, the seeing of which, as I have told thee often, will be the seeing of it no more forever. But do thou neither listen nor make answer to aught regarding thy husband. Besides, we have sown also the seed of our race. Even now this bosom grows with a child to be born to us, a child, if thou but keep our secret, of divine quality; if thou profane it, subject to death." And Psyche was glad at the tidings, rejoicing in that solace of a divine seed, and in the glory of that pledge of love to be, and the dignity of the name of mother. Anxiously she notes the increase of the days, the waning months. And again, as he tarries briefly beside her, the bridegroom repeats his warning: "Even now the sword is drawn with which thy sisters seek thy life. Have pity on thyself, sweet wife, and upon our child, and see not those evil women again." But the sisters make their way into the palace once more, crying to her in wily tones, "O Psyche! and thou too wilt be a mother! How great will be the joy at home! Happy indeed shall we be to have the nursing of the golden child. Truly if he be answerable to the beauty of his parents, it will be a birth of Cupid himself."

So, little by little, they stole upon the heart of their sister. She, meanwhile, bids the lyre to sound for their delight, and the playing is heard: she bids the pipes to move, the quire to sing, and the music and the singing come invisibly, soothing the mind of the listener with sweetest modulation. Yet not even thereby was their malice put to sleep: once more they seek to know what manner of husband she has, and whence that seed. And Psyche, simple over-much, forgetful of her first story, answers, "My husband comes from a far country, trading for great sums. He is already of middle age, with whitening locks." And therewith she dismisses them again.

And returning home upon the soft breath of Zephyrus one cried to the other, "What shall be said of so ugly a lie? He who was a young man with goodly beard is now in middle life. It must be that she told a false tale: else is she in very truth ignorant what manner of man he is. Howsoever it be, let us destroy her quickly. For if she indeed knows not, be sure that her bridegroom is one of the gods: it is a god she bears in her womb. And let that be far from us! If she be called mother of a god, then will life be more than I can bear."

So full of rage against her, they returned to Psyche, and said to her craftily, "Thou livest in an ignorant bliss, all incurious of thy real danger. It is a deadly serpent, as we certainly know, that comes to sleep at thy side. Remember the words of the oracle, which declared thee destined to a cruel beast. There are those who have seen it at nightfall, coming back from its feeding. In no long time, they say, it will end its blandishments. It but waits for the babe to be formed in thee, that it may devour thee by so much the richer. If indeed the solitude of this musical place, or it may be the loathsome commerce of a hidden love, delight thee, we at least in sisterly piety have done our part." And at last the unhappy Psyche, simple and frail of soul, carried away by the terror of their words, losing memory of her husband's precepts and her own promise, brought upon herself a great calamity. Trembling and turning pale, she answers them, "And they who tell those things, it may be, speak the truth. For in very deed never have I seen the face of my husband, nor know I at all what manner of man he is. Always he frights me diligently from the sight of him, threatening some great evil should I too curiously look upon his face. Do ye, if ye can help your sister in her great peril, stand by her now."

Her sisters answered her, "The way of safety we have well considered, and will teach thee. Take a sharp knife, and hide it in that part of the couch where thou art wont to lie: take also a lamp filled with oil, and set it privily behind the curtain. And when he shall have drawn up his coils into the accustomed place, and thou hearest him breathe in sleep, slip then from his side and discover the lamp, and, knife in hand, put forth thy strength, and strike off the serpent's head." And so they departed in haste.

And Psyche left alone (alone but for the furies which beset her) is tossed up and down in her distress, like a wave of the sea; and though her will is firm, yet, in the moment of putting hand to the deed, she falters, and is torn asunder by various apprehension of the great calamity upon her. She hastens and anon delays, now full of distrust, and now of angry courage: under one bodily form she loathes the monster and loves the bridegroom. But twilight ushers in the night; and at length in haste she makes ready for the terrible deed. Darkness came, and the bridegroom; and he first, after some faint essay of love, falls into a deep sleep.

And she, erewhile of no strength, the hard purpose of destiny assisting her, is confirmed in force. With lamp plucked forth, knife in hand, she put by her sex; and lo! as the secrets of the bed became manifest, the sweetest and most gentle of all creatures, Love himself, reclined there, in his own proper loveliness! At sight of him the very flame of the lamp kindled more gladly! But Psyche was afraid at the vision, and, faint of soul, trembled back upon her knees, and would have hidden the steel in her own bosom. But the knife slipped from her hand; and now, undone, yet ofttimes looking upon the beauty of that divine countenance, she lives again. She sees the locks of that golden head, pleasant with the unction of the gods, shed down in graceful entanglement behind and before, about the ruddy cheeks and white throat. The pinions of the winged god, yet fresh with the dew, are spotless upon his shoulders, the delicate plumage wavering over them as they lie at rest. Smooth he was, and, touched with light, worthy of Venus his mother. At the foot of the couch lay his bow and arrows, the instruments of his power, propitious to men.

And Psyche, gazing hungrily thereon, draws an arrow from the quiver, and trying the point upon her thumb, tremulous still, drave in the barb, so that a drop of blood came forth. Thus fell she, by her own act, and unaware, into the love of Love. Falling upon the bridegroom, with indrawn breath, in a hurry of kisses from eager and open lips, she shuddered as she thought how brief that sleep might be. And it chanced that a drop of burning oil fell from the lamp upon the god's shoulder. Ah! maladroit minister of love, thus to wound him from whom all fire comes; though 'twas a lover, I trow, first devised thee, to have the fruit of his desire even in the darkness! At the touch of the fire the god started up, and beholding the overthrow of her faith, quietly took flight from her embraces.

And Psyche, as he rose upon the wing, laid hold on him with her two hands, hanging upon him in his passage through the air, till she sinks to the earth through weariness. And as she lay there, the divine lover tarrying still, lighted upon a cypress tree which grew near, and, from the top of it, spake thus to her, in great emotion. "Foolish one! unmindful of the command of Venus, my mother, who had devoted thee to one of base degree, I fled to thee in his stead. Now know I that this was vainly done. Into mine own flesh pierced mine arrow, and I made thee my wife, only that I might seem a monster beside thee—that thou shouldst seek to wound the head wherein lay the eyes so full of love to thee! Again and again, I thought to put thee on thy guard concerning these things, and warned thee in loving-kindness. Now I would but punish thee by my flight hence." And therewith he winged his way into the deep sky.

Psyche, prostrate upon the earth, and following far as sight might reach the flight of the bridegroom, wept and lamented; and when the breadth of space had parted him wholly from her, cast herself down from the bank of a river which was nigh. But the stream, turning gentle in honor of the god, put her forth again unhurt upon its margin. And as it happened, Pan, the rustic god, was sitting just then by the waterside, embracing, in the body of a reed, the goddess Canna; teaching her to respond to him in all varieties of slender sound. Hard by, his flock of goats browsed at will. And the shaggy god called her, wounded and outworn, kindly to him and said, "I am but a rustic herdsman, pretty maiden, yet wise, by favor of my great age and long experience; and if I guess truly by those faltering steps, by thy sorrowful eyes and continual sighing, thou laborest with excess of love.

Listen then to me, and seek not death again, in the stream or otherwise. Put aside thy woe, and turn thy prayers to Cupid. He is in truth a delicate youth: win him by the delicacy of thy service."

So the shepherd-god spoke and Psyche, answering nothing, but with a reverence to his serviceable deity, went on her way. And while she, in her search after Cupid, wandered through many lands, he was lying in the chamber of his mother, heart-sick. And the white bird which floats over the waves plunged in haste into the sea, and approaching Venus, as she bathed, made known to her that her son lies afflicted with some grievous hurt, doubtful of life. And Venus cried, angrily, "My son, then, has a mistress! And it is Psyche, who witched away my beauty and was the rival of my godhead, whom he loves!"

Therewith she issued from the sea, and returning to her golden chamber, found there the lad, sick, as she had heard, and cried from the doorway, "Well done, truly! to trample thy mother's precepts under foot, to spare my enemy that cross of an unworthy love; nay, unite her to thyself, child as thou art, that I might have a daughter-in-law who hates me! I will make thee repent of thy sport, and the savor of thy marriage bitter. There is one who shall chasten this body of thine, put out thy torch and unstring thy bow. Not till she has plucked forth that hair, into which so oft these hands have smoothed the golden light, and sheared away thy wings, shall I feel the injury done me avenged." And with this she hastened in anger from the doors.

And Ceres and Juno met her, and sought to know the meaning of her troubled countenance. "Ye come in season," she cried; "I pray you, find for me Psyche. It must needs be that ye have heard the disgrace of my house." And they, ignorant of what was done, would have soothed her anger, saying, "What fault, Mistress, hath thy son committed, that thou wouldst destroy the girl he loves? Knowest thou not that he is now of age? Because he wears his years so lightly must he seem to thee ever but a child? Wilt thou for ever thus pry into the pastimes of thy son, always accusing his wantonness, and blaming in him those delicate wiles which are all thine own?" Thus, in secret fear of the boy's bow, did they seek to please him with their gracious patronage. But Venus, angry at their light taking of her wrongs, turned her back upon them, and with hasty steps made her way once more to the sea.

Meanwhile Psyche, tossed in soul, wandering hither and thither, rested not night or day in the pursuit of her husband, desiring, if she might not soothe his anger by the endearments of a wife, at the least to propitiate him with the prayers of a handmaid. And seeing a certain temple on the top of a high mountain, she said, "Who knows whether yonder place be not the abode of my lord?" Thither, therefore, she turned her steps, hastening now the more because desire and hope pressed her on, weary as she was with the labors of the way, and so, painfully measuring out the highest ridges of the mountain, drew near to the sacred couches. She sees ears of wheat, in heaps or twisted into chaplets; ears of barley also, with sickles and all the instruments of harvest, lying there in disorder, thrown at random from the hands of the laborers in the great heat. These she curiously sets apart, one by one, duly ordering them; for she said within herself, "I may not neglect the shrines, nor the holy service, of any god there be, but must rather win by supplication the kindly mercy of them all."

And Ceres found her bending sadly upon her task, and cried aloud, "Alas, Psyche! Venus, in the furiousness of her anger, tracks thy footsteps through the world, seeking for thee to pay her the utmost penalty; and thou, thinking of anything rather than thine own safety, hast taken on thee the care of what belongs to me!" Then Psyche fell down at her feet, and sweeping the floor with her hair, washing the footsteps of the goddess in her tears, besought her mercy, with many prayers:—"By the gladdening rites of harvest, by the lighted lamps and mystic marches of the Marriage and mysterious Invention of thy daughter Proserpine, and by all beside that the holy place of Attica veils in silence, minister, I pray thee, to the sorrowful heart of Psyche! Suffer me to hide myself but for a few days among the heaps of corn, till time have softened the anger of the goddess, and my strength, out-worn in my long travail, be recovered by a little rest."

But Ceres answered her, "Truly thy tears move me, and I would fain help thee; only I dare not incur the ill-will of my kinswoman. Depart hence as quickly as may be." And Psyche, repelled against hope, afflicted now with twofold sorrow, making her way back again, beheld among the half-lighted woods of the valley below a sanctuary builded with cunning art. And that she might lose no way of hope, howsoever doubtful, she drew near to the sacred doors. She sees there gifts of price, and garments fixed upon the door-posts and to the branches of the trees, wrought with letters of gold which told the name of the goddess to whom they were dedicated, with thanksgiving for that she had done. So, with bent knee and hands laid about the glowing altar, she prayed saying, "Sister and spouse of Jupiter! be thou to these my desperate fortunes, Juno the Auspicious! I know that thou dost willingly help those in travail with child; deliver me from the peril that is upon me." And as she prayed thus, Juno in the majesty of her godhead, was straightway present, and answered, "Would that I might incline favorably to thee; but against the will of Venus, whom I have ever loved as a daughter, I may not, for very shame, grant thy prayer."

And Psyche, dismayed by this new shipwreck of her hope, communed thus with herself, "Whither, from the midst of the snares that beset me, shall I take my way once more? In what dark solitude shall I hide me from the all-seeing eye of Venus? What if I put on at length a man's courage, and yielding myself unto her as my mistress, soften by a humility not yet too late the fierceness of her purpose? Who knows but that I may find him also whom my soul seeketh after, in the abode of his mother?"

And Venus, renouncing all earthly aid in her search, prepared to return to heaven. She ordered the chariot to be made ready, wrought for her by Vulcan as a marriage-gift, with a cunning of hand which had left his work so much the richer by the weight of gold it lost under his tool. From the multitude which housed about the bed-chamber of their mistress, white doves came forth, and with joyful motions bent their painted necks beneath the yoke. Behind it, with playful riot, the sparrows sped onward, and other birds sweet of song, making known by their soft notes the approach of the goddess. Eagle and cruel hawk alarmed not the quireful family of Venus. And the clouds broke away, as the uttermost ether opened to receive her, daughter and goddess, with great joy.

And Venus passed straightway to the house of Jupiter to beg from him the service of Mercury, the god of speech. And Jupiter refused not her prayer. And Venus and Mercury descended from heaven together; and as they went, the former said to the latter, "Thou knowest, my brother of Arcady, that never at any time have I done anything without thy help; for how long time, moreover, I have sought a certain maiden in vain. And now nought remains but that, by thy heraldry, I proclaim a reward for whomsoever shall find her. Do thou my bidding quickly." And therewith she conveyed to him a little scrip, in the which was written the name of Psyche, with other things; and so returned home.

And Mercury failed not in his office; but departing into all lands, proclaimed that whosoever delivered up to Venus the fugitive girl, should receive from herself seven kisses—one thereof full of the inmost honey of her throat. With that the doubt of Psyche was ended. And now, as she came near to the doors of Venus, one of the household, whose name was Use-and-Wont, ran out to her, crying, "Hast thou learned, Wicked Maid! now at last! that thou hast a mistress?" and seizing her roughly by the hair, drew her into the presence of Venus. And when Venus sa her, she cried out, saying, "Thou hast deigned then to make th salutations to thy mother-in-law. Now will I in turn treat thee a becometh a dutiful daughter-in-law!"

And she took barley and millet and poppy-seed, every kind of grain and seed, and mixed them together, and laughed, and said to her: "Methinks so plain a maiden can earn lovers only by industrious ministry: now will I also make trial of thy service. Sort me this heap of seed, the one kind from the others, grain by grain; and get thy task done before the evening." And Psyche, stunned by the cruelty of her bidding, was silent, and moved not her hand to the inextricable heap. And there came forth a little ant which had understanding of the difficulty of her task, and took pity upon the consort of the god of Love; and he ran deftly hither and thither, and called together the whole army of his fellows. "Have pity," he cried, "nimble scholars of the Earth, Mother of all things!—have pity upon the wife of Love, and hasten to help her in her perilous effort." Then, one upon the other, the hosts of the insect people hurried together; and they sorted asunder the whole heap of seed, separating every grain after its kind, and so departed quickly out of sight.

And at nightfall Venus returned, and seeing that task finished with so wonderful diligence, she cried, "The work is not thine, thou naughty maid, but his in whose eyes thou hast found favor." And calling her again in the morning, "See now the grove," she said, "beyond yonder torrent. Certain sheep feed there, whose fleeces shine with gold. Fetch me straightway a lock of that precious stuff, having gotten it as thou mayst."

And Psyche went forth willingly, not to obey the command of Venus, but even to seek a rest from her labor in the depths of the river. But from the river, the green reed, lowly mother of music, spake to her: "O Psyche! pollute not these waters by self-destruction, nor approach that terrible flock; for, as the heat groweth, they wax fierce. Lie down under yon plane-tree, till the quiet of the river's breath have soothed them. Thereafter thou mayst shake down the fleecy gold from the trees of the grove, for it holdeth by the leaves."

And Psyche, instructed thus by the simple reed, in the humanity of its heart, filled her bosom with the soft golden stuff, and returned to Venus. But the goddess smiled bitterly, and said to her, "Well know I who was the author of this thing also. I will make further trial of thy discretion, and the boldness of thy heart. Seest thou the utmost peak of yonder steep mountain? The dark stream which flows down thence waters the Stygian fields, and swells the flood of Cocytus. Bring me now, in this little urn, a draught from its innermost source." And therewith she put into her hands a vessel of wrought crystal.

And Psyche set forth in haste on her way to the mountain, looking there at last to find the end of her hapless life. But when she came to the region which borders on the cliff that was showed to her, she understood the deadly nature of her task. From a great rock, steep and slippery, a horrible river of water poured forth, falling straightway by a channel exceeding narrow into the unseen gulf below. And lo! creeping from the rocks on either hand, angry serpents, with their long necks and sleepless eyes. The very waters found a voice and bade her depart, in smothered cries of, *Depart hence!* and *What doest thou here? Look around thee!* and *Destruction is upon thee!* And then sense left her, in the immensity of her peril, as one changed to stone.

Yet not even then did the distress of this innocent soul escape the steady eye of a gentle providence. For the bird of Jupiter spread his wings and took flight to her, and asked her, "Didst thou think, simple one, even thou! that thou couldst steal one drop of that relentless stream, the holy river of Styx, terrible even to the gods? But give me thine urn." And the bird took the urn, and filled it at the source, and returned to her quickly from among the teeth of the serpents, bringing with him of the waters, all unwilling—nay! warning him to depart away and not molest them.

And she, receiving the urn with great joy, ran back quickly that she might deliver it to Venus, and yet again satisfied not the angry goddess. "My child!" she said, "in this one thing further must thou serve me. Take now this tiny casket, and get thee down even unto hell, and deliver it to Proserpine. Tell her that Venus would have of her beauty so much at least as may suffice for but one day's use, that beauty she possessed erewhile being foreworn and spoiled, through her tendance upon the sick-bed of her son; and be not slow in returning."

And Psyche perceived there the last ebbing of her fortune— that she was now thrust openly upon death, who must go down, of her own motion, to Hades and the Shades. And straightway she climbed to the top of an exceeding high tower, thinking within herself, "I will cast myself down thence: so shall I descend most quickly into the kingdom of the dead." And the tower, again, broke forth into speech: "Wretched Maid! Wretched Maid! Wilt thou destroy thyself? If the breath quit thy body, then wilt thou indeed go down into Hades, but by no means return hither. Listen to me. Among the pathless wilds not far from this place lies a certain mountain, and therein one of hell's vent-holes. Through the breach a rough way lies open, following which thou wilt come, by straight course, to the castle of Orcus. And thou must not go empty-handed. Take in each hand a morsel of barley-bread, soaked in hydromel; and in thy mouth two pieces of money. And when thou shalt be now well onward in the way of death, then wilt thou overtake a lame ass laden with wood, and a lame driver, who will pray thee reach him certain cords to fasten the burden which is falling from the ass: but be thou cautious to pass on in silence. And soon as thou comest to the river of the dead, Charon, in that crazy bark he hath, will put thee over upon the further side. There is greed even among the dead: and thou shalt deliver to him, for the ferrying, one of those two pieces of money, in such wise that he take it with his hand from between thy lips. And as thou passest over the stream, a dead old man, rising on the water, will put up to thee his mouldering hands, and pray thee draw him into the ferry-boat. But beware thou yield not to unlawful pity.

"When thou shalt be come over, and art upon the causeway, certain aged women, spinning, will cry to thee to lend thy hand to their work; and beware again that thou take no part therein; for this also is the snare of Venus, whereby she would cause thee to cast away one at least of those cakes thou bearest in thy hands. And think not that a slight matter; for the loss of either one of them will be to thee the losing of the light of day. For a watch-dog exceeding fierce lies ever before the threshold of that lonely house of Proserpine. Close his mouth with one of thy cakes; so shalt thou pass by him, and enter straightway into the presence of Proserpine herself. Then do thou deliver thy message, and taking what she shall give thee, return back again; offering to the watch-dog the other cake, and to the ferryman that other piece of money thou hast in thy mouth. After this manner mayst thou return again beneath the stars. But withal, I charge thee, think not to look into, nor open, the casket thou bearest, with that treasure of the beauty of the divine countenance hidden therein."

So spake the stones of the tower; and Psyche delayed not, but proceeding diligently after the manner enjoined, entered into the house of Proserpine, at whose feet she sat down humbly, and would neither the delicate couch nor that divine food the goddess offered her, but did straightway the business of Venus. And Proserpine filled the casket secretly, and shut the lid, and delivered it to Psyche, who fled therewith from Hades with new strength. But coming back into the light of day, even as she hasted now to the ending of her service, she was seized by a rash curiosity. "Lo! now," she said within herself, "my simpleness! who bearing in my hands the divine loveliness, heed not to touch myself with a particle at least therefrom, that I may please the more, by the favor of it, my fair one, my beloved." Even as she spoke, she lifted the lid; and behold! within, neither beauty, nor anything beside, save sleep only, the sleep of the dead, which took hold upon her, filling all her members with its drowsy vapor, so that she lay down in the way and moved not, as in the slumber of death.

And Cupid being healed of his wound, because he would endure no longer the absence of her he loved, gliding through the narrow window of the chamber wherein he was holden, his pinions being now repaired by a little rest, fled forth swiftly upon them, and coming to the place where Psyche was, shook that sleep away from her, and set him in his prison again, awaking her with the innocent point of his arrow. "Lo! thine old error again," he said, "which had like once more to have destroyed thee! But do thou now what is lacking of the command of my mother: the rest shall be my care." With these words, the lover rose upon the air; and being consumed inwardly with the greatness of his love, penetrated with vehement wing into the highest place of heaven, to lay his cause before the father of the gods. And the father of gods took his hand in his, and kissed his face, and said to him, "At no time, my son, hast thou regarded me with due honor. Often hast thou vexed my bosom, wherein lies the disposition of the stars, with those busy darts of thine. Nevertheless, because thou hast grown up between these mine hands, I will accomplish thy desire." And straightway he bade Mercury call the gods together; and, the council-chamber being filled, sitting upon a high throne, "Ye gods," he said, "all ye whose names are in the white book of the Muses, ye know yonder lad. It seems good to me that his youthful heats should by some means be restrained. And that all occasion may be taken from him, I would even confine him in the bonds of marriage. He has chosen and embraced a mortal maiden. Let him have fruit of his love, and possess her for ever."

Thereupon he bade Mercury produce Psyche in heaven; and holding out to her his ambrosial cup, "Take it," he said, "and live for ever; nor shall Cupid ever depart from thee." And the gods sat down together to the marriage-feast. On the first couch lay the bridegroom, and Psyche in his bosom. His rustic serving-boy bare the wine to Jupiter; and Bacchus to the rest. The Seasons crimsoned all things with their roses. Apollo sang to the lyre, while a little Pan prattled on his reeds, and Venus danced very sweetly to the soft music. Thus, with due rites, did Psyche pass into the power of Cupid; and from them was born the daughter whom men call Voluptas.

GLOSSARY – INDEX

The page references in parentheses which follow each entry refer only to the first mention of a name in any single account. Persons mentioned only in passing have been omitted, as have geographical references.

ACASTUS Son of Pelias; expelled Jason and Medea from Iolcus for murder of Pelis; purified Peleus; after his wife, Hippolyte, falsely accused Peleus, he deserted Peleus in hunt and hid his sword (*see* Peleus).

ACHAENS (AKHAIANS) The Greeks.

ACHELOÖS A river-god who could change form; took form of bull to wrestle Heracles for Deianeira's hand; Heracles won, broke off Acheloös' horn; Acheloös later recovered horn; purified Alcmaeon and gave him his daughter Callirrhoe to wife. (86)

ACHILLES Son of Peleus and Thetis; put in fire by Thetis to make him immortal; reared by Chiron; leader of Myrmidons against Troy; wounded Telephus; later healed him with rust of his spear; angry because of Agamemnon's seizure of Briseis, he stopped fighting; received embassy from Agamemnon; sent Patroclus to fight Trojans; recovered Briseis; re-entered war in armor from Hephaestus; angered river Scamander; slew Hector and allowed Priam to ransom body; buried Patroclus; shot in vulnerable heel by Apollo and Paris; married Medea in Elysium; games held in his honor and his arms contested for by Ajax and Odysseus. (25, 74, 141, 142, 143, 146, 147, 148, 149, 150, 151, 154, 156, 159, 160, 161, 162, 164, 165, 166, 167, 169, 170, 382, 383, 384, 385, 386)

ACRISIUS Son of Abas, twin of Proetus; expelled Proetus; reigned over Argos; father of Danaë; because she was fated to bear son who would kill his grandfather, Acrisius locked Danaë in bronze chamber; when she bore Perseus by Zeus he cast her and Perseus into sea (*see* Danaë); accidentally killed by Perseus at athletic games. (122)

ACTAEON A hunter; devoured by his own dogs either because Zeus was angry at him for wooing Semele, or because he saw Artemis bathing in the nude.

ADMETUS Kind king of Pherai; Apollo served him as herdsman; got Alcestis as wife with Apollo's help; Apollo persuaded Fates to let Admetus live if he could induce another to die in his stead; Alcestis volunteered and died for him (*see* Alcestis). (367)

ADONIS Son of Myrrha through incest with her father; she was pursued by her father; compassionate gods turned her into myrrh tree, from which Adonis was born; Adonis carried by Aphrodite in a chest to Persephone; because both wanted him, he divided time between Aphrodite and Persephone; killed by boar while hunting; in grief Aphrodite caused the anemone to spring up from his blood. (319, 328)

ADRASTOS King of Argos; married his daughters to exiles Tydeus and Polyneices; led Seven against Thebes to regain Thebes for Polyneices; only he of Seven was saved by his horse Arion. (132, 135)

AEETES Son of Helios and Perseis; king of Colchis; received Golden Fleece from Phrixus; promised it to Jason if he would yoke brazen-footed bulls and sow dragon's teeth; pursued Medea and Jason. (93, 95)

AEGEUS Son of Pandion; restored to Athens by his brothers; induced by Aethra's father, Pittheus, to lay with her; son Theseus was sent to him in Athens; recognized Theseus just as Medea tried to poison him; cast himself from Acropolis when Theseus forgot to change black sail after killing Minotaur. (99, 100)

AEGINA Daughter of Asopus; carried off and ravished by Zeus; bore Aracus to Zeus.

AEGISTHUS Son of Thyestes; in one account murdered Atreus and restored kingdom to Thyestes; Clytemnestra's lover; with Clytemnestra murdered Agamemnon and Cassandra; murdered by Orestes. (180, 181, 183, 184, 186, 386)

AENEAS Son of Anchises and Aphrodite; fought Greeks in Trojan War; fled Troy with father and son after war; lost wife Creusa; wandered in Mediterranean; told in dream that Italy was his goal; landed in Sicily; hurricane raised by Juno drove him to Carthage; loved by Dido; returned to Sicily at Jupiter's warning; entered underworld with Golden Bough; heard father's prophecy; well received by Latinus in Latium; married Latinus' daughter;

founded town, slew Turnus; became ruler of Latins; killed by
Rutulians; body carried up to heaven. (61, 73, 116, 237, 238,
239, 240, 242, 243, 244, 245, 248, 254, 381, 385)

AEOLUS King of Aeolia, keeper of the winds; gave Odysseus winds
in bag; married his six sons to his six daughters. (124, 135, 201,
343)

AEROPE Wife of Atreus; mother of Agamemnon and Menelaus; seduced by Atreus' brother, Thyestes.

AESCULAPIUS *see* Asklepios.

AESON Father of Jason; about to be killed by Pelias, he killed himself by drinking bull's blood. (136)

AETHRA Daughter of Pittheus; bore Theseus by Aegeus; captured by
Dioscuri when they rescued Helen, whom Theseus had carried
off to Aphidnae. (100, 171)

AGAMEMNON Son of Atreus, drove Thyestes from Mycenae and slew
his son; married Clytemnestra; father of Orestes, Electra, Iphigenia; ruled Mycenae; commanded army against Troy; sacrificed
Iphigenia to pacify Artemis; ordered Philoctetes put ashore at
Lemnos; demanded Briseis from Achilles; got Cassandra as booty
when Troy fell; returned to Mycenae; murdered by Clytemnestra
and Aegisthus. (142, 143, 145, 147, 152, 155, 156, 172, 178, 180,
181, 184, 186, 192, 382, 383, 386, 409)

AGENOR Son of Poseidon and Libya; ruled Tyre; father of Europa,
Cadmus, Phoenix, Cilix.

AIAS [1] Son of Telamon; suitor of Helen; fought against Troy;
fought Hector to a draw; sent as ambassador to Achilles; rescued
Patroclus' body; killing Glaucus, rescued Achilles' body; contended
with Odysseus for Achilles' arms; went mad and killed himself.
(147, 170, 173, 188, 384, 385, 386, 409)

AIAS [2] Son of Oileus; suitor of Helen; led Locrians against Troy;
violated Cassandra at Athena's altar; was shipwrecked and drowned
on return from Troy.

AIDONEUS *see* Hades.

AIETES *see* Aeetes.

AJAX *see* Aias [1].

ALCESTIS Daughter of Pelias; volunteered to die for her husband
Admetus; restored to life by Heracles. (367)

ALCIDES *see* Heracles.

ALCINOUS King of the Phaeacians. (222, 404)

ALCMAEON Son of Amphiaraus and Eriphyle; brother of Amphilochus; led Epigoni in capture of Thebes; killed Eriphyle in accordance with Amphiaraus' command; pursued by Erinyes for this

crime; purified by Phegeus; married Phegeus' daughter Arsinoe; gave Arsinoe necklace and robe of Harmonia; driven from Psophis, he was purified by Acheloös; married Acheloös' daughter Callirrhoe; having tricked Phegeus out of Harmonia's necklace and robe in order to give them to Callirrhoe, he was killed by Phegeus' sons.

ALCMENE Daughter of Electryon; wife of Amphitryon; seduced by Zeus in Amphitryon's likeness; bore Heracles by Zeus and Iphicles by Amphitryon but delivery delayed at Hera's instigation; gouged out Eurystheus' eyes; married Rhadamanthus. (81, 136, 157, 195)

ALCYONE Wife of Ceyx; when Ceyx drowned she mourned so piteously that she was transformed into a bird; she kissed his corpse and he too became bird. (343)

ALEXANDER *see* Paris.

ALOADS Otus and Ephialtes, giant sons of Iphimedia and Poseidon, tallest men of earth; threatened to climb to heaven by piling up mountains; bound Ares; were killed by Apollo; in variant story they killed each other while trying to kill deer which was Artemis in disguise. (399)

ALPHEUS River-god of Peloponnese; pursued nymph Arethusa to Sicily. (325)

ALTHAEA Daughter of Thestius; wife of Oeneus; mother of Meleager (and Toxeus); caused Meleager's death when he killed her brothers. (112, 118)

AMAZONS A people living beyond the earth's borders; reared only females; Heracles fought them and took Hippolyte's belt; attacked Athens; defeated by Theseus. (83, 172, 260, 261)

AMPHIARAUS Argive seer; husband of Eriphyle; father of Alcmaeon and Amphilochus; foreknew that expedition of Seven against Thebes would fail, that if he joined it, he wouldn't return; Eriphyle, bribed by Polyneices, persuaded him to join expedition; he commanded his sons to avenge his death on Eriphyle and make a second expedition; while fleeing from battle at Thebes he was swallowed into the earth; made immortal by Zeus. (135)

AMPHILOCHUS Son of Amphiaraus and Eriphyle; brother of Alcmaeon; one of Epigoni; in some versions he helped Alcmaeon kill Eriphyle.

AMPHION Son of Antiope and Zeus; twin of Zethus; became musician, with Zethus rescued Antiope from Lycus and Dirce, tied Dirce to bull; both succeeded to Theban throne; they fortified city, the stones following Amphion's lyre; Amphion married Niobe. (136)

AMPHITRITE Wife of Poseidon; sea-goddess. (30, 198)

AMPHITRYON Son of Alcaeus; received Alcmene and kingdom of Mycenae from Electryon; accidentally killed Electryon; banished from Argos; went to Thebes with Alcmene; purified by Creon; led expedition which rid Cadmea of vixen plaguing it; supported by Creon, he attacked Teleboans; Alcmene, seduced by Zeus in Amphitryon's likeness, bore Heracles; killed in battle with Minyans. (82, 136)

ANCAEUS Argonaut; killed by Calydonian boar.

ANCHISES Father of Aeneas by Aphrodite; carried off by Aeneas at sack of Troy; accompanied Aeneas to Sicily and died there. (58, 73, 240, 246, 254)

ANDROMACHE Wife of Hector; mother of Astyanax; awarded to Neoptolemus after Trojan War. (385)

ANDROMEDA Beautiful daughter of Cepheus of Ethiopia; when her mother boasted that she was more beautiful than Nereids, Poseidon sent monster to punish land; Andromeda bound to rack as sacrifice to monster; rescued by Perseus; married Perseus. (124)

ANTAEUS Libyan giant overcome by Heracles. (85, 103)

ANTICLEIA Mother of Odysseus; told him of situation at home on his journey to Hades.

ANTIGONE Daughter of Oedipus; sister of Ismene, Polyneices, Eteocles; accompanied him to Attica; buried Polyneices in defiance of Creon; was buried alive. (132, 133)

ANTIOPE Daughter of Nycteus; seduced by Zeus; escaped father's wrath by fleeing and marrying Epopeus; bore Amphion and Zethus; captured by her uncle Lycus and his wife Dirce; rescued by sons. (136)

APHRODITE Greek goddess of love, beauty, and marriage; daughter of Zeus and Dione; wife of Hephaestus; caused Dawn to be perpetually in love; afflicted Lemnian women; carried away Butes; loved by Ares; bore Harmonia by him; gave Hippomenes golden apples; caused Cinyras' daughters to cohabit with foreigners; disputed with Persephone over possession of Adonis; loved Anchises; bore him Aeneas and Lyrus; won prize of beauty by promising Paris the most beautiful woman; rescued Paris from Menelaus; wounded by Diomedes in Trojan War. (7, 47, 57, 64, 70, 90, 107, 158, 175, 176, 238, 239, 240, 266, 300, 305, 315, 318, 327, 340, 357, 361, 381, 412)

APOLLO Greek god of medicine, music, prophecy, archery, the flock; son of Zeus and Leto; Artemis' twin; killed Python and took over Delphic oracle; killed Marsyas after musical contest; wooed Marpessa; father of Asklepios by Coronis; killed Coronis for infidelity;

killed Cyclopes to avenge Asklepios' death; served Admetus as punishment; fortified Troy; defrauded by Laomedon, he sent pestilence to Troy; fought Heracles for tripod; killed Niobe's sons; reconciled with Hermes, gave him wand; loved and involuntarily killed Hyacinthus; gave Cassandra gift of prophecy but destined her never to be believed; sent two serpents as sign to Trojans; with Paris shot Achilles; defended Orestes against Erinyes. (22, 26, 28, 32, 34, 57, 66, 82, 90, 104, 115, 129, 131, 137, 143, 150, 154, 160, 163, 166, 182, 225, 246, 262, 271, 288, 293, 309, 313, 317, 354, 359, 362, 383, 387, 400, 413)

ARES Greek god of war; son of Zeus and Hera; lover of Aphrodite. (10, 57, 63, 86, 142, 148, 157, 159, 162, 167, 190, 238, 252, 263, 272, 315, 387)

ARETHUSA A nymph; when the river-god Alpheus tried to seduce her, she was transformed into a fountain to escape him. (324)

ARGO Ship used by Jason in his search for Golden Fleece.

ARGOS Dog of Odysseus; faithfully awaited Odysseus' return; died at his return. (230)

ARGUS Son of Agenor; had a hundred eyes all over his body; appointed by Hera to guard Io; slain by Hermes. (269)

ARGUS-SLAYER *see* Hermes.

ARIADNE Daughter of Minos; loved Theseus; gave him clue to labyrinth; taken by him to Naxos and deserted; in variant story he forgot her while under a charm; bride of Dionysus. (106, 111, 137, 267, 382)

ARION Lyric poet and musician of Methymna. (391)

ARISTAIOS Rustic deity; passionately pursued Eurydice who died of snakebite she received while fleeing from him; Dryads caused his bees to die; when Dryads were appeased, new swarm of bees was got from bullock's decaying carcass.

ARSINOE Daughter of Phegeus; married Alcmaeon; received necklace and robe of Harmonia from Alcmaeon; when she upbraided Phegeus' sons for killing Alcmaeon, they gave her as slave to Agapenor.

ARTEMIS Greek goddess of the hunt and of birth; daughter of Zeus and Leto; Apollo's twin; slew Orion; killed Aloads; plagued Oeneus with Calydonian boar for forgetting her sacrifice; rebuked Heracles for shooting Cerynitian hind sacred to her; seen bathing by Actaeon, she turned him into a stag; killed Niobe's daughters; shot Callisto; Atreus neglected vow to her; Iphigenia sacrificed to her by Agamemnon to appease anger for Atreus' crime; in variant Artemis rescued Iphigenia and substituted deer on altar. (31, 32,

57, 82, 91, 111, 113, 137, 156, 179, 220, 224, 271, 288, 294, 309, 319, 321, 326, 338, 358, 362, 382, 383)

ASCANIUS *see* Iulus.

ASKLEPIOS Son of Apollo and Coronis; god of medicine; raised Hippolytus from dead and therefore smitten with a thunderbolt by Zeus. (287, 294)

ASOPUS A river; pursued Zeus when Zeus carried off and ravished his daughter, Aegina, but was driven back by Zeus' thunderbolts.

ASTYANAX Son of Hector and Andromache; thrown by Greeks from battlements of Troy after Troy fell.

ATALANTA In Arcadian legend, daughter of Iasus; exposed by Iasus; was suckled by a bear; became virgin huntress; repulsed approaches by men; Milanion was woman-hater who fell in love with Atalanta when he saw her; he earned marriage to her by faithful service; they hunted Calydonian boar; were turned into lions by Zeus for making love at his altar.

In Boeotian legend, daughter of Schoeneus; excelled in foot racing; wished to remain virgin; promised to marry man who beat her in foot race; in race with Hippomenes he scattered apples of Hesperides on the way; she stopped to recover them and lost race; she married Hippomenes; both were turned into lions by Cybele for making love at her altar. (114, 135, 327, 410)

ATE Goddess of ruin and destruction. (157)

ATHAMAS Husband of Ino.

ATHENE Greek goddess of war and of intellectual and moral aspects of life; daughter of Zeus and Metis; born from Zeus' head; killed Triton's daughter, Pallas, and made image of her, the Palladium; flayed giant Pallas; gave Aeetes dragon's teeth; with Hermes purified Danaïds for murder of husbands; received Gorgon's head from Perseus; put it in shield; helped Heracles in Twelve Labors; blinded Tiresias when he saw her naked; in contest with Poseidon for Attica she planted olive trees and won; mother of Erichthonius; entrusted Erichthonius in a chest to Pandrosus; drove Pandrosus' sisters mad for opening chest; competed with Hera and Aphrodite for prize of beauty; angry with Greeks after Trojan War for Ajax's violation of Cassandra in her temple; asked Zeus to send storm on Greeks as they sailed away. (22, 32, 57, 63, 70, 84, 85, 113, 127, 144, 150, 161, 175, 178, 190, 193, 197, 220, 221, 234, 236, 259, 265, 300, 381, 385, 386, 387)

ATLAS Son of Iapetus and Asia; held up sky; got golden apples of Hesperides for Heracles while Heracles held up sky for him; father of Pleiades and Calypso. (83, 123, 286)

ATREIDAI Sons of Atreus, Agamemnon, and Menelaus. (188)

ATREUS Son of Pelops; brother of Thyestes; father of Agamemnon and Menelaus by Aerope; neglected to perform vow to Artemis and hid golden lamb in box; when Thyestes seduced Aerope, stole lamb and became king of Mycenae, sun went backward as divine sign that Atreus should rule Mycenae; Athens ousted Thyestes; Atreus murdered Thyestes' children and served them to him; killed by Aegisthus. (180, 187)

ATROPOS *see* Fates.

AUGEAS King of Elis. (83)

AURA *see* Cephalus.

AURORA *see* Eos.

BACCHAE Worshippers of Dionysus.

BACCHUS *see* Dionysus.

BAUCIS Baucis and Philemon were a poor old couple; entertained Zeus and Hermes who were in disguise; for their kindness were saved from deluge and made priest and priestess of gods; transformed into trees. (375)

BELLEROPHON Son of Glaucus; accidentally killed brother; purified of murder by Proetus; when he rejected advances of Proetus' wife, she falsely accused him to Proetus; sent by Proetus to Iobates to be killed; sent by Iobates against Chimera; shot Chimera while riding winged horse, Pegasus; conquered Solymi and Amazons; killed Lycians; married Iobates' daughter, succeeded to throne. (259, 260)

BOREAS North Wind; when his prayers for Orithyia's hand were spurned, he carried her off by force; father of Zetes and Calais by her. (18, 94, 333, 335)

BRISEIS A favorite slave-girl of Achilles; when Agamemnon was forced to surrender his slave-girl, Chryseis, he seized Briseis; Achilles refused to fight until he got Briseis back. (144, 158, 383)

BUSIRIS Egyptian king who sacrificed foreigners; killed by Heracles. (86, 103)

CACUS Italian shepherd; son of Vulcan; stole part of Heracles' cattle; discovered and slain by Heracles. (87)

CADMUS Son of Agenor; followed cow and founded Thebes; killed dragon of the spring, sowed its teeth; served Ares as atonement; married Harmonia; succeeded by Pentheus at Thebes; went with Harmonia to Encheleans, where they were turned into serpents and sent to Elysian Fields. (11, 67, 74, 131, 262, 270)

CAENIS (CAENEUS) A Lapith; after Poseidon raped her, he granted her wish to become an invulnerable man; as invulnerable man he was beaten into ground with fir trees by centaurs.

CAESAR Julius Caesar, represented by poets as the descendant of Aphrodite through Aeneas and his son Iulus. (238)

CALAIS *see* Zetes.

CALCHAS Greek seer; said Achilles was needed to take Troy; Agamemnon must sacrifice Iphigenia; said Heracles' bow needed to take Troy; was defeated in contest of seercraft with Mopsus and died. (180, 382, 386)

CALLIRRHOE Daughter of Acheloös; married Alcmaeon; coveted necklace and robe of Harmonia; at her plea Zeus caused her sons by Alcmaeon to become men, whereupon they avenged Alcmaeon's death by killing Phegeus and dedicating robe and necklace to Apollo at Delphi.

CALLISTO Artemis' companion in hunt; vowed to maidenhood; seduced by Zeus; turned into a bear by him; shot as bear by Artemis at Hera's instigation; snatched up and turned into star by Zeus; her babe rescued by Zeus.

CALYDONIAN BOAR Boar of extraordinary size and strength sent by Artemis to ravage Calydon because the king, Oeneus, forgot to make sacrifice to her; finally killed by Meleager in expedition.

CALYPSO Daughter of Atlas; received Odysseus in Ogygia; bore Latinus by him. (219)

CANDAULES King of Lydia. (392)

CAPANEUS One of the Seven against Thebes; because of impiety he was killed by a thunderbolt while scaling walls of Thebes; his wife burned herself, with his dead body.

CASSANDRA Daughter of Priam and Hecuba; granted art of prophecy by Apollo, but when she refused to lay with him he destined that her prophecies would never be believed; when Troy fell she was violated at Athene's altar by Aias, son of Oileus; awarded to Agamemnon; killed with Agamemnon by Aegisthus and Clytemnestra. (185, 381, 385)

CASTOR *see* Dioscuri.

CATTLE OF HELIOS *see* Odysseus.

CECROPS First king of Attica; born from the soil with a body half man, half serpent.

CELEUS King of Eleusis; father of Triptolemus; received Demeter kindly. (47)

CENTAURS Race of men whose bodies were part horse, part human; fought Heracles for opening their wine jar; routed by Heracles;

tried to violate Hippodamia and were attacked by Thesus and Pirithous; beat Caeneus into ground with fir trees; *see* Ixlon. (38, 76, 82, 108)

CEPHALUS Son of Deion; married Procris; in expedition led by Amphitryon their inescapable dog chased uncatchable vixen plaguing Cadmea; dog and vixen turned into stone in chase; Cephalus accidentally killed Procris in hunt; condemned to eternal banishment. (333, 335)

CERBERUS Dog-like doorkeeper at entrance to Hades; was overpowered and brought up from Hades by Heracles as one of Twelve Labors. (77, 323)

CERCYON *see* Theseus.

CERES *see* Demeter.

CEYX *see* Alcyone.

CHARIS Wife of Hephaestus. (56)

CHARON Ferryman on river Styx, the boundary of Hades; was paid to ferry dead across Styx to Hades. (426)

CHARYBDIS A rock between Sicily and Italy; near Scylla; fig tree grew on rock; under tree dwelt woman, Charybdis, who thrice a day swallowed and then threw up again waters of the sea; danger to ships. (217)

CHEIRON Son of Cronus; most just and wise of centaurs; reared Actaeon, Asklepios, Jason, Achilles; saved Peleus from centaurs; advised Peleus to seize Thetis; accidentally wounded by Heracles, wished to die; died when Prometheus assumed his immortality. (91, 142, 287)

CHIMERA Offspring of Typhon and Echidna; fire-breathing monster shaped like a lion in front, a dragon behind, and a goat in the middle; killed by Bellerophon. (260, 261)

CHIRON *see* Cheiron.

CHLORIS Wife of Neleus; mother of Nestor; also goddess of flowers. (136)

CHRYSAOR Offspring of Gorgon and Poseidon; father of Geryon.

CHRYSEIS Prize of Agamemnon at Troy; the necessity of returning her to her father Chryses led to quarrel between Agamemnon and Achilles. (143)

CICONES Tribe visited by Odysseus. (198)

CIRCE An enchantress on whose island Odysseus landed. (204, 214, 215, 217, 387)

CLASHING ROCKS Two huge cliffs in the sea which winds continuously dashed together, closing sea passage; after Argo passed through they ceased clashing.

CLEOPATRA Wife of Meleager (112)

CLOTHO *see* Fates.

CLYTEMNESTRA Daughter of Tyndareus and Leda; Agamemnon's wife; bore him Orestes, Electra, Iphigenia; corrupted by Aegisthus; with Aegisthus murdered Agamemnon and Cassandra; murdered by Orestes. (182, 185, 186, 386)

CORONIS *see* Asklepios.

CREON King of Thebes after Laius; brother of Jocasta; helped Amphitryon against Teleboans when Amphitryon led expedition in which Cephalus' dog and vixen plaguing Cadmea were turned to stone; father of Menoeceus and Haemon; gave Oedipus throne when he solved Sphinx's riddle; became Theban king when Oedipus was banished; forbade burial of Polyneices' body after war with Argives; buried Antigone alive for defying his order. (131, 133)

CREUSA Daughter of Priam and Hecuba; wife of Aeneas; mother of Iulus (Ascanius); was lost by Aeneas when he fled Troy; appeared to him as a spirit and revealed his future fate.

CROESUS Son of Alyattes; King of Lydia. (388)

CRONIDES *see* Zeus.

CRONUS Early Greek deity; son of Uranus (Heaven) and Gaia (Earth); hated Uranus; castrated and dethroned Uranus at Gaia's behest; married Rhea; since he was destined to be dethroned by his own son, he swallowed his children; Rhea hid their son Zeus, gave Cronus a rock to swallow; Cronus dethroned by Zeus. (4, 8, 24, 27, 57, 71, 75, 287, 302)

CUPID *see* Eros.

CYBELE Nature goddess; the "Great Mother." (332)

CYCLOPS Offspring of Uranus and Earth; cast into Tartarus by Uranus; released by Zeus; forged thunderbolts for Zeus; slain by Apollo to avenge Asklepios' death; in Homer, Cyclops were one-eyed monsters visited by Odysseus. (4, 200, 206, 217, 222, 373)

CYCNUS (CYGNUS) Father of Tenes and Hemithea; believing false accusation against his children, he set them adrift on the sea; learning the truth, he stoned the accuser. (82, 86)

CYPRIS *see* Aphrodite.

CYTHEREA *see* Aphrodite.

DAEDALUS Craftsman, exiled from Athens for murder of Talos; accomplice of Pasiphae; constructed labyrinth for Minotaur; made wings for himself and son Icarus; fled to Italy. (266)

DANAË Daughter of Acrisius; shut up in bronze chamber; seduced in chamber by Zeus in form of stream of gold; bore Perseus; cast into sea with Perseus by Acrisius, she drifted to Seriphus; refused Polydectes' affections; rescued from Polydectes by Perseus. (122, 291, 303)

DANAÏDS Punished in Underworld for murdering their husbands. *See* Hypermnestra.

DANAUS Father of Danaïds.

DAPHNE Follower of Artemis; vowed to virginity; killed Leukippos when she discovered him dressed as woman to be near her; fled from Apollo's advances; prayed for rescue when he began overtaking her and was turned into laurel. (308)

DAWN *see* Eos.

DEJANIRA Daughter of Oeneus; Heracles wrestled with Achelous for her; she was given poisoned blood as love charm by the dying Nessus after Heracles slew him for assaulting her; she tried to win Heracles' love back from Iole by sending him robe smeared with Nessus' love charm and thereby, unwittingly, burned him unendurably; hanged herself when she learned of his torture. (86)

DEIDAMIA Daughter of Lycomedes; bore Neoptolemus by Achilles; given by Neoptolemus in marriage to Helenus. (108)

DEIPHOBUS Son of Priam and Hecuba; brother of Paris and Hector; awarded Helen after Paris' death; killed by Menelaus when Troy fell. (177, 384)

DEMETER Greek goddess of agriculture; daughter of Cronus and Rhea; bore Persephone by Zeus; searched for Persephone when Hades carried her off; was received by Celeus at Eleusis; tried to make Celeus' child immortal; turned Ascalaphus into an owl for bearing witness against Persephone; compromised with Hades over Persephone; tried to avoid Poseidon by turning into mare; he seduced her by turning into stallion; she bore the horse Arion; was loved by Iasion. (45, 113, 220, 292, 304, 324, 421)

DEMOPHOÖN Son of Theseus; seduced Phyllis and abandoned her.

DEUCALION Son of Prometheus; husband of Pyrrha; he and Pyrrha saved from great flood of Bronze Age because Prometheus previously warned him to build ark; after flood receded, they responded to Zeus' message to throw bones of their mother over their shoulders, by throwing stones of Mother Earth over their shoulders; out of these stones sprang new race of men. (19)

DIANA *see* Artemis.

DIDO Beautiful foundress of Carthage; violently loved Aeneas at Venus' instigation; killed herself when he left. (239, 240, 242, 243, 245, 249, 250, 251)

DIOMEDES Son of Tydeus; went to wars of Thebes and Troy; suitor of Helen; Argive leader against Troy; wounded Aphrodite; exchanged armor with Glaucus; sent with Odysseus as spy, they killed Dolon and Rhesus; went with Odysseus to fetch Heracles' bow and arrows; helped Odysseus steal Palladium. (63, 82, 151, 156, 177, 192, 193, 384, 386)

DIONYSUS Greek god of wine and fertility of nature; son of Zeus and Semele; was born from Zeus' thigh; was reared as girl by Athamas and Ion; later reared by nymphs; discovered vine; driven mad by Hera, he roamed Egypt and Syria; was purified by Rhea and learned rights of initiation; was expelled by Lycurgus; caused Lycurgus' death; spread cult of vine in Thrace and India; drove Theban women mad and caused Pentheus' death; drove Argive women mad for rejecting his rites; was seized as slave by pirates whom he then turned into dolphins; married Ariadne; was finally honored as a god; raised Semele from Hades and they ascended to heaven. (65, 66, 67, 107, 110, 113, 122, 137, 267, 270, 277, 290, 303, 354, 428)

DIOSCURI Castor and Pollux; sons of Leda and Zeus; brothers of Helen; rescued Helen from Aphidnae and captured Aethra; carried off and married Hilaira and Phoebe; drove cattle from Messena; deceived by Idas; lay in wait for Idas and Lynceus; Castor was killed by Idas; Pollux was carried to heaven by Zeus; Pollux wouldn't accept immortality while Castor was dead; permitted to live together, on alternating days among gods and among mortals. (137, 173, 189, 382)

DIRCE Wife of Lycus; she and Lycus mistreated his niece Antiope; Antiope's sons, Amphion and Zethus, had Dirce dragged to her death by a bull and slew Lycus.

DRYADS Tree-nymphs.

EARTH *see* Gaia.

EARTH-BORN *see* Uranus.

EARTH-SHAKER *see* Poseidon.

ECHIDNA Monster, half woman, half serpent; offspring of Tartarus and Gaia; by Typhon she bore Orthus, Cerberus, Hydra, Chimera, Sphinx, Nemean lion, dragon of Hesperides, Crommyon sow, Prometheus' eagle.

ECHO Nymph; enabled by Hera to speak only last words spoken to her; her love repulsed by Narcissus, she hid and wasted away to a voice. In variant story she refused Pan's love; he drove shepherds to tear her in pieces, only her voice surviving. (353)

EILITHYIA Goddess of childbirth; identified with Artemis. (30, 157)

ELECTRA [1] Daughter of Agamemnon and Clytemnestra; sister of Orestes; saved Orestes from Clytemnestra and Aegisthus when they killed Agamemnon; helped Orestes kill them to avenge Agamemnon's death.

ELECTRA [2] One of Pleiades; violated by Zeus and took refuge at Palladium; bore, by Zeus, Iasion and Dardanus.

ELECTRYON Son of Perseus; king of Mycenae; gave kingdom and his daughter, Alcmene, as wife to Amphitryon; accidentally killed by Amphitryon.

ELPENOR Companion of Odysseus; died from fall on Circe's isle; not buried by Odysseus; his unresting soul met Odysseus on threshold of Hades. (214)

ELYSIUM A paradise; in earlier poets, a land of eternal perfect happiness where those who were worthy were carried without seeing death; in later poets, a part of lower world where those whom judges of the dead pronounced worthy resided.

ENDYMION Handsome man; granted wish by Zeus, he chose to be cast into perpetual sleep; in variant story he was loved by Selene who cast him into perpetual sleep so she could kiss him.

Eos Greek goddess of the dawn; daughter of Hyperion and Thia; bedded with Ares; caused by Aphrodite to be perpetually in love; loved Orion; loved and carried off Cephalus; carried off Tithonus; bore him Emathion and Memnon. (40, 61, 123, 220, 248, 282, 335, 383)

EPAPHUS Son of Io by Zeus; carried off at Hera's instigation; returned to Egypt by Io; ruled Egypt; married Memphis; father of Libya. (270)

EPHIALTES *see* Aloads.

EPICASTE *see* Jocasta.

EPIGONI Sons of Seven against Thebes; made second attack on Thebes and were victorious.

ER Pamphilian; left for dead on battlefield, he accompanied the dead on their journey; restored to life, he reported a vision of the life to come. (404)

ERECHTHEUS Son of Gaia; married Praxithea; father of Orithyia, Creusa and Procris; in war with Eleusinians he slaughtered his youngest daughter for victory; other daughters slaughtered themselves; he and his house destroyed by Poseidon. (99, 100, 333, 335)

ERICHTHONIUS Son of Hephaestus; in Hephaestus' unsuccessful attempt to rape Athene his seed fell on Earth and Erichthonius sprang up; Earth gave him to Athene who put him in a chest and entrusted the chest to Cecrops' daughters; out of curiosity Cecrops' daughters opened chest and were driven mad; Erichthonius reared by Athene; became king of Athens; set up image of Athene; instituted Panathenaea; married nymph, Praxithea; father of Pandion.

ERINYES Born of Uranus and Earth; terrible and just avengers of crime; executors of curses invoked by the wronged on the wrongdoer; pursued Orestes after he killed Clytemnestra; when Orestes was acquitted by Areopagus and Erinyes' anger against him was appeased, they became Eumenides or "well disposed goddesses." (6, 112, 120, 131, 157, 188, 239, 249, 323)

ERIPHYLE Wife of Amphiaraus; mother of Alcmaeon and Amphilochus; although forbidden by Amphiaraus to accept gifts from Polyneices, she was bribed by necklace of Harmonia; persuaded Amphiaraus to join Seven against Thebes; in some versions she was later bribed by robe of Harmonia to persuade sons to join Epigoni; killed by Alcmaeon to avenge Amphiaraus' death. (137)

ERISICHTHON Defied Demeter by felling trees sacred to her; plagued with insatiable hunger.

EROS God of love; Cupid. (3, 308, 318, 335, 358, 399, 413)

ETEOCLES Brother of Polyneices; son of Oedipus. (132, 134)

EUMAEUS Faithful swineherd of Odysseus in Ithaca; helped Odysseus kill suitors. (231)

EUMENIDES *see* Erinyes.

EUMOLPUS Son of Poseidon by Chione; thrown into sea by Chione to hide her shame; rescued and carried to Ethiopia by Poseidon; after being banished, he went to Thrace and became king; fought with Eleusinians against Erechtheus; killed by Erechtheus, whom, with his house, Poseidon then destroyed.

EUROPA Daughter of Agenor; carried off by Zeus in form of bull; bore Minos, Sarpedon, and Rhadamanthus by him; later married Asterius. (84, 262, 305)

EURYDICE Wife of Orpheus. (322)

EURYLOCHUS Companion of Odysseus. (206)

EURYSTHEUS King of Mycenae; got power over Heracles when oracle told Heracles to serve him; assigned Twelve Labors to Heracles; after Heracles became immortal, his children (Heracleidae) fled to Ceyx; Eurystheus killed by Hyllus in war to recapture Heracles' children. (82, 83, 158)

EURYTION King of Phthia.

EURYTUS Prince of Oechalia; taught Heracles to use bow; offered his daughter Iole as prize in archery contest; when Heracles won contest Eurytus refused him Iole because he had killed his former children; Heracles slew him and carried off Iole.

EVANDER King of Arcadia; settled in Italy at site of Rome; aided Aeneas. (254)

FATES Daughters of Zeus and Night (or Themis): Lachesis, Clotho, Atropos; determined each man's portion in life; often pictured as spinners spinning each man's thread of life. (8, 50, 368, 407)

FAUNUS *see* Pan.

FURIES *see* Erinyes.

GAIA (GE) Early Greek deity; sprang from Chaos at beginning; represented earth; mated with Uranus (sky); their children, the Cyclops and Titans; grieved because Uranus cast Cyclops into Tartarus, she persuaded Titans to attack Uranus; gave Cronus sickle to castrate Uranus; vexed because Zeus shut up Titans in Tartarus, she bore Giants to attack gods. (3, 71, 75, 285)

GALATEA A delicate nymph; loved Acis; Polyphemus, a Cyclops, tried clumsily to woo her; jealous, he crushed Acis with a rock; Galatea changed Acis' blood flowing from under rock into river. (373)

GANYMEDE Trojan youth who, because of his beauty, was taken to heaven by an eagle and made cupbearer of gods by Zeus. (61)

GERYON Spanish king with three bodies; killed by Heracles. (88)

GIANTS Monstrous creatures born of Uranus and Earth; roused by Earth to attack Gods; defeated by Gods led by Zeus. (6)

GLAUCE Daughter of Creon of Corinth; was married by Jason who divorced Medea; burned to death when she wore robe which Medea had poisoned and sent her as wedding gift.

GLAUCUS Son of Minos; drowned in jar of honey; found and brought to life with magic herb by Polyidus, a diviner; Minos forced Polyidus to teach Glaucus art of divination, of which Polyidus later deprived Glaucus. (259, 260)

GOLDEN APPLES OF THE HESPERIDES Tree of golden apples given by Gaia to Zeus and Hera as wedding gift; guarded by dragon and four maidens (the Hesperides); procured by Heracles with Atlas' help as one of Twelve Labors. (8, 86, 291)

GOLDEN FLEECE Golden Fleece of ram which Hermes gave Nephele; Nephele sent ram to rescue Phrixus and Helle; Phrixus gave fleece to his father-in-law, Aeetes; Jason then got fleece from Aeetes.

GORGONS Three daughters of Phorcus and Ceto; were so horrible that those who looked at them turned to stone; Medusa beheaded by Perseus.

GRACES Charites, Aglaia, Euphrosyne, Thalia; confer all grace and victory. (58, 70, 269, 272, 306, 318)

GYGES Lydian; murdered King Candaules, either with the aid of the King's wife or by means of magic ring which made him invisible. (392)

HADES Greek god of lower world; son of Cronus and Rhea; brother of Poseidon and Zeus; received world of dead as his kingdom and it took on his name; carried off Persephone. (10, 27, 44, 45, 60, 64, 71, 74, 83, 112, 133, 141, 169, 170, 205, 214, 215, 426)

HARMONIA Daughter of Ares and Aphrodite; married to Cadmus; received necklace made by Hephaestus; she and Cadmus turned into serpents and sent to Elysian Fields by Zeus. (131)

HARPIES Offspring of Thaumas and Electra; wind spirits who snatched away the living; plagued Phineus; chased away by Zetes and Calais.

HEBE Greek goddess of youth, daughter of Zeus and Hera; married to Heracles when he gained immortality. (82, 85)

HECALE Old woman who entertained Theseus near Marathon. (104)

HECATE Goddess of magic; often identified with Artemis. (45, 249)

HECTOR Son of Priam and Hecuba; married Andromache; father of Astyanax; killed Protesilaus; fought Ajax; slain by Achilles; body ransomed from Achilles by Priam. (74, 142, 146, 147, 150, 153, 154, 156, 160, 161, 162, 164, 166, 168, 169, 174, 188, 238, 368, 383)

HECUBA Second wife of Priam; mother of Cassandra, Hector and Paris; dreamed Paris to be ruin of Troy; awarded to Odysseus; turned into a bitch.

HELEN Daughter of Zeus by Leda; carried off by Theseus to Aphidnae; rescued by Dioscuri; married by Menelaus; carried off by Paris to Troy; helped Odysseus steal Palladium; assigned to Deiphobus after Paris' death; recovered by Menelaus; went with him to Elysium; in variant story real Helen carried to Egypt, phantom to Troy; real Helen recovered by Menelaus after war. (11, 142, 171, 174, 175, 176, 178, 241, 368, 381, 384, 385)

HELENUS Son of Priam and Hecuba; seer in Troy; captured by Odysseus, he told how Troy might be taken; went to Molossia with Neoptolemus; given Deidamia as wife by Neoptolemus.

HELIOS Greek god of the sun; son of Hyperion; father of Aeetes,

Circe and Pasiphae by Perseis; father of Phaethon; killed Odysseus' men for killing his cows in Erythia; gave Dragon-car to Medea; gave Heracles golden goblet in which to cross sea. (33, 41, 45, 83, 189, 204, 215, 218, 234, 249, 279, 315)

HELLE Sister of Phrixos.

HELLENES The Greeks.

HEPHAESTUS Greek god of fire; divine smith; lame; son of Zeus and Hera; cast out of heaven by Zeus; husband of Aphrodite; helped birth of Athene; nailed Prometheus to Caucasus; gave bronze-footed bulls to Aeetes; gave Talos to Minos; gave Heracles golden breast plate; gave Athene bronze castanets; father of Erichthonius in unsuccessful attempt to rape Athene; made armor for Achilles; dried up river Scamander during its conflict with Achilles. (22, 25, 35, 55, 70, 84, 88, 162, 226, 234, 251, 282, 288, 299, 306, 315, 383, 423)

HEPHAISTOS see Hephaestus.

HERA Greek goddess of marriage; jealous consort of Zeus and queen of heaven; daughter of Cronus and Rhea; mother of Ares and Hephaestus; put in bonds and hung from Olympus by Zeus; not honored by Pelias; Jason helped Eilithyia and Argonauts on voyage; persecuted Io who was in form of cow; instigated kidnaping of Epaphus; persuaded Eilythyia to retard Heracles' birth; sent serpents to kill infant Heracles; drove Heracles mad; stirred up Amazons against Heracles; sent storms against Heracles; was reconciled to Heracles; deceived Semele; drove Athamas and Ino mad for rearing Dionysus; drove Dionysus mad; blinded Tiresias because of his unfavorable decision in a dispute with Zeus; persuaded Artemis to shoot Callisto; assaulted by Ixion; competitor for prize of beauty awarded by Paris to Aphrodite. (24, 30, 58, 63, 65, 73, 75, 85, 94, 99, 144, 150, 153, 155, 157, 175, 183, 229, 237, 238, 243, 247, 249, 251, 268, 269, 272, 299, 306, 347, 381, 389, 421)

HERACLEIDAE Numerous descendants of Heracles, rulers and pretenders to rule in cities of Greece and Asia.

HERACLES (HERAKLES) Son of Alcmene and Zeus; birth delayed at Hera's instigation to rob him of destined glory; twin of Iphices; in infancy strangled two serpents sent by Hera; killed Linus; killed lion of Cithaeron; lay with Thespius' fifty daughters; dressed in lion's skin; received weapons from Athene and compelled Minyans to pay Thebes tribute; married Megara; driven mad by Hera, he killed his children; purified by Thespius; ordered by oracle to serve Eurystheus; performed Twelve Labors for Eurystheus; 1. killed Nemean lion by cutting himself club; 2. killed Lernean

Hydra and dipped arrows in gall; 3. caught Cerynitian hind; 4. caught Erymanthian boar; battled centaurs; 5. cleaned Augeas' stables and was refused reward; 6. shot Stymphalian birds; 7. caught Cretan bull; 8. caught Diomedes' horses; 9. took Hippolyte's belt; delivered Hesione from sea beast; received golden goblet from sun to cross ocean; 10. killed Geryon and drove off cattle; 11. brought up Cerberus from Hades; extorted answer from Nereus; released Prometheus; 12. relieved Atlas of burden while Atlas got golden apples of Hesperides for him; wooed Iole but was denied her; killed Iphitus in madness; purified by Deiphobus, went to Delphi and carried off tripod; sold as slave to Omphale; saved Hesione from sea monster; captured Ilium and gave Hesione to Telamon; killed Augeas; slew Meleus; slew Hippocoön; restored Tyndareus and Icarius to Lacedaemon; seduced Auge and she bore Telephus; in early expedition against Troy; Heracles' bow necessary to take Troy; rescued Alcestis from Hades; brought up Theseus from Hades; wooed Deianira and wrestled with Acheloös; killed Nessus for assaulting Deianira; captured Oechalia and carried off Iole; tortured by poisoned robe, he had himself burned; obtained immortality; married Hebe. (81, 82, 83, 85, 86, 88, 101, 136, 155, 191, 253, 301, 348, 382)

HERCULES *see* Heracles.

HERMAPHRODITUS Bi-sexual godling born of Hermes and Aphrodite; Salmacis, a nymph, loved him/her; prayed to be ever united; prayer was answered and lover and loved were united into one person, a hermaphrodite. (357, 358)

HERMES Sons of Zeus and Maia; on day of birth went to Pieria, stole Apollo's cows, made lyre, made pipe; got art of divination and golden wand from Apollo; appointed herald of gods; father of Autolycus, Cephalus, Pan; recovered the sinews of Zeus; gave ram with Golden Fleece to Nephele; on orders from Zeus he rescued Io by killing Argus; purified Danaïds with Athene; received winged sandals, wallet and cap of Hades from Perseus; restored them to nymphs; admonished Heracles in Hades; sold Heracles to Omphale; brought up Protesilaus from Hades. (33, 70, 85, 94, 104, 127, 175, 181, 188, 208, 219, 244, 248, 269, 317, 321, 357, 368, 375, 381, 423)

HERMIONE Daughter of Helen and Menelaus; betrothed to Orestes; married Neoptolemus instead; carried off by Orestes after he killed Neoptolemus; in variant story Hermione first betrothed to Neoptolemus; married Orestes; carried off by Neoptolemus who was later slain by Orestes.

HERO Priestess of Aphrodite at Sestus; Leander, a youth of Abydos, guided by lighthouse, swam Hellespont every night for love of her; one night, when a storm extinguished the light, he drowned; when Hero saw corpse, she drowned herself. (374)

HESIONE Daughter of Laomedon.

HESPERIDES *see* Golden Apples.

HESTIA Goddess of the hearth; child of Cronus and Rhea; less prominent in Greece than Rome where she was worshipped as Vesta. (57, 239)

HIPPOCOÖN King of Lacedaemon; with his sons expelled Icarius and Tyndareus from Lacedaemon; they were slain by Heracles because they had fought with Neleus against Heracles.

HIPPODAMIA Daughter of Oenomaus; offered as prize to suitor who beat Oenomaus in a chariot race; loved Pelops; was won unfairly by Pelops. (101)

HIPPOLYTUS Son of Theseus and Hippolyte; falsely accused of assault by his stepmother Phaedra, whose love he repulsed; cursed by Theseus; dragged to death by his horses, when they saw bull Poseidon sent from sea; raised from dead by Asklepios. *See* Virbius. (108, 294)

HIPPOMENES Lover who won Atalanta in race with her, aided by golden apples given him by Aphrodite. (327)

HYACINTHUS Beautiful boy loved by Apollo and Zephyros; preferred Apollo; killed by discus thrown by Apollo and blown at his head by wind which Zephyros caused; hyacinth flower sprang up where Hyacinthus' blood dropped. (313)

HYDRA Monster with a huge body and nine heads; when one head was cut off, two grew up; killed by Heracles.

HYLAS Minion of Heracles; pulled into well by water-nymphs. (86)

HYLLUS Son of Heracles and Deianira; married Iole on order of Heracles; slew Eurystheus; tried to lead reconquest of Peloponesos by Heracleidae; killed in duel with Peloponnesian leader.

HYMEN God of marriage. (127, 272)

HYPERION Father of Helios.

HYPERMNESTRA One of Danaus' fifty daughters, married to fifty cousins; saved her husband Lynceus, ignoring Danaus' order for all fifty daughters to kill husbands; later united to Lynceus by Danaus; mother of Abas, founder of Argive dynasty. (76, 77)

HYPSIPYLE Queen of Lemnos; mistress of Jason; hid her father when women massacred all men in Lemnos; when women discovered this they sold Hypsipyle into slavery; she served Lycurgus as nurse to his son Opheltes; her negligence caused child's death.

IASION Lover of Demeter. (220)

ICARIUS Son of Perieres; with Tyndareus expelled from Lacedaemon by Hippocoön; restored to Lacedaemon by Heracles; father
of Penelope; gave Penelope to Odysseus.

ICARUS Son of Daedalus; wearing wings made by Daedalus of wax
and feathers, he flew too close to sun; wings melted and he
drowned in sea. (267)

IDAS Son of Aphareus; cheated Dioscuri in cattle raid; killed Castor;
struck with thunderbolt by Zeus.

IDOMENEUS Cretan leader with Greeks at Troy. (173)

ILUS Son of Tros; father of Laomedon; founded Ilium; received
Palladium as divine sign.

INO Daughter of Cadmus; second wife of Athamas, son of Aeolus;
hated children of Athamas by Nephele, Phrixos and Helle; when
she tried to have them killed, Nephele rescued them; Ino bore
Learchos and Melikertes by Athamas; reared Dionysus as girl; in
punishment for helping Dionysus, Hera drove Athamas and her
mad; Athamas mistakenly killed Learchos in hunt; Ino ran off with
Melikertes and jumped into the sea; transformed into sea-goddess;
in variant, after Hera drove them mad Ino fled; Athamas married
Themisto; when Ino was returned Themisto tried to kill Learchos
and Melikertes; Ino replaced her children with Themisto's hence
Themisto unwittingly killed her children, then killed herself in
horror.

IO Beautiful daughter of Inachus; seduced by Zeus; to escape Hera's
wrath she was changed into cow by Zeus; cow guarded by Argus
for Hera; when Hermes slew Argus, Io was driven mad by gad-fly
sent by Hera; she wandered to Egypt; bore Epaphos; recovered
sanity and was worshiped in Egypt as Isis. (269)

IOBATES King of Lycia; received Proetus from Argus; gave Proetus
his daughter, Stheneboea; sent Bellerophon against Chimera,
Solymi and Amazons; gave Bellerophon his daughter Philonoe.

IOLAUS *see* Protesilaus.

IOLE Daughter of Eurytus; denied to Heracles when he won her in
archery contest; later captured by Heracles.

IPHICLES King of Phylace; a second Iphicles was Heracles' brother.
(136)

IPHIGENIA Daughter of Agamemnon and Clytemnestra; sister of
Electra and Orestes; sacrificed by Agamemnon to Artemis; in variant she was carried from altar by Artemis who appointed her
priestess in Taurus; escaped from savage Taurians with Orestes
when he came to rescue Artemis' image. (178, 382)

IPHITUS Son of Eurytus; supported Heracles' claim to Iole when Heracles won her in archery contest; thrown from wall by Heracles in fit of madness.

IPHIMEDEIA Wife of Aloeus; when pouring water from sea into her lap Poseidon met her and begat Aloads.

IRIS Messenger of the gods. (16, 30, 51, 150, 251, 347, 382)

ISIS Egyptian deity identified with Io.

ISMENE Daughter of Oedipus and Jocasta; sister of Antigone, Eteocles, Polyneices; would not help Antigone bury Polyneices' body. (132)

ITYLUS *see* Itys.

ITYS Son of Tereus and Procne. (272)

IULUS Son of Aeneas; originally Ascanius; ancestor of Julian family. (238, 241, 242, 243, 244, 249, 251)

IXION Husband of Dia; lured Dia's father to his death in pit of burning coals; purified by Zeus; tried to seduce Hera; impregnated cloud substituted for Hera by Zeus; cloud produced first Centaur; Ixion bound to wheel which revolves forever. (75, 77, 117, 303, 323)

JASON Son of Aeson; carried Hera in disguise of old woman across river and gained her favor; from single sandal was recognized by Pelias as man of whom oracle said to beware; sent by Pelias to fetch Golden Fleece; commanded Argo to Colchis; bedded with Hypsipyle; demanded Fleece from Aeetes; promised to marry Medea in return for help; got magic ointment from her; yoked bronze bulls; sowed dragon's teeth and defeated men who arose; led to Fleece by Medea; fled with Medea; married her; brought Fleece to Pelias; after Pelias died through Medea's treachery, Jason and Medea were expelled from Iolcus; went to Corinth; Jason divorced Medea, married Glauce; killed by falling piece of Argo's woodwork. (87, 90, 97, 115)

JOCASTA Wife of Laius; Oedipus' mother; married her son unwittingly; hanged herself when truth was revealed. (131, 136)

JOVE *see* Zeus.

JUNO *see* Hera.

JUPITER *see* Zeus.

KADMOS *see* Cadmus.

KALAIS *see* Zetes.

KENTAUROS *see* Centaurs.

Leucippus Child of Galatea.

Lotus-eaters Inhabitants of land visited by Odysseus; ate lotus-fruit, which made one desire to live only in Lotus-land. (199)

Loxias *see* Apollo.

Lucifer Son of Aurora; father of Ceyx; the morning star. (123, 282, 347)

Lycaon Son of Pelasgus; king of Arcadia; had fifty sons who were especially proud and impious; sons tempted Zeus by mixing child's bowels with sacrifice; sons were destroyed by Zeus with thunderbolt; their impiety led Zeus to send flood which destroyed men of Bronze Age, except Deucalion and Pyrrha; in variant story flood was caused by Lycaon himself, when he killed his son and served flesh to Zeus.

Lycomedes King of Scyros; Achilles had son Neoptolemus, by his daughter, Deidamia; killed Theseus.

Lycurgus [1] Son of Dryas, king of Edonians; insulted and expelled Dionysus; punished by gods with blindness and early death; in variant story he was driven mad by Dionysus and cut off son's limbs; to deliver land from ensuing barrenness, his subjects permitted his murder by horses.

Lycurgus [2] King of Nemea; bought Hypsipyle as slave, appointed her nurse to his son, Opheltes or Archemorus; once, while she guided Seven Against Thebes to a spring, dragon devoured Opheltes; Seven against Thebes celebrated Nemean games in Opheltes' honor.

Lycus Husband of Dirce.

Lynceus Husband of Hypermnestra; saved from death by her; ruled Argos; Lynceus and Hypermnestra parents of future rulers of Argos.

Maia One of the Pleiades; bore Hermes to Zeus; received Callisto's infant, Arcas, from Hermes to rear. (33)

Manto Prophetess; daughter of Tiresias; was dedicated to Apollo when Epigoni took Thebes; bore Tisiphone, and Eriphyle and Amphilochus by Alcmaeon; bore Mopsus by Apollo.

Mars *see* Ares.

Medea An enchantress; daughter of Aeetes; loved Jason; gave him magic ointment; led him to Fleece and charmed dragon; fled with Jason; killed her brother to slow Aeetes' pursuit; married Jason; beguiled Talos to his death; beguiled Pelias' daughters to murder him; expelled with Jason; went to Corinth; divorced by Jason; burned Glauce with poisoned robe; murdered her own children;

fled to Athens; married Aegeus; expelled by Aegeus for plotting against Theseus; returned to Colchis and restored kingdom to father. (95, 97, 103)

MEDUSA One of Gorgons; from her trunk sprang Chrysaor and winged horse Pegasus begotten by Poseidon; beheaded by Perseus. (124, 127)

MEGARA Daughter of Creon; married Heracles; she and children were burned by Heracles when Hera drove him mad. (86, 136)

MELAMPUS A seer; learned language of animals; the first to devise cure by drugs and purification; healed Proetus' daughters; father of Abas.

MELEAGER Son of Oeneus and Althaea; at birth Fates said he would live until the brand then on the fire burned to ashes; Althea kept brand; Meleager hunted Calydonian boar; killed Althaea's brothers; gave boar skin to Atalanta; for vengeance Althaea flung brand into fire; brand burned to ashes and Meleager died. (112, 114)

MEMNON Son of Aurora and Tithonus; killed at Troy by Achilles. (142)

MENELAUS Son of Atreus; married Helen; with Agamemnon aroused Greeks to war to recover Helen from Paris; led Lacedaemonians against Troy; fought Paris in single combat; slew Deiphobus; led Helen away; quarrelled with Agamemnon; driven by storm to Egypt; left Egypt; stranded on island; disguised as seal, captured Proteus despite his changing shapes; instructed by Proteus to sacrifice to Gods in Egypt; returned to Sparta and regained kingdom; went to Elysian Fields with Helen; in variant story Menelaus found real Helen in Egypt, phantom Helen in Troy. (173, 175, 176, 178, 181, 183, 382, 384, 385, 386)

MENESTHEUS Son of Peteos; led Athenians against Troy; went to Melos and reigned as king.

MENOETES Herdsman of Hades; told Geryon of theft of his cattle by Heracles; defeated at wrestling by Heracles in Hades.

MERCURY *see* Hermes.

METIS Daughter of Ocean; because of prophecy that she would bear son who would be lord of heaven, Zeus swallowed her after he made her pregnant; Athena then was born from his head.

MIDAS King of Phrygia; in exchange for returning Silenus, he was granted a wish by Dionysus; wished everything he touched to become gold; had favor rescinded when even his food turned to gold; possessed well in which he mixed wine; caught Satyrs who in their drunkenness slept there; his ears changed to those of an ass by Apollo; hid ears with cap but barber knew secret; barber unable to hold secret, whispered it into ground; a reed which grew up on that spot whispered the secret whenever wind blew. (291)

MILANION Woman-hater who fell in love with Atalanta and married her.

MILETUS Son of Apollo; loved by Sarpedon and Minos who fought over him; founded city of Miletus.

MINERVA *see* Athene.

MINOS King of Crete; son of Zeus and Europa; Pasiphae's husband; father of Glaucus, Ariadne, Phaedra; vowed to sacrifice bull to Poseidon, but when he saw beauty of bull Poseidon sent, he sacrificed another; hence Pasiphae bore Minotaur by the bull; recovered Glaucus from the dead through a diviner; gave Procris inescapable dog and dart for sleeping with him; captured Megara through Scylla's treachery and drowned her; ordered Athens to send seven youths and seven maids yearly for Minotaur as terms of peace; locked Daedalus in labyrinth; pursued him to Italy when Daedalus escaped; killed there by Cocalus' daughters; judge of the dead in Underworld. (74, 84, 105, 137, 266, 304, 362)

MINOTAUR Monster, half bull, half man; born by Pasiphae of a bull; placed in labyrinth; Athens sent seven youths and seven maidens yearly for Minotaur as tribute to Minos; Minotaur killed by Theseus. (105, 266)

MOIRAI *see* Fates.

MORPHEUS A spirit of sleep. (301, 347)

MUSES Inspiring goddesses of song and poetry; later goddesses of all arts and sciences; daughters of Zeus and Mnemosyne (Memory); by name, Clio, Euterpe, Thalia, Melpomene, Terpsichore, Erato, Polyhymnia, Urania, Calliope; individual muses sometimes assigned special spheres of arts and sciences. (42, 72, 269, 384, 428)

MYRTILUS Son of Hermes; charioteer of Oenomaus; bribed by Pelops to rig Oenomaus' chariot in race for hand of Oenomaus' daughter, Hippodamia; drowned by Pelops, he cursed Pelops' house.

NARCISSUS Loveliest young man; cold to all love, he repulsed Echo's love; in punishment he fell in love with his own reflection in a spring; died of longing for his reflection; turned into a narcissus. (353)

NAUPLIUS A wrecker who lured sailors to death by beacons; son of Poseidon; father of Palamedes; received Auge and sold her to

Teuthras; unsuccessfully demanded satisfaction for Palamedes' death; contrived for wives of Greek fighters to be unfaithful; lured homeward-bound Greeks onto rocks.

NAUSICAA Daughter of Alcinous; when washing clothes on shore she was appealed to by the shipwrecked Odysseus; led him to Alcinous. (222, 229)

NECESSITY Mother of the Fates. *See* Fates. (406)

NELEUS Son of Poseidon by Tyro; Pelias' twin; exposed by Tyro; with Pelias rescued Tyro from her stepmother; banished by Pelias; founded Pylus; father of Nestor; slain by Heracles. (136)

NEMESIS Goddess of retribution for evil deeds; had a temple at Rhamnus in Attica. (13, 354, 367)

NEOPTOLEMUS Son of Achilles and Deidamia (sometimes called Pyrrhus); fought against Troy; slew Priam; was awarded Andromache when Troy fell; went to Molossia; ruled Molossians; succeeded to Achilles' kingdom; carried off Orestes' wife, Hermione; was killed by Orestes (*see* Hermione for variant). (191, 384, 385, 386)

NEPHELE First wife of Athamas; bore him Phrixos and Helle; rescued Phrixos and Helle from death at hands of Athamas' second wife, Ino.

NEPTUNE *see* Poseidon.

NEREIDS The fifty daughters of Nereus; nymphs of the Mediterranean; propitious to sailors. (17, 307)

NEREUS Sea-god; son of Oceanus and Tethys; father, by Doris, of the Nereids. (142, 285, 290)

NESSUS A centaur; killed by Heracles when he tried to violate Deianira; while dying he gave Deianira his poisoned blood as love charm; blood later caused Heracles to be burned.

NESTOR King of Pylos; son of Neleus; father of Antilochos; led Pylians against Troy; honored for his wisdom and reminiscences. (116, 136, 146, 148, 181, 197, 386)

NIOBE Daughter of Tantalus; married Amphion; boasted of her superiority to Leto because she had more children; in punishment Artemis and Apollo slew her children; wept over dead children until she turned into stone from which tears constantly flowed. (271)

NISUS Son of Pandion; king of Megara; fated to die when a purple hair on his head was pulled out; Minos invaded Megara; Nisus died when his daughter Scylla, in love with Minos, pulled purple hair out; in variant story Nisus changed into bird when she pulled hair out. (362)

NYMPHS Beautiful young feminine creatures, spirits dwelling in many of the aspects of Nature. (6, 384)

OCEANUS Husband of Tethys, father of the nymphs; the ocean. (37, 45, 178, 300)

ODYSSEUS Son of Laertes and Anticlea; married Penelope; Telemachus' father; feigned madness to avoid Trojan war; detected by Palamedes; caused Palamedes' death; led Cephallenians against Troy; put Philoctetes ashore at Lemnos; sent with Menelaus to Troy to demand restoration of Helen; sent as ambassador to Achilles; sent with Diomedes as spy, they killed Dolon and Rhesus; defended Achilles' dead body; was awarded Achilles' arms; fetched Philoctetes from Lemnos; captured Helenus; fetched Neoptolemus and gave him Achilles' arms; with Diomedes stole Palladium from Troy; invented Wooden Horse; was concealed in it; got Hecuba; sailed from Troy; visited Cicones, Lotus-eaters; visiting Cyclops, he blinded Polyphemus; was given winds in a bag by Aeolus; when comrades opened bag, winds escaped and drove him back to Aeolus; visited cannibalic Laestrygones who ate most of his men; visited Circe who turned his men into beasts; Odysseus escaped her enchantments, bedded with her; father of Telegonus by her; consulted Tiresias' ghost in Hades; saw ghosts of his mother and Elpenor; having plugged his men's ears and ordered himself tied to mast, he sailed past Sirens; passed Scylla; visiting island of Helios, his comrades slew some cattle; in punishment Zeus wrecked ship; saved from Charybdis, Odysseus was washed to Calypso's island; lived with Calypso five years; washed onto island of Phaeacians; entertained by Alcinous; sent by Alcinous to Ithaca; came to Ithaca as beggar; revealed himself to Telemachus, Eumaeus, Philoetius; killed suitors; revealed himself to his father and Penelope; later slain accidentally by Telegonus, his son by Circe. (85, 147, 156, 170, 172, 176, 185, 186, 191, 193, 196, 198, 200, 203, 204, 214, 215, 216, 218, 219, 221, 229, 230, 231, 233, 234, 236, 382, 383, 384, 385, 386, 404, 410)

OEDIPUS Son of Laius and Jocasta; exposed when born; adopted by Polybus, king of Corinth; told by Delphic oracle that he would kill father and marry mother; killed Laius unwittingly; rid Thebes of Sphinx by solving riddle; succeeded to Theban throne; married Jocasta; father of Eteocles, Polyneices, Ismene, Antigone; when his incest was discovered, he was banished from Thebes; received by Theseus; at Colonus was transported into next world. (11, 130, 131, 134, 136, 338, 382)

OENEUS King of Calydon; married Althaea; the first to receive vine-plant from Dionysus; father of Meleager, Toxeus; slew Toxeus for leaping over ditch; because he forgot to sacrifice to Artemis, she sent Calydonian boar to ravage country; Meleager led expedition against boar; Oeneus married Periboea; father of Tydeus, Deianira; deposed and killed by Agrius' sons. (111, 113)

OENOMAUS King of Pisa; offered hand of his daughter Hippodamia to him who beat Oenomaus in chariot race; killed through Pelops' machinations.

OENONE Nymph; original wife of Paris; deserted by Paris when he married Helen; later, when he had been wounded by Philoctetes, she refused to help him; when he died she remorsefully hung herself.

OIDOPOUS *see* Oedipus.

OMPHALE Queen of Lydia; Heracles served her as slave to atone for murder of Iphitus; he did women's work and became very feminine in the period of his servitude.

ORESTES Son of Agamemnon and Clytemnestra; killed his mother to avenge her murder of his father. (180, 183, 386)

ORION A giant; great hunter; wooed Merope; blinded by Merope's father; healed by sun's rays; loved by Eos and carried to Delos by her; killed by Artemis; in variant when he pursued Pleiades, he and Pleiades turned into constellations. (74, 137, 220)

ORITHYIA Daughter of Erechtheus, king of Athens, and of Praxithea; seized by Boreas and carried off to Thrace, where she became the mother of Cleopatra, Chione, Zetes, and Calais. (333, 335)

ORPHEUS Musician; husband of Eurydice; she died of snakebite received while fleeing Aristaios; with music Orpheus charmed Hades to permit return of Eurydice if he didn't look back until he reached upper world; he looked back and Eurydice disappeared; became a solitary; torn to pieces by women in Dionysiac orgy. (94, 291, 322, 409)

ORPHISM A cult originating in sixth century B.C., which, under guidance of doctrines attributed to Orpheus, worshipped Dionysus; it aimed, through a mystical asceticism, to satisfy longing for spiritual elevation.

OTUS *see* Aloads.

PALAMEDES Son of Nauplius; exposed falsity of madness which Odysseus feigned to avoid Trojan War; at Odysseus' instigation he was stoned to death for treason by Greeks.

PALLADIUM Image of Pallas made in sorrow by Athene after she killed Pallas; thrown by Zeus into land of Troy; found and honored by Ilus; Troy would not be taken while Palladium remained within walls; in war with Greeks it was stolen by Odysseus and Diomedes and Troy fell.

PALLAS [1] *see* Athene.

PALLAS [2] Young ally of Aeneas; killed by Turnus. (253, 254)

PAN Greek god of flocks and shepherds; musician; goatish and sensual in appearance and character; son of Hermes; loved Syrinx in vain; she was turned into bed of reeds when Pan pursued her; cutting reeds, he made first pan-pipes; loved Pitys who was turned into pine tree when he pursued her; loved Echo and caused her death; helped Athenians at Marathon. (292, 321, 428)

PANDION [1] Son of Cecrops; king of Athens; expelled by Metionids; married daughter of king of Megara; became king of Megara; father of Aegeus, Nisus, and Lycus; his sons regained Athens. (99, 333)

PANDION [2] King of Athens; son of Erichthonius; married mother's sister; father of Procne and Philomela; gave Procne in marriage to Tereus; succeeded by twin sons, Butes and Erechtheus. (104, 272)

PANDORA First woman created by gods; made from clay and given gifts by various gods; sent by Zeus, for vengeance on Prometheus, to his brother Epimethus; he accepted her; she opened jar she carried containing evils and diseases and they escaped to plague men. (70)

PARIS Son of Priam and Hecuba; fated to cause Troy's ruin; exposed by Priam when born; rescued by bear; married Oenone; regained status in Troy; judged the three goddesses; gave prize of beauty to Aphrodite who promised him most beautiful woman; visited Menelaus; carried off Helen to Troy; in Trojan War fought Menelaus in single combat; shot Achilles; was shot by Philoctetes; refused help by Oenone, he died. (163, 174, 175, 368, 381, 384)

PASIPHAE Daughter of Helios; Aeetes' sister; married Minos; when Minos didn't sacrifice bull to Poseidon as he had promised, Poseidon caused Pasiphae to lust for the bull; disguised as a cow by Daedalus she conceived Minotaur by the bull.

PATROCLES An aide to Achilles; sent by Achilles to fight Trojans in Achilles' armor; killed by Hector; honored with funeral games. (148, 149, 150, 151, 154, 159, 163, 164, 165, 168, 169, 170, 383)

PEGASUS Winged horse; offspring of Poseidon and Medusa; sprang from Medusa's trunk, was tamed by Bellerophon with divine bridle; bore Bellerophon aloft when he killed Chimera. (128, 259)

PEITHO Goddess of persuasion. (70)

PELEUS Son of Aeacus and Endeis; brother of Telamon and Phocus; helped Telamon kill Phocus and was expelled by Aeacus; fled to Eurytion, king of Phthia; married Eurytion's daughter, Antigone; accidentally killed Eurytion; fled to Acastas in Iolcus; purified by Acastus; when Peleus spurned love of Acastus' wife Hippolyte, she falsely accused him to Acastus; Peleus' wife hanged herself; Acastus deserted Peleus in hunt and hid his sword; Peleus rescued from Centaurs by Cheiron; married Thetis; father of Achilles by her; prevented Thetis from burning away mortal part of Achilles; entrusted Achilles to Cheiron; conquered Iolcus, killed Acastus' wife; later expelled from Iolcus by Acastus' sons and died; transported to Island of the Blessed. (74, 116, 141, 142, 149, 151, 154, 381, 386)

PELIAS Son of Poseidon and Tyro; Neleus' twin; with Neleus, rescued Tyro from her stepmother; banished Neleus; father of Acastus, Alcestis; incurred Hera's wrath by not honoring her; having been warned by oracle to beware of one wearing a single sandal, he was afraid when Jason entered Iolcus wearing a single sandal; sent Jason to fetch Golden Fleece; caused death of Aeson and his infant son; was murdered by his daughters at Medea's instigation. (90, 97, 136, 367)

PELIDES *see* Achilles.

PELOPS Son of Tantalus; was boiled and served to gods by Tantalus; was restored to life by gods; brought infertility on Greece by treacherously killing Stymphalus; was loved by Hippodamia; won her in chariot race with her father, Oenomaus, when he persuaded Myrtilus to rig Oenomaus' chariot; threw Myrtilus into sea; father of Atreus, Thyestes, Chrysippus. (100, 101, 187)

PENELOPE Daughter of Icarius; Odysseus' wife; mother of Telemachus; wooed by suitors in Odysseus' absence; promised to wed when she finished Laertes' shroud; unravelled shroud nightly to hinder her progress; Odysseus returned, killed suitors, revealed himself to Penelope; later she married Telegonus and went to Elysium. (186, 194, 221, 229, 234, 386)

PENTHESILEA An Amazon; daughter of Ares; accidentally killed Hippolyte; purified by Priam; at Troy killed in battle by Achilles who then mourned her death. (383)

PENTHEUS King of Thebes; son of Echion and Agave; tried to stop Bacchic orgies; while spying on one at Dionysus' instigation, he was torn to pieces by Agave. (22, 69)

PERIPHETES Club-bearer killed by Theseus. (102)

PERSEPHONE Daughter of Zeus and Demeter; was carried off by

Hades; bound herself to lower world by eating food there; through compromise she spent part of year in Hades, part with Demeter; was wooed by Perithous; disputed with Aphrodite for possession of Adonis. (46, 73, 112, 133, 142, 214, 251, 320, 323, 422)

PERSEUS Son of Zeus and Danaë; sent by Polydectes to fetch Gorgon's head; learned way to nymphs from Phorcides; got wallet, sandals and cap, which made him invisible from nymphs; using shield as mirror, he cut off Gorgon's head; when Atlas refused him rest in his realm, he changed Atlas into mountain by showing Gorgon's head; rescued and married Andromeda; children were Alcaeus and Electryon; turned Polydectes to stone to save Danaë; gave wallet, sandals, and cap to Hermes; gave Gorgon's head to Athena; accidentally killed Acrisius, his grandfather, in athletic game. (122, 125, 303)

PERSUASION *see* Peitho.

PHAEDRA Daughter of Minos and Pasiphae; Theseus' wife; loved her stepson Hippolytus; caused his death by false accusation in suicide note. (108, 137, 294)

PHAETHON Son of Helios and Klymene; permitted by Helios to drive chariot of the sun; lost control of chariot and was slain by Zeus because of danger to the earth. (280)

PHEGEUS King of Psophis; purified Alcmaeon; tricked by Alcmaeon, he had him killed by Alcmaeon's sons.

PHILEMON *see* Baucis.

PHILOCTETES Son of Poeas; possessed Heracles' arrows which were necessary to take Troy; bitten by snake on journey to Troy, he was put ashore at Lemnos; when Trojan seer said that the Greeks could only take Troy with Heracles' arrows, Philoctetes was fetched from Lemnos; he slew Paris. (191, 383, 384)

PHILOMELA Daughter of Pandion; sister of Procne; seduced by Tereus. (272)

PHINEUS Thracian seer; son of Agenor; misled by his second wife, he blinded sons of his first wife; given choice of blindness or death as punishment, he chose blindness; Helios, enraged by his choice, plagued him with Harpies as further punishment; when Zetes and Calais delivered him from Harpies, in gratitude he revealed to Argonauts the course of their voyage.

PHOEBUS *see* Apollo.

PHOENIX Son of Amyntor; blinded and cursed by Amyntor for an affair with a slave-concubine of Amyntor; healed by Cheiron; tutor to young Achilles; sent as ambassador to Achilles in Trojan War. (148, 386)

PHORCIDS Three daughters of Phorcus and Ceto; were born old women and had one eye and one tooth among them; showed Perseus way to the Gorgons.

PHORCUS Son of Pontus (Sea) and Gaia (Earth); father of Phorcids, Gorgons, and Scylla by Ceto. (127)

PHRIXOS Son of Athamas and Nephele; brother of Helle; when Athamas' second wife, Ino, tried to kill Phrixos and Helle, Nephele sent ram with Golden Fleece to carry them off; Phrixos married Aeetes' daughter Chalciope; he gave ram's Golden Fleece to Aeetes; father of Argus who built Argo. (93)

PIRITHOUS Son of Ixion; half-brother of Centaurs; leader of Lapiths; with Theseus was bound to chair in Hades for wooing Persephone; with Theseus and Lapiths he routed Centaurs when they tried to violate his wife Deidamia at wedding. (108)

PITTHEUS King of Troezen; father of Aethra; grandfather of Theseus. (100, 171)

PLEIADES Seven daughters of Atlas and Pleione; persistently pursued by Orion; in one version Orion's pursuit of Pleione and Pleiades was stopped by pursuer and pursued being turned into constellations.

PLUTO *see* Hades.

PLUTUS God of Wealth. (55)

POLLUX *see* Dioscuri.

POLYBUS King of Corinth; adopted Oedipus when Corinthian shepherds found him. (131)

POLYCRATES Tyrant of Samos. (394)

POLYDECTES King of Seriphus; gave Danaë and Perseus shelter; Danaë rejected his affections; tried to eliminate Perseus by sending him after Gorgon's head; tortured Danaë; turned to stone when Perseus showed him Gorgon's head.

POLYDEUCES (POLLUX) *see* Dioscuri.

POLYIDUS A diviner.

POLYNEICES Son of Oedipus and Jocasta; brother of Eteocles, Antigone, Ismene; on Oedipus' departure, Eteocles and Polyneices agreed to rule Thebes alternately; Polyneices banished by Eteocles; Polyneices went to Argos; Polyneices married Adrastus' daughter, Argia; bribed Eriphyle; Polyneices led Argive attack on Thebes; brothers killed each other in combat; Polyneices' body was forbidden burial by Creon; body buried by Antigone. (132, 133, 134)

POLYPHEMUS One of the Cyclops; blinded by Odysseus; dull-witted giant; tried to woo Galatea according to later version; killed her lover Acis. (200)

POLYXENA Daughter of Priam and Hecuba; slain by Greeks on Achilles' grave. (385)

POSEIDON Greek god of the sea; son of Cronus and Rhea; brother of Hades and Zeus; received sea as kingdom; his emblem was trident; married Amphitrite; killed giant Polybotes by throwing piece of an island at him; begot Aloads by Iphimedeia; begot Pelias and Neleus by Tyro; begot Pegasus by Medusa; sent flood and monster to Ethiopia; when Minos didn't sacrifice bull Poseidon sent, he caused Pasiphae to bear Minotaur by bull; fortified Troy, but defrauded of his wages by Laomedon, he sent flood and monster; seduced Demeter in form of horse; striving with Athene for Attica, he produced sea on Acropolis; he lost and flooded Attica; father of Eumolpus by Chione; rescued Eumolpus from sea; destroyed Erechtheus and his house; in compliance with wish he had granted Theseus, he sent bull from sea to frighten Hippolytus' horses; raped Caenis and changed her into man; hindered Odysseus' journey home from Troy because of blinding of Polyphemus. (18, 22, 26, 27, 57, 66, 83, 84, 94, 101, 135, 141, 144, 150, 184, 193, 201, 227, 285, 290, 307, 317, 329)

PRIAM Son of Laomedon; king of Troy; married Hecuba; father of Paris, Hector, Cassandra, Helenus; warned that Paris would cause Troy's ruin, he exposed him; ransomed Hector's dead body from Achilles. (27, 146, 161, 163, 166, 167, 169, 171, 192, 220, 246, 385)

PROCNE Daughter of Pandion; married Tereus who seduced her sister. (272)

PROCRIS Daughter of Erechtheus and Praxithea; married Cephalus; got inescapable dog and dart from Minos for sleeping with him (in variant she got them from Artemis); killed accidentally by Cephalus while hunting. (137, 335)

PROCRUSTES *see* Theseus.

PROETUS Son of Abas; twin of Acrisius; expelled from Argos by Acrisius; went to Iobates and married his daughter Steneboea; ruled over Tiryns; his daughters went mad because they didn't recognize Dionysus' deity; Melampus cured them; Proetus purified Bellerophon; sent Bellerophon to Iobates to be killed because of his wife Antaea's false accusation. (260)

PROMETHEUS Son of Themis; father of Deucalion; tricked Zeus in arbitrating which part of sacrificial victim gods would get; told by Themis that Thetis could bear Zeus a son mightier than he; refused to tell Zeus despite tortures; created men from clay; gave men fire; Zeus took vengeance by sending Pandora with jar of evils to Prometheus' brother; Prometheus chained to rock by Zeus; his liver was torn daily by eagle and grew again nightly; rescued by Heracles (in variant released by Zeus for revealing secret of Thetis); warned Deucalion to build ark for great flood; assumed wounded Cheiron's immortality so Cheiron could die. (69, 71, 86)

PROTESILAUS Husband of Laodamia; first Greek killed at Troy. (367, 368, 383)

PROTEUS [1] Herdsman of sea; was able to change shapes; forced by Menelaus to reveal that Menelaus was staying in Egypt because he forgot to sacrifice to gods. (183, 290)

PROTEUS [2] King of Egypt; in one version he kept real Helen while Paris took phantom Helen to Troy; real Helen found by Menelaus on return from Troy. (175)

PSYCHE Beloved of Eros. (412)

PTERELAUS King of Teleboans; Poseidon made him immortal by putting a golden hair on his head; when Amphitryon attacked Teleboans, Pterelaus' daughter, Comaetho, fell in love with Amphitryon; she pulled out Pterelaus' golden hair, he died, and his kingdom fell.

PYGMALION King of Cyprus; made a statue of woman so artfully that he fell in love with it; Aphrodite made statue live; he married her (name Galatea is modern). (360)

PYLADES Constant companion of Orestes; accompanied Orestes to Mycenae and later to Taurus; married Electra.

PYRAMUS Pyramus and Thisbe were lovers; Thisbe was frightened away from rendezvous with Pyramus by lion; lion got blood on cloak dropped by Thisbe; Pyramus saw bloody cloak, thought Thisbe dead and killed himself; she returned, found him dead and killed herself; their blood touched mulberry tree and turned fruit red. (369)

PYRRHA Wife of Deucalion. (19)

PYRRHUS *see* Neoptolemus.

PYTHON Serpent which guarded oracle at Delphi; killed by Apollo when he took over oracle. (309)

QUIRINUS *see* Romulus.

RHADAMANTHUS Son of Zeus and Europa; ruled Elysium; one of three judges of the dead in Hades (others: Minos and Aiakos); married Alcmene. (74, 178, 304)

RHEA Early Greek deity; daughter of Uranus and Gaia; married

Cronus; mother of Zeus, Demeter, Hera, Poseidon, Hades; Cronus swallowed all his children; when Rhea bore Zeus, she gave Cronus a rock to swallow and hid Zeus; purified Dionysus and taught him initiation rites. (27, 29, 46, 58, 74, 332)

ROMULUS Founder of Rome; deified as Quirinus. (238, 239, 252)

SALMACIS A nymph. *See* Hermaphroditus.

SALMONEUS Son of Aeolus; father of Tyro; was killed by thunderbolt for mimicking Zeus.

SARPEDON Son of Zeus and Laodameia; leader of Lycians at Troy; killed by Patrocles. (150, 253, 262)

SATURN King of the gods in the Golden Age; predecessor of Zeus. (14, 300)

SATYRS Woodland spirits who were attendants of Dionysus; sensual creatures with animal-like features. (111)

SCAMANDER River near Troy; dried up by Hephaestus when it rushed at Achilles because he had killed many Trojans there.

SCIRON *see* Theseus.

SCYLLA [1] Daughter of Phorcus; because of attentions Poseidon gave her, Amphitrite turned her into monster encircled below waist by dogs' heads; devoured sailors passing her cave near Charybdis. (99, 217)

SCYLLA [2] Daughter of Nisus; in love with father's enemy, Minos; she killed Nisus by pulling out purple hair; was drowned by Minos; in variant story she changed into bird. (362)

SELENE Daughter of Hyperion and Thea; goddess of moon; loved Endymion.

SEMELE Daughter of Cadmus and Harmonia; loved by Zeus; at the jealous Hera's instigation she tricked Zeus into agreeing to appear in his divine splendor; when he did, she was destroyed by power of his glory and lightning; Zeus sewed her unborn child up in his thigh and bore Dionysus at proper time; Dionysus rescued Semele from Hades, ascended to Heaven with her. (65, 66, 67, 270)

SEMIRAMIS Queen of Babylon. (369)

SEVEN AGAINST THEBES Seven leaders of an army mustered by Adrastus to regain Thebes from Eteocles for Adrastus' son-in-law Polyneices; attack failed; only Adrastus survived.

SILENUS Drunken tutor and attendant of Dionysus. (111, 290)

SINNIS *see* Theseus.

SIRENS Creatures with birds' bodies and women's heads; by music they lured passing mariners to crash on rocks; they died as fated when Odysseus' ship successfully passed them. (215)

SISYPHUS Son of Aeolus; Merope's husband; outwitted Death whom Zeus had sent to fetch him; outwitted Death a second time; lived to old age; betrayed secret of Zeus' intrigue with Aegina; his punishment in Hades was to roll stone up hill only to see it roll down when he reached top. (75, 99, 260)

SLEEP *see* Morpheus.

SOLON Athenian lawgiver; one of the Seven Sages of Greece. (388)

SPHINX Monster with face of woman, body features of lion and bird; offspring of Typhon; Hera sent her with riddle to plague Thebes; Oedipus saved city by solving riddle; Sphinx killed herself. (130, 132)

STHENEBOEA Daughter of Iobates; Proetus' wife; falsely accused Bellerophon.

STYMPHALUS King of Arcadians; treacherously murdered by Pelops which brought infertility to Greece.

STYX An Oceanid whose water flows from rock in Hades forming river Styx; Zeus ordained that oaths sworn by her by gods were inviolable. (29, 50, 280, 332, 425)

SUITORS OF PENELOPE Men who wooed Penelope while Odysseus returned from Troy; deceived by Penelope; killed by Odysseus on his return.

SUN *see* Helios.

SYMPLEGADES *see* Clashing Rocks.

SYRINX Nymph loved by Pan. (321)

TALOS [1] Apprentice to Daedalus the craftsman; invented saw; in jealousy Daedalus threw him into sea and he became bird bearing his name.

TALOS [2] Bronze giant who guarded Crete; given to Minos by Hephaestus; had one vein closed up by bronze pin in his heel; when Medea entranced him and removed pin, he bled to death.

TANTALUS Father of Niobe and Pelops; tested omniscience of gods by boiling and serving up Pelops to them; was punished by being surrounded by water which receded whenever he tried to drink and fruit which blew out of reach when he tried to pick it. (75)

TARTARUS Gloomy place in Hades where the wicked were punished; Tartarus, ruler of Tartarus, father of Typhon and Echidna.

TEIRESIAS *see* Tiresias.

TELAMON Son of Aeacus; brother of Peleus and Phocus; killed Phocus out of jealousy and was expelled by Aeacus; fled to Salamis and succeeded to throne; father of Ajax by Periboea; accompanied Heracles to Troy; received Hesione as prize; father of Teucer by her. (86, 116)

TELEGONUS Son of Odysseus by Circe; sailed in search of Odysseus; in Ithaca he killed Odysseus unwittingly; took corpse and Penelope to Circe; married Penelope and they were sent to Elysium by Circe. (387)

TELEMACHUS Son of Odysseus and Penelope; tried to oust suitors in Odysseus' absence; sailed in search of clues about Odysseus; helped Odysseus kill suitors. (195, 196, 197, 215, 232, 382, 387)

TELEPHUS Son of Heracles and Auge; exposed by Auge; king of Mysia; wounded by Achilles when Greeks mistakenly landed at Mysia; at oracle's advice sought Achilles to heal wound; Achilles healed wound by rubbing with rust from the spear which gave the wound. (142, 382)

TEREUS Son of Ares; married Procne; father of Itys; seduced Procne's sister Philomela and cut out her tongue; Philomela embroidered the story for Procne; in revenge Procne killed and served Itys to Tereus; on discovering truth he tried to kill sisters but all three turned into birds. (272, 333)

TETHYS Wife of Oceanus; mother of river-gods and sea-nymphs. (300)

THAMYRIS Beautiful minstrel; first male to love males; loved Hyacinthus; engaged in musical contest with Muses; when he lost he was deprived of his eyes and minstrelsy.

THEA Daughter of Uranos and Earth; mother of Helios (Sun) and Selene (Moon) by Hyperion.

THEMIS Early Greek deity; daughter of Uranus and Gaia; mother of Prometheus; mother of Seasons and Fates by Zeus; prophesied that Thetis would bear son mightier than his sire. (4, 18, 29, 59, 71, 123, 141, 197, 338, 381)

THERSITES Greek at Troy; notorious for ugliness and abusiveness. (410)

THESEUS Son of Aegeus and Aethra; after Aegeus lay with Aethra he put sword and sandals under great rocks; Aegeus told her to send him son she would bear when son could shift rock to get tokens; in young manhood Theseus performed this task; setting out for Athens he cleared road to Athens of evildoers; killed Periphetes the Clubman; killed Sinnis the Pine-bender; slew Crommyon sow; threw Sciron into sea; slew Cercyon and Damastes (Procrustes); came to Athens; recognized by Aegeus as Medea tried to poison him; caught Marathonian bull for Aegeus; went as sacrifice to Minotaur; with Ariadne's help he slew Minotaur and found way out of labyrinth; deserted Ariadne; accidentally caused Aegeus' death; defeated Amazons, married Hippolyte; their son Hippolytus; caused Hippolytus' death with curse; carried off Helen from Sparta; bound to chair in Hades with Perithous for helping Perithous woo Persephone; rescued by Heracles; killed by Lycomedes in Scyros. (100, 102, 103, 110, 117, 137, 267, 382)

THESPIUS King of Thespiae; arranged for his fifty daughters to sleep with Heracles; all bore sons by Heracles; Thespius later purified Heracles for murder of Heracles' children.

THESTIUS Son of Ares; father of Leda, Althaea, Ephiclus and others; his sons killed by Meleager in hunt for Calydonian boar. (120)

THETIS A Nereid; with Nereids steered Argo through Wandering Rocks; Poseidon and Zeus were at first rivals for her hand; she was destined to bear son mightier than his sire; married Peleus after trying to avoid him by changing shapes; mother of Achilles; tried to burn away mortal part of Achilles; by dipping him in Styx she made Achilles invulnerable except for spot on heel where she held him; seeing that Achilles would die if he joined attack on Troy, she entrusted him in female disguise to Lycomedes; warned Achilles not to incur Apollo's enmity by killing Tenes. (24, 55, 141, 144, 151, 152, 155, 384, 386)

THISBE Beloved of Pyramus. (369)

THYESTES Son of Pelops; brother of Atreus; seduced Atreus' wife and stole golden lamb from him; unwittingly ate of his children served up by Atreus; on oracle's advice lay with his daughter to beget Aegisthus, avenger of Atreus' crime; restored to Mycene by Aegisthus; ousted by Agamemnon and Menelaus. (183, 187)

TIRESIAS Blind Theban seer; lived part of his life as a man and part as a woman; blinded by Hera for judging that women got more pleasure from love than men; then given seercraft by Zeus. (134, 170, 214, 352, 386)

TITANS Sons of Uranus and Earth; attacked Uranus at Earth's behest; made Cronus sovereign; shut up in Tartarus by Cronus; with Cronus defeated by Zeus and again shut up in Tartarus. (7, 71)

TITHONUS Son of Laomedon; loved by Eos; father of Emathion and Memnon by her; at Eos' request he was made immortal by Zeus, but wasn't made ageless; aged and suffered infirmities of age eternally. (61, 248)

TITYOS Son of Zeus and Gaia; tried to rape Leto; punished in Hades by being bound fast while vultures tore at his liver. (75, 77, 91)

TRIPTOLEMUS Son of Celeus of Eleusis; going through world in dragon-drawn chariot given him by Demeter, he sowed whole earth with grain. (48)

TRITON Son of Poseidon; sea-god. (18, 307)

TRIVIA see Artemis.

TROILUS Son of Priam; killed at Troy. (383)

TURNUS King of the Rutulians; promised Lavinia, daughter of Latinus; killer of Pallas; killed by Aeneas. (253, 254)

TYDEUS Son of Oeneus and Periboea; exiled for homicide, went to Argos; married Adrastus' daughter; Diomedes' father; one of Seven against Thebes; wounded by Melanippus in battle; slew Melanippus; sucked out his brains; Athena, in disgust, withheld immortality she had intended for Tydeus. (135)

TYDIDES see Diomedes.

TYNDAREOS Son of Perieros and Gorgophone; expelled from Lacedaemon by Hippocoön; restored to Lacedaemon by Heracles; King of Sparta; married Leda; father of Dioscuri, Helen and Clytemnestra; exacted oath from Helen's suitors to defend chosen bridegroom against any wrong; gave Helen to Menelaus; procured Penelope for Odysseus for suggesting oath; gave kingdom to Menelaus when Dioscuri became gods. (137)

TYPHON Monster begotten by Tartarus and Gaia; attacked heaven; severed Zeus' sinews; hid them in cave; pursued by Zeus when sinews were recovered; buried under Mt. Etna by Zeus; father of several monstrous offspring by Echidna.

TYRO Woman who loved river Enipeus; seduced by Poseidon disguised as Enipeus and bore twins Pelias and Neleus by him; saved by twins from persecution by her stepmother. (135, 195)

URANUS Early Greek deity sprang from Chaos at the beginning; represented Heaven; mated with Gaia (who represented Earth); their children the Cyclops, Titans; castrated and overthrown by son Cronus; from drops falling upon Earth from his severed member arose Erinyes, Giants, Meliai; from member itself, which fell into sea and gathered foam, sprang Aphrodite.

VENUS see Aphrodite.

VESTA see Hestia.

VIRBIUS Roman deity; after Artemis caused Asklepios to restore Hippolytus to life, she brought him to Aricia in Italy where he was worshipped as Virbius, she as Diana.

VULCAN see Hephaestus.

WOODEN HORSE Device invented by Odysseus to smuggle Greeks into Troy; Trojans were baffled; brought it into city; Greeks escaped from horse, destroyed Troy.

ZEPHYRUS Son of Aurora; gentle west wind. (414)

ZETES Zetes and Calais were winged sons of Boreas; fated to die when they couldn't catch a fugitive; while with Argonauts they pursued Harpies plaguing Phineus; failed to catch them and died; in variant story they were killed by Heracles. (94, 335)

ZETHUS Twin of Amphion; became cattle breeder; rescued Antiope and fortified Thebes; married Thebe. (136)

ZEUS Greatest Greek god; supreme ruler of gods and men; son of Cronus and Rhea; was hidden from Cronus by Rhea and reared in cave; defeated Titans, dethroned Cronus; brother of Poseidon and Hades; received sky as his kingdom; defeated Giants; married Hera; father of Ares and Hephaestus; seduced Metis; swallowed her, bore Athena from his head; fought Typhon; his sinews were cut by Typhon; caused Prometheus to be punished; destroyed mankind except for Deucalion by flooding earth; caused new race to spring up from stones; in form of swan he seduced Leda who bore Helen, Castor and Pollux; seduced Io; turned her into a cow; in form of stream of gold he seduced Danaë who bore Perseus; in Amphitryon's likeness he seduced Alcmene who bore Heracles and Iphicles; in form of bull he carried off Europa; begot Minos, Sarpedon, Rhadamanthus by her; loved Semele; unwillingly killed her; bore her unborn child Dionysus; father of Amphion and Zethus by Antiope; seduced Callisto; turned her into bear, then star; substituted cloud for Hera when Ixion tried to seduce her; bound Ixion to eternally revolving wheel; also father of Pan, Tityos, Hermes, Hebe, the Seasons, the Fates, Aphrodite, the Graces, the Muses, Persephone. (4, 10, 14, 22, 23, 24, 27, 28, 32, 33, 45, 57, 64, 65, 66, 67, 69, 71, 73, 74, 75, 81, 82, 84, 85, 86, 91, 93, 99, 122, 136, 141, 142, 146, 149, 150, 152, 155, 157, 161, 163, 164, 168, 174, 176, 180, 182, 188, 189, 192, 195, 197, 198, 202, 217, 220, 225, 229, 231, 233, 236, 246, 249, 252, 262, 266, 270, 271, 281, 294, 299, 305, 310, 316, 363, 373, 375, 381, 384, 385, 400, 423)